World History
Volume 2—1500 to Present
Ninth Edition

909
ANN

EDITORS

Joseph R. Mitchell
History Instructor, Howard Community College

Joseph R. Mitchell is a history instructor at Howard Community College in Columbia, Maryland, and a popular regional speaker. He received a M.A. in history from Loyola College in Maryland and a M.A. in African American History from Morgan State University, also in Maryland. He is the principal coeditor of *The Holocaust: Readings and Interpretations* (McGraw-Hill/Dushkin, 2001).

Helen Buss Mitchell
Professor of Philosophy, Howard Community College

Helen Buss Mitchell is a professor of philosophy and director of the women's studies program at Howard Community College in Columbia, Maryland. She is the author of *Roots of Wisdom* and *Readings From the Roots of Wisdom*. Both books were published by Wadsworh Publishing Company and are now in their fourth and third editions respectively. She has also created, written, and hosted a philosophy telecourse, *For the Love of Wisdom,* which is distributed throughout the country by PBS. She has earned numerous degrees, including a Ph.D. in women's history from the University of Maryland.

Contemporary Learning Series

2460 Kerper Blvd., Dubuque, IA 52001

Visit us on the Internet
http://www.mhcls.com

Mendham, NJ 07945

Credits

1. **The World and the West, 1500–1900**
   Unit photo—Phillip Coblentz/BrandXPictures/PictureQuest
2. **The Ferment of the West, 1500–1900**
   Unit photo—Royalty-Free/CORBIS
3. **The Industrial and Scientific Revolutions**
   Unit photo—Copyright 1997 IMS Communications Ltd./Capstone Design. All Rights Reserved
4. **The Twentieth Century to 1950**
   Unit photo—Public Domain image
5. **The Era of the Cold War, 1950–1990**
   Unit photo—UN Photo 172543 by Y. Nagata. Reprinted with Permission
6. **Global Problems, Global Interdependence**
   Unit photo—WHO/P. Virot

D
1

.W63

2008

V.02

Copyright

Cataloging in Publication Data
Main entry under title: Annual Editions: World History, vol. 2—1500 to the present. 9/e
1. World history—Periodicals. 2. Civilization, Modern—Periodicals, 3. Social Problems—Periodicals.
I. Mitchell, Joseph R. and Helen Buss, *comp.* II. Title: World History, vol. 2: 1500 to the present.
ISBN 13: 978–0–07–352846–5   MHID 10: 0–07–352846–3   658'.05   ISSN 1054–2779

Ninth Edition

Cover image: Comstock Images/PictureQuest and Dynamic Graphics/JupiterImages
Compositor: Laserwords Private Limited

Printed in the United States of America   1234567890QPDQPD987   Printed on Recycled Paper

Preface

In publishing ANNUAL EDITIONS we recognize the enormous role played by the magazines, newspapers, and journals of the public press in providing current, first-rate educational information in a broad spectrum of interest areas. Many of these articles are appropriate for students, researchers, and professionals seeking accurate, current material to help bridge the gap between principles and theories and the real world. These articles, however, become more useful for study when those of lasting value are carefully collected, organized, indexed, and reproduced in a low-cost format, which provides easy and permanent access when the material is needed. That is the role played by ANNUAL EDITIONS.

History is a dialogue between the past and the present. As we respond to events in our own time and place, we bring the concerns of the present to our study of the past. It has been said that where you stand determines what you see. Those of us who stand within the Western world have sometimes been surprised to discover peoples and cultures long gone that seem quite "modern" and even a bit "Western." Other peoples and cultures in the complex narrative of World History can seem utterly "foreign."

At times, the West has felt that its power and dominance made only its own story worth telling. History, we are reminded, is written by the winners. For the Chinese, the Greeks, the Ottoman Turks, and many other victors from the past, the stories of other civilizations seemed irrelevant, and certainly less valuable than their own triumphal saga. From our perspective in the present, however, all these stories form a tapestry. No one thread or pattern tells the whole tale, and all seem to be equally necessary for assembling a complete picture of the past.

As we are linked by capital, communications, and conflict with cultures whose histories, value systems, and goals challenge our own, World History can offer keys to understanding. As businesspeople and diplomats have always known, negotiations require a deep knowledge of the other's worldview. In an increasingly interconnected world, we ignore other civilizations at our own peril. As the dominant world power, we touch the lives of millions by decisions we make in the voting booth. Once powerful cultures that have fallen can offer cautionary advice. Those that survived longer than their neighbors offer hints.

When we read the newspaper or surf the Internet, we find confusing political, economic, religious, and military clashes that make sense only within the context of lived history and historical memory. The role of the United States in Afghanistan and Iraq, the perennial conflicts in the Middle East, China's emerging role as an economic superpower, the threat posed by religious fundamentalism, Africa's political future, the possibility of viral pandemics—these concerns of the global village have roots in the past. Understanding the origins of conflicts offers us the possibility of envisioning their solutions.

Periodization, or the marking of turning points in history, cannot be done universally. Cultures mature on different timetables and rise and fall independently. We have followed, in this volume, the periodization of the Western world, beginning with Exploration and Colonization, continuing through the Enlightenment and Industrial/Scientific Revolutions, examining the hot and cold wars of the Twentieth Century, and ending with Global Problems, Global Interdependence. Within this narrative of Western progress, one can find responses to imperialism and resistance to expansionism. Women emerge as citizens and even rulers. China's decision to abandon its exploration of the world as well as its competence in mechanization and mass production offers a parallel narrative to Europe's embracing of this path. And, we conclude with a survey of challenging new problems—atomic, nuclear, and chemical weapons; the so-called population "bomb"; religious zealotry and terrorism; and the largely unpredictable results of globalization.

The articles have been selected for balance, readability, and interest. They are offered to the instructor to broaden and deepen material in the assigned text as well as to provide a variety of focuses and writing styles. Our intention has been to offer the most current articles available. If you know of good articles that might be used in future editions, please use the prepaid *article rating form* at the back of this book to make your suggestions. The topic guide will help instructors navigate the volume and choose the readings that best complement a unit of study.

We would like to thank David McComb for providing a framework with so many fine readings in the previous edition of *Annual Editions: World History, Volume II*. And, Steven Varvis of the Editorial Board suggested and contributed a number of other very useful additions.

Joseph R. Mitchell
Editor

Helen Buss Mitchell
Editor

Contents

UNIT 1
The World and the West, 1500–1900

The concepts in bold italics are developed in the article. For further expansion, please refer to the Topic Guide and the Index.

UNIT 2
The Ferment of the West, 1500–1900

The concepts in bold italics are developed in the article. For further expansion, please refer to the Topic Guide and the Index.

UNIT 3
The Industrial and Scientific Revolutions

The concepts in bold italics are developed in the article. For further expansion, please refer to the Topic Guide and the Index.

UNIT 4
The Twentieth Century to 1950

The concepts in bold italics are developed in the article. For further expansion, please refer to the Topic Guide and the Index.

UNIT 5
The Era of the Cold War, 1950–1990

The concepts in bold italics are developed in the article. For further expansion, please refer to the Topic Guide and the Index.

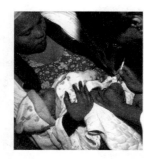

UNIT 6
Global Problems, Global Interdependence

The concepts in bold italics are developed in the article. For further expansion, please refer to the Topic Guide and the Index.

The concepts in bold italics are developed in the article. For further expansion, please refer to the Topic Guide and the Index.

Topic Guide

This topic guide suggests how the selections in this book relate to the subjects covered in your course. You may want to use the topics listed on these pages to search the Web more easily.

On the following pages a number of Web sites have been gathered specifically for this book. They are arranged to reflect the units of this *Annual Edition*. You can link to these sites by going to the student online support site at *http://www.mhcls.com/online/*.

ALL THE ARTICLES THAT RELATE TO EACH TOPIC ARE LISTED BELOW THE BOLD-FACED TERM.

Africa
5. Death on the Nile
9. New Light on the 'Heart of Darkness'
44. 10 Million Orphans
45. In God's Name: Genocide and Religion in the Twentieth Century

Americas
1. Aztecs: A New Perspective
11. Benjamin Franklin: An American in London
23. The Transatlantic Telegraph Cable
35. The Plan and the Man
40. The Common Currents of Imperialism

Asia
3. 400 Years of the East India Company
6. Coffee, Tea, or Opium
7. After Centuries of Japanese Isolation, a Fateful Meeting of East and West
8. Chinese Burns: Britain in China, 1842–1900
21. The X Factor
22. Samurai, Shoguns & the Age of Steam
26. On the Turn—Japan, 1900
28. Gandhi and Nehru: Frustrated Visionaries?
29. The Roots of Chinese Xenophobia
32. Exposing the Rape of Nanking
39. The USA in Vietnam

Business
3. 400 Years of the East India Company
6. Coffee, Tea, or Opium
7. After Centuries of Japanese Isolation, a Fateful Meeting of East and West
16. As Good as Gold?
20. The Workshop of a New Society

China
3. 400 Years of the East India Company
6. Coffee, Tea, or Opium
8. Chinese Burns: Britain in China, 1842–1900
21. The X Factor
29. The Roots of Chinese Xenophobia
32. Exposing the Rape of Nanking

Cold War
35. The Plan and the Man
36. Korea: Echoes of a War
38. Iraq's Unruly Century
39. The USA in Vietnam

Culture
1. Aztecs: A New Perspective
2. The Peopling of Canada
7. After Centuries of Japanese Isolation, a Fateful Meeting of East and West
8. Chinese Burns: Britain in China, 1842–1900
10. The First Feminist
13. This Is Not a Story and Other Stories
15. The Return of Catherine the Great
17. A Woman Writ Large in Our History and Hearts
24. A Tale of Two Reputations

Economics
3. 400 Years of the East India Company
6. Coffee, Tea, or Opium
7. After Centuries of Japanese Isolation, a Fateful Meeting of East and West
14. From Mercantilism to 'The Wealth of Nations'
16. As Good as Gold?
20. The Workshop of a New Society
21. The X Factor
35. The Plan and the Man

Environment
41. Like Herrings in a Barrel
42. The Weather Turns Wild
43. Bombs, Gas and Microbes

Europe
2. The Peopling of Canada
3. 400 Years of the East India Company
4. The Ottomans in Europe
8. Chinese Burns: Britain in China, 1842–1900
10. The First Feminist
14. From Mercantilism to 'The Wealth of Nations'
20. The Workshop of a New Society
27. Home at Last
28. Gandhi and Nehru: Frustrated Visionaries?
30. The Dirty A-Word
31. Women in the Third Reich
34. Judgment at Nuremberg
35. The Plan and the Man
45. In God's Name: Genocide and Religion in the Twentieth Century

France
2. The Peopling of Canada
13. This Is Not a Story and Other Stories
14. From Mercantilism to 'The Wealth of Nations'

Geography
1. Aztecs: A New Perspective
5. Death on the Nile
7. After Centuries of Japanese Isolation, a Fateful Meeting of East and West

Germany
30. The Dirty A-Word
31. Women in the Third Reich
34. Judgment at Nuremberg
45. In God's Name: Genocide and Religion in the Twentieth Century

Great Britain
2. The Peopling of Canada
3. 400 Years of the East India Company
5. Death on the Nile
6. Coffee, Tea, or Opium
8. Chinese Burns: Britain in China, 1842–1900
9. New Light on the 'Heart of Darkness'
10. The First Feminist
11. Benjamin Franklin: An American in London

Internet References

The following Internet sites have been carefully researched and selected to support the articles found in this reader. The easiest way to access these selected sites is to go to our student online support site at *http://www.mhcls.com/online/*.

AE: World History, Volume 2

The following sites were available at the time of publication. Visit our Web site—we update our student online support site regularly to reflect any changes.

General Sources

CNN on Line Page
http://www.cnn.com

This is a U.S. 24-hour video news channel. News, updated every few hours, includes text, pictures, and film. It has good external links.

C-SPAN Online
http://www.c-span.org/

See especially C-SPAN International on the Web for International Programming Highlights and archived C-SPAN programs.

Historical Text Archive
http://historicaltextarchive.com/

This award-winning site contains links to world history, regional or national, and topical history and resources. For speed, use the text version.

Echo Virtual Center
http://echo.gmu.edu/center/

This database of information is for cataloguing, annotating, and reviewing sites on the History of Science, Technology and Medicine site.

HyperHistory Online
http://www.hyperhistory.com/

At this Web site, click on "hyperhistory" and navigate through 3,000 years of world history. There are links to important historical persons, events, and maps.

International Network Information Systems at University of Texas
http://inic.utexas.edu/

This gateway has pointers to international study sites for Africa, India, China, Japan, and many other countries.

Military History
http://militaryhistory.about.com/

Here is a good place to start exploring military history. The site includes a timeline of major wars and links to military history by period.

Humanities Links
http://www-sul.stanford.edu/depts/hasrg/

Philosophical, cultural, and historical worldwide links, including archives, history sites, and an electronic library of full texts and documents are includes on this Web site. The resources are useful for research in history and the humanities.

United Nations System
http://www.unsystem.org/

Everything is listed alphabetically at this official Web site for the United Nations system of organizations. Examples: UNICC; Food and Agriculture Organization.

U.S. Department of State Home Page
http://www.state.gov/index.html

Organized by categories: Hot Topics (i.e. Country Reports on Human Rights Practices), International Policy, Business Services, and more.

Unit 1: The World and the West, 1500–1900

Commodore Matthew Perry
http://members.tripod.com/MickMc/perry.html

Here you will find information about Matthew Perry and his expedition to Japan. There is also a brief history of Japan and its isolation from trading and the West before Perry arrived.

The East India Company
http://www.sscnet.ucla.edu/southasia/History/British/EAco.html

The East India Company has had a long history. Explore its history and products on its official Web site.

Unit 2: The Ferment of the West, 1500–1900

The Adam Smith Institute
http://www.adamsmith.org

This company and its Web site are dedicated to the economic principles and theories of Adam Smith. Visit here to explore those theories and Smith's original texts.

Britannica.com: Mercantilism
http://www.britannica.com/eb/article?eu=53378

This entry from the online Encyclopedia Britannica explains the economic theory and practice of mercantilism. It also provides links to information and popular sites on mercantilism.

Victorian Web
http://www.victorianweb.org/

At this Web site, open up links to Victorian Times, which includes social context, visual arts, politics, and Victorianism. This is an expansive collection of links.

Unit 3: The Industrial and Scientific Revolutions

A Trip to the Past
http://members.aol.com/mhirotsu/kevin/trip2.html

www.mhcls.com/online/

This site contains art, pictures, and text concerning the Industrial Revolution. Follow the links to an essay, innovative inventions, advances in art, and modifications in medicine.

Center for Mars Exploration
http://cmex-www.arc.nasa.gov/

A starting place for an exploration of the history of Mars, with links to the Whole Mars Catalog and Live from Mars information about Pathfinder and Global Surveyor.

Sir Isaac Newton
http://www-gap.dcs.st-and.ac.uk/~history/Mathematicians/Newton.html

Newton.org is a virtual museum about Isaac Newton and the history of science.

Unit 4: The Twentieth Century to 1950

U.S. Holocaust Memorial Museum
http://www.ushmm.org/

From this site you can access the official trial records, with photographs, of the Nuremberg trials, along with complete information about the Holocaust.

World War (1914—1918)
http://www.pitt.edu/~pugachev/greatwar/ww1.html

This page is dedicated to World War I and features links to many subjects, including trench warfare, the Versailles Treaty, individual countries' participation, and lost poets of the war.

World War II on the Web
http://www.geocities.com/Athens/Oracle/2691/welcome.htm

From this page you can explore 445 links to World War II material, including Pacific War Chronology, Women at War, Rescuers During the Holocaust, and the Rise of Adolf Hitler.

Unit 5: The Era of the Cold War, 1950–1990

The Chornobyl Nuclear Accident
http://www.infoukes.com/history/chornobyl

This site contains Dr. Zuzak's Chornobyl Files, Chornobyl maps and photo gallery, and a Chornobyl bibliography. There are also essays and projects about the disaster and its ramifications.

The Marshall Plan
http://www.marshallfoundation.org

Here is a brief overview concerning the Marshall Plan.

Russia on the Web
http://www.valley.net/~transnat/

Among other links at this very complete site, click on History for a virtual tour of the palace where Nicholas II and Alexandra lived, Mikhail Gorbachev's home page, or Russian Studies on the Internet, a listing of sites related to Russian history and culture.

Vietnam Online
http://www.pbs.org/wgbh/amex/vietnam

Official Web site for the PBS series "Vietnam: A Television History," first broadcast in 1983 and repeated in 1998. It covers all phases of the war and its legacy.

WWW Virtual Library: Russian and East European Studies
http://www.ucis.pitt.edu/reesweb/

Through the NewsWeb at the University of Pittsburgh, there is a massive collection of links to both historic and contemporary information about Russia and Eastern Europe. At this Web site, there is everything from maps of the former Soviet Union to Bucharest's home page.

Unit 6: Global Problems, Global Interdependence

Africa News Web Site: Crisis in the Great Lakes Region
http://www.africanews.org/greatlakes.html

The African News Web Site on the Great Lakes (i.e., Rwanda, Burundi), Zaire (now Democratic Republic of the Congo), Kenya, Tanzania, and Uganda is found here, with frequent updates plus good links to other sites.

Africa Notes
http://www.csis.org/html/2africa.html

CSIS Africa Notes is published monthly. Check into this Web site for what's new in efforts to help sub-Saharan countries.

Amnesty International
http://www.amnesty.org/

Information about the current state of human rights throughout the world is available at this Web site.

Population Awareness
http://www.overpopulation.org/nav.html

This page contains fact sheets and statistics about population as well as answers to the questions: Why does population matter? and What are the impacts of overpopulation?

Reliefweb
http://www.reliefweb.int/

This is the UN's Department of Humanitarian Affairs clearinghouse for international humanitarian emergencies. It has daily updates, including Reuters, VOA, and PANA.

Target America
http://www.pbs.org/wgbh/pages/frontline/shows/target

Comprehensive Web site on terrorism which includes: a timeline of terrorist attacks, interviews with policy makers and newsmen, and an essay on the evolution of Islamic terrorism. It also includes related links.

We highly recommend that you review our Web site for expanded information and our other product lines. We are continually updating and adding links to our Web site in order to offer you the most usable and useful information that will support and expand the value of your Annual Editions. You can reach us at: *http://www.mhcls.com/annualeditions/.*

UNIT 1

The World and the West, 1500–1900

Unit Selections

1. **Aztecs: A New Perspective,** John M.D. Pohl
2. **The Peopling of Canada,** Phillip Buckner
3. **400 Years of the East India Company,** Huv W. Bowen
4. **The Ottomans in Europe,** Geoffrey Woodward
5. **Death on the Nile,** Simon Craig
6. **Coffee, Tea, or Opium,** Samuel M. Wilson
7. **After Centuries of Japanese Isolation,** James Fallows
8. **Chinese Burns: Britain in China, 1842–1900,** Robert Bickers
9. **New Light on the 'Heart of Darkness',** Angus Mitchell

Key Points to Consider

- How has Aztec civilization been clouded in mystery and misunderstanding? What does Pohl do to provide counterbalance to that?

- How did Canada's two colonial experiences influence their "peopling"? What affect does this have on Canada today?

- What impact, positively and negatively, did the British East India Company have on the 400 years of its existence? Who benefited most from their actions, and who was hurt most by them?

- What was the extent of Ottoman westward expansion in the 16th century? How did the Western European nations respond to this expansion?

- Why did the British wage war on the Sudanese in 1897? What resulted from this action?

- Why were British merchants allowed to transport opium to China? How were British interest affected by this? Chinese interests?

- Why was Matthew Perry's mission to Japan a turning point in Japanese history? What specifics happened as a result of it?

- How did Joseph Conrad's book influence Western policies toward Africa?

Student Web Site

www.mhcls.com/online

Internet References

Further information regarding these Web sites may be found in this book's preface or online.

Commodore Matthew Perry
http://members.tripod.com/MickMc/perry.html

The East India Company
http://www.sscnet.ucla.edu/southasia/History/British/EAco.html

Searching for trade opportunities, the small, seafaring nation of Portugal began the great European exploration of the fifteenth century. Portuguese navigators followed the western coast of Africa, eventually rounded the Cape of Good Hope, and sailed on to India and the spice islands of the Far East. They were the first Europeans to reach Japan, and they introduced the Japanese to both guns and Christianity.

The Japanese had not been very interested in the rest of the world and had gone so far as to suppress gun making in favor of honing the honored Samurai swords. It was a profound shock, therefore, when Matthew Perry of the United States arrived with his small flotilla and forced Japan to open it ports, under threat of naval gun power. However, following the forced opening of its ports, Japan undertook a large-scale industrialization that brought it power in the Far East and allowed it to avoid the humiliation visited upon China by Western nations.

Western nations, particularly Great Britain, followed the Portuguese and the Dutch to the Far East. At the end of the eighteenth century, an English delegation led by Lord George Macartney tried unsuccessfully to arrange a trade agreement with China. Meanwhile, the East India Company consolidated

British power in India with Robert Clive's victory over an Indian and French force at the Battle of Plassey during the Seven Years' War. Imperialism arrived through the dominance of a commercial enterprise.

The East India Company established trade in China and paid for the tea it bought with opium grown in India. Chinese efforts to halt this debilitating drug trade failed when the British government authorized the use of its warships to legalize the transactions. Five ports and Hong Kong fell under British influence, and other European nations moved in to join in the exploitation of China's weakness. In 1900 China's hatred of outsiders boiled over in the Boxer Rebellion. When the uprising was brutally suppressed by Western troops, China seemed on the verge of dissolution.

Britain's industrial and military might assured its dominance throughout the empire, as well as in far-flung cities where its interests were threatened. The strategic importance of the Suez Canal, the vital link with India, led the British to construct a desert railway line from the Egyptian border to Khartoum, capital of the Sudan. A local warlord who controlled the area was, of course, no match for well-trained troops with machine guns and artillery.

One example of successful resistance to European expansionism can be found in the vibrant military culture of the Ottoman Turks, whose army was the largest in Europe and whose navy ruled the shipping lanes of the eastern Mediterranean. From 1354 the Ottoman Empire had advanced westward, overrunning Constantinople in the mid-fifteenth century and renaming it Istanbul. By 1520, the Ottomans were undisputed rulers of the Muslim world and already casting their shadow over Western Europe.

Imperial cruelty and excess in Africa's Congo, fictionalized in Joseph Conrad's *Heart of Darkness,* along with press coverage of abuses in the region surrounding the Amazon, provoked public outrage and ultimately led to reform. Radical discussions from this period inspired human rights organizations such as Amnesty International and eventually led to the abolition of slavery.

European adventures in the Americas included both the Spanish military conquest of Mesoamerica and the much more incremental annexation of Canada. There, the conquest happened much more slowly and much less violently. So gradual was its takeover as first a French colony and later a British one that both cultures remain vibrant today. Although the majority of Canada is English-speaking, there is a thriving area of French language and culture in the province of Quebec.

Aztecs: A New Perspective

JOHN M.D. POHL

As the warriors stand before the Great Temple of Tenochtitlán listening to speeches given by the emperor, they gaze out over the plaza looking for the faces of their proud families among the multitude who have come to witness their triumph. One mighty veteran gets a firmer grip on the hair of the prisoner kneeling at his feet and looks up at the towering pyramid to ponder the shrine of his patron god. It is the sworn duty of every Aztec soldier to carry on the legacy of Huitzilopochtli, Hummingbird of the South; to be ever vigilant, ever prepared to protect his family and his city from those who would destroy all that his ancestors had worked to accomplish.

The captive resigns himself to his fate; he knew the fortunes of war when he joined the army of his city-state in revolt against the empire. The priests approach and the warrior makes his presentation. Now is the time for the final conflict, the triumph, the conclusion of battle to be witnessed there in the central precinct by the Aztec people themselves. The captive will reenact the role of a cosmic enemy, living proof of Huitzilopochtli's omnipotence, of his power manifest in the abilities of the warriors, his spiritual descendants, to repay him for his blessings. The captive is pulled on to his back over the surface of a stone disk emblazoned with the image of the sun. He is held down by four priests, while a fifth drives a knife into his chest. The trauma of the blow kills him nearly instantaneously. Just as quickly the priest slits the arteries of the heart and lifts the bloody mass into the air, pronouncing it to be the 'precious eagle cactus fruit', a supreme offering to the solar god.

Every time I look upon the colossal monument known as the Aztec Calendar Stone, I try to imagine such rituals following Aztec military campaigns. Thousands of people participated— to reassure themselves that their investment in supplying food, making weapons and equipment, and committing the lives of their children to the armies would grant them the benefits of conquest that their emperors guaranteed.

Aztec civilisation has been clouded in mystery and misunderstanding for centuries. For many people, knowledge of the Aztecs is confined to vague recollections of the illustrated books of youth and their graphic depictions of grisly sacrifices. This may be more true in Britain, indeed in Europe, than in North America where we have been privileged to witness a remarkable rediscovery of the Aztec culture over the past two decades. Aztec

'sacrifice', for example, once perceived as a ruthless practice committed by a 'tribe' seemingly obsessed with bloodshed, is now seen as no more or less brutal than what many imperial civilisations have done to 'bring home the war' in the words of my colleague, the Harvard professor, David Carrasco.

Today we witness war on television to confirm for ourselves that what a government claims they are doing in the interests of national security is worth the cost in resources and human life. But ancient societies had no comparable means to convey the image of battle to the heartland of their culture. Roman triumphs were a means of doing just this, and were more important than battlefields for ambitious politicians, and we should not forget that those captives who were forced to march in their thousands to celebrate the glorious commander were condemned to horrifying deaths in the Colosseum. The Aztec rituals were no different.

In their songs and stories the Aztecs described four great ages of the past, each destroyed by some catastrophe wrought by vengeful gods. The fifth and present world only came into being through the self-sacrifice of a hero who was transformed into the Sun. But the Sun refused to move across the sky without a gift from humankind to equal his own. War was therefore waged to obtain the holy food that the Sun required, and thus to perpetuate life on Earth. The Aztecs used no term like 'human sacrifice' for their rituals. For them it was next-laualli, the sacred debt payment to the gods. Thus warfare, sacrifice and the promotion of agricultural fertility were inextricably linked in their religious ideology. Meanwhile for the Aztec soldiers, participation in these rituals was a means of displaying their prowess, gaining rewards from the emperor's own hand, and announcing their promotion in society. In addition, the executions served as a grim reminder for foreign dignitaries, lest they should ever consider making war against the empire themselves.

The very name 'Aztec' is debated by scholars today. The word is not really indigenous, though it does have a cultural basis. It was first proposed by a European, the explorer-naturalist Alexander von Humboldt (1769–1859), and later popularized by William H. Prescott in his remarkable 1843 publication The History of the Conquest of Mexico. 'Aztec' is an eponym derived from Aztlan, or 'Place of the White Heron', a legendary homeland of seven desert tribes called Chichimecs who miraculously emerged from caves located at the heart of a sacred mountain far to the north of the Valley of Mexico. The Chichimecs enjoyed a peaceful existence, hunting and fishing, until they were divinely inspired to fulfill a destiny of conquest by their gods. They journeyed until one day they witnessed a tree being ripped asunder by a bolt of lightning. The seventh and last tribe, known as the Mexica, took the event as a sign that they were to divide and follow their own destiny. They continued to wander for many more years, sometimes hunting and sometimes settling down to farm, but never remaining in any one place for long. When Tula, the capital of a powerful Toltec state that had dominated central Mexico for four hundred years, collapsed, the Mexica decided to move south to Lake Texcoco.

Impoverished and without allies, the Mexica were subjected to attacks by local Toltec warlords who forced them to retreat to an island where they witnessed a miraculous vision of prophecy: an eagle standing on a cactus growing from solid rock. It was the sign for Tenochtitlán, their final destination. Having little to offer other than their reputation as warriors, the Mexica hired themselves out as mercenaries to rival Toltec factions. Eventually they were able to affect the balance of power in the region to such a degree that they were granted royal marriages. Now the most powerful of the seven original Aztec tribes, by the early fifteenth century the Mexica incorporated their former enemies and together they built an empire. Eventually they were to give their name to the nation of Mexico, while their city of Tenochtitlán became what we know as Mexico City. The term Aztec is applied to the archaeological culture that dominated the Basin of Mexico in the fifteenth and early sixteenth century, but the people themselves were ethnically highly diverse.

Tenochtitlán was officially said to have been founded in 1325 but it was over a century before the city rose to its height as an imperial capital. Between 1372 and 1428, the Mexica emperors—called huey tlatoque or 'great speakers'— Acamapichtli (r. 1376–96), Huitzilihuitl (r. 1397–1417), and Chimalpopoca (r. 1417–27) served as the vassals of a despotic Tepanec lord named Tezozomoc of Azcapotzalco. They shared in the spoils of victory and succeeded in expanding their own domain south and east along Lake Texcoco. But when Tezozomoc died in 1427, his son Maxtla seized power and had Chimalpopoca assassinated. The Mexica quickly appointed Chimalpopoca's uncle, a war captain named Itzcóatl, as emperor. Itzcóatl allied himself to Nezhualcoyotl, deposed heir to the throne of Texcoco, the kingdom lying on the eastern shore of the lake. Together the two kings attacked Azcapotzalco. The siege lasted for over a hundred days and only concluded when Maxtla relinquished his throne and retreated into exile. Itzcóatl and Nezhualcoyotl then rewarded the Tepanec lords who had aided them, and the three cities of Tenochtitlán, Texcoco, and Tlacopan formed the new Aztec Empire of the Triple Alliance.

Itzcóatl died in 1440 and was succeeded by his nephew Motecuhzoma Ilhuicamina. Motecuhzoma I (r. 1440–69), as he was later known, charted the course for Aztec expansionism for the remainder of the fifteenth century and was succeeded by his son Axayacatl in 1469. Axayacatl had proven himself a capable military commander as a prince, now he sought to capitalise on the conquests of his father by entirely surrounding the kingdom

of Tlaxcala to the east and expanding imperial control over the Mixtecs and Zapotecs of Oaxaca to the south. But by 1481, Axayacatl had died. He was followed by Tizoc, who ruled briefly but ineffectually. In 1486, the throne passed to Tizoc's younger brother, Ahuitzotl (r. 1486–1502), who proved himself an outstanding military commander. Ahuitzotl reorganised the army and soon regained much of the territory lost under the previous administration. He then initiated a programme of long-distance campaigning on an unprecedented scale. The empire reached its apogee under Ahuitzotl, dominating possibly as many as 25 million people throughout the Mexican highlands. Ahuitzotl was succeeded by the doomed Motecuhzoma II (r. 1502–20) who suffered the catastrophic Spanish invasion under Hernan Cortés.

The land mass of Tenochtitlán, the Aztec capital founded on a small island off the western shore of Lake Texcoco, was artificially expanded until eventually it covered more than five square miles. The city was divided into four districts. Each district was composed of neighbourhood wards of landowning families called calpulli, or 'house groups'. Most of the calpulli were inhabited by farmers who cultivated bountiful crops of corn, beans, and squash using an ingenious system of raised fields called chinampas, while others were occupied by craftspeople. Six major canals ran through the metropolis, with many smaller ones criss-crossing the entire city, making it possible to travel virtually anywhere by boat. Boats were also the principal means of transportation to the island. Scholars estimate that between 200,000 and 250,000 people lived in Tenochtitlán in 1500, more than four times the population of London at that time.

There were three great causeways that ran from the mainland into the city. These were spanned with drawbridges that, when taken up, sealed the city off entirely. Fresh water was transported by a system of aqueducts, of which the main construction ran from a spring on a mountain called Chapultepec to the west. The four districts each had temples dedicated to the principal gods, though these were overshadowed by the Great Temple, a man-made mountain constructed within the central precinct and topped by dual shrines dedicated to the Toltec storm god Tlaloc and the Chichimec war god Huitzilopochtli. The surrounding precinct itself was a city within a city of over 1,200 square metres of temples, public buildings, palaces, and plazas enclosed by a defensive bastion called the coatepantli or serpent wall, so named after the scores of carved stone snake heads that ornamented its exterior.

In November 1519, the band of 250 Spanish adventurers stood above Lake Texcoco and gazed upon Tenochtitlán. The Spaniards were dumbfounded and many wondered if what they were looking at was an illusion. The more worldly among them, veterans of Italian wars, compared the city to Venice but were no less astonished to find such a metropolis on the other side of the world. At the invitation of the Emperor Motecuhzoma, Hernan Cortés led his men across the great Tlalpan causeway into Tenochtitlán. He later described what he saw in letters to the Holy Roman Emperor Charles V. Cortés marvelled at the broad boulevards and canals, the temples dedicated to countless gods, as well as the magnificent residences of the lords and priests who resided with the emperor and attended his court. The Spaniard described the central market where thousands of people sold everything from gold, silver, gems, shells and feathers, to unhewn stone, adobe bricks, and timber. Each street was devoted to a special commodity, from clay pottery to dyed textiles, while a special court of judges enforced strict rules of transaction. All manner of foods were bartered: dogs, rabbits, deer, turkeys, quail and every sort of vegetable and fruit.

What happened once Cortés had entered the city is a long-familiar tale, retold from vivid reports of the Europeans themselves: though the Spaniards were initially welcomed, they seized emperor Motecuhzoma, held him hostage and forced him to swear allegiance to the king of Spain. In June 1520 Motecuhzoma was killed while trying to placate his subjects. Cortés was forced to retreat, but came back to beseige Tenochtitlán, which fell after three months in August 1521.

Some of the most dramatic recent changes to our perception of the Aztecs have come with a critical reappraisal of the histories of the Conquest itself. Spanish accounts traditionally portrayed the defeat of the Aztec empire as a brilliant military achievement, with Cortés' troops, outnumbered but better armed with guns and cavalry, defeating hordes of superstitious savages. The reality now appears far more complex. During the first year-and-a-half of the conflict, the Spaniards rarely numbered over 300 and frequently they campaigned with fewer than 150. Their steel weapons may have had an impact initially, but they soon ran out of gunpowder and by 1520 had eaten their remaining horses. So what accounted for their incredible achievement? They owed their success not so much to superior arms, training, and leadership as to Aztec political factionalism and disease.

With his publication in 1993 of Montezuma, Cortés, and the Fall of Old Mexico, Hugh Thomas exploded the myths of the Conquest, demonstrating that in nearly all their battles, the Spaniards were fighting with Indian allied armies that numbered in the tens of thousands. Initially these were drawn from disaffected states to the east and west of the Basin of Mexico, especially Tlaxcala, but by 1521 even the Acolhua of Texcoco, cofounders of the empire together with the Mexica, had appointed a new government that clearly saw an opportunity in the defeat of their former allies. The extent to which the Spaniards were conscious of strategy in coalition-building or whether they were actually being manipulated by Indians themselves is unknown. But on August 13th, 1521, when Cortés defeated Tenochtitlán, he was at the head of an allied Indian army estimated by some historians at between 150,000 and 200,000 men. Yet even this victory was only achieved after what is considered to be the longest continuous battle ever waged in the annals of military history.

By now, successive epidemics of smallpox and typhus—diseases unknown in Mexico prior to the arrival of the Europeans—were raging. Neither the Europeans nor the Indians appreciated that disease could be caused by contagious viruses. In fact successive epidemics would take away first 25, 50, and eventually 75 per cent of the population of an entire city-state within a year. By the summer of 1521, smallpox in particular had created a situation that allowed Cortés to assume the role of a kind of 'kingmaker,' appointing new governments among his allies, as the leaders of the old regimes loyal to the Mexica succumbed to sickness.

The Pre-Columbian city was totally destroyed during the siege of 1521 and the Spanish colonialists founded their own capital, Mexico City, on the ruins. After this, knowledge of Tenochtitlán's central religious precinct remained largely conjectural. The traditional belief that the Great Temple might lie beneath Mexico City's contemporary zocalo or city centre seemed to be confirmed in 1790, with the discovery of the monolithic sculptures known as the Calendar Stone and the statue of Coatlique, the legendary mother of Huitzilopochtli. Writings, drawings, and maps from the early colonial period appeared to indicate that the base of the Great Temple had been approximately 300ft square, with four or five stepped levels rising as high as 180ft. There were descriptions of dual staircases on the west side, stopping before two shrines at the summit. Only recently, however, has systematic archaeological excavation provided a more certain idea of what the Spanish invaders actually witnessed.

On February 21st, 1978, Mexico City electrical workers were excavating a trench, six feet below street level to the northeast of the cathedral, when they encountered a monolithic carved stone block. Archaeologists were called to the scene to salvage what turned out to be a stone disk carved with a relief in human form, eleven feet in diameter. The image was identified as a goddess known as Coyolxauhqui, 'She Who is Adorned with Bells'. According to a legend recorded by the Spanish friar and ethnographer Bernardino de Sahagún (1499–1590), there once lived an old woman named Coatlicue or Lady Serpent Skirt, together with her daughter, Coyolxauhqui, and her 400 sons at Coatepec, meaning Snake Mountain. One day as Coatlicue was attending to her chores she gathered up a mysterious ball of feathers and placed them in the sash of her belt. Miraculously, she found herself with child. But when her daughter Coyoxauhqui saw what had happened she was enraged and shrieked: 'My brothers, she has dishonoured us! Who is the cause of what is in her womb? We must kill this wicked one who is with child!'

Coatlicue was frightened but Huitzilopochtli, who was in her womb, called to her saying: 'Have no fear mother, for I know what to do.' The 400 sons went forth. Each wielded his weapon and Coyolxauqui led them. At last they scaled the heights of Coatepec. At this point there are many variations to the story but it appears that when Coyolxauhqui and her brothers reached the summit of Coatepec they immediately killed Coatlique. Then Huitzilopochtli was born in full array with his shield and spear thrower. At once he pierced Coyolxauhqui with a spear and then he struck off her head. Her body twisted and turned as it fell to the ground below the Snake Mountain. Then Huitzilopochtli took on the 400 brothers in equal measure and slew each of them.

Examination of the Coyolxauhqui stone led the National Institute's director of excavations, Eduardo Matos Moctezuma, to conclude that the monument had never been seen by the Spaniards, much less smashed and reburied like so many other Aztec carvings. Remembering that Coyoxauhqui's body was said to have come to rest at the foot of the mountain, the archaeologists began to surmise that Coatepec, or rather its incarnation as the Great Temple, might lie very nearby. It was not long before they discovered parts of a grand staircase and then the massive stone serpent heads, literally signifying the Snake Mountain Coatepec, surrounding the base of the pyramid itself. The Great Temple had been found by decoding a thousand-year-old legend.

Since 1980 the Mexican National Institute of Anthropology and history has carried out almost continuous excavations, uncovering at least six separate building phases of the Great Temple, as well as numerous smaller temples and palaces from the surrounding precinct. Excavations carried out by Leonardo Lopéz Luján and his associates have uncovered no fewer than 120 caches of priceless objects buried as offerings from vassal states within the matrix of the Great Temple. Further excavations, even tunnelling under the streets of Mexico City, to the north of the site have revealed an astounding new structure called the House of the Eagles (named for the stone and ceramic statuary portraying the heraldic raptor), which has yielded even greater treasures. Perhaps the most dramatic finds are frightening life-size images of Mictlantecuhtli, god of the underworld. Lopéz and his associates, examining images of Mictlantecuhtli found in pictographic books called codices, noted that they are depicted being drenched in offerings of blood. New techniques to identify microscopic traces of organic material were applied to the spot where the statues were found, that revealed extremely high concentrations of albumin and other substances pertaining to blood on the floors surrounding pedestals on which the statues once stood, a testament to the veracity of the ancient Aztec books.

One of the most remarkable discoveries was a stone box that had been hermetically sealed with a layer of plaster. Inside lay the remains of an entire wardrobe, headdress, and mask for a priest of the Temple of Tlaloc, the ancient Toltec god of rain and fertility whose shrine stood next to that of Huitzilopochtli at the summit of the pyramid. Despite the lavish depictions of Aztec ritual clothing in the codices, none was known to have survived the fires of Spanish evangelistic fervour. For the first time we have a glimpse of the perishable artefacts which played such a major role in Aztec rituals, pomp and ceremony.

During the course of excavations within the matrix-fill of the Great Temple, archaeologists have found the remains of objects very much like those well-known from earlier collections, together with hordes of other exotic materials. Investigators were initially puzzled by the discovery of hordes of shells, jade beads, greenstone masks, jaguar and crocodile bones, exquisitely painted vessels, textile fragments and quantities of other exotic materials. The clue lay in the Codex Mendoza, an pictographic book of Aztec civilisation compiled under Spanish supervision in 1541 and preserved in Oxford University's Bodleian Library. Here, the manuscript inventories the entire tribute of the empire for one year. Hieroglyphic place-signs name cities and provinces conquered throughout the fifteenth century. Pictographs for staple foods such as maize, beans, and squash appear, but the great majority of the pictographs represent precisely the same kinds of exotic goods found in the excavations.

Many ancient societies buried precious materials, including works of art. Economists argue that such practices served as levelling mechanisms when the supply of anything rare or labour intensive exceeded demand. The Aztecs compared war to a market place and it appears that there was more to this than just metaphor.

In societies like the Mixtecs and Zapotecs of southern Mexico, with whom the Aztecs fought nearly continuously for seventy-five years, the production and consumption of luxury goods in precious metals, gems, shell, feathers, and cotton was restricted to the elite. Commoners were even forbidden to wear jewellery. Royal women were the principal craft producers and the kings sought to marry many wives, not only to forge alliances but so that they could enrich themselves by exchanging the women's artistic creations through dowry, and other gift-giving networks. A king might marry as many as twenty times, so each palace could produce luxury goods to be measured by the ton. By 1200 CE, royal palaces throughout the central and southern highlands of Mexico began to engage in fiercely competitive reciprocity systems to enhance their positions within alliance networks. The greater the ability of a royal house to acquire exotic materials and to craft them into exquisite jewels, textiles, and featherwork, the better marriages it could negotiate. The better marriages it could negotiate, the higher the rank a royal house could achieve within a confederacy and, in turn, the better access it would have to materials, merchants, and craftspeople. In short, royal marriages promoted syndicates.

Historians are beginning to recognise that the Aztec strategy of military conquest was not only to secure supplies of food. It also sought to subvert the luxury economies of foreign states, forcing them to produce goods for the Empire's own system of gift exchange: rewards for military valour that made the soldiers of the imperial armies dependent upon the emperor himself for promotion in Aztec society. The outlandish uniforms seen on the battlefield must also have served as graphic proof of the kind of crushing tribute demands the Aztec empire could inflict. No less than 50,000 woven cloaks a month were sent by the conquered provinces to Tenochtitlán. For the kingdoms of southern Mexico, the prospect of being forced to subvert their artistic skills to the production of military uniforms to be redistributed to an ever more glory-hungry army of Aztec lords and commoners alike must have been a frightening proposition.

A great many Aztec artefacts were taken back to Europe by the Spanish; finely wrought jewels of gold, human skulls studded with turquoise mosaic, heraldic shields ornamented with the feathers of rare tropical birds, and dazzling codices all mesmerized the court of Habsburg Spain. Later these became highly prized by the nobility of Europe, in some cases passing between princes as ambassadorial presents. Others were seized as war booty and fell into the hands of collectors who valued them but were often at a loss to understand what they were or who had created them. It was only when a new generation of scholars and adventurers began to explore the ruins of Mexico and Central America in the nineteenth century that their meaning began to be appreciated. In November of this year, a major exhibition at the Royal Academy in London will be the first time that these have been brought together with the stunning finds of the past twenty-five years from the Great Temple site.

The Peopling of Canada

PHILLIP BUCKNER

Canada's experience of European imperialism has been both longer and more diverse than any of the major European colonies of settlement in the Americas. Indeed, parallels with those colonies are misleading for Canada alone was the creation not only of two imperial powers but of two distinct periods of European colonisation.

During the first period from the sixteenth to the eighteenth centuries all of the European colonies of settlement grew painfully slowly but none more painfully and slowly than the French colonies in Canada. Neither Acadia nor New France possessed the potential for plantation economies and the only exports that they produced of value to the mother country were fish and furs. The fisheries were of considerable economic importance, but did not require permanent settlements for their exploitation. The fur trade drew France into the interior of North America, but it could not sustain a large population base.

The French crown placed responsibility for colonisation in the hands of a succession of chartered companies until 1663 when it made a concerted effort to increase the population of New France. The costs were high and after 1672 the French monarchy returned primary responsibility for transporting colonists to French merchants. The flow of emigrants dwindled to a trickle. When Acadia was surrendered to the British in 1713, its population was about 1,000. At the time of its surrender in 1763 New France numbered around 75,000.

No more than a few hundred French settlers paid their own way across the Atlantic and there was a substantial preponderance of single, particularly single male, migrants. Peter Moogk estimates that about 10,250 migrants made their home in Canada between 1608 and 1760: 3,300 soldiers, 1,800 Acadians, 1,500 French women, 1,200 indentured workers, 900 slaves, 600 British subjects (most taken captive during the wars with the British), 500 male clergy, 250 self-financed migrants, and 200 deported prisoners. If these figures are correct, New France was even more of a military settlement than previously thought since soldiers formed a third of the total number of colonists. Since at least some of the soldiers and workers did not come from France, the origins of the population were also considerably more diverse than is traditionally assumed. The role of the French women, who had the highest retention rate of any group of migrants to the colony, was undoubtedly critical in the transmission of French culture, as was the role of the church, since all residents had to be Catholic.

Initially the chartered companies lacked incentive to colonise and the fur trade hindered agricultural development by employing large numbers of men in the interior of the colony. Yet after the first half of the seventeenth century the fur traders were aware that without a substantial base along the St Lawrence their furs and their scalps would end up decorating an Iroquois longhouse. The failure to create a larger colony had more to do with the imbalance of the sexes. Women of marital age continued to be outnumbered by men by more than two to one during the mid-seventeenth century and without a wife a male could not establish a viable farm. After 1700 the sexes came into balance but without substantial immigration New France grew slowly through natural increase.

Since half-a-million French Protestants left France between 1660 and 1710 the decision to exclude Protestants may have denied to the colony a valuable source of immigrants. Yet it is far from certain that a large number of French Protestants would have emigrated if allowed to do so. In any event the Catholic population of France was large enough to have supplied New France with all the settlers it required. Why then did they not go? One explanation emphasises the demands of the French army, which was many times larger than that of Britain's, and it is plausible that employment opportunities in the army reduced the number of potential emigrants.

But a large pool of itinerant landless labourers and unemployed artisans still existed in France and a peasant class suffering from high levels of feudal exactions and taxation. Some historians have therefore suggested that it was the land tenure system in France which discouraged emigration. In England the peasantry had lost their title to the land and had become tenants or wage labourers. In France, on the other hand, the peasants not only retained their titles but clung to the land tenaciously. But this hypothesis fails to explain why so many of those who did migrate subsequently abandoned New France. Something of the order of 27,000 French men and women emigrated but close to 70 per cent returned to France.

Historians have, in fact, been beguiled by the obvious comparisons with New England, which was created in one rush by a large number of families who came not to trade but to farm and who had the resources to establish viable communities. New France did not begin with this initial advantage and so could not offset the locational disadvantages of its climate, harsh environment and limited resources. Moreover, New France was almost continuously at war, with the Iroquois in the seventeenth century and the Thirteen Colonies in the eighteenth. It is hardly surprising that such a large proportion of the French immigrants were drawn from the military. New France began life as a fur trading post but ended it as a military outpost with a small colony attached to the base.

In the years immediately following the conquest the former French colonies received only a handful of British emigrants. Between 1763 and 1775, 125,000 emigrants from the British Isles sailed for British America, but virtually all of them went to the Thirteen Colonies. Indeed, the Thirteen Colonies, not the British Isles, was responsible for most of settlers who came to Canada prior to 1815. Americans came in three waves. The first consisted of some 7–8,000 New Englanders who occupied the lands forcibly vacated by the Acadians in Nova Scotia, and a few hundred Americans who went to Quebec. The second and largest wave were Loyalists, compelled to leave the newly established United States after 1783. Around 60,000 came to build new homes in the remnants of the first British Empire in North America. In the 1790s a third wave of American immigrants (erroneously described as Late Loyalists) came in search of land. The war of 1812–14 put an end to further migration from the United States but there was precious little about British North America that was British in 1815. By far the largest colony was Lower Canada with a population of about 335,000, of whom nearly 90 per cent were descendants of the original French emigrants. Outside of the urban areas, the French-Canadians had no need to learn English and they continued to live under their own civil law and to follow traditional inheritance practices. With virtually no migration from France for half a century French-Canadians had developed a strong sense of ethnic solidarity. In the remaining colonies the population was approaching 200,000, a substantial majority of them descendants of American migrants; most of their trade and their cultural ties were with the United States.

All this would change because of a second wave of colonisation from the British Isles after 1815. Over the next half century substantially more than a million British emigrants poured into British North America. Many did not stay but moved on to the United States. Nonetheless, the population of Canada at the time of Confederation in 1867 was around 3½ million, nearly seven times what it had been in 1815. The migration to Canada was remarkably homogeneous compared with the much larger migration to the United States in this period. Except for a small influx of Germans, almost all of the immigrants came from the British Isles.

The sheer scale of the migration, which peaked in the quarter century from 1830 to 1854, meant that every province except Quebec had a majority composed of the British-born and their children by 1867. Even in Quebec the British minority had grown to nearly 25 per cent of the population.

The vast majority of the migrants paid their own way across the Atlantic. Since none came as indentured servants and slavery never took root, British North America was developed almost entirely by free labour. Male migrants slightly outnumbered women, but the majority came as part of a family migration, even though some members of the family often had to precede others. Most migrants, even those from urban areas, sought to acquire land of their own and most ended up in rural areas occupying family farms.

The frontier experience of these immigrants was remarkably short-lived. Since the majority came after 1830 and settlement was virtually complete by the 1860s, eastern British North America was transformed from a wilderness into a series of comparatively densely populated communities within a single generation. Nor did nineteenth-century British immigrants face a prolonged conflict with native peoples. They were not a kinder, gentler people than earlier migrants, but they settled in areas where, because of the ravages of European diseases and the prolonged conflicts of an earlier period, the native peoples were too few in number to offer effective resistance to the spread of settlement.

The British immigrants also overwhelmed the earlier American migrants. Lower Canada continued to have a substantial French-Canadian majority, but even the French-Canadians were compelled to make substantial changes in their society in order to survive within the second British Empire and within a Canada in which the British immigrants and their descendants formed a numerical majority.

Although migrants came from all parts of the British Isles, the Englist Canada that came into being in the first half of the nineteenth century was more Irish and more Scottish than the mother country. The Irish formed close to 60 per cent of the emigrants. Most of what has been written about the Irish in Canada has suffered from erroneous comparison with the Irish in the United States and an obsession with the Irish Famine. In fact, the mass movement of Irish to Canada peaked earlier than to the United States and the vast majority of Canada's Irish arrived before the onset of the Great Famine in 1845. The famine years did see an enormous increase in immigrants, but most of them continued on to the United States. In the later 1850s Irish migration to Canada dropped precipitously, at a time when Irish migration to the United States was dramatically increasing. Not only did Irish migration to Canada largely precede the famine but the majority of those who settled in Canada were Protestants, not Catholics.

Early nineteenth-century transatlantic Irish migrants were rarely destitute. More typically they came from comfortable farming classes who feared a future loss of status. They migrated as part of a family movement and were destined not to become indigent labourers but to acquire land and become agricultural pioneers. In the later years the income and skill level of the migrants dropped but the vast majority of those without resources were attracted to the United States. In many of the urban centres, in the lumber and railway construction camps, there were clusters of Irish labourers, but they were not the norm. Even the Catholic Irish were not so dramatically overrepresented among the labouring classes as is usually assumed. Moreover, the Irish were significantly represented among the educated elite of the colonies; many of the judges, customs officers and surveyors were graduates of Trinity College, Dublin, and every colony had its Irish-born merchants, lawyers and doctors. In large parts of New Brunswick and the Canadas the Irish presence was so large that they did not so much overwhelm the existing settlers as absorb them.

The Scots were also disproportionately represented among the migrants, forming about 15 per cent of the total. Small numbers of Highlanders had begun to trickle into British North America before 1815. A people in transition from a clan-based society dependent upon subsistence agriculture, they moved across the Atlantic as part of communal groups under traditional clan leadership to protest against the economic transformation of the Highlands. But Highlanders composed a diminishing proportion of the migrants after 1815, because as economic conditions in the Highlands deteriorated, fewer and fewer could afford the costs of a passage. The majority of Scottish migrants came from the highly commercialised economy of the central Lowlands. By the early nineteenth century Lowland Scots were already a highly mobile people. Like the Irish, most moved as families and settled on the land as farmers, although there was a significant proportion of artisans among the migrants.

Not surprisingly, in view of the superior Scottish system of higher education and the over-supply of professionals in Scotland, Scottish university graduates played an important role in developing Canada's system of higher education and were strongly represented in the fields of law and medicine. Moreover, Scottish commercial links with British North America were strong. Scottish involvement in the fur trade increased the numbers of Scottish merchants in Quebec in the late eighteenth century but the real growth came with the expansion of the colonial timber and grain trades in the nineteenth. Scottish firms dominated the import and export trade of the colonies and provided the leadership in organising the Canadian banking system.

Less is known about the pattern of migration from England and Wales. Welsh migrants were comparatively few and probably came from groups suffering from the same kind of dislocation as the Scottish Highlanders. English migrants outnumbered Scottish, forming some 20–25 per cent of the total. They also migrated as families, though rarely as part of a community. Many were moderately successful farmers or skilled artisans and, particularly in the aftermath of the Napoleonic wars, the English influx included a substantial proportion of recently demobilised army officers. As with many of the Scottish and Irish migrants, this was probably not the first move for many of the English and in British North America many would move again to achieve eventual economic security for themselves and their families.

The migrants would take with them, and for a long time would preserve, the ethnic and regional distinctions that had divided them in the Old World. But nineteenth-century Britain was less fragmented than in the past. The prolonged wars with France had contributed to this process of unification and to the growth of a sense of British nationalism. There remained a good deal of popular unrest throughout the British Isles after 1815 but the rapid growth of the British economy in the middle decades of the nineteenth century, the opportunities offered by an expanding empire, and Catholic Emancipation in 1829 and the Great Reform Bill of 1832 channelled the discontent along constitutional lines and consolidated this new sense of British nationalism.

British immigrants carried these attitudes with them to the colonies. They were the children of the second British Empire, an empire infinitely larger and more impressive than the first. The heirs of the Loyalists already had a tradition of loyalty to crown and empire. The arrival of the British immigrants

reinforced this tradition; indeed, they appropriated it. No group was more pronounced in their loyalty than the Protestant Irish who expressed their commitment to both Protestantism and the British constitutional monarchy through the Orange Order. In Canada the Orange Order expanded far beyond its ethnic roots and by the end of the nineteenth century about one-third of all English-speaking adult Canadian males belonged to it. Many Irish Catholics did not, of course, share the enthusiasm of the other British immigrants for the imperial connection, but those most disaffected made their way to the United States. While Fenianism had its supporters in Canada, it possessed nothing like the popular appeal it had either in Ireland or in the United States and was opposed by many leading Canadian Irish Catholics.

By the time of Confederation these immigrants had transformed the landscape. In 1815, except in Lower Canada, British North America had consisted of a series of thinly populated colonies. Most settlers were engaged in subsistence agriculture, although the fisheries were important and the timber trade had begun to develop. There were few urban centres and limited contact between the tiny provincial capitals and the outports scattered around the colonies. Except for small numbers of Americans and a trickle of Scots, there were few immigrants after the 1790s and population growth occurred largely through natural increase. In the half century after 1815 the population soared. All of the good arable land—and much of the not so good—was occupied and the land cleared of trees. Villages sprung up across the countryside and were linked by roads and by the 1850s in the more densely populated regions by canals and railroads. The newcomers were used to a competitive market economy and they quickly turned to the production of timber and wheat, the two great staple industries of early nineteenth-century Canada. They were encouraged to do so by the rapidly expanding British market in which colonial wheat and timber had a comparative advantage because of the system of protective duties imposed during the Napoleonic wars. Of course, subsistence agriculture persisted in remoter or less well endowed areas, but it usually had to be combined with some kind of wage labour in order to purchase manufactured goods, most of them now imported from Britain.

The commercial system was based on a chain of credit that stretched back to the mother country. Britain had a larger volume of trade with the United States than with Canada but there was not the same degree of dependency in the United States on the British market, which continued to absorb the bulk of British North America's exports even after the protective duties were removed. Most of British North America's imports also came from Britain, as did the capital that financed the railways of the 1850s and 1860s. British North America was not settled by small self-sufficient farmers gradually inching along the frontier. It was settled in one great influx by British immigrants who were quickly integrated into the nineteenth-century imperial economy.

The benefits of that integration were not universally shared. There was upward mobility in British North America. The earlier settlers benefited from later expansion and the inflation in land prices, but those who came out to the colonies with even small amounts of capital possessed an enormous advantage over those who did not. The latter group might eventually acquire land but it was more likely less desirable land suitable only for subsistence agriculture. By the 1860s many rural communities contained a class of backland farmers who were compelled to supplement their incomes by off-farm labour. In those industries requiring greater capital investment, such as the fisheries and the timber trade, most of the profits inevitably remained in the hands of British merchants and their colonial partners. In the urban centres disparities of wealth were even more pronounced. Social mobility was for those with capital or at least connections. Indeed, the real beneficiaries of economic growth were the colonial merchants, lawyers and administrators who acted as intermediaries for British merchants and investors. Inevitably they were largely drawn from among the British immigrants and quite naturally they were the most enthusiastic supporters of the imperial connection.

The colonies not only imported British manufactured goods and capital but also British engineers and technology, British troops to defend them during boundary disputes with the United States, British lawyers and judges to shape and to run the legal system, doctors from British medical schools to establish standards for the medical profession, British university graduates to teach in their colleges, British textbooks to use in their schools, and British architectural designs for their public buildings, their churches and even their homes. Particularly in the period after 1830, when most of the immigrants arrived, Britain was in the words of George Kitson Clark 'an expanding society', spreading its influence across the globe, but few countries experienced the force of this pressure as Canada did. British North Americans were not immune to influences from the United States, but the distance between Britain and her North American colonies shrank during the middle decades of the nineteenth century. The passage across the Atlantic became easier and quicker. Colonial newspapers carried regular reports of events in Britain and they were seldom more than a few days out of date after the laying of the Atlantic cable.

The British North American elites frequently crossed the Atlantic to lobby British politicians, to arrange for loans from British bankers, to strengthen commercial alliances with British merchants, to visit friends and relatives they had left behind, or simply as tourists. A number of prominent British North Americans retired in Britain and members of the colonial elites eagerly sought titles and honours from the imperial government. Loyalty to the empire did not, of course, mean subservience, for British North Americans considered local self-government as part of their birthright and all of the colonies received the institution of an Assembly.

In Upper Canada and Lower Canada disputes between the Assemblies and the imperial Government led to rebellions in 1837. These rebellions reflected the growing anxiety felt by groups who did not want to see British North America more closely integrated into the second British Empire. French Canadians were legitimately fearful of the growth of a substantial British community in their midst and the rebellion of 1837 in Lower Canada was born of those fears. In Upper Canada the rebellion was a much smaller affair supported primarily by descendants of the pre1815 American migrants. In Lower Canada the rebellion was crushed by the combined might of imperial forces and the British minority; in Upper Canada the rebellion was so weakly supported that no imperial troops were required. In the aftermath of the rebellions the British Government soon realised that to retain the loyalty of its subjects, including the ever larger British-born population, it would have to give them control over their own internal affairs. The solution was the adoption of the principle of responsible government, a principle gradually extended to all of the colonies of settlement. The British Government would continue to play a part in the running of the colonies, but British North Americans now had the power to shape their own future as part of the larger empire to which they quite happily belonged.

Even most French Canadians came to accommodate themselves to the imperial connection. In 1846 one French-Canadian politician predicted that:

> We will never forget our allegiance till
> the last cannon which is shot on this
> continent in defence of Great Britain is
> fired by the hand of a French Canadian.

Not all French Canadians shared this enthusiasm but as the economy of Quebec became increasingly commercialised and the French Canadian bourgeoisie benefited from the prosperity generated by the imperial connection, the elite certainly did.

In 1867 British North Americans decided to unite into a single political unit, but they did not do so in order to create an independent state. Indeed, the majority of the immigrants of the post-Napoleonic period and their offspring felt themselves to be part of a common British culture. To them Confederation was seen as the best way of preserving the imperial connection. More British immigrants went to the United States than to British North America in the nineteenth century but there they became, in Charlotte Erickson's words, 'invisible immigrants', forced to adapt to a society and a political culture that had been shaped by the descendants of those who had emigrated during the first period of European colonisation. In Canada, however, British immigrants came in such large numbers during the nineteenth century that they were able to overwhelm the existing settlers and lay the foundation for an enduring imperial connection.

400 Years of the East India Company

Huw V. Bowen asks whether the East India Company was one of the 'most powerful engines' of state and empire in British history.

HUW V. BOWEN

The year 2000 marks the 400th anniversary of the founding of the English East India Company, the trading organisation that acted as the vehicle for British commercial and imperial expansion in Asia. For over two hundred years, the Company stood like a colossus over trade, commerce and empire, and contemporaries could only marvel at its influence, resources, strength and wealth. Writing at the beginning of the nineteenth century, the political economist David Macpherson was unequivocal in his assessment that the Company was 'the most illustrious and most flourishing commercial association that ever existed in any age or country.'

Today even the most powerful firm pales by comparison in terms of longevity and wide-ranging economic, political and cultural influence. In an era before fast travel and instant communication, the East India Company established a far-flung empire and then set about governing, controlling and exploiting it from a great distance in London. It managed to do this until it was finally rendered obsolete by the tumultuous events surrounding the Indian Mutiny in 1857.

The Company was granted its first charter by Elizabeth I on the last day of 1600, and it had to survive an uncertain first century or so as it sought access to Asian markets and commodities. At home, it was restructured several times, notably between 1698 and 1708 when an 'old' and 'new' East India Company co-existed before merging to form the United Company of Merchants Trading to the East Indies. In the East, the Company came under such pressure from its Dutch rivals during the mid-seventeenth century that it was obliged to shift the main focus of its activities from the Malay archipelago and the Spice Islands to South Asia. Over time, it managed to establish a commercial presence in India centred upon three 'presidencies' established at Madras, Bombay and Calcutta. These tenuous footholds were fortified and defended by the Company as it sought to consolidate its position in an often hostile commercial and political world. This in turn gave rise to the growth of a small private army that was eventually to rival the regular British army in terms of size and manpower. The Company's role in India was thus defined by both commercial activity and a military presence: it was considered legitimate to use force in support of trade, and the overseas personnel were organised and deployed accordingly. In the words of one contemporary, it was a 'fighting company'.

By the mid-eighteenth century, the Company had begun to assert itself over rival European companies and Indian powers alike, and this placed it in a position from which it could begin to carve out an extended territorial and commercial empire for itself. The actions of men such as Robert Clive (1725–74), Warren Hastings (1732–1818) and Charles Cornwallis (1738–1805) helped to transform the Company from trader to sovereign, so that during the second half of the eighteenth century millions of Indians were brought under British rule. As William Playfair put it in 1799:

Figure 1 The frontispiece of Isaac Pike's Journal of the Stringer (1713) showed the Company robustly defending its trading position.
Note: HT Archives

From a limited body of merchants, the India Company have become the Arbiters of the East.

The Company created the British Raj, and as such it has left a deep and permanent imprint on the history and historiography of India. The story, once almost universally described as the 'rise of British India', not so long ago formed part of the staple reading diet of British schoolchildren and students. In the post-colonial era, when imperial history has ceased to be fashionable, the legacies of British India are still hotly debated and contested. It is within this context that the history of the East India Company remains to the fore.

Today's casual observer finds few signs of the leading role the Company once played in the life of the nation.

Rather less obvious, perhaps, is the part played by the East India Company in the domestic development of Britain. Indeed, today's casual observer finds few signs of the leading role it once played in the nation's business, commercial, cultural and political life. In terms of architecture, for example, there is little surviving evidence in London of the Company's once-extensive property empire. The London docklands, home to the East India dock complex, has been reshaped. Although Commercial Road and East India Dock Road—the purpose-built link with the City—survive, the docks themselves have been filled in and redeveloped, leaving only a few poignant reminders of the Company's once formidable presence in the area. To the West, the great fortress-like warehouses built by the Company at Cutler Street were partially demolished and refurbished in controversial circumstances during the late 1970s. There is no trace remaining whatsoever of the Company's headquarters in Leadenhall Street. Charles Dickens once described the 'rich' East India House 'teeming with suggestions' of eastern delights, but it was unceremoniously pulled down in the 1860s, and in its place today stands the new Lloyd's Building, also a monument to commercial capitalism, but displaying rather different architectural qualities. In recent years, the only obvious local clue to the Indian connection was provided by the East India Arms, a tavern in nearby Lime Street, but that too has now fallen victim to the modern re-naming and re-branding process. As a result, the East India Company is now out of sight and out of mind.

It was not always like this. During the late eighteenth century, the Company played a key role in London's economy, employing several thousand labourers, warehousemen and clerks. Returning fleets of East Indiamen moored in Blackwall Reach, before their Indian and Chinese cargoes were transferred via hoys and carts to enormous warehouses where they awaited distribution and sale in Britain's burgeoning consumer markets. The profile of the Company in London was always high and the eyes of many were on Leadenhall Street. Political infighting at East India House regularly captured the attention of the metropolitan chattering classes. The Company itself was repeatedly subjected to inquiry by a Parliament uneasy about the turn being taken by events in the East.

The Company's domestic tentacles extended well beyond London, however, and its influences were widely felt across the south of England. Provincial outposts were established in the form of the agencies in ports such as Deal, Falmouth, Plymouth and Portsmouth. Over the years the Company maintained camps for its military recruits at Newport in the Isle of White, Warley in Essex and at Chatham in Kent. Educational establishments were set up for the purpose of preparing those destined for service overseas. During the first half of the nineteenth century, the East India College at Haileybury in Hertfordshire educated boys for the civil service, while Addiscombe Military Seminary near Croydon trained military cadets.

More generally, the Company touched many sectors of British society and the economy, as some contemporaries acknowledged. In 1813, for example, a friend to the Company, Thomas William Plummer, set about identifying what 'proportion of the community' had a connection with the Company. Without mentioning several million purchasers of tea, spices, silks, muslins and other Asian commodities, he listed investors, Company employees of many types, tradesmen, manufacturers, shipbuilders, dealers, private merchants, military personnel and ship crews, before concluding that:

> Scarcely any part of the British community is distinct from some personal or collateral interest in the welfare of the East India Company.

There was more than a grain of truth in what Plummer wrote, and by the beginning of the nineteenth century many interests across the country had been tied closely to the Company. This was particularly the case with the several thousand or so well-to-do individuals who chose to invest in Company stocks and bonds. For much of the eighteenth century East India stock was the most attractive investment available in the nascent stock market, not least because it always paid out an annual dividend of more than 5 per cent. The India bonds that provided the Company with its short-term working capital were also highly prized, with one early stock market analyst describing them as 'the most convenient and profitable security a person can be possessed of'.

The fortunes of Company and nation had become so tightly intertwined that they had begun to move in tandem with one another as those who took a broad view of political and economic matters were able to see. When the Company flourished, the nation flourished. Equally, as Edmund Burke put it, 'to say the Company was in a state of distress was neither more nor less than to say the country was in a state of distress'. Such logic dictated that the effects of any crisis or catastrophe experienced by the Company in India would be deeply felt in Britain and the wider British Empire, and this was well understood by close observers of the imperial scene. One pamphleteer wrote in 1773 that the loss of India would occasion a 'national bankruptcy' while the imperial theorist Thomas Pownall suggested that such an event would cause 'the ruin of the whole edifice of the British Empire'. These concerns lay behind the increased levels of government anxiety about Company adventurism, misrule, and mismanagement in India that became evident after 1760.

By the 1770's the Company was akin to a semi-privatised imperial wing of the Hanoverian state.

Late eighteenth-century concerns about events in the East reflected the fact that the East India Company was no longer an ordinary trading company. It had evolved into an immensely powerful hybrid commercial and imperial agency, and after the conquest of Bengal it fundamentally reshaped its traditional commercial policy based upon the exchange of exported British goods and bullion for Asian commodities. Instead, the Company concentrated its efforts on the collection of territorial and customs revenues in northeast India. The right to collect these revenues had been granted by the Mughal Emperor Shah Alam II in 1765, an event which both confirmed British military supremacy in the region and served to elevate the Company to the position of *de facto* sovereign in Bengal and the neighbouring provinces of Bihar and Orissa. Thereafter, trade was used to facilitate the transfer of 'tribute' from Asia to London as surplus revenue was ploughed into the purchase of Indian and Chinese commodities for export to Britain. As Edmund Burke later remarked, this marked a 'revolution' in the Company's commercial affairs.

The Company's empire had now become self-financing to the point that further military expansion could be sustained, but it was also believed that generous payments could be made to domestic stockholders and the British government alike. This proved to be a vain hope, but the transfer of tribute helped to define the essential characteristics of the late-eighteenth-century state-Company relationship. Successive ministers declared the state's 'right' to a share of the Bengal revenues, but in return for the promise of annual payments into the public treasury they allowed the Company to continue in its role as the administrator, defender and revenue collector of Bengal. This brought the British government the benefits of empire without any expensive administrative or military responsibilities. It was a welcome and convenient arrangement at a time when the national debt was spiralling ever-upwards and parts of the Empire, most notably North America, were proving increasingly difficult to control and subdue.

By the 1770s the Company thus found itself as something akin to a semi-privatised imperial wing of the Hanoverian state, with its operations being defined by the dual pursuit of both private and public interest. It was charged with the protection, cultivation, and exploitation of one of Britain's most important national assets, and contemporary observers described its new role accordingly. In 1773 the prime minister, Lord North, declared that the Company was acting as '[tax] farmers to the publick', while a late-century pamphleteer suggested that the Company had become 'stewards to the state'. In this scheme of things, there was a greater need for the Company to become more accountable, efficient, and reliable, and this desire lay behind the reforms embodied in North's Regulating Act of 1773 and Pitt's India Act of 1784.

The Company's importance to the British state was not, however, simply to be assessed in terms of its role as the licensed agent through which metropolitan administrative, fiscal and military influences were brought to bear upon the Indian empire. The Company had been present at the birth of the eighteenth-century state during the troubled period following the 'Glorious Revolution' of 1688–89. As a hard-pressed nation struggled to cope with the demands of the Nine Years' War, ministers had drawn heavily on the financial resources of the 'new' East India Company that had received its charter in 1698. This meant that when the United Company was established in 1709 it was already deeply embedded in both the public finances and the City of London where, together with the Bank of England, it formed part of the 'monied interest'.

The financial relationship between state and Company took several different forms, all of which were a variation on a theme that saw the Company's monopoly privileges periodically confirmed or extended by the Crown in return for loans or payments made to the public purse. Indeed, by the 1720s the entire paid-up share capital of the Company, almost £3.2 million, was on long-term loan to the state at 5 per cent interest. This sizeable advance was extended to £4.2 million before prime minister and chancellor Henry Pelham's restructuring of the national debt in 1749–50 saw the reduction of interest payments to 3 per cent and the creation of the East India annuities. This extensive underwriting of the post-settlement regime was such that a Chairman of the Company, Jacob Bosanquet, was later to borrow a phrase from Adam Smith and declare that the Company, together with the Bank of England, had become one of the 'most powerful engines of the state'. As Chairman of a company under great pressure from critics by 1799, Bosanquet was hardly likely to say anything else, but his comments were not altogether inaccurate. His organisation had established itself as a cornerstone of the City of London, and as such it had played a key role in supporting the state and public credit.

By the end of the eighteenth century, apologists were thus arguing that the Company formed part of the very foundations of Britain's state and empire, yet within sixty years it had ceased to exist at all. What happened to make the great 'engine' run out of steam so rapidly?

There are a great many answers to this question but the most basic one is undoubtedly the most important. Quite simply, in economic terms the Company failed to deliver what it had promised since the 1760s. As the military and administrative costs of empire multiplied, the Company proved itself unable to generate a revenue surplus for transfer to Britain. A great many attempts were made to remodel the Company's fiscal and commercial operations but successes in one area were always off-set by failures and setbacks elsewhere. Only the striking growth of the China tea trade offered the Company any prospect of success, but that in itself was not enough to satisfy the demands of profit-hungry stockholders and ministers. Indeed, the annual flow of 'tribute' to the state Treasury promised by the Company in 1767 had dried up almost at once. By 1772 the Company was teetering on the edge of bankruptcy, having failed to master the complexities of its new role in India, and a degree of desperation forced it into the measures that ultimately led to the Boston Tea Party the following year. Thereafter, the Company staggered from crisis to crisis, requiring government loans to enable it to continue functioning. In effect, this meant that roles had been reversed, and the Company had become dependent upon the state for financial support.

The Company failed to argue convincingly that it offered the best way forward for the Anglo-Asian connection.

A dose of economic reality, coupled with widespread metropolitan unease about 'despotic' Company government in India, caused many commentators rapidly to reassess their views of Britain's eastern empire. Nowhere was this more evident than with Edmund Burke who became one of the Company's harshest critics and campaigned long and hard for reform and the punishment of British misdemeanours in India. Initially, though, Burke had been as captivated as any observer by the prospect of Britain gaining very real material advantage from the Company's successes in Bengal. He had outlined the economic potential of India to the House of Commons in 1769 before concluding that 'The Orient sun never laid more glorious expectations before us.' This type of view was commonplace during the 1760s, but it was replaced by much gloomier assessments of the situation in the decades that followed. Commentators soon tired of hearing about the promise of Indian wealth being used to the advantage of the metropolis, and began instead to expose the flaws that were evident in the Company's calculations and methods. The figures did not seem to add up, leaving one MP, George Tierney, to complain that 'Our Indian prosperity is always in the future tense'.

Criticism such as this only strengthened the case of those in Britain who were campaigning vigorously for the East India trade to be opened up to free competition. Just as the utility of the Company to the nation began to be discussed, old mercantilist assumptions about the organisation of trade were being called into question. Taking a lead from Adam Smith, who had condemned chartered companies as being 'nuisances in every respect', critics exposed the Company to searching analyses of its methods and practices.

Under such attack, the Company proved unable, indeed almost unwilling, to answer the charges levelled against it. Although it began to emphasise the contribution it made to intellectual and scientific life in Britain, it failed to argue convincingly that it alone offered the best way forward for the further development of the Anglo-Asian connection. Part of the reason for this was that the Company believed it had already taken the organisation of its commercial and financial affairs to the highest possible level. It proved to be remarkably complacent and, together with a deep-rooted institutional conservatism, this meant that any change was regarded with the deepest suspicion. As one director of the Company put it, 'Innovations in an established system are at all times dangerous'. Few friends of the Company could see any need to alter an organisation that was thought to be beyond improvement, and this case was restated time and again. Most would have agreed with Thomas Mortimer who argued during the 1760s that the Company had 'brought the commerce and mercantile credit of Great Britain to such a degree of perfection, as no age or country can equal.' To alter anything would be to invite trouble. Sustained failure and. disappointing performance, however, flew in the face of such opinion, and this ensured that pressure for change continued to grow from outside the Company.

In the end, the Company's failure was essentially two-fold as far as many of those in the metropolis were concerned. It failed to deliver to Britain the great financial windfall that had been anticipated after the conquest of Bengal; and because of this it was unable to sustain much beyond 1760 its position as one of the major institutional and financial props of the Hanoverian state. When charges related to misrule, despotism, unfair monopoly practices and a host of other complaints were added to the scales, they served eventually to tip the balance of political opinion.

The immediate and outright abolition of the Company, however, was never an option because the state did not possess the resources, skills or will necessary to govern a large empire in India. Instead, successive breaches were made in the Company's commercial position. Trade with the East was opened up to a limited degree in 1793; the Indian monopoly was ended in 1813; and the exclusive trade with China was abolished in 1833. The Company survived for another twenty-five years as Britain's administrative and military representative in India, but by then it was a trading company in name only. The Company had achieved the full transition from trader to sovereign, amply fulfilling Adam Smith's prediction that trade and government were incompatible within a 'company of merchants'.

The Company ended its days in the aftermath of the Indian Mutiny when no case at all could be advanced for its survival in any form. Its powerful legacy endured in India for many more years in the form of the Indian army and civil service, but sight was soon lost of the importance of its contribution to the development of the metropolitan state and to imperial Britain itself. Today the Company has been almost entirely removed from the geographical and historical landscape and it has been more or less erased from our national consciousness. As the 400th anniversary of the founding of the Company approaches, this makes it all the more necessary for us to reflect on the deep, but now hidden, impression left on British history by this quite extraordinary institution.

For Further Reading

H.V. Bowen, 'Investment and Empire in the Later Eighteenth Century: East India Stockholding, 1756–1791', *Economic History Review* (1989); K.N. Chaudhuri, *The English East India Company: The Study of an Early Joint-Stock Company* (Cass, 1965); John Keay, *The Honourable Company: The History of the English East India Company* (Harper Collins, 1991); Philip Lawson, *The East India Company: A History* (Macmillan, 1993); Martin Moir, *A General Guide to the India Office Records* (British Library, 1996); Jean Sutton, *Lords of the East: The East India Company and its Ships* (Conway Maritime Press, 1981). Information about the records of the East India Company can be found on the British Library's website http://www.bl.uk/ (follow the links to the Oriental and India Office collections).

HUW BOWEN is Senior Lecturer in Economic and Social History at the University of Leicester and the author of War and British Society 1688–1815 (Cambridge UP, 1998).

This article first appeared in *History Today*, July 2000, pp. 47–53. Copyright © 2000 by History Today, Ltd. Reprinted by permission.

The Ottomans in Europe

GEOFFREY WOODWARD

Introduction

> *'Now shalt thou feel the force of Turkish arms*
> *Which lately made all Europe quake for fear.'*

Christopher Marlowe's observation in Tamburlaine (1587) held true for most of the sixteenth century. The Ottoman army was the largest in Europe, its navy ruled the shipping lanes of the eastern Mediterranean, and its capital Istanbul was five times the size of Paris. Its resources seemed limitless, and its capacity to sweep aside opposition in the name of Islam gave the Turkish Empire an awesome presence. Indeed between 1520 and 1565 its momentum seemed unstoppable. Well might Christians in western Europe 'quake for fear'. This article sets out to trace some of the ways in which Europeans were affected by the Turkish Empire in the course of the sixteenth century. First, it considers the impact on the Balkans and the consequences for the Holy Roman Empire. Second, it looks at how Spain, Portugal and Venice were affected by the maritime expansion. Third, consideration is given to the argument that important military changes occurred in Europe as a result of Ottoman expansion. Finally, the strength of its Empire is evaluated and the question posed: did it really present a serious threat to Europe?

Ottoman Western Expansion

Since 1354 the Ottoman Turks had been advancing westwards, overrunning Constantinople (and renaming it Istanbul) in 1453, gaining control of the Black Sea and the main routes to the Balkans and driving on to the eastern Adriatic. Owing to the exploits of successive Sultans, the Ottomans were, by 1520, the undisputed leaders of the Muslim world. For the rest of the century they cast their shadow over western Europe.

Suleiman 'the Magnificent' (1520–66) seized Belgrade in 1521 and, upon capturing Rhodes, evicted the Knights of St John and removed the last remaining obstacle to his domination of the eastern Mediterranean. The effect upon Europe was dramatic. The Holy Roman Emperor, Charles V, absent in Spain and Italy for most of the 1520s, delegated the administration and defence of his Austrian lands to his brother Ferdinand. It proved a timely move as Suleiman thrust aside the Hungarian armies at Mohacs, killed King Louis II of Hungary and, three years later, moved to the gates of Vienna. Though severe weather conditions led the Ottomans to withdraw after a two-month siege, Ferdinand

and his court had been forced to flee and he never forgot how close he had been to losing his capital. In 1532 Charles himself stood in the way of the largest army ever seen in Europe and repelled its assault on Guns, 60 miles south of Vienna. This, however, was to be a temporary respite and Suleiman's only military setback. In 1541 Ferdinand was forced out of Buda and six years later at Adrianople agreed to pay the sultan an annual tribute of 30,000 ducats in return for holding a small strip of western Hungary. Another abortive attempt to expel the Ottomans from Transylvania in 1550 confirmed that the Balkan frontier would remain 80 miles from Vienna and the Austrian Habsburgs would be treated as a tributary power.

In the second half of the century, the Habsburg emperors strengthened their frontier defences in anticipation of further Ottoman attacks and, apart from desultory fighting between 1552 and 1568, Austria was spared. In the wake of Suleiman's death in 1566, Selim the Sot (1566–74) and his successor, Murad III (1574–95), called a halt to the landward advances and, for much of this period, the Turks concentrated on defence rather than expansion. Like other European states, they were feeling the strain of administering their massive empire, a fact reflected by the state debts recorded every year after 1592. Indeed, peace would have probably lasted longer if Emperor Rudolf had not refused to continue paying his tribute. When Murad retaliated, war began again.

The Long War (1593–1606) started badly for the Ottomans with revolts occurring in their own vassal states. Dnieper Cossacks pillaged their supply lines and, worst of all, Persia invaded Anatolia in 1599. Moreover, at Mezokeresztes (1596), Hungarian troops demonstrated superior firepower and inflicted upon the Turks their first military setback for over a century. Hungarian and Transylvanian towns were won and lost in a series of sieges until all sides agreed upon a treaty in 1686 at Zsitva-Torok. The Habsburgs were confirmed in their possession of western Hungary, their tribute was annulled and Transylvania granted its independence. The Austrian-Turkish frontier had not moved since 1529 and it was now apparent that the western limit of the Ottoman Empire had been reached.

(i) Turkish Rule in the Balkans

The impact of Turkish rule upon all sectors of Balkan society was profound. Most of its aristocracy were killed though a minority was absorbed into the ruling class when, in keeping with Ottoman practice, the sultan took over their lands. In contrast, the peasantry, who worked the land, paid most of the taxes and were liable for military service, were treated much better than before. They were protected by the new landlords and had their feudal services abolished. Apart from the frontier regions, most of the Balkans were spared that cultural and religious destruction usually associated with armies of occupation. Christians, though encouraged to convert to Islam, were allowed religious toleration and mixed marriages, and the comparative freedom and contentment enjoyed by its people is one of the most important explanations why the Balkans remained under Ottoman rule for over 400 years.

(ii) The Impact on the Holy Roman Empire

Largely for reasons of geography, Charles V suffered more than most west European rulers. As 'the Most Catholic' King of Spain (1516–56) and Holy Roman Emperor (1519–58), he took his obligations seriously. The Ottomans were intent on a holy war against Christianity and the western Empire looked to him to counter them, but his political commitments consistently distracted him and forced him to confine his efforts to stemming the Turkish advance in north Africa. In this respect, he was spectacularly unsuccessful, losing at Tunis (1534), Algiers (1541), and Tripoli, Bougie and Penon de Velez in the 1550s. To add to his problems, German princes skillfully exploited the Ottoman threat by forcing him to make political and religious concessions. Charles himself later admitted that the Turkish threat had forced him to put aside religious issues. Indeed, at times of greatest peril—in 1527, 1532 and 1541—Charles compromised religion to attend to the Turks, and significantly his only triumph against the Lutherans in 1547 was secured in the knowledge that Suleiman was engaged in wars against Persia. The Turks also received considerable help from France. It was Francis I who first encouraged them to attack the Habsburgs and allowed them free access to the ports of Marseilles and Toulon to reduce the Emperor's power. Indeed, it can safely be said that the Ottoman Empire's western expansion owed a great deal to the political and religious disunity of Europe.

Spain, Portugal and Venice

(i) Spain

The effects of Ottoman expansion were felt as far west as Spain in the early sixteenth century. To reduce the possibility that Granadan Moriscos would receive help from Muslims in north Africa, King Ferdinand seized five coastal settlements, including Tripoli and Algiers, and secured Spain's sea routes between Sicily, Sardinia and Tunisia. However, the creation of a powerful Turkish fleet enabled it to conquer Egypt and renewed the threat to Spain's possessions. And the situation became critical when Barbarossa defected to the Ottoman fleet: Tunis and Algiers were lost and several north African settlements seized in the 1550s. Not only were Spanish communications with

Milan, Naples and Sicily endangered but the mainland towns of Malaga, Cadiz and Gibraltar also suffered raids from corsair pirates. It was just as well that the main Ottoman army was pre-occupied with Persia.

Philip II of Spain responded to the Muslim threat in 1560 when his troops occupied the island of Djerba preparatory to an attack on Tripoli, but the expedition ended in disaster: 27 galleys were lost and 10,000 men were taken prisoner to Istanbul. The recovery of Penon in 1564 renewed Spanish spirits but celebrations were curtailed with the news that Malta was being besieged by 40,000 troops and 180 Ottoman warships. The subsequent relief of the island in September 1565 by the viceroy of Naples saved Sicily as well as Malta and marked the limit of Ottoman expansion in the western Mediterranean but, in spite of Suleiman's death the following year, its maritime power remained formidable. In 1570 Tunis, recovered by Spain in 1535, was again captured by the Turks and the Venetian island of Cyprus was attacked.

A Christian fleet, which was mainly Venetian but commanded by a Spaniard, Don John, met the Ottomans at Lepanto in the Gulf of Corinth. The ensuing battle (October 1571) saw two of the largest navies ever assembled and resulted in victory for the Christians. Though they lost 10 of their 208 galleys and 15,000 men, this was nothing compared with the losses sustained by the Turks. 117 out of 270 Ottoman ships were captured, 113 sunk and 30,000 men killed. It was their worst defeat since 1402 and dispelled the myth of invincibility. Most historians have viewed Lepanto as a crucial battle, that ended the long conflict between Muslims and Christians. Thomas Arnold has recently argued that: 'After Lepanto, the Ottoman navy never recovered its earlier near-mastery of the Mediterranean'. The extant evidence in the Turkish archives, however, does not bear out this judgement, at least not in the short term. The sultan's reaction to defeat was to rebuild his fleet and double his resolve to control north Africa and the sea routes via Malta and Sicily. Just six months after Lepanto, the Turks had built 200 new galleys and captured Cyprus—a reminder that their potential to inflict a serious blow was still formidable. In 1574 a massive Turkish fleet seized Tunis and put the Spanish garrison in La Goletta to flight. Yet just when it seemed that the Ottomans were resuming the initiative, Selim died, and with him passed the last competent sultan for over a hundred years. Western Europe had been saved by a hair's breadth.

The expansion of the Ottoman Empire had two further direct effects upon Spanish affairs. For 20 years after Philip II's accession (in 1556), the problem had drawn resources away from the Netherlands and northern Europe and enabled the Dutch Revolt to gather momentum. Second, there was widespread belief in the 1560s that the Spanish Moriscos were in secret contact with the Muslims and the Ottoman court in Istanbul. Though some 4,000 Turkish and Berber troops fought alongside the Granadan Moriscos in their rebellion of 1598–70, letters from local Turkish rulers in 1574 suggest that the sultan was indeed contemplating a coordinated attack on Spanish lands. Philip II and the Inquisition continued to investigate reports of collusion.

Though nothing was proved, it served to perpetuate the myth of the 'Turkish menace'.

(ii) Portugal

Portuguese interests were affected both positively and negatively. Portuguese merchants in their search for gold had developed an alternative route to the Far East and Spice Islands that avoided the Turkish controlled east Mediterranean. This gave Portugal in the late fifteenth and early sixteenth centuries 'premier league' status. But its territorial and commercial expansion came at a price. Its long sea routes needed defending from the Turks, who had also reached the Red Sea by 1500 and the Indian Ocean by the mid-sixteenth century, and they were equally keen to secure the lucrative pepper trade with the Far East. Portugal, however, was more than up to this challenge. Its efficiently designed and well defended barracks saw off Turkish galleys which were less manoeuvrable in ocean waters, but the struggle for dominance of the spice trade was not won quickly or cheaply. Moreover Portugal had limited resources. As competition with Spain increased, it could ill-afford a struggle with the Ottomans for mastery of the Indian Ocean. It was precisely this threat of overstretch which made Portugal so vulnerable in the late sixteenth and early seventeenth centuries, due not so much to any Turkish incursion—this had long since passed—but to English, Dutch and French colonials, merchants and privateers.

(iii) Venice

The Turkish threat to Mediterranean trade in general and to Iberian possessions in particular receded in the last quarter of the sixteenth century, but its impact was none the less considerable. A principal beneficiary for much of this period was the city-state of Venice. Since 1479 it had paid a tribute to gain access to the Middle East overland routes to Aleppo and Alexandria, and under Ottoman sufferance it remained the major maritime power in the eastern Mediterranean, handling most Ottoman trade with the west and successfully competing with Portugal for control of the pepper trade. Of course, Ottoman wars in the Red Sea, Persian Gulf and Mediterranean had disrupted trade but for most of the sixteenth century Venice itself avoided armed conflict. Indeed, by strengthening its fortresses and doubling the size of its fleet, it enjoyed rising profits from trade at least until the 1570s. However, the loss of Cyprus in 1571, rich in grain and wine, and Venice's failure to recover it, proved a turning-point in its history. In 1573 it gave up its claims to Cyprus and Dalmatia, returned lands in Albania and agreed to pay a large indemnity to normalise its trade arrangements with the sultan. The 1570s also brought new trading competitors when first French and then English merchants received Turkish 'capitulations' or privileges to compete with Venetian traders. By 1600, French merchants had displaced Venetians in the Levant, Dutch traders had won control of the east African trade and the English East India Company was ready to exploit the weakening condition of Spain, Portugal, Venice, and the Ottoman Empire.

The Turks and the 'Military Revolution'

Historians have long recognised the significance of the wars with the Turks as an important, if not vital, element in the development of the 'military revolution' of western states. Victory for the cross over the crescent carried more than ideological and religious superiority. It proved, at least as far as west Europeans were concerned, that their military and naval tactics, equipment and application were also second to none.

There were some important differences between European and Turkish military developments. One lay in the line of fortifications built by several Christian towns in the 1520s which were modelled on the trace Italienne: these were earthen ramparts, low-walled bastions, and strategically located cannons which could repel the main Turkish assaults whether human or artillery. Although some fortresses fell to the Turks—Szigeth in Hungary (1566), Nicosia in Cyprus (1570)—they were the exceptions to the rule, and Vienna, Guns, Corfu and Malta all successfully withstood lengthy sieges.

A second important difference was that European armies placed more emphasis on drill and discipline, on practising defensive infantry formations of squares of pikes and arquebusiers, and of combining infantry, artillery and cavalry, confident that they could repel a Turkish cavalry and infantry attack. Treatises on military tactics encouraged generals to believe the way forward was to innovate. In one writer's opinion, a well-trained pike and arquebus detachment could withstand a Turkish cavalry assault, and another author claimed that a disciplined infantry would enable 'a few men to defeat the great multitudes of the Turks'. Although contemporaries could not prove it—there were no battles between Turks and Europeans in the sixteenth century—their confidence was not misplaced, as campaign after campaign confirmed in later centuries.

Third, the Turkish navy never developed the flexibility in ship design or strategy achieved by its European counterparts. As the Spanish and Portuguese adapted their ocean-going galleons to sail the Mediterranean and modified their galleys into three-masted carracks capable of both trading and fighting, so they were able to counter the Ottoman fleet and merchant shipping which was composed solely of galleys. Though the Turks almost always put more ships to sea, the Christians had a better fleet and superior cannon fire. After Lepanto, Turkish fleets warily avoided further engagements.

Ottoman Decline?

To decide whether the Ottomans were in decline by the end of the sixteenth century, we must realise that ever since the seventh century the Turkish Empire had been expanding. As it did so, it became a military state geared for conquest and holy war. The sultan exercised, at least in theory, unlimited authority. The only conceivable challenge to his position came from his family, and such threats were negated by the traditional Ottoman practice of fratricide. By 1520, the Ottoman Empire was self-sufficient in food, minerals and land; the Islamic faith bound its people together and its army was second to none. Suleiman possessed the best field artillery, 87,000 devoted cavalry (known as sipahis) and 16,000 highly disciplined infantry (janissaries), whose sole objective was to wage war. Its western vassal states formed a buttress to defend the core principality of Anatolia, and so, of necessity, its frontier was in a permanent state of war. Since the fourteenth century, the Ottoman family had provided very able sultans. It was they who gave the Empire its dynamism. Under Suleiman, who fought 13 successful campaigns and some 40 battles, they had a leader capable of putting the fear of Allah into all Christians. Indeed, only his death in September 1566 prevented an estimated 300,000 troops from advancing upon the Austrian-Habsburg lands. The last naval engagement between Christians and Muslims may have been in 1573, but Spain's north African and Italian possessions remained vulnerable targets and Philip II considered it prudent to keep a fleet in excess of 100 ships in the Mediterranean for the rest of his reign.

The Ottoman Empire's strengths, nevertheless, hid long-term weaknesses. First, the sultans Selim, Murad and Mohammed, who followed Suleiman, began a line of ineffectual rulers whose authority was seriously undermined by a series of palace revolts. Second, by fixing Istanbul as the administrative capital, the Ottomans had unknowingly established limits to their western and eastern Empire. Some 99 days were needed to transport 100,000 troops from Istanbul to Hungary. This reduced the campaigning season to a few months at best, and made communications and supply lines difficult to sustain. Similarly, to reach Malta by sea entailed a journey in excess of a thousand miles, which raised questions as to the point of wanting to sail beyond it. Third, the Ottomans were beginning to fall behind western Europe in naval and military technology and tactics. In fact, it can be argued that only the lack of political and spiritual unity within Europe prevented western states from exploiting Ottoman weaknesses. Already by the end of the sixteenth century Turkey's northern frontier of Azerbaijan and its central Asian trade were being challenged by the emerging state of Muscovy and its eastern frontier was threatened by the Safavids of Persia. For much of the century, the Ottomans had seen off challenges from these old rivals but victory eluded them in the Long War. It now seems clear that when both its western and eastern frontiers ceased to advance, the Ottoman state was vulnerable, and this was its condition at the end of the sixteenth century.

Conclusion

The impact of the Ottoman Turks on sixteenth-century Europe was far-reaching. This explains why Charles V regarded them as a greater threat to Christendom than Luther; why Ferdinand II devoted the best part of his life to defending the Austrian heartlands; why Spain feared for its trade and dominions in the western Mediterranean and became paranoid over suspected links with Granadan Moriscos; why Portugal was prepared to neglect its transatlantic trade and colonies in order to defend its pepper monopoly with Asia; and why Venice saw its livelihood hang by a thread as Turkish fleets threatened to cut off its sea-borne trade. It also contributed to the 'military revolution' as European armies and navies learned how first to defend and then to defeat superior numbers and, in so doing, forged ahead of their eastern rivals. In this, as in so many other ways, the Turks played an important part in shaping European history.

Death on the Nile

SIMON CRAIG

It was 1897, the year of Queen Victoria's Diamond Jubilee, the apogee of the Empire on which the sun never set. It would not have dared. For imperial integrity was assured by the Royal Navy, its global supremacy unchallenged since Trafalgar; and where land fighting was necessary, the British infantry square was impenetrable to native armies.

Well, nearly so. Rudyard Kipling, bard of empire, had recently written in grudging admiration of one especially resolute imperial foe: An' 'ere's to you, Fuzzy-Wuzzy, with your 'ayrick 'ead of 'air

You big black boundin' beggar—for you broke a British square!

He was referring to an embarrassing incident which had taken place at the beginning of 1885.

General Charles Gordon—popularly known as "Chinese Gordon" following his success in crushing the Taiping Rebellion in China in 1864—was besieged in Khartoum by the Mahdi's Dervishes and was fast running out of time. Responding to the urgency of the situation, General Wolseley (Sir Garnet, later Lord Wolseley, a renowned imperial general) took the danger-ous step of splitting his relieving force which was on its way up the Nile from Egypt. He sent part of it from the relative safety of the river to reach Gordon the quick way, across the desert. It was this column which met a large force of Dervishes at Abu Klea, 320 kilometres north of Khartoum.

In the savage battle which ensued the British square was penetrated, and Tommy Atkins learned a healthy respect for the "Fuzzy-Wuzzy." In the end, disaster was averted and the battle won, but Gordon still perished when Khartoum fell 10 days later, just before the relief force could arrive. Gordon was already a national hero and his death was regarded as a calamity. Prime Minister Gladstone was held responsible, and the blow to his prestige almost certainly contributed to his fall from power a few months later.

The strange thing about all this is that Britain had never really felt much interest in Sudan, but was dragged in by events further north in Egypt. Here the interest was clear: to hold Egypt was to hold the Suez Canal which since its opening in 1869 had been the lifeline to Britain's greatest imperial possession—India.

From Britain's point of view all was well until the compliant regime of the Khedive in Egypt fell to a national rising in 1881. Gladstone, the great anti-imperialist, tried hard to avoid military involvement, but his hand was eventually forced. In 1882 British troops suppressed the rising and, despite nominal

independence, Egypt became effectively a British colony. Henceforth Cairo's problems were London's too, and Sudan ranked high among them.

It was an Egyptian province, but the links between Cairo and Khartoum were now highly tenuous. Long years of corrupt administration had led to rebellion against Egypt, which no lon-ger controlled events there.

The rebel leader was Mohammed Ahmed, a quint essen-tially Middle Eastern Islamic figure known to all as the Mahdi, the promised leader, whose coming was to herald a new era of righteousness.

The obliteration by the Mahdi in 1883 of an Egyptian force of 10,000 under the command of a British officer, Colonel Hicks, persuaded London to abandon the Sudan altogether. Gordon's task in Khartoum had been simply to evacuate Egyptian offi-cials and their families. This he could not or would not do, and his death was confirmed in The Times of 13 February 1885. Wolseley's relief force went home, and for more than a decade Sudan was abandoned to the rule of the Mahdi and his successor, the Khalifa. The capital moved across the river from Khartoum to Omdurman, and from there the vast land was governed inde-pendently of Egypt and Britain.

But the situation could not last. In the 1880s and 1890s the so-called scramble for Africa was turning the whole continent into a patchwork quilt of European colonies and spheres of influence. And although the Sudan was not in itself of great value to the colonisers, it was nonetheless of enormous poten-tial significance, as Egypt's security depended on control of the Nile. And while the Dervishes lacked the technical resources to interfere with its flow, the Europeans certainly did not. The British government became increasingly anxious.

And so in 1896, Egypt, controlled by Britain, took a some-what hesitant first step towards reconquest. General Kitchener, with the title of Sirdar, or commander-in-chief, reclaimed the northern province of Dongola. But it was not until New Year's Day 1897 that work started on the desert railway line from Wadi Halfa on the Egyptian border to Abu Hamed and ultimately to Atbara. There could be only one reason for building such a line: a decision had been taken to end the Mahdist Empire and reas-sert Egyptian control over the entire Sudan.

Of course the obvious way to transport an army from the Mediterranean to Khartoum and Omdurman was by the Nile, but the six cataracts which lie between Aswan and the Khalifa's capital made this impossible. What was needed was a railway line running from Wadi Halfa to a point from which the river was navigable all the way south to Khartoum. The tale is told in detail by Winston Churchill in The River War, his account of the entire campaign.

Kitchener's task was essentially logistical; success was assured, provided that he could get his army and its equipment to the war zone intact. It was really all a matter of technology. The Khalifa's forces had no hope of prevailing against Kitchener's.

It was nonetheless a massive undertaking. Thomas Cook steamers, designed for ferrying tourists to the Valley of Kings, were commandeered to bring troops to the railhead at Wadi Halfa. Several powerful gunboats were brought out in sections and fitted together in Sudan.

The railway was not completed until 3 July 1898, almost a year after the action at Abu Hamed. The terminus had been secured after a fierce battle on 8 April, a large-scale engagement which left no doubt as to the superiority of the Sirdar's forces. From now on, it was only a matter of time. As Churchill put it: "On the day that the first troop train steamed into the fortified camp at the confluence of the Nile and the Atbara rivers the doom of the Dervishes was sealed." The Sirdar's gunboats could now reach to Khartoum and far beyond, and his troops could go with them.

The denouement came at Omdurman on 2 September in a battle lasting almost five hours. Kitchener's forces numbered 26,000, two-thirds of whom were Egyptian and Sudanese (by no means did all Sudanese favour the Khalifa). The Dervishes had perhaps twice as many men, but were hopelessly out-gunned. Kitchener repulsed two determined charges before slaughtering the hapless Mahdists with machine guns and artillery. There was even an old-fashioned cavalry charge by the 21st Lancers, later vividly described by Churchill, himself a participant.

In truth, however, accounts of the action make depressing reading. It was not a battle but a massacre. The Dervish losses have been estimated at 10,000, a similar number wounded and some 5,000 taken prisoner. Kitchener's casualties totalled around 500.

Gordon had been avenged, and the Sudan was not to taste independence again for nearly 60 years. But now came a trickier task, getting the other colonial powers to recognise Egyptian (that is British) supremacy over that part of the Sudan through which the Nile flows.

In the end it was the French who disputed the territory. While the Sirdar had been pursuing his inexorable course from Wadi Halfa to Omdurman, a small French expedition under Major Marchand had pressed across Africa from the Atlantic coast. It had reached Fashoda (now Kodok), on the left bank of the White Nile, on 10 July 1898.

Marchand was left in undisputed possession of Fashoda for a little over two months before Kitchener arrived. There ensued a tense stand-off lasting nearly three months, at the end of which the French backed down under orders from Paris. In retrospect it seems inevitable, for it was clearly Kitchener who had the power to impose his will at Fashoda.

So Kitchener won all the way. The Mahdists were crushed and the French faced down. Britain had ensured the security of Egypt and thus of the Suez Canal, the lifeline of the Empire.

No nation has ever been so powerful as was Britain at the end of the 19th century. But the glory was transient. Within 20 years the slaughter of the Great War would destroy European self-confidence and its huge cost would make far-flung colonies impossible in the long term to retain. Men who had fought with Kitchener would live to see the Empire dwindle almost to nothing, Egypt and Sudan become independent, and the Suez Canal pass out of the control of Britain.

Kipling foresaw it all in 1897, the year construction of the desert railway began, the glorious year of the Diamond Jubilee. Sooner or later, he wrote, the sun would indeed set on the British Empire as it had done on all others.

From *Geographical*, Vol. 71, No. 8, August 1997. Copyright © 1997 by Geographical Magazine. Reprinted by permission.

Coffee, Tea, or Opium?

In 1838, a Chinese drug czar confronted the Age of Addiction

SAMUEL M. WILSON

In 1839, China's commissioner for foreign trade, Lin Zexu (Lin Tse-hsü), was running out of diplomatic options. Traders from the East India Company and other European enterprises were pressing him ever more forcefully to turn a blind eye to the illegal importation of opium into his country. They were implicitly backed by Britain's heavily armored warships—such as the *Blenheim* and *Wellesley,* carrying seventy-four cannons each—which could crush China's navy and lay waste to her ports. But the opium trade was damaging public health and bleeding China of her wealth. In 1838, the Manchu emperor had given Lin extensive power and ordered him to control the demand of China's people for opium and force the barbarian merchants to cut off the supply.

After his appointment, Lin began to study European culture, looking for clues to barbarian behavior. He obtained a partial translation of Emer de Vattel's 1758 *Le Droit des Gens* ("The Law of Nations"), and he bought and studied the British ship *Cambridge.* Although it was not the largest of the "East Indiamen"—big defended freighters—and although it had been stripped of its guns and its intricate rigging was a mystery to Lin's sailors, the ship was ample evidence that these British were clever at naval warfare.

Lin also visited Macao, the Portuguese trading entrepôt near Canton, and carried out some anthropological fieldwork:

> As soon as I entered the wall of Macao, a hundred barbarian soldiers dressed in barbarian military uniform, led by the barbarian headman, greeted me. They marched in front of my sedan playing barbarian music and led me into the city. . . . On this day, everyone, man and woman, came out on the street or leaned from the window to take a look. Unfortunately the barbarian costume was too absurd. The men, their bodies wrapped tightly in short coats and long "legs," resembled in shape foxes and rabbits as impersonated in the plays. . . . Their beards, with abundant whiskers, were half shaved off and only a piece was kept. Looking at them all of a sudden was frightening. That the Cantonese referred to them as "devils" was indeed not vicious disparagement. [Chang Hsin-pao, *Commissioner Lin and the Opium War* (Cambridge: Harvard University Press, 1964)]

Although the Chinese forbade opium importation, willing trading partners were easily found among the Chinese merchants. And if trade became too difficult for the foreigners in the principal port of Canton, there were a thousand miles of coastline, and thousands of miles more of inland borders, through which opium could be transported. Lin saw that the opium trade was ruining China. Informed by his reading of de Vattel and by his extensive dealings with the British representatives, in early 1839 he appealed to Queen Victoria, attempting to conceal the sense of superiority that the Chinese rulers felt toward Westerners:

> We have heard that in your honorable nation, too, the people are not permitted to smoke [opium], and that offenders in this particular expose themselves to sure punishment. . . . Though not making use of it one's self, to venture nevertheless to manufacture and sell it, and with it to seduce the simple folk of this land, is to seek one's own livelihood by exposing others to death, to see one's own advantage by other men's injury. Such acts are bitterly abhorrent to the nature of man and are utterly opposed to the ways of heaven. . . . We now wish to find, in cooperation with your honorable sovereignty, some means of bringing to a perpetual end this opium, so hurtful to mankind: we in this land forbidding the use of it, and you, in the nations of your dominion, forbidding its manufacture. [Chang Hsin-pao, *Commissioner Lin and the Opium War*]

The British were the biggest traders in China, but merchants from the United States were present too. Lin considered petitioning this other, possibly significant state, but understood that twenty-four chiefs governed the American people, and thought that communicating with them all would be too difficult.

In his letter to Queen Victoria, Lin sought to explain the situation logically. Earlier communications from the Chinese government had not been so diplomatic. The commander of Canton had sent an edict to the Western traders demanding, "Could your various countries stand one day without trading with China?" This threat came in part from the Chinese leaders' delusion that the British would die if deprived of tea, China's largest export (a delusion the British may have shared). The same edict took note that, according to the Western press,

> your motives are to deplete the Middle Kingdom's wealth and destroy the lives of the Chinese people. There is no need to dwell on the topic that the wealth of the Celestial Empire, where all five metals are produced and precious deposits abound, could not be exhausted by such a mere trifle, but for what enmity do you want to kill the Chinese people?

China had withstood barbarian traders without difficulty for two thousand years. But now it was feeling the after-shock of the Western encounter with the Americas and with the closely related expansion of European influence across the globe. The importation of opium reached staggering pro-portions in the early nineteenth century after the British-run East India Company took control of the drug's production in India. During the trading season of 1816–17, about forty-six hundred 150-pound chests of opium entered China. This number rose to 22,000 by 1831–32 and 35,000 by 1837–38. That was more than 5.25 million pounds of opium, the care-fully collected and dried sap extruded from 4.8 trillion opium poppies.

The period from the seventeenth century to the present could be termed the Age of Addiction, for the international economy and the fortunes of nations depended on trade in addictive or semiaddictive agricultural products. The young United States exported tobacco, the habit for which spread rapidly across Europe, Africa, and Asia. The Spaniards carried the New World practice of tobacco smoking to Europe and the East Indies, and as its popularity spread, the plant came to be widely cultivated throughout the Old World. In their Indonesian colonies the Dutch tried filling their pipes with a combination of opium and tobacco. The Chinese continued to smoke the opium, but left out the tobacco.

The British became addicted to the carefully processed leaves of *Camellia sinensis,* or Chinese tea (originally, China was the only exporter). Caffeine-rich coffee was another drug for which Europeans and others developed a craving. A native plant of Ethiopia, coffee's range of cultivation expanded hand in hand with European colonialism. Perfect growing conditions were found in both the New World and Southeast Asia, giv-ing rise to the exotic names for coffee familiar today: Jamaica Blue Mountain, Mocha Java, Guatemalan, Sumatran, and Colombian. These and other nonessential but deeply desired plant products—cocaine, chocolate, and marijuana—have cap-tured huge markets.

Addictive substances are wonderful exports for the coun-tries that produce and ship them. They are highly valuable and compact agricultural products that can be exchanged for hard currency, and the demand of addicts is—for physiological reasons—what economists would call highly inelastic. Farmers get much more from their land and effort than they would by growing things for a local market, and middlemen on both sides of the border get rich. The losers in the transaction—apart from the users themselves—are the importing countries, which run up uncontrollable trade deficits.

From the opening of the Silk Road in the Middle Ages, Western countries were eager to obtain Chinese spices, fab-rics, and tea, viewing them as superior to European products. The problem for England and other nations was that they had very little that China wanted, so they had to pay in the most respected and accepted international currency, Spanish silver dollars. With good reason, the Chinese thought the British could not live without tea. About all China would take in trade was British woolen and cotton cloth. American merchants, lacking England's textile manufacturing infrastructure, struggled still more to find anything the Chinese would take in trade. They too paid mainly with Spanish silver, but they also brought natural products—sealskins and other furs from the Northwest Coast, aromatic wood, cotton, wild American ginseng—with which to trade (*see* "Yankee Doodle Went to Canton," *Natural History,* February 1984).

By capitalizing upon a massive addiction to smoked opium in China—and in substantial measure helping to create it—England and the other Western nations shifted the balance of trade in their favor. As social historian Fernand Braudel put it, "China was now literally being paid in smoke (and what smoke!)." Most of the rest of what England traded was woven cotton, also grown and spun in India. In return, at the time of Commissioner Lin's appeal to Queen Victoria, the Chinese were trading about 60 percent tea, 12 percent silks, and most of the rest, about 25 percent, silver and gold.

The opium trade was not the only alarming foreign influence in Lin's day. The barbarians seemed to have designs on Chinese territory. The port of Canton lay thirty miles upriver from the great Gulf of Canton, twenty miles wide and fifty miles long. At the western approach to the bay was the Portuguese trading colony of Macao, which the Chinese had allowed to exist since 1557. On the other side of the gulf lay the island of Hong Kong, which the British sought to turn into a secure headquarters for their trading operations. Even if the Europeans had lacked naval superiority, they could have defended both places from invasion by land or sea. China had always insisted that barbarians of any stripe carry out their trade and then leave, but instead of acting as temporary visitors, the Western traders were staying longer and longer, becoming in effect permanent residents.

Another major grievance was that the foreigners would not submit to Chinese laws when in China. Some European sailors murdered Chinese citizens, but their leaders would not turn over the culprits to the Chinese magistrates. Lin's research revealed that foreigners in England were required to obey British law, but when he confronted the British commanders with this double standard, they merely conceded that he had a case and again refused to turn over British subjects to almost certain execution. Other European and American traders acted similarly.

Despite the barbarian offenses, Lin preferred negotiation and reasoned discussion to fighting a battle that he felt would be difficult to win. In a final, carefully worded letter to Queen Victoria, he wrote:

> Let us suppose that foreigners came from another country, and brought opium into England, and seduced the people of your country to smoke it. Would not you, the sovereign

of the said country, look upon such a procedure with anger, and in your just indignation endeavor to get rid of it? Now we have always heard that Your Highness possesses a most kind and benevolent heart. Surely then you are incapable of doing or causing to be done unto another that which you should not wish another to do unto you. [Chang Hsin-pao, *Commissioner Lin and the Opium War*]

Moral persuasion has not, historically, proved very effective in dealing with drug smuggling or rulers who sanction it. Unofficially, the contents of the letter were probably widely known but, as with his previous attempts, Lin received no official response. Britain was determined that the opium trade would continue, by force if necessary, and because China had been unwilling to open formal diplomatic channels, the British government would not accept a letter to the queen from a commissioner.

Lin's efforts to rein in the barbarians and subdue the Chinese appetite for opium were ultimately unsuccessful, and the emperor harshly accused him of failing:

Externally you wanted to stop the trade, but it has not been stopped. Internally you wanted to wipe out the outlaws, but they are not cleared away. . . . You are just making excuses with empty words. Nothing has been accomplished but many troubles have been created. Thinking of these things I cannot contain my rage. What do you have to say now?

Lin replied that the Chinese should address the threat and fight the British, falling back to the interior and fighting a guerrilla war if necessary. He warned the emperor not to attempt to placate the British: "The more they get the more they demand, and if we do not overcome them by force of arms there will be no end to our troubles. Moreover there is every probability that if the English are not dealt with, other foreigners will soon begin to copy and even outdo them."

In June of 1839, Lin had 20,000 chests of opium destroyed in Canton, and the foreign merchants fell back to Macao. The British sent a fleet of their most powerful warships on a punitive expedition, and they overwhelmed the Chinese fleet whenever they faced it. Among their warships were the "ships-of-the-line," massively armed vessels that demonstrated the advantage of superior technology over superior numbers in modern warfare. In the summer of 1842, China was forced to sign the humiliating Treaty of Nanking, which required $21 million in reparations, opened five ports to British trade (including Canton and Shanghai), and ceded Hong Kong, surrounding islands, and part of the mainland to Queen Victoria. China also agreed that future Chinese–British relations would be on terms of "complete equality." This condition seems ironic, because the terms of the treaty were certainly in the Western merchants' favor. This wording was insisted upon by the British, however, because previously China had dealt with Westerners as barbarian traders, never recognizing them as official representatives of foreign governments. Nowhere did the treaty mention opium, but everyone knew that the drug had been at the heart of the war.

One hundred fifty years later, China still feels the sting of this defeat. The recently negotiated treaty for the return of Hong Kong in 1997 is viewed as just a fraction of the restitution owed. In 1990, writing in the *Beijing Review,* historian Hu Sheng, president of the Chinese Academy of Social Sciences, lamented the cost of the war in terms of Chinese health, hard currency, and national honor. He also observed that for the next hundred years China was under continuous attack by the West and Japan, but because the emperors were willing to tolerate their presence, the people were unable to rise up and throw out the foreigners. In his view, and in that of many Chinese, "Only the Chinese Communist Party could do this."

For his failure to curb the barbarians, Lin Zexu was demoted and disgraced, and spent the last few years before his death supervising irrigation projects and the repair of dikes. In retrospect, he is regarded as a hero. "The Chinese army, commanded by Lin," writes Hu, "resisted the invaders together with the local people. However, the corrupt Qing court was unable to continue the resistance and succumbed to the invaders."

Commissioner Lin would no doubt feel vindicated, and perhaps even take some pleasure in the way many Western nations are now on the receiving end of the drug policies they helped invent.

SAMUEL M. WILSON teaches anthropology at the University of Texas at Austin.

After Centuries of Japanese Isolation, a Fateful Meeting of East and West

When Japan's rulers finally let in Yankee trade and technology, they changed the history of their country and of the world

JAMES FALLOWS

From the deck of the USS *Susquehanna* the sailors watched the sea around them fill with little boats. The *Susquehanna* and its sister ships—the *Mississippi,* the *Saratoga,* the *Powhatan*—had been traveling for more than half a year. From Norfolk, Virginia, they had sailed in the late fall of 1852 across the Atlantic, then down around Capetown, and across the Indian Ocean to the South China Sea. Through the spring of 1853 they labored northward past Macao, Hong Kong, Okinawa and the Bonin island chain—Iwo Jima and Chichi Jima—toward the main islands of Japan.

On the evening of July 8, 1853, they rounded a promontory and came to the entrance of the Uraga Channel, itself the entrance to Edo Wan, now known as Tokyo Bay. At the head of the bay, less than a day's sail away, lay Edo itself, Japan's largest city, insulated from foreign contact for nearly 250 years.

The Japanese guard boats that teemed around the American flotilla in the Uraga Channel were made of wood, with sharply angled prows. Sweating oarsmen propelled the boats through the ocean chop. Above the rowers' heads flapped the geometric- or floral-patterned standards of the Tokugawa shoguns who ruled Japan. The American sailors could not understand the shouts that came to them in Japanese. Yet every crew member knew that in the past, uninvited visitors to Japan had often been jailed, tortured or decapitated.

As the lead guard boat approached the *Susquehanna,* the Americans peering down from the deck found, with relief, that they could make out a few familiar characters from the Roman alphabet, rather than the gracefully swirling *hiragana* of Japanese phonetic writing or the intricate *kanji* ideograms the Japanese had adapted from written Chinese. As the guard boat drew closer still, sharp-eyed crewmen sounded out the first word: *"Départez!"* The entire message was in French, not English. It said, "Depart immediately and dare not anchor!" The two nations that would become the main Pacific powers made their first significant contact in a language neither really understood.

The Lengthened Shadows of Two Men

Japan's rulers had not in any way invited the encounter; indeed, the more imminent it had become, the more it filled them with dread. America forced the encounter on Japan for a confused tangle of reasons, many of which the American instigators did not honestly discuss among themselves. Yet the after effects of this moment prepared Japan for the most impressive feat in its history, and one of the most surprising in the history of any nation. At the same time American interests were more shrewdly advanced by the man who sat hidden in his cabin on the *Susquehanna* than by other American leaders almost any time in U.S. history. Ninety years afterward, Japan and America would be at war, but that was not the fault of the two men who guided this encounter on a hot summer day in 1853; Masahiro Abe, in the shogun's council at Edo, and Matthew Calbraith Perry, in command of the vessels known today in Japan as *kuro-fune,* "black ships."

Matthew Perry, bearing the title not of Commodore but of "Commander in Chief, United States Naval Forces stationed in the East India, China, and Japan Seas," was 59 years old when his fleet reached Uraga. For the era, that was old—especially for a man undertaking a prolonged voyage to an essentially unknown destination. Perry suffered from arthritis and other maladies that confined him to his cabin during much of the long trip. Even at age 25 he had been remarked on for his gravitas; as he grew older he took on the air of a mandarin. This demeanor proved a great asset. Like Douglas MacArthur, another American too regal to fit easily into his home culture, Matthew Perry was well prepared by training and temperament for negotiations in Japan. An aw-shucks, unassuming manner might be an asset on the American frontier, but not surrounded by little boats in Tokyo Bay.

Perry's career, indeed his whole life, was devoted to the expansion of the U.S. Navy. His older brother, Oliver Hazard

Perry, had become a hero at the Battle of Lake Erie before Matthew was out of his teens. Matthew, by contrast, spent his early career in a peacetime navy "where members of a small clique of senior officers scrambled for the limited command opportunities, where feuding, backbiting, and even dueling were a way of life," as Peter Booth Wiley puts it in *Yankees in the Land of the Gods.* "During the navy's first fifty years, thirty-three officers were killed in duels." Perry's first important mission, in 1819, was to transport freed slaves to Africa during the founding of Liberia. He did not see combat until he was in his 50s, at the Battle of Veracruz in the Mexican War, as the nation kept expanding westward toward a second sea frontier on the Pacific.

One great struggle over America's maritime future turned on the relative future roles of clipper ships versus steam-powered vessels. By the 1850s the fast and graceful clippers had given America the lead in the shipping trade. But the British were outbuilding America in steamships, and by the 1840s, Britain's steam-powered Cunard line was winning the battle for passengers and valuable freight on the transatlantic route.

Steam power required coal, and at the time no ship was large enough to carry all the coal it needed to cross the vast Pacific. Clipper ships had to choose routes to China on the basis of favorable winds, but steamers could be more deliberate, following a "great circle" route up toward Alaska and then down the Japanese archipelago. With coaling stations along the way, the great circle route would be possible, and in 1851 Americans learned that Japan had deposits of coal. "The moment is near when the last link in the chain of oceanic steam navigation is to be formed," said Senator Daniel Webster of New Hampshire, not stinting on rhetoric, as he endorsed an American expedition to Japan. The point of this link would not be to buy from the Japanese their own handicrafts and manufactures but to obtain a "gift of Providence, deposited, by the Creator of all things, in the depths of the Japanese islands for the benefit of the human family"—that is, Japan's coal.

The desire to expand a coal-using, steam-powered navy was not the only reason for the expedition to Japan. Beyond lay China, where Americans hoped to find markets to develop and souls to convert. For a century before the age of steamships, American whalers had worked the waters of the North Pacific surrounding Japan. Frequently the ships did not come home. American sailors stranded by typhoon or shipwreck had washed ashore in Japan since the late 1700s. Often they were executed; usually they were jailed; a few were forced to perform ritual disrespect to Christian symbols, for instance by walking on a portrait of the Virgin Mary.

Getting the Jump on Dutch, French and English

These icons of the Blessed Virgin were leftovers from Portuguese Jesuits, who had proselytized in Japan for nearly a century before being driven out in the early 1600s. The shipwrecked Americans, mainly Protestants, found this ordeal less excruciating than the Japanese expected, yet news of such episodes, especially one involving the whaler *Lagoda,* filtered back to America, where at a minimum they stirred a passion for better protection for whalers, and among some people a desire to make the "pagans" atone. "If that double-bolted land, Japan, is ever to become hospitable, it is the whale-ship alone to whom the credit will be due," Herman Melville wrote in *Moby-Dick* in 1851.

The British had won their Opium Wars against China. From the north came Russian vessels. Swarming around were the French and the Dutch. The expansionist U.S. Government watched these plans with care. Finally to establish America's presence first, the Administration of Millard Fillmore, in by far its most consequential step, commissioned the Japan Expedition and convinced Matthew Perry to command it. For nearly two and a half centuries, since the great warlord Hideyoshi took steps that led to the policies known as *sakoku,* or "closed country," Japan's officials had isolated themselves from the world—and wondered apprehensively when the isolation might end.

In 1549 a Portuguese Jesuit, Francis Xavier, had come ashore on the island of Kyushu. Initially tolerated, even supported by some local noblemen, the Jesuits had in the next 50 years made tens of thousands of Japanese converts. By the end of the century Hideyoshi, weakened by a costly and failed attempt to conquer Korea, and chastened to learn that savage conquistadors had often followed the cross in Latin America, had expelled all missionaries. Soon, the Tokugawa shogunate launched its radical policy of seclusion. As far as possible, Japan and its leaders would function as if there were no world beyond Japan's seacoast. "So long as the Sun shall warm the earth, let no Christian dare to come to Japan," said the shogun's expulsion order of 1638. If contact with foreigners was unavoidable, it would be handled through an enclave of Dutch traders, concentrated in an island ghetto called Deshima, near Nagasaki in the far southern extreme of the country—hundreds of miles from the great, protected centers of Kyoto and Edo.

The sakoku policy worked for a while—indeed, for as many years as the United States has now existed as an independent country. Yet in the early 1800s, as Japan began its third century of near-total isolation, the strains were evident. "In 1642, the year Isaac Newton was born, the last Japanese priest had been crucified and Japan had closed like an oyster," one American historian has written. But the leaders who made the decision "could hardly guess that Japan, which went into seclusion as one of the two or three strongest nations on the globe, would emerge from it, centuries later, as a distinctly second-class power."

The same whalers and fishermen who were inconvenient when washed onto Japanese shores inevitably brought news of the Industrial Revolution and other advancements outside Japan. A young Japanese fisherman named Manjiro Nakajima was himself shipwrecked and picked up by an American whaler in 1841. Under Japan's seclusion law, it was a capital offense to leave the country—or to come back, if one had escaped. But after spending a decade in New England, under the name John Mung, Manjiro decided to risk returning to Japan.

The *daimyo,* or lord, of the southern province of Satsuma realized, as Samuel Eliot Morison puts it, that decapitating Manjiro would not only sever his head but also "would cut off an important source of information." Instead, the daimyo sent him to Nagasaki, "where officials pumped Manjiro dry of everything he knew about the United States." Among the facts Manjiro revealed (as Walter McDougall wrote in *Let the Sea Make a Noise . . .*) was that Americans were lewd by nature, and that in their country "toilets are placed over holes in the ground. It is customary to read books in them."

Officially the Japanese rulers faced news of foreign developments with redoubled sternness. In 1825, as whaling traffic increased, the shogun issued an edict forbidding any foreign ship to land. When a foreign ship came into view, the order read, it was crucial to shoot at it first and ask questions later. "Have no compunctions about firing on [the Dutch] by mistake," the order went on. "When in doubt, drive the ship away without hesitation. Never be caught off guard."

Behind this bravado was a debate, based on very little information but heated because the Japanese felt the very survival of the nation was at stake. In the town of Mito, a day's walk to the northeast of Edo, the "Mito School" of theorists said that an increased threat required increased determination to resist. Japan must shore up its coastal defenses, girding itself for the inevitable battle to the death that would keep the foreigners away. "Today the alien barbarians of the West, the lowly organs of the legs and feet of the world, are . . . trampling other countries underfoot, and daring, with their squinting eyes and limping feet, to override the noble nations," one such scholar wrote in 1825. With such a foe, no compromise could be possible.

Could Japan Bend Without Breaking?

In the other camp were the Rangakusha, or "masters of Dutch learning," so called after Holland's role during the closed-country years as the vehicle for all learning from overseas. A realistic assessment of the circumstances, said members of this camp, required Japan to bend so as to avoid being broken. They had evidence of weakness inside the country. Taxes, levied in rice, were becoming oppressive. In several centuries of peace the samurai class had grown large and dependent; in 1850 Edo alone supported some 17,000 bureaucrats, compared with 1,500 in Washington, D.C.

Evidence of the strength of potential invaders was even more dramatic. In 1846, seven years before Matthew Perry's arrival, Commodore James Biddle of the U.S. Navy had reached the mouth of the Uraga Channel. He had retreated with humiliating loss of face, after letting Japanese sightseers and officials inspect every inch of his ship and after accepting a letter from the shogun telling him never to return. Yet the shrewder Japanese officials of the era carefully noted the size and power of his ships, and of the American guns. Biddle's vessels represented destructive potential of a sort Japan had barely imagined.

Most of all the Japanese realists noticed what had happened to China—noticed, and were appalled. China was not just another country but the Middle Kingdom, the Central Country. Its emperor had historically referred to Japan's emperor as "your little king." A new China had been carved up by Westerners, debauched by opium and left totally unprotected by either the

Ch'ing dynasty or armed force. If the British and French could polish off China, what hope was there for little Japan—against Britain, France, Russia and the United States? Japan could try to enforce its seclusion law, said one of its very shrewdest leaders after the Biddle affair, but if "the foreigners retaliated, it would be a hopeless contest, and it would be a worse disgrace for Japan."

This leader was Masahiro Abe, the senior counselor for the shogun's government. As the shogun was the power that ruled Japan in the emperor's name, so Abe was the strategist who made plans on behalf of the weakened shogun, Tokugawa Ieyoshi, who was in place when Perry arrived. Abe was a generation younger than Perry, only 34 years old as Perry's flotilla of Black Ships neared Edo. Raised in a scholar's family, he had through force of intellect made himself one of the shogun's most influential advisers while still in his 20s.

In the split between the hard-liners and compromisers in the shogun's court, Abe sided initially with the hard-liners. But after extensive consultation among the daimyos of Japan, he and his allies came up with a brilliant compromise. Japan would open itself to the Western traders—but only for a time—placating them just long enough to learn how to rebuild its own navies and arsenals. Naosuke Ii, the most influential of all the daimyos, reminded the shogun that, even as Japan had earlier used Dutch traders as its bridge to the outside world, it was time to use the Americans and other foreigners as another, broader bridge. Across this bridge new discoveries could flow into Japan—providing the country, in the long run, with means to rearm itself, learn from outside technology, and ultimately "gain a complete victory" over the foreigners.

Some of the American politicians promoting the Japan Expedition had cast it in missionary terms, a chance to open the Orient to faith and flag. "I am sure that the Japanese policy of seclusion is not according to God's plan of bringing the nations of the earth to a knowledge of the truth," Samuel Wells Williams, a missionary traveling with Perry as cultural expert and interpreter, wrote in his journal as the expedition neared Edo. Perry himself, pious enough, never described his duties in these terms. Instead he concentrated on how to deploy his men, his ships and himself for maximum effect. Before the trip began, Perry foresaw that his fleet's substantial armament "would do more to command their fears, and secure their friendship, than all that the diplomatic missions have accomplished in the last one hundred years." In a set of "Instructions" for the voyage, Perry said that the Commander "will be careful to do nothing that may [compromise] his own dignity or that of the country. He will, on the contrary, do every thing to impress them with a just sense of the power and greatness of this country and to satisfy them that its past forbearance has been the result, not of timidity, but of a desire to be on friendly terms with them."

Gifts to Show a Nation's Strength

Like Masahiro Abe, Perry had studied the sad history of Commodore Biddle, who had been forced out of Edo Bay in 1846. In Perry's view, Biddle never recovered from setting

Figure 1 Of gifts given, those from Japanese were more decorative, while Perry's aimed to impress Japan with industrial might. Baby steam engine was biggest hit, but offerings included plow, scythe, grindstone.

Note: United States Naval Academy Museum, Annapolis

his first foot wrong with the Japanese: rather than insisting on retaining a mysterious distance, he had let them climb onto his ship and, in effect, imprison it with guard boats. Speaking of himself in the third person, in his memoir of the voyage Perry said, "The Commodore . . . was well aware that the more exclusive he should make himself, and the more unyielding he might be in adhering to his declared intentions, the more respect these people of forms and ceremonies would be disposed to award him." He would meet only with officials of "the highest rank" in Japan. He would make a threat only when he was absolutely certain he could carry it out.

Power could be demonstrated through generosity as well as reserve. Perry had prepared gifts to demonstrate the range of strengths his nation possessed. Editions of Audubon's *Birds of America* and *Quadrupeds of America* that had cost $1,000 apiece—a decade's earnings for an average American family at the time. Champagne, perfume and mirrors. Whisky, liqueurs, and small weapons from the Colt factory. And, most important, American machines: plows, a telegraph, a crude camera, even a nifty little quarter-scale steam-powered railroad train.

This was the man who appeared in the Uraga Channel in July 1853. He was not one to be driven away by instructions to *"Départez!"* Sweating alone in his cabin, unwilling to present himself prematurely to the crowd of Japanese, he issued his orders. The *Susquehanna* and sister ships were to repel, with

all necessary force, any Japanese who attempted to board the boats. They would proceed up the channel, toward Edo, until their wish to meet a truly senior official, one who could speak for the ruler, was fulfilled. After the failure of the French message, a Japanese official had neared the *Susquehanna* and yelled out, in English, "I can speak Dutch!" To him the Americans conveyed their wish to meet someone truly in command.

Throughout Edo, news of the Black Ships' arrival created near-panic. Some citizens fled, carrying their possessions to the countryside, fearing pillage and war. The shogun's council met to consider bleak-seeming alternatives. The usual reflexive responses to outside pressure—asking the foreigners to come back again in a few years, telling them to go on to Nagasaki, the only site where Japan had done business with foreign representatives through the sakoku years—seemed to have lost their potency. The Americans would not retreat—in fact, they kept sending surveying ships farther up the bay, ignoring Japanese assertions that this violated local law and saying that they needed to be sure about anchorages, for "the next time."

As the governing council quarreled, Abe pushed them toward a decision: the Americans must be placated, at least for now. Perry had been asking to meet the emperor; that was out of the question, of course. Indeed, to this point the Americans were not even aware that a real emperor existed, hidden in Kyoto. When they said "emperor," they were referring to the shogun;

their official goal was to present him with letters from President Fillmore.

Clearly some meeting was essential, and so on July 14, after elaborate arguments over protocol, Matthew Perry himself came ashore at the town of Kurihama.

In retrospect this result seems inevitable. America was a country on the rise. Japan could not wall itself off eternally. Each party had a stake in negotiating reasonably with the other: Perry because he was outnumbered on the scene; the Japanese, because other Americans could come back and exact retribution if anything went wrong. But at the time it was very much touch and go. More than once Perry's men came to the brink of violent confrontation. Crewmen on the *Mississippi* had to level a loaded musket at a Japanese official's chest to keep him from climbing aboard. A small American survey boat, commanded by Lieut. Silas Bent, found itself surrounded by three dozen Japanese guard boats. Bent prepared for hand-to-hand combat, instructing his small crew to fix bayonets—until the mighty *Mississippi* steamed into view and the Japanese retreated.

And so, on the night before Perry's scheduled landing in Kurihama, his crew members watched apprehensively from their decks as more and more Japanese troops filled the shore. Perry considered the possibility that the proposed meeting was really an ambush. After his surveyors reported that Kurihama's harbor was deep enough, Perry ordered his gunboats brought in close to shore, where they could bombard the Japanese if anything went wrong. On the long night before the meeting, 250 American sailors were chosen by lot for the dangerous mission of accompanying their commander ashore. The Japanese worked through the night to prepare a pavilion for the meeting—and to increase the boats guarding the entrance to Edo Bay, in case the Americans were planning a sudden, treacherous assault.

On the morning of July 14, the American boats drew near to shore. Members of the landing party, dressed in their formal uniforms, were issued 20 rounds of ammunition apiece and carefully loaded their muskets and pistols. On the shore they saw three new pavilions, covered with the bright flags and standards of Japanese officialdom. Surrounding the pavilions were files and files of soldiers, armed with swords, bows and arrows, and a few antique firearms.

At 10 o'clock barges full of Americans began arriving on the shore. Miscalculations at this moment might have had historic consequences; long after the event, one of the Japanese commanders revealed that ten swordsmen had been hiding under the floor of a pavilion, with orders to leap out and slaughter the foreigners if they made the slightest aggressive move.

As their numbers grew on the beach, Perry's men formed a double line, through which their commander, arriving at last, marched toward the waiting Japanese. Ahead of Perry was a Marine officer walking with sword in hand. On either side of him were two of the largest men from his ship, both black stewards, loaded with all the weapons they could carry and towering over every other person on the beach. Once Perry was safe ashore, tension eased a bit. He was met by two Japanese governors, to whom the stewards presented large rosewood boxes. Inside were small solid-gold cases, which in turn contained Millard

Fillmore's letters requesting that Japan open itself to the world. The governors, in return, presented Perry with a letter said to be from Japan's ruler. When translated, it turned out to contain warnings that the Americans had broken Japanese law by landing in Kurihama and must not come back. Perry said that, with his mission accomplished, he was leaving Japan—but he would be back the next year to hear the Japanese government's response. With quite as many ships? the interpreter asked. "All of them," Perry replied. "And probably more, as these are only a portion of the squadron."

After the meeting in Kurihama, Perry had compounded Japan's sense of threat by sending surveying parties even deeper into Edo Bay. Then his departing fleet retraced the route it had taken toward Japan, visiting Okinawa and the Bonin Islands before stopping for repairs and refitting in Macao. He studiously ignored suggestions from Washington that he wait and assemble a much larger force before his return trip. Perry knew that French and Russian missions would soon be heading to Japan. He was suffering terribly from arthritis; a winter passage back to Edo would be dangerous and unpleasant. Yet to forestall all other navies and force action from the Japanese, Perry set sail northward from Macao in the middle of January 1854.

Back in Edo everything was still uncertain. What did the Americans really want? What compromise would be enough to make their warships go away? Suppose the shogun's government offered to give the Americans half the trading rights now monopolized by the Dutch? Or dragged out the negotiations themselves over five or ten years; after which time the Americans might lose interest or Japan might come up with a new plan?

Fight It Out or Face Up to Progress

Masahiro Abe had ordered Japan's coastal defenses fortified as soon as Perry's flotilla headed south after its first visit. He engineered the repeal of a law—enacted at the start of the sakoku era—that prohibited Japanese citizens from building seagoing vessels, and he opened negotiations with the Dutch about buying some steam-powered warships from them. All factions in Japan agreed that negotiations should be strung out as long as possible. Yet when the moment of choice arose, should Japan fight to the death, as influential figures like Tokugawa Nariaki, daimyo of Mito, were advocating? Or should it bow to the reality of superior force and instead plan for long-term survival, and future revenge?

The issue was forced in the middle of February when American ships arrived once more in the Uraga Channel. This time Perry's flotilla numbered three steam-powered frigates, seven ships under sail, and combined crews totaling more than 1,500 men. Overcoming bitter accusations that he was betraying Japan, Abe at last forced through a decision. Japan would greet the Americans with conciliation. It would accept a code of conduct for shipwrecked whalers and seamen. It would let the Americans obtain coal in Shimoda, near Edo, and trade with them at sites other than the traditional foreigner's ghetto in Nagasaki. It asked only for a transition period of a few years before the full agreement came into effect.

There were still points of detail to be negotiated—how many ports would be open to trade, what tariff the Japanese could impose. But under Abe's guidance Japan had given in. Matthew Perry, confined by disease and dignity to his Black Ship cabin, was ready by early March to deal face-to-face with his Japanese counterparts. On March 8 he came ashore at Yokohama for a detailed, though still touchy, negotiating session.

On March 13 Perry went ashore once again for the first gift-exchanging ceremony. One by one he gave away the marvels of artistry and engineering he had stowed aboard his ships nearly two years before. The Japanese onlookers were entranced by the scale-model locomotive pulling a train. The passenger coach, complete with interior benches and curtains, was too small for human passengers, but samurai and shogun's officials took rides sitting on top of the train. In their turn, the Japanese offered gifts. But because they thought that valuable gifts might be insulting—suggesting the possibility of a bribe or the need to reply in kind—their gifts were modest, though artistic and of fine workmanship. Perry regarded them as trifling. More impressive were their mammoth sumo wrestlers. Perry watched as the *sumotori* strode in, heavy sacks of rice atop their heads. One of the wrestlers approached Perry, who accepted the invitation to punch the immense stomach and feel its strength. Samuel Wells Williams, Perry's missionary-interpreter, who was generally quite admiring of Japan and who despaired of his crewmates' insensitivity to foreign ways, nonetheless wrote in his diary that the spectacle demonstrated the clash of two cultures: the "success of science and enterprise" on the American side, the "brute animal force" on Japan's.

A final disagreement arose over Perry's desire to walk the streets of the capital city. Here the Japanese held firm: Perry could, if he chose, view Edo from the deck of his ship, but must not come ashore. Perry accepted, sailed to the top of Edo Bay for a look, and then, on April 14, headed south again.

Negotiations between Japan and the United States were just beginning. For most of the next decade an American counsel, Townsend Harris, would accuse Japanese officials of backsliding, dissembling and attempting to evade the treaty's terms. More than a century later in the debate over trading issues, Japanese and American officials have assumed roles very similar to those first played in Uraga and Kurihama, with the Japanese debating the merits of acquiescence or defiance, and the Americans, far less powerful now, attempting to display impressive and intimidating force.

Perry's role in Japan was complete. It was to be a profound role and, though deeply unwished for by the Japanese, in the long run it had quite positive effects. Although Japan had been forced to make concessions and accept "unequal treaties," it had avoided outright defeat—and had prepared for the rapid modernization that began with the Meiji Restoration of 1868. For this progress Japan could, with mixed emotions, thank Perry and the shock he delivered with the Black Ships.

Perry thought he would be lionized by his countrymen on his return, but he was not, in part because his countrymen were preoccupied with tensions over slavery that would lead to the Civil War. Retiring to his town house in New York, the Commodore worked methodically on his *Narrative of the Expedition,* which he submitted to the publisher at the end of 1857. Masahiro Abe, who had skillfully guided Japan through its greatest challenge of the 19th century, died while still in his 30s, a few months before Perry completed the manuscript. On March 4, 1858, shortly before his 64th birthday, Matthew Perry died at home, of rheumatism and heart failure. His cortege was led down Fifth Avenue by the men with whom he had sailed to Japan—the men, that is to say, with whom he had changed history.

JAMES FALLOWS, Washington editor of the *Atlantic Monthly,* has published *Looking at the Sun,* a study of Japanese and East Asian economic systems.

Chinese Burns:
Britain in China, 1842–1900

Robert Bickers shows how the history of British and European imperialism in China helps explain the ferocious Boxer War of 1900.

The Boxer rising began in the obscurity of the north-west regions of China's Shandong province in 1899. It finished as an international crisis. The Chinese siege of the foreign legations in the capital city Beijing from June 20th to August 14th, 1900, gripped the world's press. It fed and still feeds a steady stream of memoir and narrative to willing publishers.

The 'Boxer' became an international figure. But the episode began in 1899 when young Shandong farm boys, made idle as drought followed flooding, started practising 'spirit boxing', a martial art which was acquiring new features including individual 'spirit possession' and invulnerability rituals. They then set out to right a world gone wrong. Boxer beliefs, circulated through placards and pamphlets and rehearsed in doggerel and rumour, restated common prejudices and exacerbated long-standing rural tensions by scapegoating Chinese Christian converts and their foreign missionary mentors. They believed that church spires pierced the sky and prevented the rains and that the withdrawal of converts from communal ritual life unbalanced the world. Exterminating the foreign would surely bring the rain and also save their Qing rulers from foreign aggression.

The rains came in early July, but by August 14th, 1900, British and other armed forces had also arrived and were camped in the ruins of Beijing, having lifted the fifty-five-day siege of the legations and of the city's Roman Catholic Northern Cathedral (the Beitang). The port city of Tianjin, gateway to the capital, was levelled after its own siege. Numerous small towns and villages on the north China plain had seen vicious destructive warfare, and foreign troops launched raids to 'punish' residents living in the sites of alleged Boxer activity deep into 1901. Russian troops would not be evacuated from Manchuria until forced out in a Russo-Japanese war fought mostly on Chinese territory. The Qing court—which had taken the Boxers as allies and declared war on imperialism on June 21st, 1900—fled to China's north-west city of Xian, where it remained until October 1901. At least 220 foreign missionaries were dead, some executed at the order of Qing officials, while hundreds of foreign soldiers and probably tens of thousands of Chinese Christians, soldiers and civilians were killed in battle or cold blood, or died of disease or starvation as the conflict disordered north China. 'Invulnerable'

Boxers had been cut down by foreign soldiers (who would not spare any captives) and by Qing troops angry at the impotence of Boxer magic or cynically using them as cannon fodder. The September 1901 Boxer Protocol imposed a huge indemnity on the Qing state and established permanent foreign garrisons in the capital to guard a legation district that was removed from Chinese control and turned into an internationalised enclave.

Popular xenophobia and elite opportunism have often been blamed for the outbreak of what even one sympathetic foreign observer, the Inspector-General of China's Maritime Customs Service, Ulsterman Sir Robert Hart, called 'mid-summer madness'. But there was much method and deliberation in such elite and mass 'madness', and while attention in recent years has focused on understanding the anthropology of the Boxer movement and its roots in Shandong popular culture, research is in progress on the rational deliberations which led a powerful coalition at the Qing court to align itself with a mass movement in a bid to be rid of the foreign peril. It is as well, then, to focus on the history of foreign intrusions which fed Chinese worries. After all, British forces had camped out at Beijing before, in 1860, and had first seen Tianjin from their warships in 1840. Popular and elite resistance had cost Britons dearly at times, but British power had always won out. The use of armed force in China was wearisomely familiar to British diplomats, but its origins lay not in any lack of formal relations between the Qing empire and the British state, but in fact from the very intimacy of the relationship.

That intimacy is easily forgotten. The handover of the former British Crown Colony of Hong Kong to the People's Republic of China in 1997 was accompanied on the Chinese side by an unprecedented barrage of noisy propaganda that stressed the place of Hong Kong in the imperialist assault on China after 1840. Where British observers stressed the triumphs of the Hong Kong economy and its legislative and legal foundations as legacies of British rule, the Chinese debate mostly emphasised the illegality of the seizure in the first place, rooted as it was in the 'unequal' 1842 Treaty of Nanjing that ended the First Opium War. There was little common ground. British memories of colonialism tend to be short and roseate, and many Britons were surprised that memories of the nineteenth century were alive and well in China in 1997. The importance for modern Chinese nationalism and the national psyche of what is construed in China as 'national humiliation' is indeed singular. The seizure of the obscure island of Hong Kong was one such humiliation, the occupation of Beijing in 1900 was another.

Hong Kong was just one part of a network of leased territories, British concessions and settlements and international settlements in China. British gunboats patrolled Chinese rivers as part of the Royal Navy's China Station (established in 1844). British steamship companies ran coastal and river services while trading firms operated national business networks. Efficient conditions for foreign trade were guaranteed, as foreign observers saw it, by the creation after 1858 of a foreign-run Maritime Customs Service. Sir Robert Hart was a servant of the Chinese state, but his tenure of the Inspector-Generalship was rightly seen as an indicator of British control. Missionary organisations made opportunistic use of treaty clauses to set up stations in the Chinese interior and proselytise through a range of evangelical, educational and medical initiatives. Underpinning this British presence was the principle of extraterritoriality, by which British subjects in China came under the jurisdiction of their own consular representatives rather than Chinese law. The system was open to abuse and was extended in practice to include British-owned property and even British goods in the hands of Chinese agents.

Shanghai developed a distinctively militaristic settler culture, which was fiercely protective of its independence.

By 1900 British interests still formed the largest sector of the overall foreign presence, but the treaty port world was international, and most favoured nation clauses were granted to all who had signed treaties with China. So when farmers in Shandong started to practise Boxer rituals and then to attack Christian converts, they were in part reacting to the growth in China over the sixty years since the Nanjing treaty of this network of concessions and settlements, as well as to local manifestations of the foreign presence. The direct impact on small rural communities might be minimal but the claustrophobia and fear this foreign web caused was quickly communicated throughout the country to all levels of society.

The foreign impact was most visible and potent in the coastal cities. Although the British Minister was based in Beijing, and Hong Kong was formally incorporated into the British empire, the capital city of the British presence in China was Shanghai. By 1900 2,691 Britons (half of those resident in China outside Hong Kong) lived in the city's British-dominated International Settlement, which formed one of its three administrative units, the others being a French concession and the Chinese-administered city and suburbs. The Shanghai Municipal Council, which administered and policed the settlement, was staffed mostly by Britons and answered to nine representatives (seven Britons, one American and one German) elected

by the foreign ratepayers. In 1900 the council was chaired by Edbert Ansgar Hewett (P & O), and contained representatives of such China interests as Jardine Mathesons, E.D. Sassoon and the Chartered Bank, and local British settler interests including the waterworks and a dockyard firm. A Chinese population of 352,000 (out of about 900,000 in the city as a whole) effectively lived under foreign rule. In 1899 the council had extended its territory from 2.75 to 8.35 square miles, bringing more Chinese residents into the settlement, and some hothead local lobbyists wanted to see further extensions, preferably in the context of a British-dominated Yangzi protectorate.

In the International Settlement British residents mixed the pan-imperial pomp of Britain's eastern empire (Sikh policemen, colonial architecture) with institutions of local administration imported directly from the UK. Like colonial communities elsewhere they laid out a *bund* (a raised riverside embankment), built clubs, schools, hospitals and a cathedral (Holy Trinity), marked out race tracks, patronised theatres, joined Masonic lodges, walked in their public gardens and listened to the municipal band. The city had the headquarters of the China Inland Mission, as well as leading commercial firms and the Hong Kong and Shanghai Bank. It had its newspapers (the *North China Herald,* founded 1850), a library, commercial publishers such as Kelly and Walsh, cultural societies and sports clubs. In its learned societies there were discussions and debates on Chinese history and culture, while for those less academically-minded the Amoy Road gaol (built in 'solid lasting British style') could hold 140 prisoners. There were foreign department stores (Lane, Crawford and Co., Hall & Holtz), watchmakers, restaurants, dairies and a full range of service industries (law, insurance). Shanghailanders organised a Shanghai Volunteer Corps, a local militia charged with the task of protecting the settlement if need be until British forces could be landed from naval vessels or dispatched from Hong Kong. They were inspected annually by a representative of the commanding officer of British forces in China and Hong Kong, who found them in April 1900 to be 'a fine body of citizen soldiers in whose hands the great mercantile interests of Shanghai are in good keeping'. A distinctive settler culture, typical of that created by overseas Britons, developed—militaristic and fiercely protective of its independence.

As the population figures suggested, however, Shanghai remained a Chinese city. On the surface there was much that was European, especially the buildings reflecting the variegated nature of the foreign community, but appearances were deceptive. The International Settlement was built on Chinese labour, expertise and capital. Shanghai was a lively and important centre of Chinese cultural and commercial innovation. Foreign trading firms sought access to supplies and markets by establishing alliances with Chinese businessmen. Other foreign entrepreneurs—such as Briton Ernest Major, who founded Shanghai's first Chinese newspaper the *Shenbao* (1872) and the illustrated magazine the *Dianshizhai huabao* (1884)—created and fed new Chinese markets. Real estate firms made fortunes from Chinese residents or for Chinese investors. Foreign companies sought capital as well as market expertise and raised finance through share issues. It gets difficult in fact to distinguish between British and Chinese interests. Yet such intimacies often co-existed with informal social segregation and, quite frequently, there was an absence of meaningful communication between Chinese and Briton. Meanwhile the British-dominated authorities discriminated against its Chinese residents by denying them access to municipal parks and gardens, and by refusing them the right to vote or stand for election to the council. The International Settlement prided itself on being a 'model settlement', and Chinese observers looked to it for demonstrations of the practices of Western municipal administration, but the relationship between the foreign and the Chinese was uneasy. 1900 passed off peacefully in Shanghai, but local tensions over the settlement erupted into violence in 1905.

Chinese intellectuals in 1900 feared that the hour of national extinction had arrived.

Shanghai's lobbyists talked loosely about their ambitions for greater autonomy, and their actions and words rightly worried Chinese observers. But the foreign danger was not confined to the coastal cities. Mission societies were active in treaty ports such as Shanghai, but their chosen field was rural China, and the impact of the missionary sector of the British presence was felt most strongly there. The modern mission presence in the country dated back to September 1807 when the Protestant missionary Robert Morrison arrived in Canton. His twenty-seven years in China produced a path-breaking Chinese-English dictionary but no more than a dozen converts. Yet the treaty of Nanjing facilitated the extension of Protestant and Catholic activities. Missionaries set up operations (including churches, schools and printing presses) in the newly opened treaty ports. The Qing state was forced to accept toleration of Christianity in 1858, while under a clause in the 1860 Sino-French treaty missionaries acquired the right to reside in the interior and purchase land and buildings. By the end of the century there were around 530,000 Catholic and some 80,000 Protestant converts. These numbers were insignificant in relation to the population of the Qing empire, but the impact was intense.

In the twenty years before 1900 Protestant missionary activity greatly intensified as 272 new centres were opened, while the number of stations rose from 132 to 498. Few parts of China were without some form of mission presence, or without some form of resistance, sometimes bloody, to that presence. Reports of 'mission cases' bedevilled smooth diplomatic relations. In the most spectacular incident—the Tianjin massacre of 1870—ten French nuns, one priest, the French consul, his deputy and sundry other French and Chinese unfortunates were killed in an incident related to local rumours about child kidnapping and the removal of eyes by the nuns at a Catholic orphanage. British and French churches were destroyed and gunboats quickly despatched. War with France was feared, and the Qing court was soon riven by divisions over how to deal with the incident, which was eventually settled by a mission of apology to France. Most incidents were smaller in scale and in implications, and the majority involved tensions between converts and their local communities. In fairness, it should be said that the mission record was hardly uniformly negative, and Chinese converts were not all 'rice-Christians' seeking economic or other benefit from their relations with Westerners. Most missionaries did not see themselves as agents of broader British interests in China, but it was impossible to disentangle their activities and impact from that of the broader British and foreign presence.

The British establishment in China, then, was multifaceted and divided. It included official representatives in the consular service and armed forces, missionaries and the traders, bankers and landlords who filled the ranks of the Shanghai oligarchs, together with their servants of empire: shop clerks, engineers and police constables. Baghdadi Jews from India, overseas Chinese from the Straits Settlements, Sikh policemen and Eurasians from Hong Kong all lived and worked under British protection in China. There was a confident sub-imperialism, articulated and served by such aggressive all-rounders as J.O.P. Bland (1863–1945), who worked in the Customs, for settler imperialism through the Shanghai Municipal Council, and later for finance imperialism through the British and Chinese Corporation. Bland also worked from 1896 to 1910 as a contributor to *The Times,* and as a freelance author and commentator thereafter. He lobbied for a British 'forward policy' on the Yangzi in the 1890s, noting the movements and gains of Britain's European rivals, but was on leave during much of the Boxer crisis: otherwise his shrill voice might have been heard arguing for further settlement extension in Shanghai, bent as he ever was on 'stratagems and spoils for the glory of the Raj'. There was also fear and uncertainty about the British position of course, but in the first fifty years of the British presence in China there seemed little limit to potential spoils for such Shanghai adventurers.

These British certainties as well as the nineteenth-century treaty settlement were destabilised by the entry of aggressive new actors onto the scene in the 1890s: firstly Japan, and then Russia and Germany. In the aftermath of the 1894–95 Sino-Japanese war, a punitive indemnity imposed on China set off a scramble among European loan consortia to lend China the funds it needed. The lobbying support of national governments was earnestly sought, and to British surprise a Franco-Russian group was awarded the first such loan in 1895, although an Anglo-German group at least secured the second. Such loans threatened the British status quo. Competition intensified in late 1897. On November 1st, two German Catholic missionaries were hacked to death by Chinese assailants in an incident rooted in local ill-feeling towards the mission presence in that part of Shandong. The Kaiser happily seized this opportunity to order German warships to occupy the port of Jiaozhou. A Sino-German treaty of March 6th, 1898, confirmed the seizure and granted preferential rights in Shandong to Germany. German expansion thereafter was effectively stymied by the local Chinese authorities, but with the German navy-administered colony of 'Kiautschou' (Jiaozhou) another slice of the Chinese melon had been taken. Before too long Russia had seized Dalian (Port Arthur), and Britain the port of Weihaiwei, which was ruled as a leased territory until 1930. These moves also accelerated the feeding frenzy for railway and other concessions.

Chinese intellectuals feared that the hour of national extinction had arrived.

This was the situation into which the Boxers emerged. It explains the vacillations and hesitancies of the official Qing response—and the ultimate decision of the court to try to use the opportunity presented by the popular rural movement to strike back at foreign aggression. But it also explains why British military personnel were already on the spot, why they had few qualms about storming and seizing the Dagu (Taku) forts which protected the route to the capital, and why Britain's Admiral Seymour launched his expedition to relieve the legations on June 10th, thereby effectively invading China's sovereign territory and giving the Qing a perfectly legitimate *casus belli*. Seymour provided the immediate reason for the formal Boxer war, but the treaty system itself and the pressures exerted by Shanghai settlers and foreign diplomats alike had served to raise tensions. Regardless of the established practice of the Qing state and its predecessors of making foreigners administer themselves, it is impossible to argue that the establishment of foreign-controlled enclaves on Chinese soil was anything but derogatory to its sovereignty and increasingly to its dignity. The men and boys from Shandong who targeted the foreign legations certainly did not have the treaty establishment in mind, but the overall impact of such encroachments, and latterly the heightened activities of concession hunters and diplomats, was profoundly unsettling for the local and national Chinese elites who took the Boxers as allies.

The robustness of the identities of these British communities was underlined by the ways in which the Boxer events became integral parts of the communal myths they lived by until their demise after the Second World War. 1900 seemed to give the China-British an imperial legitimacy, and it was taken as their own equivalent of the 1857 Sepoy mutiny. One telling event took place on June 17th, 1931, when a memorial service was held at the Canton Road cemetery in Tianjin. Military officials, consular representatives, military detachments and a band gathered together with other foreign residents in the city for a ceremony: the playing of Chopin's *'Marche Funèbre'* was followed by the recital of a 'Memorial Prayer', the singing of Rudyard Kipling's poem 'Lest We Forget' and the decoration of gravestones with potted flowers by Boy Scouts and Girl Guides. What was not being forgotten was the siege of the Tianjin foreign concessions by Boxer forces and regular Chinese troops between June 17th and July 13th, 1900. This act of communal remembrance was in itself hardly striking or unusual, but noting it reminds us that British relations with China were more than abstract or confined merely to diplomatic exchanges.

In Beijing, British diplomats maintained one bullet-riddled wall in the legation, on which someone had daubed that ubiquitous injunction 'Lest We Forget' as a physical memorial of the siege. The motto was carefully tended and periodically repainted until, in the interests of diplomacy, it was removed in 1947. At least one public British memorial remains. Towards the Admiralty arch end of the Mall in London is a statue dedicated to Royal Marines Light Infantry casualties in South Africa and China. On the sides are bas-reliefs of fighting during the siege of Tianjin. Like many such British memorials it is submerged into the London background. We are perhaps more conscious of the empty plinth in Trafalgar Square than of the mute mementoes that surround us and remind us of the colonial centuries. In China the emphasis lies squarely with remembrance, in Britain with forgetting.

For Further Reading

Robert Bickers, *Britain in China: Community, Culture and Colonialism, 1900–49* (Manchester University Press, 1999); Sabine Dabringhaus, 'An Army on Vacation? The German War in China, 1900–1901', in Manfred F. Boemeke, Roger Chickering and Stig Förster (eds), *Anticipating Total War: The German and American Experiences, 1871–1914* (Cambridge University Press, 1999); Jürgen Osterhammel, 'Britain and China 1842–1914' in Andrew Porter (ed), *The Oxford History of the British Empire, Volume III: The Nineteenth Century* (Oxford University Press, 1999); Frances Wood, *No Dogs and Not Many Chinese: Treaty Port Life in China, 1843–1943* (John Murray, 1998); Peter Fleming, The Siege at Peking (Rupert Hart-Davis, 1959).

Robert Bickers is Lecturer in History at the University of Bristol.

New Light on the 'Heart of Darkness'

A century after the publication of Joseph Conrad's novel, Angus Mitchell reflects on the grim reality underlying the fiction, and the fight against slavery it inspired.

ANGUS MITCHELL

In the spring of 1899, when Heart of Darkness was serialized in Blackwood's Magazine, its author, Joseph Conrad, could scarcely have predicted that he had penned one of the most provocative and controversial literary works of the next century. For a hundred years now this short novel has been a window through which Europeans have glimpsed the scramble for Africa by their empire-forging ancestors. Behind Marlow's river journey in search of Kurtz lie the great conflicts that seethed beneath the jingoism of Empire. The struggles between civilisation and savagery, nature and progress, cannibalism against culture, Christianity versus magic: all these opposites and others battle in the dense undergrowth of the narrative. Heart of Darkness was the first novel to attack concepts of Western progress and question dubious social Darwinist attitudes that were used to justify many brutal facets of Empire-building.

The debate over Heart of Darkness has grumbled on unabated ever since—to a point where it is now something of a cliche to mention it at all. The theme has attracted and sometimes obsessed the creative mind. Orson Welles adapted the story for radio. Film director Francis Ford Coppola made Apocalypse Now (1974), reinterpreting the weird nightmare to fit the psychedelic madness of American folly in Vietnam. Radical critics of Empire like Edward Said and the African writer Chinua Achebe have praised and lambasted the book respectively. A metaphyiscal dimension to Heart of Darkness makes it a hard book to pin down. The literary debate and the 'Conrad controversy' will doubtless continue for another century. Africa still lives in the shadow of horror and the significance of Heart of Darkness has matured with the vintage of the years.

But what worth has Conrad's imagining of Heart of Darkness for the historian? Was there an historical Heart of Darkness? Can it now be identified in history? Certainly in recent years there has been an effort to try and configure the fiction with fact. A number of African adventurers have been singled out as possible prototypes for 'the universal genius' Kurtz, whose great skill in collecting ivory at an up-river station eventually sends him over the edge: he turns from being the 'civilizer' into the savage.

The story begins on the banks of the Thames—the Imperial artery of commerce and civilization—but the main arena for the tale is another river altogether—the Congo. The historical framework of the narrative is set within and specifically alludes to the horror that lay beneath the surface of the Belgian King Leopold II's Congo Free State. Leopold is never mentioned by name in the novel, but he lurks in the shadows nonetheless.

Heart of Darkness appeared at a moment when horror began to take on a new graphic dimension in the European imagination and ideas on slavery demanded redefinition. During the 1890s rumours started to circulate widely that aspects of imperial policy were going terribly wrong. Conrad's ostensibly imaginative work gave these reports intellectual force. Following its publication new attitudes towards Africa emerged among radical humanitarian thinkers. Some started to wonder just where the flag of Imperial progress was leading.

The opening up of the tropical heart of Africa had been a rapid process. In 1800 Africa's interior south of the Sahara was unmapped terra incognita. At the Berlin conference in 1884–5 the colonial powers carved up Africa amongst themselves. Much of the territory by then had been traversed. The names of the epic adventurers responsible for opening up the interior: Sir James Bruce, John Hanning Speke, Sir Richard Burton, David Livingstone and Sir Henry Morton Stanley echo through classrooms even today. Their travel writings helped appropriate African territories in the Victorian imagination. Adventure stories sold newspapers. Adventurers, whether soldier-explorers, naval officers, missionaries or entrepreneurs, were the empire's own superstars.

But during the 1890s it became increasingly clear that the altruistic spirit that justified expansion for the European empire-builders was faltering. Atrocity stories began to percolate back through the ports. It was a horror more often sensed than witnessed. Clearly some aspects of the white man's administration had gone badly amiss. Imperial expansion had become a cover for ventures that increasingly subverted local life. There was much questionable military behaviour, and occasional military blunders. Some missionaries appeared to be tacit accomplices to the skullduggery, and the evangelising methods of muscular Christianity were also questioned. The leash constraining greed and exploitation was severed. The equation of commerce and Christianity that had helped to abolish the slave trade had given way to a new horror: an unspeakable horror committed by Europeans in the name of civilisation.

In response, nineteenth century humanitarian endeavour was forced to reform. Traditions of thought condemning slavery and defending tribal lands and rights against foreign invasion—ideas rooted in the sermons of the church fathers Bartolome de las Casas and Antonio Vieira—found a new voice in Britain and elsewhere in Europe among emerging socialist and radical groups, Two societies had surfaced during the nineteenth century as self-appointed guardians of the rights of 'native people': The British and Foreign Anti-Slavery Society and The Aborigines' Protection Society. Both had to adapt to the new age of human rights abuse.

The Anti-Slavery Society was founded in the 1820s through the political drive of the 'Clapham Sect', Quaker beliefs and the work of a number of politicians including William Wilberforce and, later, Sir Thomas Fowell Buxton. Through a committee including a number of politicians, peers and bishops, it exerted enormous political pressure in both chambers at Westminster and in the corridors of the Foreign Office. In 1900 the future king, Edward VII, was the Society's patron. Its list of corresponding members included Joaquin Nabuco, the statesman and architect of abolition in Brazil.

Editions of its quarterly publication The Anti-Slavery Reporter at the turn of the century show that while its main centre of interest remained the 'native question' in Africa, its effectiveness was diminishing. There were sporadic and brief reports on slavery-related issues such as race relations in the United States, the system of Latin American slavery known as peonage, convict-leasing and Chinese labour. Coverage of countries such as Burma and Fiji showed that slavery was a global problem. Wherever slavery was discussed within the realms of the Empire, such as the desperate abuses against the aborigines of Western Australia, coverage was awkward. An obvious propagandist element clouded the views of the Anti-Slavery Society and is evident in stereotypical coverage of slave labour markets in Muslim lands such as Persia, Morocco, Zanzibar, Egypt or in Portuguese and German Africa.

The more effective outfit, after the abolition of the slave trade, was the Aborigines' Protection Society. Following the publication of a government Blue Book in 1837 drafted by William Gladstone, the A.P.S. was established in 1838 to stand up to 'the enormous wrongs inflicted on Aborigines by European colonization'. In its opening report it had targeted 'the restless spirit of adventure' and emigration arising from Europe's 'superabundant population' as two of the main reasons for escalating abuses. Again its committee attracted important politicians, churchmen and businessmen. By the late 1890s it had emerged as the most informed voice as a result of the active participation of members such as the radical Liberal politicians Sir Charles Dilke and James Bryce, the philosopher Herbert Spencer, and another rising Liberal, Augustine Birrell. Its asthmatic secretary, H.R. Fox Bourne, appointed in 1889, was prepared to stick his neck out on a number of issues; one of them was the Congo question.

In the aftermath of the Boer War attitudes to the Empire changed. A new humanitarian spirit was born, partly from popular objections to government policy in South Africa, including the use of concentration camps and the burning of Boer farms, partly through the inspiration of anti-imperialist campaigners like Emily Hobhouse. Humanitarian work was still seen as important to the advancement of political careers. Perhaps in an effort to divert attention away from the embarrassing excesses of British conduct in the Boer War, discussion catalysed around the Congo question. The search for a Heart of Darkness evident in fact inspired a series of Marlowesque river journeys by individuals intent on exposing the lie at the heart of the white man's civilisation. It also helped put the humanitarian movement on a new and more radical ideological footing.

In 1900 the African Society was founded in memory of the writer, ethnographer and traveller, Mary Kingsley, whose travels in West Africa in the 1890s had done much to increase public awareness of the rich cultural traditions of tribal life in the region. The new Society's honorary secretary, and the moving force behind its establishment, was the historian Alice Stopford Green, wife of J.R. Green, author of the popular History of the English People. The honorary treasurer was George Macmillan, proprietor of the publishing house. Among its committee members was the future Liberal prime minister, Herbert Asquith; Gladstone's disciple and biographer, John Morley; the anthropologist J.G. Frazer, author of The Golden Bough; and the governor of the Gold Coast, Matthew Nathan. The society's members were motivated above all to build up 'respect for native customs' and change public understanding on Africa and Africans.

In April 1903 a young, crusading journalist, E.D. Morel, began a weekly newspaper, The West African Mail. A founding principle of the paper was to supply 'reliable and impartial business intelligence' on West African issues and the inaugural issue ran a large picture of Winston Churchill—a recent convert to Liberalism from the Tories—accompanying a letter from him supporting Morel's venture. There were further good wishes from the two Liverpool shipping line owners Sir Alfred Jones and John Holt. Alice Stopford Green's name was also on the paper's masthead. But beside covering commercial news, Motel's deeper intention was to improve public awareness of atrocities in the Congo and expose the escalating stories of slavery emerging from the interior.

The Foreign Office decided to act when in March 1903 the House of Commons passed a resolution 'to abate the evils' in the Congo. They selected their most capable consul in Africa, Roger Casement, to carry out the investigation on their behalf. Casement had already spent almost twenty years in Africa, ten of them officially connected to the Foreign Office in a series of consular postings. But his consular position was a convenient cover for intelligence work. Early on in his consular career he had undertaken such work for both the War Office Intelligence Department and another department—whose activities have gone largely unrecorded—Commercial Intelligence, part of the Board of Trade. During the Boer War he had devised an unrealised 'special mission' to attack the Boer railway lines.

Casement's voyage into the interior in several ways mirrored Marlow's journey. The consul chartered a river boat and spent two months navigating and traversing territories he had travelled through in 1897, compiling evidence from victims and perpetrators of atrocities. On his return to London he met both Morel and Conrad. His report was published in February 1904 in an abridged and edited form and represented the official government line. The national press grabbed at the story. There was an outcry across Britain. Casement himself handed the first cheque for 100 [pounds sterling] to Morel to set up the Congo Reform Association that over the next decade became the most radical humanitarian force in the Empire. It questioned fundamental principles of Imperial policy and ultimately forced Leopold II to surrender his personal control in the Congo.

Prominent journalists and radical-liberal newspapers and journals began to condemn the horrors that were happening in the name of imperialism across the globe. German atrocities against the Herreros in South West Africa (now Namibia); Japanese actions in Formosa (Taiwan); the hemp-kings of Yucatan and the slavery that had maintained Porfirio Diaz's long presidency in Mexico; reports about the US treatment of rebels in the Philippines—all built up a picture of global atrocities committed by the so-called civilisers.

The British journalist H.W. Nevinson made an investigation of slavery in Portuguese West Africa (Angola) published as A Modern Slavery (1906). Expensive libel suits by companies defending commercial practices in imperial enclaves attracted leading lawyers such as Rufus Isaacs and Sir Edward Carson. Public indignation was further excited by the contribution of other important literary heavyweights. Mark Twain wrote King Leopold's Soliloquy. Arthur Conan Doyle penned The Crime of the Congo. Thousands attended Congo Reform rallies across the country.

The publication of Red Rubber by E.D. Morel in 1906 made it clear that the worst atrocities had been committed to meet the spiralling demand for rubber as the burgeoning automobile and bicycle industries moved into top gear. 1906 was the year when Henry Ford started production of his Model T—the first mass-produced motor car. Demand for rubber now began to far outstrip the supply. As a result of both its insulating qualities for electrical wiring and circuitry and its use in the motor car industry, rubber became the defining commodity in imperial policymaking. In those crucial years between 1892 and 1914 when rubber was still tapped from tropical forests, before cultivated plantation rubber became the main supply source, desperate crimes were committed. The story of wild rubber is one of horror on an apocalyptic scale. Manipulation of the rubber market ignited a series of genocidal episodes across the twentieth century. It changed the face of the tropical regions of the world forever. Although in Heart of Darkness Conrad's character Kurtz's reputation had been built on his great renown in collecting ivory, it was the collection of wild rubber that led to the greatest tribal and environmental cataclysm of modern times. There were countless Kurtz-like white men imposing rubber tapping on indigenous populations across tropical Africa and the Amazon.

In 1909, in an effort to strengthen the front against abuse in Africa, the Anti-Slavery Society amalgamated with the Aborigines' Protection Society to produce the Anti-Slavery and Aborigines Protection Society. A former Baptist missionary who had spent many years in Africa, the Rev. John Harris, was elected as acting secretary. Within months of the merger the restructured society was involved in a new slavery scandal, this time in the disputed frontier region of the north-west Amazon bordering Colombia, Brazil, Peru, and Ecuador. It was an episode that became known to history as 'the Putumayo Atrocities', and, once again it was Casement, by this time British Consul-General in Rio de Janeiro, who was recruited by the Liberal Foreign Secretary, Sir Edward Grey, to investigate the matter on an official level. Casement made two voyages to the Amazon in 1910 and 1911, again very much in the manner of Marlow; both journeys were cloaked in official secrecy. He uncovered a horror that paralleled and even exceeded the cruelty he had witnessed in the Congo. Again with press co-operation, the matter occupied newspaper columns around the world for many months.

The humanitarian work and achievement of both Morel and Casement was celebrated during 1911. By then both men were household names throughout the Empire. On May 29th, 1911, a public presentation was made to Morel in the Whitehall Rooms at the Hotel Metropole. Lord Cromer, the famous Imperial pro-consul in Egypt, presided. There were dozens of letters from those unable to attend and rousing speeches from those who were present. The Bishop of Winchester said:

> Every candid and well-informed man knows now, and public men of all parties agree, that there had grown up on the Congo, and in its administration, one of those moral monsters which deface history and laugh in the face of the conscience of mankind. It might easily have gone on unknown: and even if dimly known behind the veils of distance and darkness, it might easily, even when known, have gone unattacked, except by some futile words of protest. That it did not do so was due, and due entirely, to Mr Morel. I am not ashamed to believe and say that for a great moral emergency the providence of God gave us the man.

The luncheon brought together a dozen bishops and as many peers and captains of industry. Andrew Carnegie, W.H. Lever, William Cadbury and John Holt were four of the better known industrialists who lent their names to the occasion. It became the defining humanitarian meeting of the age.

A few weeks later Casement received news of his knighthood, and in early August he embarked on a further trip up the Amazon to try and arrest the perpetrators of atrocities. Of Casement's three Marlowesque river journeys this remains the shadiest voyage of all. As he went up river Casement witnessed the end of the Amazon rubber boom and the collapse of the veneer of civilization built on the back of the rubber economy. Yellow fever had started to attack the three main communities at Belem do Para, Manaos and Iquitos. Rubber prices had slumped. Those who could afford to were leaving. On his return down-river Casement went to Washington and spent a few days with the British Ambassador, James Bryce, and also had a private meeting with US President William Howard Taft.

The publication of Casement's Amazon reports in a Blue Book in July 1912 brought the discussion in the newspapers to a height. Prime Minister Herbert Asquith was obliged to establish a Parliamentary Select Committee Enquiry and many of the corrupt practices supporting imperial commerce were exposed.

Rome issued a papal encyclical. Two years later legislation was passed by the Commons making British company directors responsible for their company activities abroad.

On the outbreak of war in 1914 many of those who had been united by humanitarian endeavour since the start of the century were divided in views and loyalty. Within hours of the outbreak of hostilities, Morel founded the Union of Democratic Control (UDC) along with James Ramsay MacDonald, Norman Angell and Charles Trevelyan. It became the most effective voice of dissent criticising the British government's entry into the First World War and attacked the official version of how the war had come about, accusing the Liberal government of deliberately spreading falsehoods. The loudest objections were raised against the practice of secret diplomacy and the control of foreign policy by a narrow clique of political insiders. Among those attracted to this movement was Bertrand Russell, and it says something for its influence that nine of its members became ministers in the first Labour cabinet of 1924.

Casement's career took a more revolutionary path. After his resignation from the Foreign Office in August 1913 he set about recruiting Irish Volunteers in response to the arming of the Ulster Volunteers by the Unionist leaders, Sir Edward Carson and F.E. Smith. When he left Ireland in July 1914, a month before the outbreak of the First World War, he had an army of over 12,000 volunteers at his disposal. A few days after he reached America the first shipment of guns for those volunteers was landed at Howth by Erskine Childers. The plan for this gun-running exploit had been hatched in the house of Alice Stopford Green in Grosvenor Road in London. In America Casement raised further funds and planned open rebellion against the British Empire. In the autumn of 1914 he returned to Europe in an effort to get German support for the Irish independence movement. But the German high command prevaricated and a propaganda campaign began in the British press to blacken Casement's reputation in the public mind.

In April 1916, having failed to recruit Irish prisoners of war to join a pro-independence Irish Brigade, Casement returned to Ireland in a German U-boat, but British Naval Intelligence had intercepted a cypher detailing his plans for rebellion. His landing was expected and his capture at an Iron Age fort near Ardfert in County Kerry began the tragic chain of events of Easter week 1916. Many of those who had campaigned alongside Casement and Morel for Congo reform, such as Asquith, Sir Edward Grey, Winston Churchill, Herbert Samuel, and Sir Matthew Nathan, became the figures who now demanded Casement's execution for treason. Following a state trial Casement was the last of the sixteen Irish rebel leaders to be executed in the wake of the Rising.

In 1917 Morel was imprisoned under the Defence of the Realm Act for his continuing campaign against the war. Imprisonment seriously weakened his health and in November 1924 he died prematurely. The ethical policy that Casement and Morel had forced upon the Foreign Office and which galvanised radical liberal politics before 1914 has since then been conspicuously absent. In 1914 Britain and Belgium were allies in war and the whole matter of Congo reform hung in the air like an embarrassing smell. It was only during the 1980s that the Belgian state archive finally released important source material detailing the scale of the horror in the Congo. In Britain it was as recently as 1995 that the Open Government Initiative allowed proper independent historical examination of a number of aspects of the circumstances surrounding Casement's extraordinary career as an imperial intelligence operator-turned-humanitarian-turned-revolutionary.

At the end of Heart of Darkness, Marlow returns to Brussels in order to tell Kurtz's intended bride about his death. But instead of telling her the truth he lies and claims that it was her name that Kurtz had muttered with his dying breath. The humanitarian work that united many intellectual, political and religious figures before 1914 has remained a neglected region of history: a number of aspects of the story have been suppressed until today. Lies were told which survive as part of the historical record.

It is high time that this whole matter was better understood by historians. The ideals and action that gave rise to the anti-slavery movement and the efforts to protect indigenous peoples in the Congo, Amazon and elsewhere became the foundations upon which current humanitarian and human rights organisations, including Amnesty International and Survival International, were founded. Ideas of ethical foreign policy that are currently promoted as a motivating force behind New Labour's foreign policy can also be traced back to the radical discussions of this period.

The Congo reform movement and the Putumayo atrocities, that together provoked so much public anger between 1903 and 1914, were perceived as the last chapter in the long crusade against slavery, although that chapter is yet to be written up as history. Their significance has been deliberately obscured partly because of Morel's anti-war stance and his importance in the rise of the British Labour party, but more as a consequence of Casement's involvement with advanced revolutionary activities. What the story of this period reveals, however, is that Conrad's fictional narrative Heart of Darkness reflected both a truth and a horror at the core of Empire that some hoped would never be exposed by the facts.

For Further Reading

Joseph Conrad, Heart of Darkness, edited by D.D.R.A Goonetilleke (Broadway Literary Texts, 1995); Frederick Karl and Laurence Davies, The Collected Letters of Joseph Conrad (Cambridge University Press); Marvin Swartz, The Union of Democratic Control in British Politics During the First World War (Clarendon Press, Oxford 1971); Wm Roger Louis. 'The Triumph of the Congo Reform Movement 1905–1908' in Boston University Papers on Africa; Roger Anstey, 'The Congo Rubber Atrocities—A Case Study' in African Historical Studies—Vol, IV, 1 (1971).

ANGUS MITCHELL edited *The Amazon Journal* of Roger Casement (Anaconda Editions, 1998).

UNIT 2

The Ferment of the West, 1500–1900

Unit Selections

Key Points to Consider

- Does Mary Wollstonecraft deserve to be called "The First Feminist"? Make a case for both sides of the argument.

- Why did Benjamin Franklin display divided loyalties while living in London? Why did he eventually choose the colonial side?

- What were Denis Diderot's intellectual accomplishments during his lifetime? How did he continue to influence Europe after his death?

- How did Jean-Baptiste Colbert and Adam Smith both influence the history of economics? How were they different in their approaches to economic problems?

- What reforms did Catherine the Great initiate to help the Russian people? How successful was she in achieving these reforms?

- Why is money referred to as a "medium of exchange"? What else has served as mediums of exchange in our nation's history? Do you think someday we may be able to survive without money?

- In which ways did George Sand influence the lives of European women?

Student Web Site

www.mhcls.com/online

Internet References

Further information regarding these Web sites may be found in this book's preface or online.

The Adam Smith Institute
http://www.adamsmith.org
Britannica.com: Mercantilism
http://www.britannica.com/eb/article?eu=53378
Victorian Web
http://www.victorianweb.org/

The European voyages of exploration in the fifteenth and sixteenth centuries are representative of the spirit of adventure, curiosity, and greed that carried Western civilization to the ends of the earth. The unique character of Western civilization was shaped by many events, ideas, and people. Skillful manipulation of economic systems, the articulation of a secular worldview based in law, and the proclamation of democratic values had combined to create the West's legacy to the world.

Adam Smith, the first great economist, laid the foundations for the industrial revolution. He argued that if left alone (laissez-faire) the marketplace would be self-regulating. The invisible hand of market forces would regulate the economy. Manufacturers would produce all the goods that people wanted—and in the correct amounts. Without government interference, an oversupply would drop prices and provide a disincentive to suppliers. In times of scarcity, the reverse would occur, with demand driving prices up and inspiring suppliers to provide needed goods.

Smith's law of supply and demand has been modified by later conditions such as social welfare and the creation of large, multinational corporations, more powerful than governments. However, capitalism has not been overthrown by oppressed workers, as Karl Marx predicted. Instead, it has turned out to be a flexible economic system, more successful than either socialism or communism at present.

The free trade that Smith advocated has been modified as well. When Jean-Baptiste Colbert, finance minister for Louis XIV, used mercantilism to provide France a favorable balance of trade, other monarchs paid attention. Mercantilism called for the accumulation of bullion gold and silver as marks of a great nation. And, of course, mercantilism rested on the exploitation of colonies. When modern countries suppress free trade or try to protect their industries with tariffs, there are predictable protests at meetings of the World Trade Organization. Today, gold is no longer used as a form of money and most of us receive our paychecks and pay our bills electronically, using electric current as our modern form of currency.

Another major shaper of the Western worldview was the movement toward secularism. When Denis Diderot of France set out to catalog the knowledge of the Western World as it existed in the 18th century, he had a hidden agenda. His goal was to replace a hierarchical, religious, monarchical world with a secular and more democratic one. Nature would replace an anthropomorphic deity as source of all that is; and, Man, through the use of his reason, would reign supreme within nature.

Catherine the Great of Russia, although a believer in absolute rule, also advocated "law-based" monarchy. A contemporary of Diderot's, she was one of a group of leaders who came to be known as enlightened despots. Paradoxically, perhaps, she intentionally had no children, ensuring that her successors would be through the male line. Apparently, she considered herself unique.

One of the great ideological and political struggles at the end of the eighteenth century occurred in a peripheral frontier nation that would later become the United States. Victory over Britain unleashed a vigorous, capitalistic, argumentative people, determined to make democracy work. Benjamin Franklin, chief American representative at the Treaty of Paris negotiations that ended the War of American Independence, had hoped to avoid a break with Great Britain. Equally at home in London and Philadelphia, Franklin eventually came to see that America must shake off her shackles in order to fulfill her destiny as a great nation.

Mary Wollstonecraft championed another standard of freedom in the same period with her able defense of equality for women. Arguing that women were treated as children and denied even a basic education, she advocated a rational shaping of both male and female minds. Her most potent argument was a practical one—society would benefit by having enlightened wives and mothers. Although most women of her century led secluded lives, Wollstonecraft made a career of writing and led an emancipated life. She was the first feminist, and the struggle for equality that she initiated is ongoing, around the world and even in the West.

The First Feminist

In 1792 Mary Wollstonecraft wrote a book to prove that her sex was as intelligent as the other: thus did feminism come into the world. Right on, Ms. Mary!

SHIRLEY TOMKIEVICZ

The first person—male or female—to speak at any length and to any effect about woman's rights was Mary Wollstonecraft. In 1792, when her *Vindication of the Rights of Woman* appeared, Mary was a beautiful spinster of thirty-three who had made a successful career for herself in the publishing world of London. This accomplishment was rare enough for a woman in that day. Her manifesto, at once impassioned and learned, was an achievement of real originality. The book electrified the reading public and made Mary famous. The core of its argument is simple: "I wish to see women neither heroines nor brutes; but reasonable creatures," Mary wrote. This ancestress of the Women's Liberation Movement did not demand day-care centers or an end to women's traditional role as wife and mother, nor did she call anyone a chauvinist pig. The happiest period of Mary's own life was when she was married and awaiting the birth of her second child. And the greatest delight she ever knew was in her first child, an illegitimate daughter. Mary's feminism may not appear today to be the hard-core revolutionary variety, but she did live, for a time, a scandalous and unconventional life—"emancipated," it is called by those who have never tried it. The essence of her thought, however, is simply that a woman's mind is as good as a man's.

Not many intelligent men could be found to dispute this proposition today, at least not in mixed company. In Mary's time, to speak of *anybody's* rights, let alone woman's rights, was a radical act. In England, as in other nations, "rights" were an entity belonging to the government. The common run of mankind had little access to what we now call "human rights." As an example of British justice in the late eighteenth century, the law cited two hundred different capital crimes, among them shoplifting. An accused man was not entitled to counsel. A child could be tried and hanged as soon as an adult. The right to vote existed, certainly, but because of unjust apportionment, it had come to mean little. In the United States some of these abuses had been corrected—but that the rights of man did not extend past the color bar and the masculine gender was intentional. In the land of Washington and Jefferson, as in the land of George III, human rights were a new idea and woman's rights were not even an issue.

In France, in 1792, a Revolution in the name of equality was in full course, and woman's rights had at least been alluded to. The Revolutionary government drew up plans for female education—to the age of eight. "The education of the women should always be relative to the men," Rousseau had written in *Emile*. "To please, to be useful to us, to make us love and esteem them, to educate us when young, and take care of us when grown up, to advise, to console us, to render our lives easy and agreeable; these are the duties of women at all times, and what they should be taught in their infancy." And, less prettily, "Women have, or ought to have, but little liberty."

Rousseau would have found little cause for complaint in eighteenth-century England. An Englishwoman had almost the same civil status as an American slave. Thomas Hardy, a hundred years hence, was to base a novel on the idea of a man casually selling his wife and daughter at public auction. Obviously this was not a common occurrence, but neither is it wholly implausible. In 1792, and later, a woman could not own property, nor keep any earned wages. All that she possessed belonged to her husband. She could not divorce him, but he could divorce her and take her children. There was no law to say she could not grow up illiterate or be beaten every day.

Such was the legal and moral climate in which Mary Wollstonecraft lived. She was born in London in the spring of 1759, the second child and first daughter of Edward Wollstonecraft, a prosperous weaver. Two more daughters and two more sons were eventually born into the family, making six children in all. Before they had all arrived, Mr. Wollstonecraft came into an inheritance and decided to move his family to the country and become a gentleman farmer. But this plan failed. His money dwindled, and he began drinking heavily. His wife turned into a terrified wraith whose only interest was her eldest son, Edward. Only he escaped the beatings and abuse that his father dealt out regularly to every other household member, from Mrs. Wollstonecraft to the family dog. As often happens in large and disordered families, the eldest sister had to assume the role of mother and scullery maid. Mary was a bright, strong child, determined not to be broken, and she undertook her task energetically, defying her father when he was violent and keeping her younger brothers and sisters in hand. Clearly, Mary held the household together, and in so doing forfeited her own childhood. This experience left her with an everlasting gloomy streak, and was a strong factor in making her a reformer.

At some point in Mary's childhood, another injustice was visited upon her, though so commonplace for the time that she can hardly have felt the sting. Her elder brother was sent away to be educated, and the younger children were left to learn their letters as best they could. The family now frequently changed lodgings, but from her ninth to her fifteenth year Mary went to a day school, where she had the only formal training of her life. Fortunately, this included French and composition, and somewhere Mary learned to read critically and widely. These skills, together with her curiosity and determination, were really all she needed. The *Vindication* is in some parts long-winded, ill-punctuated, and simply full of hot air, but it is the work of a well-informed mind.

Feminists—and Mary would gladly have claimed the title—inevitably, even deservedly, get bad notices. The term calls up an image of relentless battleaxes: "thin college ladies with eyeglasses, no-nonsense features, mouths thin as bologna slicers, a babe in one arm, a hatchet in the other, grey eyes bright with balefire," as Norman Mailer feelingly envisions his antagonists in the Women's Liberation Movement. He has conjured up all the horrid elements: the lips with a cutting edge, the baby immaculately conceived (one is forced to conclude), the lethal weapon tightly clutched, the desiccating college degree, the joylessness. Hanging miasmally over the tableau is the suspicion of a deformed sexuality. Are these girls man-haters, or worse? Mary Wollstonecraft, as the first of her line, has had each of these scarlet letters (except the B.A.) stitched upon her bosom. Yet she conformed very little to the hateful stereotype. In at least one respect, however, she would have chilled Mailer's bones. Having spent her childhood as an adult, Mary reached the age of nineteen in a state of complete joylessness. She was later to quit the role, but for now she wore the garb of a martyr.

Her early twenties were spent in this elderly frame of mind. First she went out as companion to an old lady living at Bath, and was released from this servitude only by a call to nurse the dying Mrs. Wollstonecraft. Then the family broke up entirely, though the younger sisters continued off and on to be dependent on Mary. The family of Mary's dearest friend, Fanny Blood, invited her to come and stay with them; the two girls made a small living doing sewing and handicrafts, and Mary dreamed of starting a primary school. Eventually, in a pleasant village called Newington Green, this plan materialized and prospered. But Fanny Blood in the meantime had married and moved to Lisbon. She wanted Mary to come and nurse her through the birth of her first child. Mary reached Lisbon just in time to see her friend die of childbed fever, and returned home just in time to find that her sisters, in whose care the flourishing little school had been left, had lost all but two pupils.

Mary made up her mind to die. "My constitution is impaired, I hope I shan't live long," she wrote to a friend in February, 1786. Under this almost habitual grief, however, Mary was gaining some new sense of herself. Newington Green, apart from offering her a brief success as a schoolmistress, had brought her some acquaintance in the world of letters, most important among them, Joseph Johnson, an intelligent and successful London publisher in search of new writers. Debt-ridden and penniless, Mary set aside her impaired constitution and wrote her first book, probably in the space of a week. Johnson bought it for ten guineas and published it. Called *Thoughts on the Education of Daughters*, it went unnoticed, and the ten guineas was soon spent. Mary had to find work. She accepted a position as governess in the house of Lord and Lady Kingsborough in the north of Ireland.

Mary's letters from Ireland to her sisters and to Joseph Johnson are so filled with Gothic gloom, so stained with tears, that one cannot keep from laughing at them. "I entered the great gates with the same kind of feeling I should have if I was going to the Bastille," she wrote upon entering Kingsborough Castle in the fall of 1786. Mary was now twenty-seven. Her most recent biographer, Margaret George, believes that Mary was not really suffering so much as she was having literary fantasies. In private she was furiously at work on a novel entitled, not very artfully, *Mary, A Fiction*. This is the story of a young lady of immense sensibilities who closely resembles Mary except that she has wealthy parents, a neglectful bridegroom, and an attractive lover. The title and fantasizing contents are precisely what a scribbler of thirteen might secretly concoct. Somehow Mary was embarking on her adolescence—with all its daydreams—fifteen years after the usual date. Mary's experience in Kingsborough Castle was a fruitful one, for all her complaints. In the summer of 1787 she lost her post as governess and set off for London with her novel. Not only did Johnson accept it for publication, he offered her a regular job as editor and translator and helped her find a place to live.

Thus, aged twenty-eight, Mary put aside her doleful persona as the martyred, set-upon elder sister. How different she is now, jauntily writing from London to her sisters: "Mr. Johnson . . . assures me that if I exert my talents in writing I may support myself in a comfortable way. I am then going to be the first of a new genus. . . ." Now Mary discovered the sweetness of financial independence earned by interesting work. She had her own apartment. She was often invited to Mr. Johnson's dinner parties, usually as the only female guest among all the most interesting men in London: Joseph Priestley, Thomas Paine, Henry Fuseli, William Blake, Thomas Christie, William Godwin—all of them up-and-coming scientists or poets or painters or philosophers, bound together by left-wing political views. Moreover, Mary was successful in her own writing as well as in editorial work. Her *Original Stories for Children* went into three editions and was illustrated by Blake. Johnson and his friend Thomas Christie had started a magazine called the *Analytical Review*, to which Mary became a regular contributor.

But—lest anyone imagine an elegantly dressed Mary presiding flirtatiously at Johnson's dinner table—her social accomplishments were rather behind her professional ones. Johnson's circle looked upon her as one of the boys. "Wollstonecraft" is what William Godwin calls her in his diary. One of her later detractors reported that she was at this time a "philosophic sloven," in a dreadful old dress and beaver hat, "with her hair hanging lank about her shoulders." Mary had yet to arrive at her final incarnation, but the new identity was imminent, if achieved by an odd route. Edmund Burke had recently published his *Reflections on the Revolution in France,* and the book had enraged Mary. The statesman who so readily supported the quest for liberty in the American colonies had his doubts about events in France.

Mary's reply to Burke, *A Vindication of the Rights of Men,* astounded London, partly because she was hitherto unknown, partly because it was good. Mary proved to be an excellent polemicist, and she had written in anger. She accused Burke, the erstwhile champion of liberty, of being "the champion of property." "Man preys on man," said she, "and you mourn for the idle tapestry that decorated a gothic pile and the dronish bell that summoned the fat priest to prayer." The book sold well. Mary moved into a better apartment and bought some pretty dresses—no farthingales, of course, but some of the revolutionary new "classical" gowns. She put her auburn hair up in a loose knot. Her days as a philosophic sloven were over.

Vindication of the Rights of Woman was her next work. In its current edition it runs to 250-odd pages; Mary wrote it in six weeks. *Vindication* is no prose masterpiece, but it has never failed to arouse its audience, in one way or another. Horace Walpole unintentionally set the style for the book's foes. Writing to his friend Hannah More in August, 1792, he referred to Thomas Paine and to Mary as "philosophizing serpents" and was "glad to hear you have not read the tract of the last mentioned writer. I would not look at it." Neither would many another of Mary's assailants, the most virulent of whom, Ferdinand Lundberg, surfaced at the late date of 1947 with a tract of his own, *Modern Woman, the Lost Sex.* Savagely misogynistic as it is, this book was hailed in its time as "the best book yet to be written about women." Lundberg calls Mary the Karl Marx of the feminist movement, and the *Vindication* a "fateful book," to which "the tenets of feminism, which have undergone no change to our day, may be traced." Very well, but then, recounting Mary's life with the maximum possible number of errors per line, he warns us that she was "an extreme neurotic of a compulsive type" who "wanted to turn on men and injure them." In one respect, at least, Mr. Lundberg hits the mark: he blames Mary for starting women in the pernicious habit of wanting an education. In the nineteenth century, he relates, English and American feminists were hard at work. "Following Mary Wollstonecraft's prescription, they made a considerable point about acquiring a higher education." This is precisely Mary's prescription, and the most dangerous idea in her fateful book.

"Men complain and with reason, of the follies and caprices of our Sex," she writes in Chapter 1. "Behold, I should answer, the natural effect of ignorance." Women, she thinks, are usually so mindless as to be scarcely fit for their roles as wives and mothers. Nevertheless, she believes this state not to be part of the feminine nature, but the result of an equally mindless oppression, as demoralizing for men as for women. If a woman's basic mission is as a wife and mother, need she be an illiterate slave for this?

The heart of the work is Mary's attack on Rousseau. In *Emile* Rousseau had set forth some refreshing new ideas for the education of little boys. But women, he decreed, are tools for pleasure, creatures too base for moral or political or educational privilege. Mary recognized that this view was destined to shut half the human race out of all hope for political freedom. *Vindication* is a plea that the "rights of men" ought to mean the "rights of humanity." The human right that she held highest was the right to have a mind and think with it. Virginia Woolf, who lived through a time of feminist activity, thought that the *Vindication* was a work so true "as to seem to contain nothing new." Its originality, she wrote, rather too optimistically, had become a commonplace.

Vindication went quickly into a second edition. Mary's name was soon known all over Europe. But as she savored her fame—and she did savor it—she found that the edge was wearing off and that she was rather lonely. So far as anyone knows, Mary had reached this point in her life without ever having had a love affair. Johnson was the only man she was close to, and he was, as she wrote him, "A father, or a brother—you have been both to me." Mary was often now in the company of the Swiss painter Henry Fuseli, and suddenly she developed what she thought was a Platonic passion in his direction. He rebuffed her, and in the winter of 1792 she went to Paris, partly to escape her embarrassment but also because she wanted to observe the workings of the Revolution firsthand.

Soon after her arrival, as she collected notes for the history of the Revolution she hoped to write, Mary saw Louis XVI, "sitting in a hackney coach . . . going to meet death." Back in her room that evening, she wrote to Mr. Johnson of seeing "eyes glare through a glass door opposite my chair and bloody hands shook at me. . . . I am going to bed and for the first time in my life, I cannot put out the candle." As the weeks went on, Edmund Burke's implacable critic began to lose her faith in the brave new world. "The aristocracy of birth is levelled to the ground, only to make room for that of riches," she wrote. By February France and England were at war, and British subjects classified as enemy aliens.

Though many Englishmen were arrested, Mary and a large English colony stayed on. One day in spring, some friends presented her to an attractive American, newly arrived in Paris, Gilbert Imlay. Probably about four years Mary's senior, Imlay, a former officer in the Continental Army, was an explorer and adventurer. He came to France seeking to finance a scheme for seizing Spanish lands in the Mississippi valley. This "natural and unaffected creature," as Mary was later to describe him, was probably the social lion of the moment, for he was also the author of a best-selling novel called *The Emigrants,* a farfetched account of life and love in the American wilderness. He and Mary soon became lovers. They were a seemingly perfect pair. Imlay must have been pleased with his famous catch, and—dear, liberated girl that she was—Mary did not insist upon marriage. Rather the contrary. But fearing that she was in danger as an Englishwoman, he registered her at the American embassy as his wife.

Blood was literally running in the Paris streets now, so Mary settled down by herself in a cottage at Neuilly. Imlay spent his days in town, working out various plans. The Mississippi expedition came to nothing, and he decided to stay in France and go into the import-export business, part of his imports being gunpowder and other war goods run from Scandinavia through the English blockade. In the evenings he would ride out to the cottage. By now it was summer, and Mary, who spent the days writing, would often stroll up the road to meet him, carrying a basket of freshly gathered grapes.

A note she wrote Imlay that summer shows exactly what her feelings for him were: "You can scarcely imagine with what pleasure I anticipate the day when we are to begin almost to live together; and you would smile to hear how many plans of employment I have in my head, now that I am confident that my heart has found peace. . . ." Soon she was pregnant. She and Imlay moved into Paris. He promised to take her to America, where they would settle down on a farm and raise six children. But business called Imlay to Le Havre, and his stay lengthened ominously into weeks.

Imlay's letters to Mary have not survived, and without them it is hard to gauge what sort of man he was and what he really thought of his adoring mistress. Her biographers like to make him out a cad, a philistine, not half good enough for Mary. Perhaps; yet the two must have had something in common. His novel, unreadable though it is now, shows that he shared her political views, including her feminist ones. He may never have been serious about the farm in America, but he was a miserably long time deciding to leave Mary alone. Though they were separated during the early months of her pregnancy, he finally did bring her to Le Havre, and continued to live with her there until the child was born and for some six months afterward. The baby arrived in May, 1794, a healthy little girl, whom Mary named Fanny after her old friend. Mary was proud that her delivery had been easy and as for Fanny, Mary loved her instantly. "My little Girl," she wrote to a friend, "begins to suck so manfully that her father reckons saucily on her writing the second part of the Rights of Woman." Mary's joy in this child illuminates almost every letter she wrote henceforth.

Fanny's father was the chief recipient of these letters with all the details of the baby's life. To Mary's despair, she and Imlay hardly ever lived together again. A year went by; Imlay was now in London and Mary in France. She offered to break it off, but mysteriously, he could not let go. In the last bitter phase of their involvement, after she had joined him in London at his behest, he even sent her—as "Mrs. Imlay"—on a complicated business errand to the Scandinavian countries. Returning to London, Mary discovered that he was living with another woman. By now half crazy with humiliation, Mary chose a dark night and threw herself in the Thames. She was nearly dead when two rivermen pulled her from the water.

Though this desperate incident was almost the end of Mary, at least it was the end of the Imlay episode. He sent a doctor to care for her, but they rarely met again. Since Mary had no money, she set about providing for herself and Fanny in the way she knew. The faithful Johnson had already brought out Volume I of her history of the French Revolution. Now she set to work editing and revising her *Letters Written during a Short Residence in Sweden, Norway, and Denmark,* a kind of thoughtful travelogue. The book was well received and widely translated.

And it also revived the memory of Mary Wollstonecraft in the mind of an old acquaintance, William Godwin. As the author of the treatise *Political Justice,* he was now as famous a philosophizing serpent as Mary and was widely admired and hated as a "freethinker." He came to call on Mary. They became friends and then lovers. Early in 1797 Mary was again pregnant. William Godwin was an avowed atheist who had publicly denounced the very institution of marriage. On March 29, 1797, he nevertheless went peaceably to church with Mary and made her his wife.

The Godwins were happy together, however William's theories may have been outraged. He adored his small stepdaughter and took pride in his brilliant wife. Awaiting the birth of her child throughout the summer, Mary worked on a new novel and made plans for a book on "the management of infants"—it would have been the first "Dr. Spock." She expected to have another easy delivery and promised to come downstairs to dinner the day following. But when labor began, on August 30, it proved to be long and agonizing. A daughter, named Mary Wollstonecraft, was born; ten days later, the mother died.

Occasionally, when a gifted writer dies young, one can feel, as in the example of Shelley, that perhaps he had at any rate accomplished his best work. But so recently had Mary come into her full intellectual and emotional growth that her death at the age of thirty-eight is bleak indeed. There is no knowing what Mary might have accomplished now that she enjoyed domestic stability. Perhaps she might have achieved little or nothing further as a writer. But she might have been able to protect her daughters from some part of the sadness that overtook them; for as things turned out, both Fanny and Mary were to sacrifice themselves.

Fanny grew up to be a shy young girl, required to feel grateful for the roof over her head, overshadowed by her prettier half sister, Mary. Godwin in due course married a formidable widow named Mrs. Clairmont, who brought her own daughter into the house—the Claire Clairmont who grew up to become Byron's mistress and the mother of his daughter Allegra. Over the years Godwin turned into a hypocrite and a miser who nevertheless continued to pose as the great liberal of the day. Percy Bysshe Shelley, born the same year that the *Vindication of the Rights of Woman* was published, came to be a devoted admirer of Mary Wollstonecraft's writing. As a young man he therefore came with his wife to call upon Godwin. What he really sought, however, were Mary's daughters—because they were her daughters. First he approached Fanny, but later changed his mind. Mary Godwin was then sixteen, the perfect potential soul mate for a man whose needs for soul mates knew no bounds. They conducted their courtship in the most up-to-the-minute romantic style: beneath a tree near her mother's grave they read aloud to each other from the Vindication. Soon they eloped, having pledged their "troth" in the cemetery. Godwin, the celebrated freethinker, was enraged. To make matters worse, Claire Clairmont had run off to Switzerland with them.

Not long afterward Fanny, too, ran away. She went to an inn in a distant town and drank a fatal dose of laudanum. It has traditionally been said that unrequited love for Shelley drove her to this pass, but there is no evidence one way or the other. One suicide that can more justly be laid at Shelley's door is that of his first wife, which occurred a month after Fanny's and which at any rate left him free to wed his mistress, Mary Godwin. Wife or mistress, she had to endure poverty, ostracism, and Percy's constant infidelities. But now at last her father could, and did, boast to his relations that he was father-in-law to a baronet's son. "Oh, philosophy!" as Mary Godwin Shelley remarked.

If in practice Shelley was merely a womanizer, on paper he was a convinced feminist. He had learned this creed from Mary Wollstonecraft. Through his verse Mary's ideas began to be disseminated. They were one part of that vast tidal wave of political, social, and artistic revolution that arose in the late eighteenth century, the romantic movement. But because of Mary's unconventional way of life, her name fell into disrepute during the nineteenth century, and her book failed to exert its rightful influence on the development of feminism. Emma Willard and other pioneers of the early Victorian period indignantly refused to claim Mary as their forebear. Elizabeth Cady Stanton and Lucretia Mott were mercifully less strait-laced on the subject. In 1889, when Mrs. Stanton and Susan B. Anthony published their *History of Woman Suffrage,* they dedicated the book to Mary. Though Mary Wollstonecraft can in no sense be said to have founded the woman's rights movement, she was, by the late nineteenth century, recognized as its inspiration, and the *Vindication* was vindicated for the highly original work it was, a landmark in the history of society.

Benjamin Franklin: An American in London

Esmond Wright recalls the life of the American philosopher, scientist and man of letters in his years in a street near Charing Cross.

Benjamin Franklin, a poorly-educated Boston boy who ran away from home to find his fortune in Philadelphia as journalist, editor, printer and publisher, founder of its University and of the American Philosophical Society, was the nearest to a genius of all the Founding Fathers of the United States. He was a practical man as well as a theorist. He was fascinated by natural phenomena, and constantly asked the question 'Why?'. When a steady succession of appalling winters and dry summers hit Europe in the 1780s, he traced the cause to a volcanic eruption in Iceland. These climatic conditions produced famines across Western Europe and were among the causes of the French Revolution. From his frequent journeys across the Atlantic, Franklin discovered and mapped the Gulf Stream. From his observations of climate he concluded that lightning was electricity. He devised and played the harmonica, his 'musical glasses'. He realised—though he never fully explored the reasons for—the contagious character of the common cold. He was, in the Italian phrase, *l'uomo universale,* a renaissance man, or, as the Scots put it, 'a man o' pairts'.

For seventeen years (1757–75) he lived in London, in 'four rooms and very genteel', as he put it. In these years, though he was proud to be an American, he was, also, in his own phrase, 'an Old England man' and proud of that too. He sought to avert the political separation that he saw coming. When it came to war, he went to Paris to secure the support of France that ensured American success. He was present in 1787 in Philadelphia at the Convention that drew up the Constitution.

When Mary Munn of Philadelphia married the 10th Earl of Bessborough in 1948, perhaps she did not realise that in London she would renew acquaintance with the most famous Philadelphian of all, Benjamin Franklin. Or maybe she did: The 2nd Earl of Bessborough in the eighteenth century as Postmaster General had been in charge of Franklin's activities as a colonial post officer-in-chief. For the last thirty years Lady Bessborough and a group of trustees have campaigned to raise money in the US and in the UK to restore the house in which Franklin lived during his London years as the agent for Pennsylvania (and eventually for Massachusetts, New Jersey and Georgia) from 1757 to his return home on the outbreak of the War for American Independence in 1775.

He made 36, Craven Street in the Strand a home from home. Franklin was as much at ease in London as he was in Philadelphia in the hurly-burly of business. Goods were landed from the river at the foot of the street and transported to the Hungerford Market at the top, where it meets the Strand. As the wits put it, there was craft on the river, and craft on the street; and Franklin, a strong swimmer, was at ease with both, the lawyers and journalists at one end, the tradesmen—and the tides—at the other. Opposite 36, Craven Street then stood the large and daunting Northumberland House, the town-house of the Dukes of Northumberland, and a thriving social centre—on the site of what is now Charing Cross Station.

His domestic circle included not only his landlady, Mrs Stevenson, and Polly, her daughter, but Franklin's grandson, Temple, and Sarah Franklin, daughter of one of his Northamptonshire cousins. The latter lived in Craven Street, and was as a second daughter to him.

The *Craven Street Gazette,* a newspaper which he produced for fun, testifies to his contentment. It is clear that he ruled over his 'Court'—at least in 'Queen Margaret's' infrequent absences—as 'Big Man', 'Great Person' and 'Dr Fatsides'. He hoped that Polly might marry his son, but they both had other ideas. Polly married a surgeon, William Hewson, but became in fact the 'intellectual daughter' that his own daughter Sarah (back in Philadelphia) never was. William had jettisoned his fiancée in Philadelphia, became a devotee of the Northumberland House connection—he visited it more often than the Inns of Court, where he was nominally a student—and in 1762 was appointed royal Governor of New Jersey; and stayed a Loyalist to the end. Polly would be persuaded to spend a winter with Benjamin in France when he was there, and finally moved to Philadelphia with her own family—her husband having died in 1774—and was with him there when he died in 1790.

Franklin was a man who attracted friends very easily, wherever he happened to be. He was so happy on the British 'side of the Water' that he had decided in 1762

> to settle all my Affairs [in America] in such a Manner, as that I may then conveniently remove to England, provided we can persuade the good Woman [his wife Deborah] to cross the Seas.

Speaking of London, Franklin said there were opportunities of displaying one's talents among the 'Virtuosi of various kingdoms and nations'. The conversation, he said, was not only agreeable but 'improving'. As he told his son William in 1772, he found in Britain,

> a general respect paid me by the learned, a number of friends and acquaintances among them with whom I have a pleasing intercourse; a character of so much weight that it has protected me when some in power would have done me injury . . . my company so much desired that I seldom dine at home in winter, and could spend the whole summer in the country houses of inviting friends if I chose it. Learned and ingenious foreigners, that come to England, almost all make a point of visiting me, for my reputation is still higher abroad than here; several of the foreign ambassadors have assiduously cultivated my acquaintance, treating me as one of their corps, partly I believe . . . that they may have an opportunity of introducing me to the gentlemen of their country who desire it.

Figure 1 'The Charing Cross Evening Frolick' by L.P. Boitard, 1756, shows a party of drunken revellers passing a coffee stand by the statue of Charles I, late one night.

Note: HT Archives

This happiness was reinforced by another factor, the political respect in which (we now forget) not only the government of Britain, but the monarchy itself, was held in what became the United States. Franklin came in 1757 to persuade the British government to abrogate the proprietary charter of Pennsylvania. He wanted royal government, not the domination of the Penns. The Penn family had ceased to live in Philadelphia, and had become Anglicans. He saw opportunities for America in royal government rather than in government by a proprietor, or by anything more democratic. He hoped that the loyalty that he felt for Britain could be translated into a general loyalty, in the concept of a royal colony.

The almost universal 'respect for the mother country, and admiration of everything that is British' on the part of the colonists, Franklin wrote in *The London Chronicle* in 1759, was 'a natural effect' not only of their constant intercourse with England, by ships arriving almost every week from the capital' but also, and more importantly, of an ingrained loyalty to a country that, for all free whites, permitted far more liberty than was enjoyed by the colonists of any European power. 'Delegates of British power' in the colonies might indeed lose the respect of and 'give Jealousy to' the colonists, either by their corrupt behaviour, or 'by continually abusing and calumniating the People'. But such actions did not diminish colonial faith in imperial institutions. 'Confidence in the Crown' remained 'as great as ever', and Parliament was held in the highest esteem as the ultimate protector of British liberty—in the colonies as well as in Britain.

This was linked to Franklin's awareness of the importance of the West. He told Lord Kames, one of his closest friends, with whom he stayed in Scotland, that the expulsion of the French from Canada in 1763 would mean that,

all the Country, from the St Lawrence to the Mississippi will in another Century be fill'd with British People; Britain itself will become vastly

more populous by the immense Increase of its Commerce; the Atlantic Sea will be cover'd with your Trading Ships; and your naval Power

Figure 2 Savaged by a dead sheep? A trade card for Robert Crow's warehouse for men's clothes, near Hungerford Market and a stone's-throw from Craven street.

Note: HT Archives

then continually increasing, will extend your Influence round the whole Globe, and awe the World.

There is no republican here, nor an American either. This is British imperialism as Joseph Chamberlain would have understood it, or American imperialism as Teddy Roosevelt would have understood it: a sense that the future rested with the empire 'on that side'. Franklin was ridiculed by Josiah Tucker in one of his pamphlets, who said that Franklin's constant plan had actually been to remove the seat of government of the British Empire to America. Although he never quite said that, Franklin did have his plan for a colony in the West. Called variously the Ohio Scheme or Vandalia, Franklin's expectation was that there would be a post or posts for him or his friends, the Washington family, and the Morgans of Philadelphia. This grand Ohio plan failed, primarily because of the opposition of Lord Hillsborough, afraid of the emigration of his Irish tenants to the New World. In 1768 Hillsborough became Secretary of State for American Affairs, a newly created department. There were other reasons for hesitation about a western colony; a British colony without seaports would mean a colony beyond naval control; its products would be sold primarily inside North America, and it would not therefore fit into the colonial system. So there were many reasons why, seen from a rather narrow-focused London point of view, this was a dangerous step; but Franklin saw his British Empire as much on the Ohio as on the Thames: it was a great misfortune for him that nothing came of Vandalia.

Tucker ridiculed Franklin, claiming his intention was to remove the seat of government of the British empire to America.

There was, of course, another good reason why Franklin was an 'Old England man', devoted to the throne. His son William was not only a royal governor throughout these years, but a very good one, as his father heard John Pownall, the permanent secretary of the new American Department, testify to Lord Hillsborough. Sadly, from an American point of view, William stayed a Loyalist when war broke out in 1776, and was imprisoned; his wife was not allowed to see him again, and she died without doing so. William's Loyalism destroyed the relationship between father and son. There was never any forgiveness. Benjamin Franklin, full of blarney and craft, was ruthless about Loyalists, even his own son.

In 1768 a new department was set up. There is no direct evidence, but my own reading suggests that Benjamin Franklin hoped he would become a permanent secretary at that new American desk, the department for North American Affairs (the post that went to John Pownall). Of course it would fold up again in 1782 after the war was over, but it was a post that might have made a profound difference. It might even have averted the War for American Independence.

As late as 1769 Franklin still believed that,

> nothing that has happened or may happen will diminish in the least our Loyalty to our Sovereign, or Affection for this Nation in general. I can scarcely conceive a King of better Dispositions, or more exemplary Virtues, or more truly desirous of promoting the Welfare of all his Subjects. The experience we have had of . . . the two preceding mild Reigns, and the good Temper of our young Princes so far as can yet be discovered, promise us a Continuance of this Felicity. The Body of this People too is of a noble and generous Nature, loving and honoring the Spirit of Liberty, and hating arbitrary Power of all Sorts.

'While I have been thought here too much of an American, I have in America been deemed too much of an Englishman.'

To this one has to add—and here the pattern begins to change and is less orthodox—Franklin's pride in being a member of an empire was rooted in his faith in American population growth, whatever his

Figure 3 The 'Colonies Reduced', a card designed by Franklin in late 1765, with which he lobbied London's 'Men of Power' about the injustice of the Stamp Act.

Note: HT Archives

criticisms of some British political and mercantile policies. His great optimism about the connection between England and America stemmed from the knowledge that the rate of population increase was so much greater in the New World than in the Old. He had written in 1751 his famous *Observations concerning the Increase of Mankind,* in which he calculated that in due course the daughter colony would become very much more populous, successful and prosperous than the mother country.

Franklin lived a long life. He moved on to other places, notably Paris, and did other things. Indeed it is said that he would have been asked to write the Declaration of Independence but for the risk that he would have put a joke in it. For all his affection for Britain, he was a man who was at times unable to read the portents, and who was unaware in 1764 of the coming conflict over stamp duty that was going to erupt within eighteen months in Boston and most of the coastal ports, and who was keen to appoint his friends to jobs as stamp distributors. Maybe the very affluence which he enjoyed in London hid such matters from him. His best friends in London—'Straney' (his name for William Strachan, the publisher and editor), Sir John Pringle, Caleb Whitefoord—were Scots, or, like Price and Priestley, Dissenters; outsiders looking in. In London, as in Philadelphia, Franklin was an addict of newspapers and gazettes, replying to criticisms of America and Americans, regularly contributing, both openly and under pen-names, often printing tall tales and spoofs as he had done in his own *Pennsylvania Gazette.* It went down well among coffee-house gossips; but it was not the way to acceptance by the decision-making aristocratic Establishment. Again, perhaps his appointment to the agency for Massachusetts in 1770, as well as that for Pennsylvania, pushed him in more radical directions than he would naturally have gone.

In London in January 1760, Franklin heard of Wolfe's seizure of Canada from the French, and wrote to Lord Kames,

> No one can rejoice more sincerely than do I on the Reduction of Canada: and this, not merely as I am a Colonist, but as I am a Briton. I have long been of Opinion that the Foundations of the future Grandeaur and Stability of the British Empire, lie in America; and tho', like other Foundations, they are low and little seen, they are nevertheless broad and Strong enough to support the greatest Political Structure Human Wisdom ever yet erected.

It might have been so. If so, it is likely that a *pax Anglo-Americana* would have been obtained. But in the eighteenth-century the Atlantic was not an easy ocean to bridge; and in 1768, as again in 1774, Franklin was not given the chance to try to do so. As it was, he paid the price of every man who tries too long to sail down the middle of the stream. 'Hence it has often happened to me, that while I have been thought here [in England] too much of an American, I have in America been deemed too much of an Englishman', as he ruefully complained.

Franklin wrote to his former good friend, Lord Howe, who in 1776 was in charge of the British forces sent to put down the American rebellion,

> Long did I endeavour, with unfeigned and unwearied zeal, to preserve from breaking that fine and noble china vase, the British Empire, for I knew that, being once broken, the separate parts could not retain even their shares of the strength or value that existed in the whole, and that a perfect reunion of those parts could scarce ever be hoped for.

By this time, Franklin charged, the Empire had become devoted to war, conquest, dominion, and commercial monopoly rather than the true interest of the mutual advantage of colonies and mother country.

> Her Fondness for Conquest, as a warlike Nation, her lust of Dominion, as an ambitious one, and her wish for a gainful Monopoly, as a

commercial One, (none of them legitimate Causes of War), will all join to hide from her Eyes every view of her true Interests, and continually goad her on in those ruinous distant Expeditions, so destructive both of Lives and Treasure, that must prove as pernicious to her in the End, as the Crusades formerly were to most of Nations in Europe.

Equally stimulated by absence and by that distance that lends enchantment, Franklin came more and more to express often his love for his 'dear Country'. A new note was now emerging: of pride in America as a distinct entity.

> Upon the whole, I have lived so great a part of my life in Britain, and have formed so many friendships in it, that I love it, and sincerely wish it prosperity; and therefore wish to see that Union, on which alone I think it can be secured and established. As to America, the advantages of such a Union to her are not so apparent. She may suffer at present under the arbitrary power of this country; she may suffer for a while in a separation from it; but these are temporary evils that she will outgrow. Scotland and Ireland are differently circumstanced. Confined by the sea, they can scarcely increase in numbers, wealth and strength, so as to over-balance England. But America, an immense territory, favoured by Nature with all advantages of climate, soil, great navigable rivers, and lakes, must become a great country, populous and mighty; and will, in a less time than is generally conceived, be able to shake off any shackles that may be imposed on her, and perhaps place them on the imposers. In the meantime every act of oppression will sour their tempers, lessen greatly, if not annihilate the profits of your commerce with them, and hasten their final revolt; for the seeds of liberty are universally found there, and nothing can eradicate them. And yet, there remains among that people, so much respect, veneration and affection for Britain, that, if cultivated prudently, with kind usage, and tenderness for their privileges, they might be easily governed still for ages, without force, or any considerable expense. But I do not see here a sufficient quantity of the wisdom, that is necessary to produce such a conduct, and I lament the want of it.

Next door to number 36 Craven Street lived the Scotsman, David Whitefoord, with whom Franklin had many a drink in the coffee-houses on the Strand. Ironically, Whitefoord in 1783 was a member of the British negotiating team which drew up the terms of the Treaty of Paris, which ended the War of American Independence, and which recognised the independence of the United States. The friendship of Franklin, the chief American negotiator, and Whitefoord, made the peace-making much easier. At the signing ceremony, and looking at the French team, Whitefoord said prophetically, 'And remember that the colonists, now independent, and their descendants will all speak English'.

For Further Reading

Esmond Wright, *Franklin of Philadelphia* (Harvard UP, 1986); Edmund Morgan (ed.), *Prologue to Revolution* (Chapel Hill, University of North Carolina, 1959); A.O. Aldridge, *Benjamin Franklin and Nature's God* (Duke UP, 1967); Bernard Bailyn, *The Ideological Origins of the American Revolution* (Harvard UP, 1967); Jonathan Dull, *Franklin the Diplomat* (American Philosophical Society, 1982); Claude Lopez, *Mon Cher Papa: Franklin and the Ladies of Paris,* (Yale UP, 1966). William Randall, *A Little Revenge: Benjamin Franklin and his son.* (Little, Brown, Boston, 1984); Sheila L. Skemp, *William Franklin, son of a Patriot, servant of a King,* (OUP, 1990).

ESMOND WRIGHT, Emeritus Professor of US History in the University of London, is former Director of the Institute of US Studies in London. He is the historical adviser to the Benjamin Franklin House project.

George Mason: Forgotten Founder, He Conceived the Bill of Rights

STEPHAN A. SCHWARTZ

It had rained over the weekend, breaking the sweltering heat that had made Philadelphia a cauldron for most of the summer of 1787. The air was cool and fresh on the Monday morning the delegates to the Constitutional Convention gathered for a last time at the war-worn State House (now Independence Hall). They had argued among themselves up to the last minute, and even now not one of them was entirely happy with the results they had achieved.

The new Constitution, professionally copied out on parchment, lay on a small baize-covered table at the front of the room. Next to it was a silver inkstand and a newly trimmed goose quill. The delegates sat in silence as the fruit of their summer's labor was read to them. Then Benjamin Franklin, knowing how fragile the consensus for acceptance was, rose to try to explain why he was prepared to sign. At 81, he was not up to the physical task, though, and his younger colleague James Wilson had to read his words. Franklin confessed there were several parts of the Constitution "which I do not at present approve."

Nathaniel Gorham of Massachusetts immediately asked to speak, offering at this final hour an amendment that would increase the size of the House. The meeting stood at a parlous point; it could easily spiral back into acrimonious debate. George Washington, one of the seven delegates from Virginia, stood to speak for the first and only time. Through the weeks of the debate, although the presiding officer, he had sat silently in front of the assembly. By his silence he had made himself the vessel of their commitment to integrity. His request that Gorham's change be approved, and that events move on, was irresistible. Finally, they lined up by state, with the New Hampshire delegation at the head. Franklin had to be helped to the small table and was said to be silently weeping as he wrote his name. Washington signed with almost unapproachable dignity, knowing, as they all did, that he would be the first President.

This wise Virginian was a friend to four future presidents, yet he refused to sign the Constitution.

Only three present refused to sign. One of them was George Mason who, more than any other individual, would influence all three American documents: the Declaration of Independence, the

Constitution and the Bill of Rights. Sixty-two, of moderate height, with a round face and chestnut hair, this gouty and irascible militia colonel with large Virginia landholdings had been a slaveholder for most of his life. Yet now, because the Constitution created a federal government he felt might be too powerful, and because it did not end the slave trade and did not contain a Bill of Rights, he withheld his support from the document he had played so large a role in crafting.

His decision not to sign baffled some and alienated others, as he must have known it would. We will never know whether he appreciated what his refusal would cost him, but it is hard to believe that a man so aware of nuance in so many other public matters would have been unaware of what his stand would mean.

He had been born to George and Ann Thomson Mason in 1725, on a Potomac River plantation in what is now Fairfax County, Virginia, near today's Washington, D.C. His father drowned in a boating accident when George was 10, and the responsibility for his upbringing from then on was shared by his mother and his uncle, John Mercer.

In the 18th century, books were rare and valuable. Most families owned only a Bible and perhaps two or three other books, and even wealthy gentry might have no more than a few dozen. Mercer possessed more than 1,500 at the time of his death. Being given the run of such an extraordinary library afforded young Mason a significant opportunity. Mason, like his friend George Washington, would receive little formal training. Mercer's library was his real education.

In 1746, when he was 21, Mason assumed control of approximately 20,000 acres of prime land, broken into farms scattered across several counties in Virginia and Maryland. He proved to be successful at running colonial plantations, and his neighbors soon knew it. At his death he owned 80,000 to 100,000 acres, and unlike many planters of the Revolutionary era, he was not crippled by debt.

Somewhere along the line, they discussed with Mason the latest information on events in the country.

Four years after taking control of his legacy, Mason married Ann Eilbeck, a planter's daughter. In an age when marriage was still largely seen through the prism of connections, theirs was a love match that lasted until Ann's death, 23 years later. They had 12 children together, nine of whom lived past childhood: five sons and four daughters. Although he was considered by many to be a difficult man, George's love for Ann was passionate, tender and unwavering. Years later he chose to be buried next to her even though he had remarried.

Midway through their first decade together, Ann and George began the construction of a new home. Mason's Gunston Hall, like Jefferson's Monticello and Washington's Mount Vernon, became an extension of the man. Given Mason's wealth and station it is surprisingly small—simple and restrained on the outside and very well appointed and elegant on the inside.

Mason's choice of the location for the new house also says a lot about the man. He could have sited Gunston Hall anywhere on his thousands of acres. He chose to put it near the main road that ran between Williamsburg—Virginia's colonial capital and most important urban center—and Philadelphia, then America's leading and most cosmopolitan city. Turning aside from their journeys, colonial leaders rode up the drive to spend a day or a week sitting in his gardens looking out at the Potomac, riding over his land, eating at his well-stocked table or gambling at loo or whist in his drawing room. Somewhere along the line, they discussed with Mason the latest information on events in the country. Jefferson, greatly influenced by him, called Mason "a man of the first order of wisdom." "My private intercourse with him," James Madison said, "was chiefly on occasional visits to Gunston when journeying to & fro from the North, in which his conversations were always a feast to me."

What may have made the advice Mason offered acceptable to many of the other Founding Fathers was not only its wisdom but that it came from someone who, unlike most of them, was not a competitor for office or public notice. Mason loved the philosophy of governance, and liked shaping it, but acknowledged that he had no tolerance for the jostling camaraderie of public political life, describing some officeholders as "Bablers."

Consulting Mason, however, was not for those put off by plain speaking. Fellow Virginian Edmond Randolph said, with some irony, that Mason was not "wantonly sarcastic," but Jefferson was blunter; "His elocution was neither flowing nor smooth; but his language was strong, his manner most impressive, and strengthened by a dash of biting cynicism, when provocation made it seasonable."

One person who didn't seem to mind was Mason's near neighbor, George Washington. When they got together they and their wives talked about farming, and fashion, and about the slaves, whose presence was inextricably intertwined with their lives. It is hard for us today to understand slavery; the concept is so repugnant that even educational reenactments at living historic sites such as Williamsburg excite controversy. But 200 years ago slavery seemed a fixture of life. By the mid-18th century, however, some in the colonial elite to which the Washingtons and Masons belonged held deeply conflicting feelings about it.

Washington's final views on slavery were still forming, but even early on Mason's had become clear and characteristically acerbic: he had grown to loathe what the next century would call "the peculiar institution." In his typically blunt style he wrote, " . . . that slow Poison, [slavery] . . . is daily contaminating the Minds & Morals of our People. Every Gentleman here is born a petty Tyrant. Practical

in Acts of Despotism & Cruelty, we become callous to the Dictates of Humanity. . . . And in such an infernal School are to be educated our future Legislators & Rulers."

For all their inner conflict, though, neither man had any clear idea what to do about slavery. To the 21st century mind the answer is easy: free your slaves! But the 18th century was a different world, with different values. Even simple human considerations were complex on this issue. Freed slaves often had to leave the state, tearing apart lifelong relationships. Freeing them in the slave culture of Virginia, and its surrounding states, also meant making them vulnerable to, at best, exploitation and, at worst, recapture and re-enslavement. For the plantation owner, mass manumission also meant financial, and thus social, suicide.

As the years passed, the issue for Mason grew more and more intolerable. He came to believe that the importation of slaves should be stopped immediately. At the same time, according to one source, he felt that before emancipation could even be considered, a program of education should be begun so that the slaves could at least read and write.

Both Georges saw public service as a responsibility, but their approaches were very different. Washington, who was both ambitious and physically commanding, viewed public office as part of his life's plan. Mason, by disposition, was a backroom man. While Washington was careful in his choice of words, famously in control of himself and rarely offended, Mason never shied away from controversy and was an early proponent of the separation of church and state, and a firm opponent of taxation without representation.

In 1773, when he was 48 his wife Ann died, leaving Mason devastated, and he tried to withdraw even further from public life. But a year later, Mason went up to spend the night at Mount Vernon. The invitation from Washington was more than social. The port of Boston had been closed, and the Virginia colonists felt a powerful need to somehow support the people of Massachusetts. To meet that need Mason and Washington got together at Mount Vernon and wrote the Fairfax Resolves, outlining the colonists' constitutional grounds for their objections to the Boston Port Bill. It was the beginning of Mason's public writing on constitutional issues.

When Washington was named Commander in Chief of the Continental Army in 1775, the Virginia Legislature asked Mason to take Washington's seat in that body. Almost immediately he was an "elder" to whom other members turned. Constant consultation, plus his natural affinity and passion for the subject, forced Mason to grapple in earnest with the relative rights of citizens and government, and how this might play out in the sweaty compromises of politics.

In 1776, Virginia delegates met at a convention whose purpose was to replace the House of Burgesses, the colonial legislature. Mason, now 51, was among those selected that year, and he felt he could not decline. Arriving late at the convention, he found himself already appointed to a committee charged with drafting a "Declaration of Rights" and a constitution.

On Saturday, May 4, little Rhode Island seceded, the first colony to declare its freedom from England. The news electrified the Virginians. Mason began work on May 18 filled with enthusiasm, but it didn't last. He complained to one of his closest friends, Richard Henry Lee, that the committee was "overcharged with useless Members . . . [who would draft] a thousand ridiculous and impracticable proposals. . . ." By the end of the first week, he had more or less pushed most of them aside. It is a measure of the respect in which he was held that the other delegates went along with this.

Madison and Jefferson were close, both seeing Mason, for all his crankiness, as a man of wisdom.

Edmund Pendleton, president of the Virginia Convention that year, wrote to Jefferson, then in Philadelphia representing Virginia at the Continental Congress. "The Political Cooks are busy in preparing the dish, and as Colo. Mason seems to have the Ascendancy in the great work, I have Sanguine hopes it will be framed so as to Answer its end . . . but I am yet a stranger to the Plan."

The Plan began with the Enlightenment philosophy of the Englishman John Locke (1632–1704), whose work Mason had likely first encountered in his uncle's library. Locke argued that government's sole purpose was to protect the natural rights—life, liberty and property—of the people. And he enumerated most of the rights Mason would later list. But it was Mason who saw why it was important to make Locke's abstractions law. He had come to a then-radical insight: that a republic had to begin with the formal, legally binding commitment that individuals had inalienable rights—rights that came from the Creator and were superior to any government.

One other committee member did play a significant role: James Madison, just 25 and beginning his public career. At first glance he made an odd contrast with the stout, acerbic Mason, twice his age. Madison, slight of stature, was a university-educated, bookish man of modest means who spoke with a soft voice. Yet, like Mason, Madison did his homework, knew his citations and could marshal his thoughts into a compelling argument. And he never babbled.

That summer spent working with Mason on Virginia's Constitution and Declaration of Rights would become the precursor event upon which Madison would build his own place in history 11 years later when, only 36, he would be the principal architect of the U.S. Constitution.

But that wasn't all. Madison and Jefferson were close, communicating regularly and candidly, both seeing Mason, for all his crankiness, as a man of wisdom. Madison understood the implications of what Mason was doing and kept Jefferson apprised of their work. Virginia's Declaration of Rights would be an unprecedented political statement; nowhere in modern times had a government acknowledged such a concept as individual inalienable rights, let alone formalized it as a limitation on its own power.

Events, however, were moving almost faster than their correspondence. In the midst of Madison and Mason's work in Williamsburg, the Virginia Convention sent Richard Henry Lee to Philadelphia, where he introduced a measure declaring the colonies' independence. It was well received, and with the usual legislative courtesy of the day, Lee would have been made the chairman of the committee charged with drafting the declaration. But Lee learned his wife was sick, and asked permission of the Congress to return home. In his place that Tuesday, June 11, Thomas Jefferson was appointed. Jefferson, only 33, thought John Adams, as the more senior member of the committee, should draft the declaration. Adams soon made it clear that he felt Jefferson was the man for the job.

"Why will you not [write the declaration]?" Jefferson asked of Adams. Replied Adams, "First, you are a Virginian, and a Virginian ought to appear at the head of this business. Second: I am obnoxious, suspected and unpopular. You are very much otherwise. Third: You can write ten times better than I can."

We credit Jefferson, but the impulse and content were clearly formed by George Mason.

But what to write, and how to write it? Part of the answer would soon arrive by courier from Williamsburg. The day after Jefferson was appointed, Mason's Virginia Declaration of Rights was adopted in Williamsburg on Wednesday, June 12. The first article of the work began, "That all men are by nature equally free and independent, and have certain inherent rights . . . namely, the enjoyment of life and liberty, with the means of acquiring and possessing property, and pursuing and obtaining happiness and safety." Jefferson's Declaration of Independence, with minor corrections from Franklin, Adams and others, came to include the immortal words that make up what may be the most famous political statement in history: "We hold these truths to be self-evident, that all men are created equal, that they are endowed by their Creator with certain unalienable Rights, that among these are Life, Liberty and the pursuit of Happiness." We credit Jefferson, but the impulse and content were clearly formed by George Mason.

On June 29 the Virginia Constitution Mason had principally authored was adopted, freeing him to return to Gunston Hall. The war, however, soon made any hopes for a private life impossible. During the Revolutionary War years, in addition to serving in the Virginia House of Delegates, Mason raised the funds for equipping a county militia. (He had been a militia colonel before the war, which fixed the rank to his name; thereafter, he was known as Colonel Mason).

Throughout the war, Mason had watched Washington's struggles with the Continental Congress and Robert Morris' attempts to raise money, and seen everything he despised about politicians confirmed. Still planning to spend time at home, he proposed to Sarah Brent, also in her 50s, of the nearby wealthy Brent planter family. It was to be a marriage of friendship and mutual comfort, but not the passionate romance he had had with Ann.

Mason found once again, however, that a completely private life was not to be his. A consensus had emerged that something had to be done about the Articles of Confederation, and a Constitutional Convention was planned. Franklin, who had deep respect for Native American cultures, called it the "Great Council Fire." It would be held in Philadelphia, and seven Virginians agreed to represent their state: Washington, Madison, George Wythe, Edmund Randolph, Dr. James McClurg, John Blair—and Mason. And so, at 62, he rode down his drive and onto the road as it snaked through the loblolly pines on a May morning in 1787. It was the longest trip Mason had ever made.

Many of the delegates, and certainly their appointing state committees, believed the purpose of the convention was to jigger with the Articles. But Madison had something very different in mind: he wanted to write an entirely new national constitution. Convincing his fellow Virginians to support him in this was not a trivial undertaking, and convincing the entire convention, even harder. One of the first people Madison turned to was Mason.

Mason's positions throughout the summer were consistent with his principles, even when, as was sometimes the case, they were against his own self-interest, or the interests of his Virginia. He argued against the interests of the rich when they abrogated the rights of the individual. He supported the power of the common man against the elite, arguing for popular elections. He fought his fellow delegates who sought to hold on to power, arguing for the admission and full equality of any new Western states. He worried about the power of a federal form of government, and argued against the slave trade.

The unwillingness of the delegates to deal with slavery was only one of Mason's disappointments. By August, he was saying he would "rather chop off my right hand than put it to the Constitution as it now stands."

Toward the end of the convention, he proposed that a bill of rights preface the Constitution, but when the state delegations caucused—each state had only one vote—it quickly became evident that most of the delegates did not get his point. When his proposal was defeated ten states to none, it was a dreadful blow.

Mason made a last effort to explain his reasons for the positions he had taken, sending to some friends 16 written objections. When his objections were still ignored, he turned his face against the new Constitution, and refused to sign it. Because of his active involvement throughout the convention, and his long association with constitutionalism, this refusal caused disappointment and consternation to the signers.

Assent of 9 of the 13 states was needed for ratification of the Constitution. Virginia cast the tenth affirmative vote. Among the Anti-Federalists in Virginia were Mason, Richard Henry Lee, future President James Monroe and Patrick Henry. Among the Federalists, or supporters of the Constitution, were Washington, Madison, George Wythe and John Marshall. After an unusually bitter debate, Virginia ratified the Constitution by an 89–79 vote. On "the first Wednesday in March"—March 4, 1789—the Constitution went into effect.

For Mason, his rejection of it had been a calculated act of public sacrifice; particularly painful to him was the effect his action had on Washington, who would be governing under the new Constitution. We do not know Washington's exact feelings, but his actions make it clear he felt betrayed. If Franklin could sign, why not Mason? But Mason could see no way to avoid what he believed must be done: "You know the friendship which has long existed (indeed from our early youth) between General Washington and myself," he would write, ". . . [but] I would not forfeit the approbation of my own mind for the approbation of any man or all the men upon earth."

He and Washington never visited each other again. Shortly before Mason's death five years after the convention, Washington referred to him as his former friend.

"I have received much Satisfaction from the Amendments to the federal Constitution. . . ."

Mason retired to Gunston Hall for the last time, even as the perspective about him was changing—at least within the state and national leadership. He was invited to become one of Virginia's senators in the first U.S. Senate, but he declined. During the months since the convention, Mason's sacrifice had had its effect. At the first session of the first Congress, Madison introduced a bill of rights that paralleled Mason's Virginia declaration. Mason commented from Gunston Hall: "I have received much Satisfaction from the Amendments to the federal Constitution, which have lately passed. . . . With two or three further Amendments . . . I cou'd chearfully put my Hand & Heart to the new Government."

Sometime in late September Mason contracted what was called "the fever of the Season," probably malaria, which was endemic in Virginia during the late summer and early fall each year. He died at home on October 7, 1792. In his will he did not free his slaves, as Washington would several years later. Although it would be hard to prove, it is interesting to speculate as to whether Mason's views influenced Washington. Born into a slave-owning world, he did not initially question its order. By the time he became President, however, Washington had begun to see slavery as wrong. He made provision in his will for the freeing of his slaves, and made arrangements for the elderly among them.

Why Mason did not do this we will never know, but if he remained true to his convictions, and it is hard to imagine Mason doing anything else, perhaps he did not free them because he could not see how a single planter acting alone could effect a solution in a matter the nation as a whole should address. In the end it may have been as simple as this: family was more important even than principle. Mason was unwilling to bankrupt his children. It cannot have been an easy decision. Washington, who had no children, did not have to face that choice.

Although recognized by his fellow Founding Fathers, Mason never overcame the public's disregard for him as the result of his stand at the Constitutional Convention, and the events that flowed out of it. His obituaries were small, and as time passed he was largely forgotten, except as a name on high schools and a university in Virginia.

But to those few who have looked deeply into America's democracy, Mason's star has never dimmed, nor has his influence waned. In the House chamber his marble relief hangs with those of other great lawgivers: Moses, the Babylonian king Hammurabi and Thomas Jefferson. When the United Nations was founded his ideas were echoed in its Universal Declaration of Human Rights. In October 1949, President Harry S. Truman wrote to a correspondent, "Too few Americans realize the vast debt we owe [George Mason]. His immortal Declaration of Rights in 1776 was one of the finest and loftiest creations ever struck from the mind of man. . . . Our matchless Bill of Rights came directly from the amazing wisdom and far-seeing vision of this patriot. . . . That is why I say that George Mason will forever hold a special place in our hearts."

Virginia-based writer **STEPHAN A. SCHWARTZ** plans a book on George Mason.

This Is Not a Story and Other Stories

EUGEN WEBER

Langres, where Denis Diderot was born in 1713, shortly before the death of Louis XIV, floats high above the chalky plains of east Champagne, a cold, windy, not very welcoming town, whose chief industries 200 years ago were cutlery and the Church. Diderot's father was a master cutler: the men of the family had been artisans or taken holy orders as far back as memory wished to press. A brilliant student of the Jesuits, young Denis tried the former craft and found it too demanding, flirted with the latter but found it too constricting. In Paris, where he had gone to continue learning, he learned too much, fell into bad ways, lost his vocation, abandoned his studies, began to hang about cares where other dissipated youths played chess (that's how he met Rousseau, another addict), chased skirts and ended up marrying one.

Marriage meant children, even though most of them died: of his four, only the last girl survived. He had to earn some money to keep the meager home, the fragile children, the wife who nagged about his wayward ways: "a grumbler and a scold," her fond daughter called her when defending her from worse charges. He scrabbled as other contemporary bohemians scrabbled, by hack journalism, sermon writing, confidence trickery and making ill-paid translations from English. "There is no need," he remarked at a later stage, "to understand a language to translate it, since one translates it only for people who understand it not."

In 1746, with Denis in his 30s, the bookseller-publishers he worked with thought of a larger project: translating the Scotsman Ephraim Chambers's groundbreaking Cyclopaedia. Diderot came cheap, and in this sphere he could be relied on. But he began to feel his oats; translation became creation. He would direct an encyclopedia of his own, bring in a distinguished mathematician, Jean Le Rond d'Alembert, as co-editor, recruit friends and acquaintances—Rousseau, Condillac, Montesquieu, Voltaire and others less well known—to contribute articles. The son of an artisan, he would take responsibility for writing or commissioning articles on the arts, and on the crafts also then regarded as arts, whose underrated social and economic importance would be demonstrated by the scale of attention devoted to them.

The epigraph to the Encyclopaedia refers to "the power of order and connection." Its contents, ranged in an alphabetical order not then taken for granted, so that Theology came after Technology, affirmed democracy over traditional hierarchies; and cross references suggested sardonic connections

("Anthropophagy: see Eucharist, Communion, Altar, etc."). Gastronomical articles on Asparagas, Almond and so on were lifted wholesale from a popular recipe book. Denounced, they were eventually dropped after the third volume. But that lay in the future. In 1751 the first volume of the work, covering the letter A, appeared to much acclaim. Two thousand, then 4,000, subscribers guaranteed the success of the series. By 1765, when the seventeenth volume of text appeared (the eleven volumes of plates took longer), the monument contained 60,660 articles.

Incoherent, uneven in the quality of its articles, unsettling in its juxtapositions, exciting in its subversions, the Encyclopaedia was to become the major war machine of that party of humanity whose militants were, like Diderot and his friends, "philosophers." As with other parties, this one's message, when listened to in detail, sounds like cacophony. Its core, however, was simple: it was time for a secular, more democratic world to replace a hierarchical, religious one. Nature was to replace anthropomorphic God. Nature came first and within Nature, Man came first, a social animal, perfectible, and selfperfectible by the application of Reason. To philosophers, says P.N. Furbank in his splendid book, "Reason was what Grace is to the Christian." Which meant that thought had to range freely. Furbank does not quote Diderot's quip that "original sin might be no more than an original way of sinning." Flippancy of this sort helps explain why right-thinking folk in what was still a Christian society looked on the philosophes as libertines, and why booksellers included pornography among their "philosophic books."

Some philosophes would have reversed the image. It was not their writings that were (or were about) harlotry, a social menace; the Great Whore was the Church, its rule, pornocracy. Most members of the philosophical clan, among them the skeptic and atheist Diderot, were more moderate. Yet all were anticlerical. For enlightened men (and philosophy was by definition enlightened as religion was by definition obscurantist), organized religions, Christianity above all, were enemies of progress, the Church a parasite on society, the chief inspiration and support of despotic rule. Nature was about Liberty. Children of Nature, "Maniacs of Freedom," abhorred slavery and slave drivers. Their hands, as one of Diderot's ballads sang, launching a trickle of quotable imitations, "would knot the guts of priests to strangle kings."

For Diderot, whose younger sister had become a nun and died in a state of religious mania, whose elder brother, a priest, was an intolerant bigot, this seemed a good idea. His religious foes responded in kind, and their powers of enforcement were greater than any that enlightened wordsmiths could have hoped to wield. Diderot's writings were burned by the public hangman. Contributors to the Encyclopaedia were hounded, the enterprise banned by the king, prohibited by the pope, condemned by the high court of Parliament ("Is there no justice against men of law?").

Friends urged Diderot to take refuge abroad. He did not, though the royal privilege by which the Encyclopadia was printed and sold in France was rescinded, and volumes only continued to appear at great risk to all involved thanks to the protection of the royal censor and of the chief of police. As absolutism was allegedly limited by satirical ditties, so censorship was mitigated by personal sympathies. Yet freedom remained severely circumscribed, and self-censorship could prove more dire than the official kind. In 1764, on the eve of the work's completion, Diderot found that his editors, fearing the wrath of authority, had bowdlerized and emasculated controversial articles, many his own; behind his back they had removed anything that could cause trouble.

The hard core of philosophical activities was found in a few salons. Writing in a dreamier age, Lytton Strachey painted the finely powdered ladies and gentlemen in their silks and jewels at these assemblies of the night. "Within, the candles sparkled, and the diamonds, and the eyes of the company sitting round in gilded, delicate chairs. And then there was supper, and the Marquise was witty, and the Comte was sententious, while yet newer vistas opened of yet happier worlds, dancing on endlessly through the floods of conversation and champagne." The image is not without justification. But for a social group, many of whom like Diderot himself were trammeled by slender budgets and skimpy lodgings, the hospitality of a generous host was crucial on the elementary material level. Dinners, receptions and drawing rooms, open on regular days, offered more than harbor: light from expensive candles enhanced by costly mirrors, lavish food and wine, freedom from dark, dust, dirt, cold hearths and the din of uninsulated quarters.

Salons provided a firm base for the cultural dog fights of the day, and a forum for intense sociability. The cacouacs, as a hostile pamphlet dubbed them, lived in each other's laps. In Furbank's pages we find everyone discussing their own affairs and everybody else's affairs as well. With lots of itchy people waiting to be scratched right way or wrong, tiffs between friends were many. Bitter accusations were resolved in floods of tears, hugs, kisses or in deadly feuds like the one that ended Rousseau and Diderot's long friendship. Everyone discussed virtue, friendship, duty, god (or its absence); everyone lavished advice on others. Diderot was good at that, and he enjoyed it. As indiscreet as he was helpful, he could not bear not to tell anyone in range, at length, what was best for them.

He was an energetic talker, physically invasive, grabbing his interlocutors or hugging them, patting, squeezing, slapping, pounding them to emphasize his points. The Empress Catherine reported that, after a conversation (and they had quite a few), her thighs were black and blue from his emphatic smacks. "I've had to put a table between him and me to keep myself and my limbs out of the range of his gesticulation." But he knew himself and he knew his kind. He loved mankind and most of all himself. He also loved their foibles. The typical man of genius, explained Rameau's Nephew, "is good at one thing only and perfectly unaware of what it means to be a citizen, a father, mother, brother, relative or friend." In any case, genius or no, "we are never sorry except for ourselves." As for Public Opinion (which Voltaire just then was busy mobilizing to right injustices), it was "a hopeless tribunal, weak, venal and feather-headed, swayed by herd-instinct . . . and instant emotion." That being so, prudence was wisdom. We must "speak against insane laws until they are reformed, but in the meantime obey them." Or at least break them cautiously. All thoughts are good to think, not all are good to publish.

That may be why so many of Diderot's writings were published in Holland—like The Indiscreet Jewels of 1748, with place of publication variously given as Monomotapa or Peking. Some, like The Nun and others that Furbank outlines and discusses, were circulated in samizdat form in his friend Melchior Grimm's Correspondance litteraire, a manuscript newsletter dispatched every two weeks by diplomatic channels to a very select list of some fifteen subscribers like the queen (later the king) of Sweden, the king of Poland and the Russian empress. Others, like Jacques the Fatalist and Rameau's Nephew, were published only after the author's death—sometimes long after.

That also applies to the five short stories or colloquial essays that Furbank has translated—notably "This Is Not a Story" and the "Supplement to Bougainville's Voyage" in the little book to which the former lends its title. The dialogue mode that Diderot liked to use is sometimes stilted and sometimes less than fascinating; but the narrative moves fast, the wit sparkles, the skepticism is modern. No wonder that the stories were much admired by the likes of Schiller and Balzac, let alone by Goethe, who translated Rameau's Nephew into German, so that its first French publication, when it came in 1821, was a garbled translation back from Goethe's German. Like them or not, though, the stories are full of pearls, as when, in Diderot's conversation with his father, the son whispers as he kisses him: "Father, the truth is, there are no laws for the wise man." The father whispers back: "Not so loud."

The father's principle evidently informed the son's practice. But there was a lot of publication all the same. Diderot was fascinated by the theater; he had strong ideas on acting and on the cool detachment that, he believed, made for better acting. "Sensibility makes mediocre actors, extreme sensibility makes hidebound actors, cool thinking makes sublime actors." By way of his effect on Lessing, Furbank holds, Diderot must count as a rounding father of German national drama. He was also fascinated by the plastic arts, wrote art criticism that was widely read in narrow circles ("We laugh at portraits of our ancestors and never think how our nephews will snigger over ours"), recommended his friend EtienneMaurice Falconet to sculpt the splendid statue that still gestures grandly in St. Petersburg today. He frequented painters, admired Ghardin and, equally, Greuze, whose "moral painting" he praised warmly. He called for styles more suggestive than exhaustive: "When we write, must we write all? When we paint, must we paint everything? Please leave something to my imagination." This when discussing a

Boucher sheepfold aswafro with the fleecy beasts. He also, as her Paris agent, bought so many important collections for the Empress Catherine that Furbank regards him as "to a considerable degree, the founder of the Hermitage collection."

In 1784, when he was 70 years old, Diderot suffered a stroke. The doctors applied blisters and plied him with emetics. "You use very nasty things to keep me alive," he commented, as we would today. At Catherine's behest, his friend Grimm rented an apartment worthy of humanity's friend in the rue de Richelieu. He did not long enjoy it. He had time to tell his daughter that "the first step toward philosophy is incredulity." At dinner the next day he ate heartily, in his usual way, and died while reaching for the cherry compote.

It is a pity that Furbank annexed This Is Not a Story to title his handsome little collection of Diderot's minor but revealing writings. He should have used that as the subtitle of the larger book. It is not really a biography, nor does it quite claim to be one, but a series of wise and knowledgeable disquisitions on aspects of literary activity in eighteenth-century Paris, from the editing of dictionaries to the writing of plays and novels, all set in the context of several lives—Diderot's, of course, but also those of his friends, loves and relations. Diderot is not so much the center of the book as the thread on which Furbank's discourse is strung. And narrative plays second fiddle to analysis—hence the subtitle, "A Critical Biography." Furbank has played fair with his readers and there is nothing wrong with this approach, as long as amateurs of mere biography are warned. This is an excellent critical biography.

It is not Furbank's fault if the frequent and copious quotations from his hero's writings, private and public, seem verbose. They did not seem so in Diderot's time, and they offer the flavor of his writing, although not quite the spice. I do demur, however, at the surfeit of quotation marks in the critical passages that recount and discuss Diderot's works. The philosopher, who liked the specificity of real-life names, often pictured his friends and himself in imaginary conversations. He does so, for example, in D'Alemberts' Dream, to which a chapter of the biography is devoted. Furbank, who gives an excellent account of the fictional debate at that essay's core, quotes the parties as "Diderot" and "D'Alembert," which, as the two men talk, litters the page with little curlicues. More materially, while Diderot's wisdom is well brought out, his wit is less so. The man who observed that love robs some of their wit and bestows it on those who have none does not appear. Nor does the one who asked, "What is more common than to think one's face has two noses, and to deride those who think their arse has two holes?"

But these are quibbles. "That great magician Diderot," as Michelet once called him, has inspired one more worthy monument to keep memory alive. He bustles out of Furbank's pages, sturdy, sociable, easygoing, playful, greedy, ebullient, vociferous, impetuous, ardent and overflowing. He knows how to coin a phrase. The man of feeling, he says, speaking of actors but thinking quite likely of himself, lacks presence of mind: "He loses his head and only recovers it at the foot of the stairs"—the source of the wonderful French expression esprit d'escalier, staircase wit. He knows many facts, and he knows that facts aren't everything. The man who insists that "a single demonstration strikes me more forcibly than a hundred facts" knows about stocking frames and knows about the "earths," gums, calcined bones, crushed stones and metallic limes that then made up the painter's palette. He knows many things that, until his Encyclopaedia, many had not thought worth knowing, and he made it possible for others to know them:

Nature and Nature's laws lay hid in night. God said "Let Denis be" and all was light.

Furbank has etched a bourgeois of genius, a middling, sensual man who was yet exceptional. Diderot was cowardly yet brave, constant, perseverant, moderate in tastes, immoderate in intellectual passion, excessive in behavior, sensible in reasoning but incapable of withstanding an idea. Ideas were like women: irresistible. They blew through his head like the winds of Langres, exhilarated him and turned him into stormwind himself, the hurricane that before long blew down the world in which he died.

EUGEN WEBER is the author most recently of *My France: Politics, Culture, Myth* (Harvard University Press).

From Mercantilism to 'The Wealth of Nations'

The Age of Discovery gave rise to an era of international trade and to arguments over economic strategies that still influence the policies of commerce.

MICHAEL MARSHALL

W e live in an era when continual economic growth is almost considered a birthright, at least in the developed world. It has become the benchmark of the health of a society, guaranteeing an ever-expanding prosperity. The current president of the United States even finds that his extensive misbehavior is overlooked by a majority of Americans because he happens to be presiding over an extended period of economic growth and optimism.

If annual growth drops below about 2 percent, planners and politicians start to get nervous, while a recession (negative growth) is considered a serious crisis. Where will it all end? Can such growth continue—with periodic setbacks, of course—indefinitely? We do not know and usually do not care to ask.

One thing is clear, however. It was not always so. For most of human history it has not been so. In western Europe in the period 1500–1750, output increased by a mere 65 percent, by one estimate, or an average of 0.26 percent a year, even though the population grew about 60 percent. For most of this period, 80 percent or more of the population worked the land. Studies of wage rates in England and France suggest that the working poor had to spend a full four-fifths of their income on food alone.

So this was not an economically dynamic society. There was relatively little disposable income, that being enjoyed by the prosperous elite of landed aristocracy and, increasingly in this period, merchants. Consequently, there was no prospect of creating a mass domestic market for new products. Most wealth was still tied up in the relatively static commodity of land, and agriculture was the major measure of a country's wealth.

Yet in the period from the voyages of discovery in the late fifteenth and early sixteenth centuries [see "Columbus and the Age of Exploration," THE WORLD & I, November 1998, p. 16] up till the Industrial Revolution there occurred what has been called a "commercial revolution."

The story of that revolution, which I will tell here, weaves together a number of significant themes. The upshot of the Age of Discovery was the emergence of a network of global trade. The consequences of that trade, and the measures taken by increasingly centralized European governments [see "The Ascent of the Nation-State," THE WORLD & I, March 1999, p. 18] to control and direct it, produced the system later labeled, most notably by Adam Smith, mercantilism. This was the practice of imperial rivalry between European powers over global trade, and it gave impetus to the disagreements between Britain and its American colonists that led to the American Revolution. Critical consideration of these issues gave birth to Smith's theoretical study of economics, which culminated in the publication of his masterwork *The Wealth of Nations*.

Protecting Bullion Reserves

Smith wrote: "The discovery of America and that of a passage to the East Indies are the two greatest and most important events recorded in the history of mankind." No doubt he exaggerated, but nothing was more important in the unfolding of this story. The Spanish conquistadores went to the New World in search of El Dorado. They found little gold but plenty of silver at Potosi in Peru and in northern Mexico. This silver became the lubricant of the machinery of an emerging global economy.

It flowed into Spain, from where much of it went to the rest of Europe, especially Holland, to pay the debts the Hapsburg rulers had incurred through the religious and dynastic struggles in their German possessions and in the Spanish Netherlands. Some of it then flowed to the Baltic to pay for the timber, rope, and other shipbuilding materials that the region supplied, especially to Holland and Britain. The bulk of it, though, went to Asia to satisfy the growing European demand for spices, silk, Indian calico, and later, Chinese tea.

Without the silver that demand could not have been satisfied: Europe had nothing that Asia wanted to import in exchange. That situation would not change until after the Industrial Revolution, when clothing from the Lancashire cotton industry in the north of England found a market in Asia. Even then problems remained. The economic reason for the shameful opium trade in the early

The Commercial Revolution

Voyages of discovery in the fifteenth and sixteenth centuries resulted in a growing network of international trade. Silver from the New World became the lubricant for the machinery of an emerging global economy.

Fearing the success of their rivals, European governments imposed trade restrictions to protect their national interests.

Viewing commerce as an arena of conflicting national interests at times thrust competing European powers into war.

Advocates of free trade criticized mercantilist policies, suggesting peace could arise from mutually beneficial terms of trade.

Clashes over trade were significant factors in the antagonisms that led to the American Declaration of Independence.

The growth of economic relations between America and Britain after the Revolutionary War suggests that the free traders were right.

and mid-nineteenth century, when opium grown in India was exported illegally to China, was to earn exchange to pay for tea without having to export silver.

Silver was not without problems. So much of it flowed into Europe in the sixteenth century that it caused serious price inflation. The Spanish economy, in particular, was considerably disrupted, a significant factor in Spain's gradual decline. During the seventeenth century, from a peak around 1600, the supply of silver began to decrease. The demand for goods from Asia, however, did not. The result was a net outflow of silver bullion from Europe, a shrinkage of the money supply, and as a result, economic recession.

No economic theory existed at the time, and no contemporary thought argued that governments should not regulate such matters affecting national wealth in the national interest. So they did. The ad hoc system of tariffs and other measures influencing trade and manufactures that came to be known as mercantilism began to emerge.

The context in which this happened was one of increasingly centralized emerging nation-states that were spending a greater portion of the total national income than in the past, especially in the frequent times of war. They exercised closer control over more aspects of life in pursuit of national policy than in the past, especially through the taxation needed to fund wars. Trade with the New World nurtured the idea that commerce could be a source of national wealth and strength just as much as agriculture and should be developed to that end.

Spain, Britain, and France all banned the export of gold or silver bullion, but this proved to be like trying to stop water from running downhill. The belief was that bullion represented the national wealth or treasure, and that trade should be conducted so as to amass a surplus of it. A country would then have a reserve to cushion itself from the economic effects of adverse fluctuations in the supply of gold and, especially, silver.

Underlying this thinking was the assumption that markets and the amount of trade were relatively fixed, and that gaining a larger share of the pie necessarily meant depriving another country of part of its share. Trade was thus conceived as an arena of national competition and even conflict, a form of war by other means.

Colbert and French Mercantilism

Advocates of free trade in the late eighteenth and the nineteenth centuries strongly criticized this aspect of mercantilist policy. They proposed that peace was one of the benefits of free trade, since it tied trading partners in mutually beneficial exchanges that could only be lost through war. Neither side was totally right. Circumstances always affect cases, and the mercantilist policymakers were pragmatists who reacted to the situation before them.

The most systematic practitioner of mercantilist policies was undoubtedly Jean-Baptiste Colbert, finance minister for France's Louis XIV in the later seventeenth century. Colbert used the considerable power of the Sun King's state to increase its wealth through the promotion of French trade and manufactures. He certainly banned the export of bullion, but his policy was aimed at replacing bullion as the means of payment for necessary imports with the earnings from the export of French manufactures.

To that end he developed selected industries by state subsidies and bringing in skilled foreign artisans. He particularly encouraged high-value products such as quality furniture, glass, and tapestries, and the quality of French workmanship in these areas became legendary throughout Europe. He used tariff barriers to protect industries that faced serious foreign competition. Wanting to develop the French cloth industry in the face of the well-established British cloth trade, he doubled the duty on imports.

Thus emerged the classic mercantilist pattern that, because it came about in a piecemeal, pragmatic manner, has only existed in its complete form in the writings of historians. The export of domestic raw materials was largely discouraged, so that domestic manufacturers could enjoy their use. The export of sheep and raw wool from Britain, for example, was heavily regulated for the benefit of the domestic textile industry. The export of manufactures was encouraged as the means to a favorable balance of trade and the bullion inflows that came with it.

The import of foreign manufactures was restricted since this adversely affected the balance of trade. Raw material imports were looked on favorably to the degree that they could be used in or support domestic manufactures, although a large agricultural country like France, under Colbert, aimed at as much self-sufficiency as possible.

Colbert realized that encouraging French industry had little point if its products could not then be exported. That meant commercial shipping and a navy to protect it. Colbert had before him the example of the Dutch. They were the dominant economic power in Europe in the early and mid-sixteenth century through their skills in trade and shipping.

The Dutch dominated North Sea fishing, annoying the British by taking huge catches of herring from Britain's east coast, developing a factory-style industry for salting the catch, and then exporting it throughout Europe. They dominated the carrying trade from the Baltic to western Europe, were major carriers of imports to Europe from the Americas and from the East, and grew rich through their control of the lucrative reexport of those imports throughout Europe from their initial port of entry in Amsterdam.

To support these efforts the Dutch dredged and improved their rather shallow harbors and developed specialized forms of shipping, both for fishing and for moving bulk materials. They also developed financial instruments to ease the flow of trade and extend the use of credit. Most notably, they established the Bank of Amsterdam, a public bank that offered a source of capital very different from the government funding of chartered companies that had marked the enterprise of discovery and trade in the sixteenth century.

Colbert built up a merchant marine to rival that of the Dutch and ensure that French trade was carried in French ships. Under his direction the merchant fleet grew from a mere 60 ships of 300 tons or more to over 700 ships of that size. He provided for the protection of French maritime commerce by building up the French navy from 20 ships to 250 by the time of his death in 1683.

He always viewed commerce as an instrument of national policy, and merchants had little say in his decisions. This was unlike the situation in England, where various merchant groups formed influential lobbies on the Crown's commercial policies. The prizes of commerce remained for him a zero-sum game: France's gain must be someone else's loss. He created a successful glass industry in Paris by inviting Venetian glassblowers to teach their skills. He later boasted that the successful royal mirror factory that resulted was depriving Venice of one million livres a year.

Commerce and Conflict

Colbert's attitude was much derided by the later free-trade economists, most notably Smith. The Scottish philosopher David Hume, a contemporary and good friend of Smith's, wrote on the subject: "I shall therefore venture to acknowledge that, not only as a man, but as a British subject, I pray for the flourishing commerce of Germany, Spain, Italy and even France itself."

It was an irony, too, and one that later critics did not fail to point out, that a considerable contribution was made to the growth of French transatlantic exports by industries that did not receive Colbert's nurturing support. Iron and coal, hardware, and the cheaper cloths produced by the textile industry in Normandy all developed through their own enterprise.

Advocates of free trade proposed that peace was one of its benefits.

Nevertheless, Colbert's legacy was a foundation for rapid and successful French commercial development in the eighteenth century. Between 1715 and 1771 the total value of French foreign trade grew eightfold until it almost matched British trade. The value of French exports multiplied more than four times between 1716 and 1789. Colbert must have been doing something right.

Nor were the policymakers of the time completely wrong in their view of commerce as conflict to gain the largest share of a fixed prize. It is certainly true that bilateral trade is mutually beneficial. If a country wants to export its goods, its potential trading partners must have the means to pay for those goods. So it is in the exporter's interest that partners have their own successful export markets, perhaps in the original country's own home market, to generate the revenue needed to buy its exports.

This is not true of the carrying and reexport trade, however. The Dutch had grown rich on this trade, and the British and French set out to take it away from them. Both ended up fighting trade wars with the Dutch over the issue. In the second half of the seventeenth century, Britain passed a series of Navigation Acts, which required that goods shipped in and out of British ports, and to and from British colonies, had to be carried in British ships.

This struck at the heart of the Dutch trade, hence the tensions that led to war. At issue was who would distribute the new colonial imports throughout the rest of Europe. The Dutch gradually lost out to the French and British. Between the 1660s and 1700 British exports grew by 50 percent. Half of that increase came from the reexport of colonial imports, mostly to Europe.

As a result, the eighteenth century was the Anglo-French century in terms of commerce. I have already mentioned the spectacular growth in French trade. The value of British trade grew threefold between 1702 and 1772, and British shipping grew at a similar rate, reaching over one million tons by 1788. This phenomenal growth represented a tremendous amount of new wealth, most of it associated with colonial trade, especially that of the New World.

The bulk of British trade in 1700 was still with Europe, but by 1776 two-thirds of its overseas trade was outside Europe. Between 1700 and 1763 the value of British exports to America and the West Indies multiplied fivefold, while the value of imports from those areas grew fourfold. Anglo-French rivalry resulted in a number of wars throughout the century. It is small wonder, given the importance of colonial trade, that parts of those wars were fought in North America and in India, over strategic control of its sources.

'Badges of Slavery'

The Atlantic trade not only was the most substantial but it also formed an interlocking network. From the plantations of the southern colonies of America, the Caribbean, and the Brazilian coast, tropical staples—tobacco, cotton, sugar, coffee, cocoa, rice—flowed to Europe. European manufactures flowed back west, supplying the plantation economies with necessities they did not produce themselves. European cities, especially those on the Atlantic, grew and prospered on this trade. From Cadiz and Lisbon in the south, through Bordeaux and Nantes in France, to Bristol, Liverpool, Glasgow, and the burgeoning entrepôt of London in England, they all became part of the Atlantic economy.

A city like Liverpool benefited from importing, refining, and reexporting sugar and tobacco. It also benefited from a new and increasingly significant part of the Atlantic economy—slavery. Plantation agriculture is labor intensive, and the plantations of the Americas looked to West Africa to supply that need. Ships from Liverpool or Bristol, or Lisbon for that matter, would sail to West Africa and trade cheap manufactured items to local chiefs in return for live bodies.

Figure 1 Slaves on the deck of the bark *Wildfire,* brought into Key West, Florida, on April 30, 1860. Carrying 510 slaves, the ship violated the 1809 slave trade law that prohibited slave importation. This engraving was made from a daguerreotype for *Harper's Weekly,* June 2, 1860. Blacks were rarely allowed on deck except for occasional "exercise."

Note: Library of Congress

These were then shipped across the Atlantic—the Middle Passage—to the Caribbean or the American South, where those still alive after the horrors of the voyage were sold. The ships then returned home laden with cotton, tobacco, or sugar. In the case of Portuguese ships, they would sail to Brazil and return with Brazilian produce.

European manufactures were also exported to the settler societies of the Americas. The half million Spanish settlers in Mexico and Peru paid for these with silver. As the supply of silver slackened and Latin American society became increasingly self-sufficient, this trade became less important.

The North American trade continued to burgeon. European manufactures were paid for by the products of the region. The question arose as to what those products were to be, and who should determine that: the colonists or the government in London? At this point, questions of mercantilist policy become questions about the future of the American colonies, in other words questions about

independence. Adam Smith addressed both sets of questions in *The Wealth of Nations.*

He described the regulations by which London sought to control the American economy as "impertinent badges of slavery." They were intended to ensure that the American economy would complement the British economy, but that, of course, also meant subordinating the one to the other. The American colonies were viewed as a supplier of those staples mentioned above and a protected market for British manufactures.

The colonies were by no means expected to develop industries that might compete with those in Britain. In 1699, Britain sought to ban the woolen industry in America and prevent any intercolony trade in woolen goods. In 1750 a similar ban was applied to steelmaking and the manufacture of finished products from iron.

The role of the New England colonies was to reduce British reliance on the Baltic region for naval materials and certain types of shipbuilding timber. Thus, these strategically sensitive materials—essential for building the ships of the Royal Navy that protected British commerce—would be under British political control. These products were allowed into Britain duty-free, as was pig iron, in that case to reduce British reliance on Swedish and Russian sources. But the pig iron was not to be any further refined in the colonies, lest it compete with the British iron industry.

Being true Englishmen jealous of their liberties, the colonists chafed under these restrictions. Political conflict inevitably resulted, and many commentators in Britain considered that the costs of that conflict outweighed any economic benefit from trying to restrict the natural economic development of the colonies. Matters came to a head in 1776, the year in which both the Declaration of Independence and *The Wealth of Nations* were published.

New Economic Directions

Smith had definite views on the American economy and on the system of tariffs and trade regulations that had helped produce the conflict. Unlike the views advocated by other contributors to the debate, however, his arose from the context of an extensive theoretical consideration of how wealth is created. It is only a slight exaggeration to say that he invented economic theory.

He can certainly be considered the originator of classical economics. It was his ideas that were first developed and interpreted by David Ricardo and then by John Stuart Mill in *Principles of Political Economy.* At the end of the nineteenth century they were revived and revised as "neoclassical" economics by Alfred Marshall. Even the economic ideas of Karl Marx and, in this century, John Maynard Keynes, started from the principles first enunciated by Smith, although they then moved in very different directions.

His book discusses systematically the basic economic questions: a theory of price or value; wages, profits, and rents; the role of labor; how wealth is distributed among owners of the different factors of production; the role of capital, money, and the banking system; and taxation and the national debt. He famously introduced the concept of the division of labor, explaining how it increases productivity and also is limited by the extent of the market.

He held a dynamic view of the economy. National wealth resulted from the flow of income over time rather than from the size of the stock of capital held. His theory anticipated the actuality of burgeoning economic growth produced by the Industrial Revolution. It differed significantly from the assumptions that lay behind mercantilist policies.

Smith and his good friend Hume refuted the argument that trade should be managed in such a way as to maintain a positive balance so as to earn bullion. Hume pointed out that if bullion flowed out of a country its prices would fall, which would render its exports more competitive, thus increasing the flow of export earnings into the country until balance was restored. In other words, Hume and Smith thought of the economy as a dynamic self-regulating system. In Smith's most famous phrase, it was as if an "invisible hand" harmonized individual economic actions pursued out of self-interest into an overall balance that served the public good. It worked best without government interference.

Economic historian Peter Mathias sums up Smith's arguments on this topic admirably, saying that

> a system of freely operating market prices, under naturally competitive conditions, would ensure the lowest effective prices to the consumer and produce the most efficient allocation of resources between the different branches of economic activity. The ultimate test of efficiency and welfare thus became a freely moving price level not distorted by legislative interference.

On the basis of this argument, Smith launched into a critique of tariffs, subsidies, and monopolies, all the tools of the commercial policy of the era that he dubbed mercantilism. "Consumption," he argued, "is the sole end and purpose of all production," yet under the mercantilist system the consumers' interest was sacrificed to that of producers, who sought special favors from the government for their particular industries.

With such views he could not help but be critical of contemporary British policy toward the American colonies. He thought that Britain could rightly impose its own taxation system on the colonies but only in the context of colonist representation at Westminster. (He was, incidentally, a friend of Benjamin Franklin's, and the two discussed these issues when Franklin was in London.) He thought, too, that Britain could extend its customs laws to America provided that *all* internal barriers to trade were abolished.

Smith thus conceived of the British Empire as a vast and free internal market for each and all of its component regions. He even envisaged that the seat of the empire should not remain fixed in London but should move "to that part of the Empire which contributed most to the general defense and support of the whole."

The Discussion Continues

Economic relations between Britain and America after the Revolutionary War suggested that the free-trade arguments promoted by Smith and his fellow critics of the system of colonial regulation were right. After 1782, British exports to the United States began to grow more rapidly than those to any other region. By 1836 about a quarter of Britain's total exports went there, while the United States provided 80 percent of Lancashire's cotton.

Such evidence boosted free-trade ideas, which became increasingly influential in the nineteenth century, especially in Britain—whose manufacturers, of course, stood to gain the most by them. But the argument that Smith first articulated against mercantilist policy is still going on today. Countries still remain very sensitive about their balance of trade. In the United States, a Republican presidential candidate, Pat Buchanan, argues for greater protection for American industry, in the face of widespread free-trade thinking in both parties.

Back in the 1970s, the Carter administration bailed out Lee Iacocca's Chrysler Corporation because it was thought that the damage to the economy as a whole and the social cost of the resulting unemployment were worse than paying the cost of a bailout. Right now the United States is entering into a tariff war with western Europe over Caribbean bananas. The Europeans want to reserve 25 percent of their banana market for producers in their former colonies. Without that guaranteed market those producers probably could not survive. The United States is arguing for unrestricted free trade in bananas, which would benefit the mighty Dole Corporation. Whoever is right in the argument, its roots lie in the system of Atlantic trade and colonies that developed in the seventeenth and eighteenth centuries.

The "commercial revolution" of the eighteenth century generated a huge increase in trade and wealth. This all happened under a system of mercantilist policy. Whether that policy nurtured the development or, as Smith argued, it took place despite the policy is a question that can probably never be resolved.

What can be said is that the commercial revolution was an important prelude to the Industrial Revolution. Some of the capital generated from trade found its way into the new manufacturing industries. Perhaps more important was the development of extensive new global markets, for it is questionable whether in the absence of those markets European domestic demand could have grown enough to sustain the rapid growth of the new industries. As it was, those industries found an already established international network of markets through which their new products could flow.

MICHAEL MARSHALL is executive editor of *The World & I*.

The Return of Catherine the Great

Tony Lentin

After seventy years of neglect and dismissal in the Soviet period as a foreign adventuress, hypocrite and poseur, indifferent to the needs of 'the people' and marginal to the pre-occupation of Marxists with 'class struggle' and revolution, Catherine the Great (1762–96) is suddenly sweeping into favour in Russia as a focus of unprecedented interest both at the popular and the scholarly level. New lines of enquiry or the re-investigation of older ones have been set in motion. Revisionism, rehabilitation and research proliferate.

The process of rehabilitation began under the impact of glasnost, in the late 1980s and early 1990s with the publication of more positive assessments of Catherine by Alexander Kamensky and Oleg Omel'chenko. (See John Alexander, 'Comparing Two Greats: Peter I and Catherine' in A Window on Russia. Papers from the Vth International Conference of the Study Group on Eighteenth-Century Russia, edited by Maria di Salvo and Lindsey Hughes, La Fenice, 1996, pp. 43–50, and Kamensky's article, in Russian, 'The significance of the reforms of Catherine II in Russian history', ibid., pp. 56–65.) The wave of scholarly interest that followed culminated in August 1996 in an international conference in St Petersburg to mark the bicentenary of Catherine's death. Held under the auspices of the Academy of Sciences and a host of associated organisations, the conference was supplemented by an exhibition of paintings and artefacts at the Hermitage devoted to the Age of Catherine the Great. (See abstracts of conference papers in Mezhdunarodnaia konferentsiia. Ekaterina Velikaia: Epokha Rossiiskai Istorii, St Petersburg, 1996. Conferences have also been held in Germany: at Zerbst, Potsdam and Eutin.)

While it is true that Catherine never lost her German accent, Lydia Kisliagina puts her 'foreignness' into perspective by pointing out that she spent only the first fourteen of her sixty-seven years in Germany: the remaining fifty-three she lived in Russia, thirty-four of these as empress. In his opening address to the St Petersburg conference, Alexander Kamensky discussed Catherine's extraordinary political skills, her adroit management of power and people, her psychological penetration and ability to spot talent and draw it out and to inspire lasting confidence and loyalty. He reminds us that she provided three and a half decades of political stability and ministerial continuity with little significant opposition to her rule despite the constant and obvious claims of her son, Paul. This in itself was an extraordinary achievement, especially after nearly forty years of palace-revolutions in the period preceding her accession.

Catherine directed her formidable tactical skills to particular ends. 'Russia is a European power' she declared in her equivalent of a political manifesto, the Nakaz or Instruction of 1766. Intended as a guideline for the drafting of a new code of law by a representative assembly duly summoned by Catherine in 1767, the Nakaz was banned in France as subversive. Catherine's emphatic assertion about Russia and Europe was full of political, cultural and social implications about the norms of thought, conduct and legality which she hoped to see established in Russia and about her own claims to be considered an exponent of 'enlightened absolutism'. (See O.A. Omel'chenko, '"Enlightened absolutism" in Russia', Coexistence, 32, 1995, pp. 31–38.)

Catherine is once more being taken seriously as an intellectual, engagee and writer (an inveterate 'scribbler', as she called herself and a ruler addicted to 'legislomania'). Committed to the values of the philosophes, she believed fervently in the power of enlightened ideas and legislation and energetically strove to put theory into practice by influencing and forming a 'public opinion' in Russia sympathetic to her objectives. She wrote moral tales for her grandchildren, school syllabuses and mildly satirical periodicals and comedies for her subjects in the lasting basic conviction that common sense, reason and moral conduct could lead to social progress and nurture a responsive and responsible 'civil' society in Russia. Education and enlightenment would create 'true sons of the fatherland' and even 'a new species of humankind'. In 1769 she founded the Smol'ny Institute, Russia's first girls' school, for the daughters of the nobility and bourgeoisie. In modelling the Institute on the latest pedagogical theories she showed a concern for the education of women as active (though not equal) contributors in the process of civilising society.

An international essay competition on the question of serfdom was intended to show that the empress held strong abolitionist views and to stimulate thinking in the same direction: the prize essay, recommending abolition, was chosen by Catherine in 1765. By her own very public example of inoculation against smallpox (in contrast to the royal families of France, Spain and Austria who refused to undergo it on religious grounds), she sought both to save lives and to demonstrate the real benefits of the Enlightenment faith in scientific empiricism and humanitarian zeal. Hospitals and the Foundlings' Home (1764) which she established also saved young lives which, in turn, she intended to turn into useful lives. (See Janet Hartley, 'Philanthropy in the

Reign of Catherine the Great: Aims and Realities' in Russia in the Age of the Enlightenment. Essays for Isabel de Madariaga, edited by Roger Bartlett and Janet M. Hartley, Macmillan, 1990, pp. 167–202.)

Just as she also sponsored scientific expeditions to investigate Russia's natural resources and thereby benefit state and society, so the Russian Academy, which Catherine founded in 1783, was intended to make her subjects more conscious of the beauties of their language by systematising its rules and compiling a Dictionary of the Russian Language in order to place Russian on a par with Western and classical languages. Catherine herself contributed both to a burgeoning Russian literature and to the historical studies which she sought to encourage. Her enthusiastic approach towards her adoptive tongue may be contrasted with Frederick the Great's dismissive attitude towards the German language and letters.

Just as Russian scholars are at last able to acknowledge Western research on Catherine, so emerging studies in Russia are bound to make their impact on historical thinking on Catherine in the West. At present the leading monographs remain the work of Western scholars. The classic example is Isabel de Madariaga's monumental Russia in the Age of Catherine the Great (Yale University Press, 1981), reoffered in a popular abbreviated form as Catherine the Great. A Short History (Yale, 1990) and still more compendiously as an essay, 'Catherine the Great', in Enlightened Absolutism. Reform and Reformers in Later Eighteenth-Century Europe, edited by H.M. Scott (Macmillan, 1990, pp. 289–311). John T. Alexander tells a good story with verve and telling quotation in his Catherine the Great. Life and Legend (Oxford University Press, 1989), but has annoyed feminists by his detailed discussion of Catherine's life with her favourites.

Soviet historians have tended previously to emphasise Russia's spectacular territorial expansion in the period without considering Catherine's own crucial role in the formulation and direction of a dynamic foreign policy. In 1990 H.M. Scott examined Catherine's striking success in increasing Russian influence and prestige abroad, her remarkable flair for turning situations to advantage and her ever 'escalating ambitions' for influence not only at the expense of Turkey and Poland, but in the world generally. She brought Russian influence into the heart of Europe by acquiring the status of mediator in the War of the Bavarian Succession, holding the balance between Austria and Prussia; and to the Atlantic world through her promotion of the League of Armed Neutrality. (See H.M. Scott, 'Russia as a European Great Power', in Russia in the Age of the Enlightenment, pp. 7–39.)

Herself a bookworm, bibliophile and writer. Catherine believed passionately in the power of the printed word. She encouraged book production and the translation of foreign works into Russian as an obvious vehicle for spreading enlightenment. She decentralised publishing, hitherto a state monopoly, from state control by her decree of 1783 authorising the establishment of free presses in Russia, and by encouraging satirical journalism in the spirit of Steele and Addison. It is well known that by the time of the French Revolution she felt obliged to clamp down on several Russian writers and publishers of whom she had hitherto approved and to re-impose tight censorship. (See W. Gareth Jones, 'Novikov and the French Revolution', in Literature, Lives, and Legality in Catherine's Russia, edited by A.G. Cross and G.S. Smith, Astra Press, Nottingham, 1994, pp. 121–26.)

What is significant in current Russian historiography is that it does not play down her initial sustained efforts in this vein or dismiss them as insincere. Catherine personally brought her subjects into touch with the ideas and authors of the Enlightenment. No sooner did Marmontel publish his portrait of an enlightened ruler in Belisaire (1766) than Catherine had it translated and herself took part in the work of translation. After Voltaire's death in 1778, when flattering him could no longer be of the issue, she asked to be sent a hundred sets of the latest edition of 'my master's works, so that I can have them distributed everywhere. I want them to serve as models; I want them to be studied, learned by heart; I want them to provide food for thought'.

Historians have always been uneasy about Catherine's fondness for the public image, the theatricality of her court and what Joseph II called the 'Catherinisation of the Princess of Zerbst'. There is no doubt that in the cultivation of her own legend she was obsessively concerned both with contemporary applause and with her future reputation. (See David Griffiths, 'To Live Forever: Catherine II, Voltaire and the Pursuit of Immortality' in Russia and the World of the Eighteenth Century. Proceedings of the Third International Conference organised by the Study Group on Eighteenth-Century Russia, edited by R.P. Bartlett, A.G. Cross, K. Rasmussen, Slavica Publishers, Ohio, 1988, pp. 446–68.) Yet as we see from Peter Burke's The Fabrication of Louis XIV (Yale, 1992), the cultivation of an image of gloire and grandeur through the arts and in ceremony could play the central part in enhancing the credibility and effectiveness of absolute monarchy. (For an outline of Catherine's use of the arts, see Allen McConnell, 'Catherine the Great and the Fine Arts' in Imperial Russia 1700–1917. State, Society, Opposition. Essays in Honor of Marc Raeff, edited by Ezra Mendelsohn and Marshall Shatz. Northern Illinois Press, 1988, pp. 37–57.)

Catherine's flair for the grand occasion should be seen as a counterpart to her detailed instructions on protocol to her ambassadors abroad: it transmitted her own prestige and Russia's, it spread the message of Russia's enlightenment and power. If she laid it on with a trowel, this probably also reflected her consciousness of a lack of lawful claim to the throne and the unprepossessing circumstances of her accession. (On the murder of her husband, Peter III. Oleg Ivanov has published some important articles in Moskovsky Zhurnal, Nos. 9, 11–12, 1995 1–3, 1996.)

This murky background had not merely to be lived down but transcended and magicked away by the grandeur of her chosen figurative persona as 'Minerva Triumphant' and 'All-wise Mother of the Fatherland', suggesting the advent of wisdom and enlightenment in the person of the spiritual descendant of Peter the Great. Catherine's victory celebrations over Turkey were breathtaking demonstrations of state power, while Oleg Nesterov reminds us of the ambitious symbolism of naming her grandsons after Alexander the Great and Constantine the Great.

Yet Catherine could successfully combine imperial grandeur and its neo-classical expression in architecture and the arts with a cluster of more intimate attitudes associated with Roman humanitas and Enlightenment humanite and a personal informality that set strangers at their ease. Natal'ia Vulich explains how the buildings which Catherine commissioned from Charles Cameron were intended to combine symbols of stoic greatness with ideas of epicurean friendship. The recent conference in St Petersburg began and ended in Catherine's private Hermitage Theatre at the Winter Palace, designed for her by Quarenghi and combining classical splendour with informality and agreement. The conference closed with a performance of items from a grandiose Russian 'historical drama' set to music by eighteenth-century Italian and Russian composers to a libretto written by Catherine herself in 'imitation of Shakespeare'. It was first performed in the self-same theatre in 1790.

On the vexed problem of serfdom, which, whatever her original hopes clearly expressed in the Nakaz, nevertheless reached its apogee in her reign, Alexander Kamensky took a swipe at the cliches of Marxist historiography and insisted on Catherine's absolute sincerity in wishing to mitigate serfdom, but pointed out that at the time of her accession the nobility had only just consolidated a near total monopoly in serf-ownership and did not take lightly to attempts to infringe their newly won privileges. Catherine attacked serfdom at her peril. She could try persuasion, but ultimately her powers were limited and she always recognised the need to take public opinion with her.

The Pugachov rebellion of 1773–4 made her particularly sensitive to the risk of any fresh shocks to the social or political order, and she came to accept the inevitability of gradualness. (See Roger Bartlett, 'The Question of Serfdom: Catherine II and the Russian Debate and the View from the Baltic Periphery' in Russia in the Age of the Enlightenment, pp. 142–66, and 'Defences of Serfdom in Eighteenth-Century Russia' in A Window on Russia, pp. 67–74.)

What went wrong? Despite her unflagging energy and conscientiousness, Catherine became increasingly aware from experience of the enormity of what she had taken on with such initial confidence. Russian historians still suggest answers in terms of the unfavourable reactions of her advisers to some of the proposals in the Nakaz; of the lack of a 'third estate' which she hoped to nurture; of the upheaval of the Pugachov rebellion and of the French Revolution, which made her perceive dangers in some of the ideas which she had formerly encouraged. Nevertheless, both Kamensky and Omel'chenko emphasise the extent and depth of her overall achievements across the reign and her fidelity to her original aims. She used the information gleaned from the Legislative Commission as the groundwork for the reorganisation and regularisation of provincial and municipal government on a solid basis, so that, as Omel'chenko claims, 'the law reforms of "enlightened absolutism" were basically realised in 1774–87'.

Throughout her reign Catherine remained an avowed believer in absolute rule as a historical and political necessity in Russia, even if, as Omel'chenko argues, she was at the same time 'the greatest theoretician and practician of "law-based" monarchy' in eighteenth-century Europe, who laid down guidelines for the exercise of power and in 1787 even contemplated introducing some form of 'fundamental law'. At all times she remained true to her Nakaz, where she declared that 'the ruler of Russia is absolute: for no power, other than that concentrated in his person, can operate with the effectiveness required by such a vast state . . . Any other form of government would be . . . fatal to Russia'.

Catherine tempered her exercise of power with fact and affability. 'Be gentle, humane, accessible, sympathetic and liberal', she urged in a set of maxims intended for herself and copy of Fenelon's Telemaque), adding, however, 'and never let this kindness undermine your authority'. Her own touch remained sensitive and sure. All her proposed measures were most carefully prepared, going through many drafts at her hands, were referred by her to special advisory commissions and tested out on her advisers.

The classic victim of her reaction against her earlier optimism was Alexander Radishchev, exiled to Siberia after the publication in 1790 of his Journey from St Petersburg to Moscow, which hit out at absolutism and by implication at her own government. Even before that she revealed occasional hints of depression and doubts about the durability of her achievements. In a note of 1787 she minuted: 'will not my labours, care and warm concern for the good of the Empire be in vain, for I do see that I cannot make my frame of mind hereditary'.

Mikhail Safonov, however, dismisses the persistent rumour that Catherine intended to exclude Paul from the succession in favour of her grandson, Alexander. On the contrary, according to Safonov, she wished to establish the succession on the firm basis of primogeniture in the male line (the principle enacted by Paul himself). If this is so, it is a paradox, that this legendary woman sought to prevent any other of her sex from following her own example.

ANTONY LENTIN is Reader in History at the Open University. His latest book is an edition and translation of *Peter the Great: His Law on the Imperial Succession,* 1722. The Official Commentary. (Headstart History, Oxford, 1996).

As Good as Gold?

Not always. Money in America has gone from crops to bullion to greenbacks to electronic markers—igniting political and economic crises along the way

T. J. STILES

It's a typical Friday for a typical American—and that means payday. Over her lunch hour, she makes a pilgrimage to the bank; on the screen of an automatic teller machine, she sees the reassuring numbers: her employer has deposited her wages into her checking account. She spends the rest of the hour paying her bills—settling some through the Internet, by authorizing deductions from her bank balance. Her employer has automatically subtracted her health-insurance premium, her retirement-plan contribution and her taxes.

In a few hours she has participated in numerous transactions involving thousands of dollars, yet she has not handled one slip of physical currency. She organizes her entire life around this day—and she never gives a thought to the invisibility of her money. A few numbers on a computer screen, a poorly printed ATM receipt and a computerized voice on the phone are all the evidence she needs that the money is there.

So what exactly *is* money? It's a question that has become harder to answer, as we use less and less actual cash. Maybe one place to go for a solution is 80 feet beneath the steel and concrete forest of Manhattan's financial district, inside the international gold vault. Maintained by the Federal Reserve Bank of New York, it contains the largest hoard of monetary gold on the planet. A quarter of the world's reserves lie there, stacked floor to ceiling, bar after very heavy bar, in dozens of locked cages according to country.

Impressive as this pile may be, it suffers from a serious problem: it really isn't money anymore. Today, we cannot walk into a store, plunk down a chunk of gold and buy something. A debit card will do, but not bullion. It is not, as the economists say, a generally accepted means of payment.

And those two little words, "generally accepted," hold the secret meaning of money—and how it has melted from some of the heaviest of metals to mere electronic markers. Money is not merely a measuring system for value; it is also a thing that everyone is willing to accept for payment for everything else, all the time.

But what happens when a large proportion of the public remains on the ledge, refusing to make that leap of faith? The answer is crisis—and just such a crisis dominated much of American history, shaping politics and tearing apart communities. The fight over how to define money created political parties, made and destroyed Presidential candidates and rang in depressions.

This long debate tells us a great deal about the nature of money, because at the center of the argument was the question of how abstract it should be. A substance intrinsically valuable, or an item we invent as needed? The issue dogged Americans for some 300 years, because we faced a critical problem: a drastic, ongoing shortage of cash.

Consider Gov. Thomas Dudley of Massachusetts Bay. In 1624 he met with two ambassadors from the Pequots, the colony's powerful Native American neighbors, who came to discuss reparations for the recent murder of an Englishman by the tribe. Dudley's demands: a few dozen furs and a large cash payment—specifically, some 2,400 feet of wampum.

Wampum—strings of shell beads—served an important ceremonial function among the Native American nations of the Northeast. And when the Indians began to ask for it as payment for their furs, it became almost as important to the colonists. Soon after Governor Dudley's talks with the Pequots, Massachusetts made wampum legal tender.

Wampum was not the colonists' first choice for cash. In the world they left behind, money was mostly gold and silver coin. But throughout the colonial era, the British government banned the export of coin across the Atlantic. Even when colonists began to acquire Spanish silver through trade with the West Indies, much of it went straight to England to pay for imports. Colonists made a few attempts to establish their own mints, but London quickly quashed them. The result was an often catastrophic shortage of money.

"We were in the Years 1721 and 1722," declared the Pennsylvania legislature, "so effectually drained of our Coin . . . that the Inhabitants of every Degree were reduced to the greatest Straits; Debts could not be discharged, nor Payments be made; the Rents of Houses fell, many whereof were deserted; Artificers and Traders were obliged to quit the Country."

In desperation, the colonies began to invent money for themselves. At first, they made existing commodities the official standard. In South Carolina, rice, peas, beef and even pork were used as monetary commodities; Virginia began to set prices in terms of tobacco as early as 1619, and shortly afterward made it legal tender. The colony established warehouses where it stored bales of tobacco; it settled bills by paying out receipts for the leaf deposited there. Taxes, even salaries were paid in these "tobacco notes," which circulated publicly and privately as a kind of paper money.

Some colonies turned to paper currency or bills of credit. Generally speaking, the issuing government would make the bills legal tender, set a terminal redemption date (usually five years or so) and establish a special tax to build a fund to pay off the notes in coin at that time.

In the Western world, legal-tender paper money (first issued by Massachusetts in 1690) was an American innovation. Despite plenty of problems, the coin-poor public loved it. In fact, one of the lesser-known provocations leading to the Revolution was an act of Parliament in 1764 that banned the issuance of paper currency in all the colonies (a band had been issued for New England in 1751). Many colonists saw the law in the context of the Sugar Act, the Stamp Act, the Quartering Act and the Townshend duties—which seemed to be a determined program by Parliament to suppress American autonomy.

Once the colonies organized the Second Continental Congress in 1775, Americans got more paper money than they ever wanted. Congress tried to finance the war of independence by issuing notes called continentals. It pledged to print no more after the first batch—then proceeded to flood the economy with more than $200 million by 1780. These legal-tender bills became virtually worthless. In desperation, Congress turned to one of the wealthiest—and shrewdest—men in the new Republic, Robert Morris of Philadelphia.

Almost from the beginning, Morris served as the financial godfather of the Revolution. In early 1777, for example, right after George Washington won a great victory at Trenton, New Jersey, the general saw a chance to strike a second blow against the British—but many of his troops had reached the end of their terms of enlistment. Washington promised a $10 bounty to each man who stayed on for six more weeks; then he wrote a frantic appeal to Morris for the money. "I am up very early this morning to despatch a supply of $50,000 to your Excellency," Morris wrote back. The general scored another success at Princeton.

Morris accomplished a similar feat in 1781, during the critical Yorktown campaign. This time Washington was desperate for supplies. Morris mobilized his wealthy friends, pledging his personal fortune as security for purchases of flour, cattle and boats.

By the time Washington won that final victory of the war, Congress had named Morris the Superintendent of Finance. Once again, he put his own good credit to work as he rebuilt that of the government. At one point, he even circulated his own notes, backed by his personal wealth. His bills were considered as good as precious-metal coin in the marketplace (thanks to Morris' vast fortune).

He took the oath of office with two bullets in his body—and had once killed a man in a duel.

But Morris had no intention of bankrolling the new nation. He persuaded the Continental Congress to begin construction of a financial infrastructure. In 1781 Congress established the Bank of North America—the first federally chartered bank on these shores. It made loans to Congress, to be redeemed at specific intervals, allowing Morris to anticipate revenues and maintain sufficient cash flow.

After the disastrous experience with continentals, the Founders got out of the legal-tender business. They wrote a prohibition on state-issued currency into the Constitution, and Congress rested content with minting gold and silver coins. Paper money was left to banks. Usually banks would take deposits in gold and silver coin (or "specie," to use the technical term) and make loans by issuing paper notes. The public paid each other with these privately printed bills, assuming they could be redeemed at the issuing bank for precious-metal coin (or cash—as in "cold, hard cash"). Banks multiplied the supply of money; they issued paper worth two or three times their specie reserves, since it was unlikely all their notes would be returned at once.

All this raised the abstraction of money to bewildering proportions. Gold and silver coin was still there at the heart of the system, tangible and real. But it tended to settle in the bellies of banks, which digested it and regurgitated paper notes. All kinds of notes. By 1860 there were no less than 1,562 state-chartered banks, and almost every one distributed its own variety of bills.

When that private-enterprise paper hit the marketplace, it fluctuated in value depending on how easily the notes could get "real" money (that is, specie). A merchant might insist on steeply discounting a note, when taking it as payment, because of the issuing bank's reputation. Distance mattered too: the farther away the bank, the harder to return its notes for coin.

This diverse, ad hoc currency aroused distrust and distaste—a sentiment expressed most belligerently by Andrew Jackson. No one better expressed American belligerence itself, for that matter: he once killed a man in a duel, and he was undoubtedly the only President who took the oath of office with two bullets in his body and then had one of them removed (without anesthesia) while in office. In one of his most famous acts as President, he crushed the Second Bank of the United States, a federally chartered giant that towered over the nation's financial structure.

But Jackson hated the entire currency system. He saw paper bills as a lot of mysterious mumbo jumbo, and bankers as a bunch of unproductive thieves who lived by other men's sweat. In 1836 Jackson drew up the Specie Circular, which decreed that federal lands would be sold only for coin—not the banknotes used by most westward-marching migrants. When consumers rushed to get specie for their notes, banks went down like dominoes, ushering in a stark depression that lasted until 1843.

That crisis was merely a bonfire compared with the firestorm of the Civil War—a conflagration that consumed everything in its path, including the country's currency. As the military and financial situation worsened in 1861, panicked note holders rushed to banks and demanded gold. By December, banks had stopped redeeming their notes. With previous metals hoarded and hidden, paper money depreciated radically.

Figure 1   Personnel inside the international gold vault at the Federal Reserve Bank of New York, which stores more than 600,000 bars of bullion from 60 countries, tally up a shipment.

Note: Federal Reserve Bank of New York

It fell to Congressman Elbridge G. Spaulding, a banker, to solve the crunch. He authored an act for a national paper currency that became known as legal-tenders, or, more commonly, greenbacks. After July 1, 1863, these notes were used for all debts except customs duties, and they could not be redeemed for specie.

The immensity of this innovation can easily be missed, as we look back from our specie-free society. But at the time it was stunning. Unlike virtually every other paper note in American history, the greenback did not represent an underlying commodity. It could not be redeemed in gold or silver—or tobacco, or wampum—then or in the future.

Probably the first thing the greenback purchased was outrage. "Gold and silver are the only true measure of value," one influential banker thundered. "These metals were prepared by the Almighty."

"I prefer gold to paper money," agreed Senator John Sherman. "But there is no other resort. We must have money or a fractured Government." But critics found plenty of ammunition in a rather peculiar market in New York City that the greenback created, known as the Gold Room.

For the first time, gold had a price. The law recognized the greenback and the old gold dollar as equals, but in the Gold Room (officially established in 1864), traders exchanged the two kinds of money, paying extra greenbacks for the rarer gold. The market, in fact, was an economic necessity, since international

purchases were made in the yellow metal, while the domestic economy used paper money almost exclusively.

For Jay Gould, the market would be a hunting ground. In 1869 the famed financier and his friend and partner, James Fish, Jr., had just made their mark on Wall Street by besting Cornelius Vanderbilt in a fight for the Erie Railroad. Now Gould led his friend to the Gold Room.

On the surface, Gould's plan was simple: he would corner the market. That is, he would create a general craze for gold by purchasing massive quantities and convincing brokers and the public that the price would keep climbing. As buyers joined the frenzy, the price of gold would shoot up.

The primary threat to Gould's scheme was the U.S. Treasury, the biggest player in the market. It could undercut the price of gold through its large sales of the specie it acquired through customs duties. So Gould spun a web of intrigue around the new President, Ulysses S. Grant. The financier bribed Grant's brother-in-law, Abel Corbin, to argue for a freeze on U.S. gold sales. Gould corrupted Daniel S. Butterfield, the assistant treasurer in New York, for inside information.

On June 15, 1869, Gould and Fish lobbied Grant himself on a passage to Boston aboard one of Gould's steamships. "We went down to dinner about nine o'clock," Fisk recalled, "intending while we were there to have the thing pretty thoroughly talked up, and, if possible to relieve him of any idea of putting the price of gold down." They came in for a shock: Grant was not interested.

But Gould knew that perception was as important as reality in the markets, so he created the impression that Grant was solidly behind them. Apparently, Gould even set up an account for First Lady Julia Dent Grant. "Mr. Gould," Fisk later told Congress, "sold $500,000 of gold belonging to Mrs. Grant . . . leaving her a balance of about $27,000." In September, the price of the precious metal went up, thanks in part to the two financiers' purchases and shrewd use of the press. Desperate to drive the market still higher, the conspirators pressured Abel Corbin to send the President one last plea for a moratorium on Treasury gold sales.

Gould had gone too far. Grant, too, had heard the rumors of his own complicity; when Corbin's note interrupted a croquet game, Grant angrily ordered his wife to write back and tell Corbin, "My husband is very much annoyed with your speculations. You must close them as quick as you can!"

"Mr. Corbin, I am undone if that letter gets out," Gould said. "If you will remain in and take the chances of the market I will give you my check for $100,000." Then the mogul left for the Gold Room, where he bid the price to new heights.

Then, unknown to everyone—even his partners—Gould began selling the bulk of his gold. And for good reason: Grant quickly ordered his Treasury secretary to dump gold on the market to stop the craze. A sale of $4 million in government specie was all it took to shatter the confidence of speculators. The market crashed on September 24, 1869, a day immediately dubbed Black Friday. Fisk later summed up the disaster succinctly: it was "each man drag out his own corpse." Gould, however, strolled away, very much alive, with a rumored $11 million in profits.

Black Friday added to a growing sense that America's money had become too abstract, too detached from the physical and metaphorical weightiness of precious metals. Congress suffered from nagging worries that the greenback was somehow dishonest—that, with the war over, a proud nation should redeem its currency in gold. The debate had even permeated the impeachment trial of Andrew Johnson in 1868. Many Republican senators had been reluctant to convict him because his designated successor, Senator Benjamin Wade, was a "soft money" man who wanted to print more greenbacks.

But to cash-starved Westerners and Southerners, legal tenders meant relief. When the Supreme Court declared the legal-tender laws (and thus greenbacks for certain debts) unconstitutional in 1870, Grant won popular acclaim by adding two new appointments to the Court to overturn the decision in 1871.

The fight between hard money and soft money dominated politics, due to the continuing money shortage after the Civil War: in 1879 there were only $72 per person in existence. While hard-money men pleaded for the honesty of the gold standard, soft-money advocates believed that there just wasn't enough specie to keep up with economic expansion.

Such conditions led to the rise of the descriptively named Greenback party. It briefly proved to be one of the most successful third-party movements in history: it won a million votes in 1878, electing 14 Congressmen. Nevertheless, the nation went back on the gold standard in 1879. Then a strange thing happened: the debate suddenly ended. The former Greenbackers gave in to the idea that paper currency had to be backed up by

precious metals. True, they still wanted to expand the money supply; but now they argued that silver should be added to gold as the specie basis of the currency—an idea called bimetallism. William Jennings Bryan, for example, won the Democratic nomination for the Presidency in 1896 with his "Cross of Gold" speech, which summed up Western and rural fury with Eastern gold-standard purists. But despite the intensity of the debate, the real war of ideas was over: the dollar, they agreed, had to be intrinsically valuable.

Ironically, money was simultaneously becoming more and more abstract in actual practice. The culprits were the banks, which spread rapidly into even rural areas after the Civil War. Banks, in fact, were becoming the medium of the medium of exchange, as the checking account began to replace actual notes.

Money was now largely a matter of ledger books, not stacks of gold or even paper notes. The establishment of the Federal Reserve System (known as the Fed) in 1913 confirmed this trend. Its 12 regional banks held the reserve accounts for member institutions; when checks cleared between banks, the Fed would make a ledger entry, deducting one reserve account and crediting another.

As a result of the New Deal reforms, American money is more abstract than ever.

The Fed also controlled the supply of paper currency: the new Federal Reserve note, the first version of the bills we use today. More importantly, the Fed could make it more or less costly for banks to expand their reserves and thus their loans. This system is still largely in place today.

But the cable that held the drifting supply of money to the deadweight of gold had not yet been cut. Each bank still had to maintain a fund for redeeming notes in specie; the amount of gold set an absolute limit on the number of dollars in circulation—as the nation would soon learn.

On October 24, 1929, the greatest financial panic in American history rolled across the economy like a tsunami, leaving behind a wrecked and desolate country. Endless debates have raged over the causes of the crisis, but the results were all too clear: the money supply simply shriveled. Frightened depositors emptied their accounts to get cash; frightened banks called in loans. For many, even Federal Reserve notes weren't good enough: they handed them over for gold, which they hoarded. By 1933 the money supply had shrunk by at least a quarter; more than 5,000 banks had come crashing down.

As Franklin Delano Roosevelt entered the White House that March, he realized that the currency had to be freed from the anchor of gold. Soon after taking the oath of office, he issued an extraordinary executive order that nationalized the nation's coin and bullion: gold was to be handed over to the Treasury, in return for Federal Reserve notes (which were more likely to circulate). With Congress's help, Roosevelt made it illegal to own gold (except for industrial and artistic purposes); he also stopped minting gold coins and redeeming paper dollars for gold.

But behind the scenes more subtle and much farther-reaching plans were being prepared. For all of the psychological importance of specie and Federal Reserve notes, the real job of making new money fell not to government printing presses but to the loan offices of banks.

In earlier times, consumers needed to trust in specie redemption before they would accept paper notes; now they had to trust in the durability of banks before they would make deposits, take out loans, or write and accept checks. So the federal government quietly poured a billion dollars into bank stocks and established the Federal Deposit Insurance Corporation (which reassured consumers that they would not lose their savings if a bank went belly-up).

As a result of the New Deal reforms, American money is more abstract than ever before. It also works better than it ever has. Since the end of the Great Depression, the United States has not suffered a single financial panic—a stretch of more than 60 years, the longest in history.

Most dollars today have no physical existence. Even ledger books began to disappear in the 1960s and '70s, replaced by computer records. The Federal Reserve System processes an average of $2.1 trillion each day through an electronic network known as Fedwire. Meanwhile, credit card companies, insurance companies, mortgage firms and retirement funds (among others) compete with banks to generate loans.

The gold standard has sunk without a trace in this vast and complex sea of financial institutions—but it did not immediately die off in 1933. Under the Bretton Woods accord of 1944, the value of the dollar was set at $35 per ounce of gold, but only dollars held by foreign officials could be redeemed for U.S. specie (most of which was, and is, kept at Fort Knox, Kentucky). At the gold vault under the Federal Reserve Bank of New York, countries could pay each other simply by shifting so many bars from one cage to another. But a severe drain on American gold reserves caused the United States to restrict and ultimately halt specie payments, leading to the end of the international gold standard in 1971.

Today, the New York gold vault sits mostly in silence. Although individual transactions are kept secret, those that occur are generally withdrawals, as nations sell bullion on the open market. A lot of its daily activity consists of visits by tourists—a fitting reminder that the vault is essentially a curiosity, a throwback to the age when Americans believed that money had to be something valuable in and of itself. Now money is largely a unit of account—it exists simply because we say it is there. And gold is just another asset like stocks, bonds or real estate—except it is less popular as an investment.

In American history, money has gone from tobacco to gold to greenbacks to ledger books to electrons. Today our institutionalized, interconnected economy resembles an electronic circuit, with money constantly flowing through it like an electric current. No, not *like* an electric current—it *is* an electric current, powering our globally wired world.

T. J. STILES began the study of money and banking as part of his research for his forthcoming biography of *Jesse James*.

A Woman Writ Large in Our History and Hearts

The free-spirited author George Sand scandalized 19th-century Paris when she defied convention and pioneered an independent path for women

ROBERT WERNICK

It can be plausibly argued that one of the critical steps toward the emancipation of women and the expansion of their world was taken one afternoon in November 1830, at the lovely chateau of Nohant in the center of France. Today, thousands of pilgrims visit that literary shrine each year, arriving from the world over to pay their respects to the famous writer who spent half her life there, George Sand.

The visitors find everything so peaceful here, the 18th-century architecture so airy and comfortable and elegant, the dining table set so properly with its place cards for M. Flaubert and M. Turgenev and Prince Jerome Napoleon. The walls are so stately with their family portraits and pale-blue paper, the views so lovely of the rich fields and woodlands of the old province of Berry, that it is hard to associate this gracious place, recently subject to a loving restoration, with a revolutionary event. George Sand's stand for freedom, taken in these spacious rooms, could be said to have had greater consequences than that year's uprising in Paris, which had overthrown the last of the Bourbon kings.

George Sand was not yet George Sand in 1830. She was the baroness Aurore Dudevant (née Dupin), 26 years old, a handsome, hot-blooded, thoroughly unhappy woman living with her husband and two little children on the estate she had inherited from her grandmother. She was rummaging through her husband's desk that day, looking for some paper she had misplaced, when she came across a bulky envelope with her name on it and written below it the words "Only To Be Opened After My Death." Since it was addressed to her, she saw no reason not to open it. The missive turned out to be full of violent abuse, all the resentments and disapprovals that had been simmering for the eight years of a marriage between two people who had nothing in common.

It was perhaps the pretext she had been looking for; in any event, something snapped inside her at that moment. She summoned her husband and told him that she was tired of living with a drunken oaf who fell asleep when she talked about books

or played the piano, and that she was moving to Paris to make a living there by writing books. She would live her own life in her own way. She needed his consent to do it, for though the property and most of the money was her own, the law decreed that a married woman was incapable of handling her own business affairs and that all the checks had to be signed by the husband. This particular husband was a great hunter and a heavy drinker, but he was no match for her in character. She bullied him into accepting her terms and giving her a small allowance when she went off to Paris. He could have had no idea that he was helping to inaugurate a new era in human history.

Within a few weeks, the baroness had packed her bags and kissed her children goodbye. (She and Casimir would manage to share custody of the children for a while; eventually, they would live with her.) She took the diligence for Paris, where she attracted immediate attention by wearing masculine attire, featuring trousers, top hat and cravat, a sight calculated to turn heads anywhere. Almost immediately, she began selling articles and short stories to newspapers and became an active member of a hitherto all-male circle of talkative, turbulent students and artists. She was living in rooms overlooking the Seine with a curly-haired young man named Jules Sandeau; they had met at a party the previous year and Sandeau had told her that he was a writer.

They agreed to collaborate and in short order had written two novels that were snapped up by a publisher. Sand did not want her given name on the title page, for the public would not take such a book seriously, and so they concocted a joint asexual pseudonym, J. Sand. When she realized that she was doing most of the work, she decided to strike out on her own.

She produced a remarkable novel called *Indiana,* about a beautiful young bride married to a dull brute. Her heroine is wooed by a cynical cad for whom she is willing to sacrifice all, but he prefers instead to make a safe and conveniently profitable marriage. In the end, she discovers her true love and disregards opprobrium in order to run off with him. Indiana, wrote

Sand, represented "Choice at odds with Necessity; she is Love blindly butting its head against all the obstacles set in its path by civilization."

A friend suggested that she might lure all the J. Sand fans into buying the book by changing a single letter, which no one would be likely to notice. So the author's name became G. Sand, and the *G,* she decided, would stand for George. It was the name by which she was to be known forevermore. *Indiana* was an instant success. She wrote another novel, and then another.

That was to be only the beginning of her aspirations.

The pants she wore were primarily a matter of practical convenience: you could not work in newspaper offices and run around with all the bright young writers and artists or even sit in the orchestra at theaters (ladies were supposed to sit in expensive boxes) if you were hobbled by ballooning skirts. They were also, like the cigars she smoked, an unmistakable signal of revolt: they announced her intention to turn law and society and traditional modes of thought upside down and put an end to the age-old tyranny of men over women.

She was going to live like a man, make money like a man, have love affairs the way every famous man from Saint Augustine to Lord Byron had done, and do it all without giving up any of what the world regarded as traditional feminine attributes: she would be a good cook and housekeeper, managing half a dozen servants and a sizable estate. She would be a good mother, and she would be flighty and flirty, letting emotion run her life when the right lover came along.

She was only trying to be completely honest and completely independent: "I ask the support of no one, neither to kill someone for me, gather a bouquet, correct a proof, nor to go with me to the theater. I go there on my own, as a man, by choice; and when I want flowers, I go on foot, by myself, to the Alps." After all the millennia of female servitude, she would be Spartacus showing the way to freedom.

She was not quite as radical as she sounded to the horrified conservatives of her day. She did not propose to do away with marriage; she only wanted the wife to have equal rights with the husband. She wanted marriage to stop being a business arrangement between families and become a loving union between two human beings.

Since she was a child of the Romantic Age, she had high standards for love. She maintained that life should be ruled by emotion and instinct, by the heart rather than the brain. In practice, however, she was not quite that simpleminded.

She would follow her heart anywhere, but the love she dreamed of had to involve the complete "embrace of twin souls." Such accords and embraces were as hard to come by in the 19th century as they are in the 20th, and it is no wonder that her love life was marked by a series of disillusionments. So was her political life, where her hatred of oppression and poverty led her to join revolutionary causes with boundless enthusiasm, only to find that when her heroes came to power, after years of shouting for the people, they soon began to think only of Me Me Me.

Underneath the swirling tides of her romantic impulses was a bedrock of common sense. Where other Romantics like Lord Byron and Alfred de Musset would turn from unattainable ideals to cynical debauchery and early death, she had the capacity for looking over her ideals coolly and, finding them wanting, going on to something else. But she never lost her faith that the future was brighter than the past and that the future did indeed mean freedom. "My profession," she said, "is to be free."

A proposal to live by this code was amazing enough coming from a somnolent backwater in the hidebound society of early 19th-century France. Still more amazing was that she got away with it. By the time she died in 1876 at the age of 72, mourned by adoring grandchildren and local villagers, she was universally recognized as one of the giant figures of the era. Though little of her vast output is still read today, she counts as one of the notable writers of France.

She understood, cannily, that literature was one of the few domains where women had the slightest chance of getting ahead in the world. There was no hope in the church or the state or commerce, but there was a long if subdued tradition of women in the arts. A handful of successful women novelists had received grudging recognition: Fanny Burney, Madame de Staël, Jane Austen. They had all operated on the sidelines.

Aurore Dupin was going to get into the thick of the professional literary world. She knew she could write well and she had plenty to write about. Few novelists have had so much family and youthful background to draw upon.

On her mother's side, she came from the back alleys of Paris, where her grandfather had peddled birds. On her father's, she was related to the last three Bourbon kings of France, through her great-great-grandfather Frederick Augustus, elector of Saxony and king of Poland. By his favorite mistress, Countess Aurora von Koenigsmark, the most beautiful woman of her time, Augustus produced the most famous of his 360 or so illegitimate children, the Maréchal de Saxe.

De Saxe was one of the most successful of French generals—there is a great broad avenue named for him in the heart of Paris. He in turn had numerous offspring, including one Aurore de Saxe. She married a rich tax collector named Dupin de Francueil and became one of those handsome free-thinking, art-loving aristocratic ladies who set the tone of French life in the 18th century. She was a friend of Voltaire and Rousseau; she used to tell her granddaughter that, in the days before the revolution, living well was an art: everyone went on enjoying good food, savoring intellectual conversation, delighting in good music every day of their lives. (As her granddaughter observed, it was a great life if you were assured of a steady income of 500,000 francs a year.)

Aurore de Saxe had one son, Maurice, who served in the military, fighting for the revolution and for Napoleon. After the battle of Marengo he met up with the beautiful Sophie Delaborde, who had made what living she could in cabarets, dancing and meeting army officers. He married her a month before the birth of their daughter, and despite the efforts of his mother to annul the marriage, the little girl was born with an honest name, Aurore Dupin.

By the time she married the baron Casimir Dudevant at the age of 18 in 1822, Aurore Dupin had lived in a Paris garret, in her grandmother's chateau, in a palace in Madrid (when her father was aide-de-camp to General Murat, who had just gobbled up Spain for his brother-in-law Napoleon Bonaparte). She had, from afar, witnessed a battle and seen Napoleon review his troops. She had experienced the tragedy of her father's death: he had been killed when his wild Spanish stallion threw him against a tree near Nohant on his way home one night. She had fed pigs with the neighboring peasant children and had spent three years in a school for young ladies of good family run by English nuns in Paris.

The convent was the very place inhabited by her grandmother during the Reign of Terror. Then it was a jail, and Madame de Saxe was locked up there. (One day, or so one story goes, her 15-year-old son had come to whisper to her how he and his tutor had crept in the dead of night to the apartment from which they had been expelled, and had detached the seals that the police had put on the doors. They searched out and burned compromising documents that would have sent her to the guillotine and resealed the doors without waking up a soul.)

Aurore Dupin knew how to gallop astride a horse (to the outrage of respectable neighbors who expected her to ride sidesaddle like a lady). She knew how to sew, draw and play the piano. She could speak fluent English and had a command of Latin. And she could tell stories that would hold her mother and her aunt spellbound.

She also had inherited a remarkably robust constitution from the kings and tavern-keepers who were her ancestors. She could walk for miles in a day and delighted in hiking the Alps. In her later years, she swam in the Indre River at what was then the very advanced age of 70.

She had a truly extraordinary capacity for work. Whatever was going on at any time in the breakneck pace of her complex life—whether it was Chopin or Liszt playing piano in the living room, or revolutionists being shot down on their barricades outside her window in a Paris street, or Jules Sandeau climbing a ladder to her bedroom while her husband snored down the hall, or 18 people coming to dinner—she was never far from her writing desk. She herself might be traversing the countryside collecting plants and flowers or nursing sick neighbors. She might discourse into the small hours with artists, actresses, revolutionary agitators. Or she might design and sew the costumes for her son's marionette theater, or stay up all night talking and drinking and running her fingers through some young poet's hair. No matter: she unfailingly turned out her 20 or more pages a day. Even so, the royalties were hardly ever sufficient to pay for her lavish hospitality, her boundless generosity to friends, lovers, neighbors, political causes.

The work did not exhaust her energy. "Unceasingly I see her hovering anxiously over me," wrote Chopin of the ghastly winter they spent in Majorca, where it rained all the time, where he spat blood and people avoided them like lepers, "nursing me all by herself, for God preserve us from the doctors of that country, making my bed, cleaning my room, depriving herself of everything for me, watching over the children as well . . . add to this, that she continues to write." In fact, she finished a novel in Majorca.

Balzac would write after a visit to Nohant: "She lives almost exactly as I do. She goes to bed at six in the morning and gets up at midday, whereas I go to bed at six in the evening and get up at midnight. But naturally I fitted in with her arrangements,

and during three days we talked from five in the evening after dinner, until five in the morning." By keeping such hours, the burly Balzac wore himself out and died before he was 52. Little (barely five feet) George Sand took it all in her stride. She was working on yet another novel (she wrote about 70 in all) when she died in 1876 at the age of 72.

She had written, in addition, many short stories, 24 plays, ten volumes of autobiography, essays, book reviews, political pamphlets and an estimated 40,000 letters, of which 22,000 have been printed. Her complete works now number 160 volumes, and they do not include hundreds of newspaper and magazine articles, or the thousands of lost letters, some of which were burned by their recipients to keep them from the eyes of their children.

She wrote about everything that came to hand: love, adventure, foreign lands and secret societies, Roman prelates and rapacious pirates, corrupt noblemen and hardworking peasants, absolutely anything that she fancied.

In her day she was one of the half dozen most widely read novelists of the Western world. She was extravagantly admired by people as different as Dostoyevsky, Walt Whitman and Elizabeth Barrett Browning (who wrote two sonnets dedicated to "Thou large-brained woman and large-hearted man, Self-called George Sand!" She was extravagantly denounced as well: by the Vatican, which repeatedly put her on the index of books no good Catholic was allowed to read, and by Charles Baudelaire, who called her a "latrine," a "great fool" and a "stupid creature."

Her reputation as a writer has not stood up very well, and though feminist scholars have revived interest in her works, it is unlikely that she will ever regain the worldwide popularity she acquired in her lifetime. Librarians and booksellers report few requests for her books. She is too long-winded and preachy, her optimism too syrupy, for modern tastes. Witness this passage from *Indiana,* wherein the heroine decries the wrongs visited upon her: "The law of this country has made you my master. You can bind my body, tie my hands, govern my actions. You are the strongest, and society adds to your power—but with my will, sir, you can do nothing. God alone can restrain it and curb it. Seek then a law, a dungeon, an instrument of torture, by which you can hold it—as if you wished to grasp the air, and seize nothing." But there are many unexpected pleasures to be derived from dipping at random into that immense mass of work, for she had a keen eye and a warm heart and a lively forthright style.

She may seem old-fashioned today, a writer of "charming improbable romances for initiated persons of the optimistic class," as Henry James called her, but in her time she was hailed, or reviled, as an innovator, bringing something radically new into literature. She was one of the first novelists, male or female, to treat marriage not as the goal and fulfillment of a maiden's desire, but as a fact of life, which in most cases meant a commercial contract leading to a life of submission and servitude.

She was a trailblazer, too, in dealing with a class of people that had largely been neglected by playwrights and novelists and historians alike: the working poor.

George Sand was among the first serious writers to attempt an account of their lives. She knew perfectly well that, even in a fairly prosperous region like Berry, the rural poor were condemned to a hard, squalid, stifling life. She didn't dare to show all the squalor, for fear of alienating her bourgeois readers, whom she wanted to make aware of the fundamental decency and dignity of these people. So her picture of the life of poverty is apt to seem sentimental to the modern reader.

She never had the gift for creating unforgettable characters like her contemporaries Balzac and Dickens—at least in her novels, for in real life she did create one character that seems sure to live on indefinitely. That character is, of course, George Sand, a fascinating and complex mixture of passion and reason, wildness and domesticity, frankness and hypocrisy.

In the summer of 1833 she wrote her friend and confidant the critic Sainte-Beuve: "I have fallen in love, and this time very seriously, with Alfred de Musset. . . . You may, perhaps, think that a woman should conceal her feelings: but I beg you to realize that I am in a quite exceptional situation, and am compelled, from now on, to live my private life in the full light of day."

These are words that would come naturally from the lips of any Princess of Wales or Hollywood starlet today. In 1833 they were—for a woman—quite revolutionary indeed.

She was not, like so many of today's celebrities, just putting on a show for the public. She was always following her heart, or her good sense when she realized her heart had led her astray. One way or the other, it made good copy everywhere.

The whole world was watching as she departed with Alfred de Musset, the delicate dandified poet six years her junior, for Italy, land of dreams and desire, from the moment they got aboard a paddle steamer in Marseilles on December 20, 1833. Coldly summarized, the couple's voyage looks as if it had been scripted a hundred and fifty years later by Woody Allen. The Mediterranean was rough, and George strode the deck blowing smoke at the elements. Alfred, who was sick as a dog, wrote a furious little quatrain to protest the reversal of traditional gender roles.

He got his revenge when they arrived in Venice at the hotel Danieli and George contracted a bad case of dysentery that knocked her out for days. Alfred went out night after night to drink and gamble, and pick up girls along the canals. A handsome young doctor named Pietro Pagello came to bleed George regularly.

Back in the hotel after she was healed, Alfred collapsed with what different biographers describe as typhoid, or perhaps brain, fever. He saw George and Pietro Pagello drinking tea out of the same cup. In his fever he saw much more, and threw a violent jealous fit.

Alfred gallantly went back to Paris alone. George stayed on happily in Venice till summer, then took Pagello back to Paris with her and introduced him to her friends as a famous archaeologist. (As usual, the romance did not work out.) Alfred eventually threw himself back into George's arms. There were passionate midnight meetings, the inevitable Sturm und Drang, and finally they broke up for good.

George, who had written two novels, a novelette and two essays about Venice during her stay there, eventually wrote a book about the whole experience. So did Musset. So did Alfred's

brother, and the actress who succeeded George in Alfred's affections. Doctor Pagello lived on in Venice till the age of 91, a local celebrity because of his liaison with the famous, or infamous, George Sand.

Within a month of her finally writing off Musset, she was passionately in love with a married man, a well-known lawyer named Michel de Bourges. Unlike most of her other lovers, he was quite a bit older than she was, and ugly and bald. But he had a golden tongue. He helped win the case against Baron Dudevant for separation (there was no such thing as divorce in France at that time).

But in 1837, less than two years into the affair, she broke things off. She had learned that, among other transgressions, her beloved had already taken another mistress.

Shortly afterward, she sat down to write a letter to herself coolly analyzing the impossibility of remaining attached to a man who wanted only her devotion and submission, who was not going to leave his wife or his comfortable way of life for her. That was the end of Michel de Bourges, and in 1838 she was willing and ready to take on Frédéric Chopin.

Chopin was a delicate, tubercular, morbidly punctilious, morbidly jealous genius, "frail as a snow-drop," said an American visitor, Margaret Fuller. To him George Sand would play alternately lover, muse, worshipful mother and devoted nurse for eight years. They were the years during which he wrote most of his best piano compositions and she some of her best novels, including the one that has been the most popular down to the present day, *La Mare au diable* (The Devil's Pool). It is a simple tale of love in the Berry countryside, of love triumphant over social convention, which she wrote in four days.

They were also years of squabbles with her daughter, Solange, now an adolescent with a roving eye. When it roved to Chopin and he responded, a tangle of jealousies and resentments ensued, also involving her son, Maurice, and Augustine, a poor cousin whom Sand had adopted. Augustine fell in love with Maurice, to the intense annoyance of Solange. She managed to turn Maurice against Augustine, Chopin against Maurice, George against Chopin. Solange married a brute of a sculptor who once attacked Maurice and George with a hammer. Everyone blamed everyone else, and the affair with Chopin, which might have gone on till his death a couple of years later, petered out unpleasantly.

Political turmoil followed domestic. Revolution erupted in 1848, spurred on by a wide variety of malcontents, from conservative republicans to socialists of various stripes. Sand, sympathetic to the plight of the people, poured out revolutionary rhetoric in countless pamphlets and open letters. A brief republic soon gave way, in a series of stages, to a Bonapartist dictatorship, headed by the nephew of Napoleon I, Louis-Napoleon Bonaparte. Republican and socialist hopes alike were dashed.

But as Sand grew older, she was losing her taste for adventure. She spent more and more time in Nohant, and it was a quieter time than any she had ever known. She had the longest lasting of all her love affairs, 15 years with a young painter named Alexandre Manceau, a devoted companion to whom she was very attached. She even left her estate for a time, moving with Manceau to a Paris suburb until 1865, when he died of tuberculosis.

She settled into an active old age at Nohant, playing with her grandchildren, writing and producing elaborate marionette shows with her son, entertaining guests by the dozen and writing novels steadily. She was an international celebrity by now; people came to see her from Russia, from America, everywhere. And although young people continued to adore her as a standard-bearer of revolt and liberation, her views of the world had calmed down considerably: she had in due course grown to detest radicalism; now she was all for moderation.

She never gave up her capacity to "live life as it is, without being ungrateful, fully aware that joy is neither enduring nor assured." Her last great affection, a purely platonic one this time, was for Flaubert. He admired her wholeheartedly, though he could never understand her taste for playing rowdy practical jokes when he wanted to talk about literature.

And when he wrote to her from the Swiss mountains where he had been sent to calm his nerves, "I am not a *man of nature,* I would trade all the glaciers in the world for the Vatican Library," she snapped back that he himself was a part of nature and he had better get used to it.

Nature was with her to the end. Almost the last words she uttered, when she was dying in agony of an intestinal cancer, were *"laissezverdure,"*—"let greenery"—perhaps because she was thinking for the last time of the great cedar trees at Nohant, planted at the birth of her two children almost half a century before.

If she had a time machine and were to come back to Nohant today, she might find much to displease her in modern life, but Nohant itself would undoubtedly have its consolations. Her house is much the way she left it, and so are the rolling grainfields and woodlands around it. The sturdy farmhouses of her neighbors look much the same; the farmers are little changed, though they now use tractors instead of teams of oxen for their planting.

She would be saddened by the loss of so many traditions: the ox-cart ruts that are now paved roads, the people who have been taught by their television sets to speak French instead of the throaty Berrichon patois she loved.

But then she was a creator of tradition, too, and she would take a generous delight in watching the women drive up on their visits to what is now a national monument, women who may keep house the way she did but also have careers such as she made for herself, as doctors, lawyers, cabinet ministers, professors of gender studies and presidents of international conglomerates. She would recognize them all as her grandchildren. "One day," she had predicted, "the world will understand me, and if this day never comes, no matter, I will have opened the way for other women.

The cedar trees still stand on the grounds of her estate.

Frequent contributor **ROBERT WERNICK** has written recently on sound bites and on the nativist political party of the mid-1800s, the Know-Nothings.

UNIT 3

The Industrial and Scientific Revolutions

Unit Selections

Key Points to Consider

• Why was it important to know about eyes and light? How did this affect later thinking?

• What were Isaac Newton's major contributions to the history of science? How does his work continue to influence our world today?

• What factors made the Industrial Revolution possible? What positives and negatives did it create?

• How was China able to develop a prototype for an Industrial Revolution? Why did it not last?

• What changes took place in Japan during the Meiji Regime during the last half of the 19th century? What role did the nation's first railroad play in these new developments?

• What obstacles had to be overcome before the transatlantic telegraph cable could be completed? What benefits were derived from such an accomplishment?

• What was controversial about the scientific achievements of Charles Darwin and Sigmund Freud? Why is the latter's work criticized more today?

• What major accomplishments have been made in the past century's scientific and technical changes? What problem, however, threatens to undo all the good that has been created?

Student Web Site

www.mhcls.com/online

Internet References

Further information regarding these Web sites may be found in this book's preface or online.

A Trip to the Past
   http://members.aol.com/mhirotsu/kevin/trip2.html
Center for Mars Exploration
   http://cmex-www.arc.nasa.gov/
Sir Isaac Newton
   http://www-gap.dcs.st-and.ac.uk/~history/Mathematicians/Newton.html

The roots of these two revolutions lie in a dramatic shift away from authority and toward observation, away from concept and toward evidence. When Abu Ali al-Hasan, a scientist living in what is now Basra, Iraq, solved the riddle of light, roughly a millennium ago, he refuted both Ptolemy and Aristotle. With a simple appeal to experience—asking people to look at the sun—he established that the source of light is outside the eye.

Sir Isaac Newton continued this pragmatic tilt with his explanatory laws—each based originally in keen observation. Watching an apple fall from a tree led him to postulate the existence of gravity. His most extraordinary discovery was that the same laws that held under the apple tree applied throughout the universe. Humans had come to realize their ability to understand the cosmos. Armed with the confident expectation that the basic laws underlying natural processes could be deciphered, human ingenuity set to work solving human problems.

We should not think of the industrial and scientific revolutions the way we think of political revolutions, such as the French and American Revolutions. Both of those were relatively quick and definitely dramatic. What we call the industrial revolution was, instead, centuries in the making, reaching back to the Middle Ages for its fundamental concepts. Powerful intellectual and religious assumptions needed to be modified before individuals dared to probe nature's deepest mysteries.

The mechanization of labor began in England, where resources, need, and opportunity combined to spur invention. Having used up its forest resources, Britain turned to coal for fuel. As miners dug deeper for coal, water accumulated in the pits, hampering progress. Thomas Newcomen, in the early eighteenth century, designed a practical steam engine to pump and drain the water. From coal mining and steam power had come a source of portable energy—more reliable than either wind or water power had been.

Ironically, Chinese scientists had developed the concepts of mechanization and mass production as early as the eleventh century. Unlike the British, however, the Chinese chose not to pursue their initial advantage. For reasons that remain unclear, the implications of this technology were never explored. Within a relatively short time, China fell behind in the race toward technological mastery. Japan, by contrast, imported industrial technology and used it to build a modern rail system that revolutionized and modernized the country. The decision of the Meiji government to modernize Japan on its own terms led to the introduction of the telegraph, telephone, and wireless radio.

It was the West, however, that fully exploited the possibilities of industrial technology. A good example of this is the laying of the transatlantic cable that connected nations on both sides of the Atlantic Ocean in 1866. This stunning achievement provided instant communication among Western nations and around the world, forever altering political and economic realities. Living in what has been called an "information age," we can easily see how the flow of information determines success or failure in business, military, and social systems.

Equally revolutionary in the history of ideas were the theories of Charles Darwin and Sigmund Freud. As technology speeds up communications, and as we have access to greater and greater quantities of information, we remain puzzled about our own place in the cosmos. Darwin's claim that humans are descended from apes was deeply shocking to people who had come to think of themselves as a little lower than the angels. And, Freud's contention that we are prisoners to our subconscious urges further eroded assumptions of human uniqueness and intellectuality.

Our scientific and technological progress has been amazing. But, we have yet to match that progress in the development of our social systems. Are we more enlightened than our counterparts of 500 years ago? Have we surpassed them in morality? It seems that the "full human and humane heritage" of the scientific and industrial revolutions remains unexplored.

Eyes Wide Open

When an obscure Arab scientist solved the riddle of light, the universe no longer belonged to God.

RICHARD POWERS

B y any human measure, a millennium is a considerable chunk of time. It is the longest fixed unit of time with a distinct name in common usage. At the beginning of our spent millennium and at frequent intervals throughout it, vexed to nightmare by the calendar, believers have awaited Christ's imminent return to rule over a new heaven and earth in a kingdom that was to run for the unthinkable span of a thousand years. Near the millennium's end, the Nazis, refiners of another one of the period's most persistent concepts, predicted their own third kingdom would last for a thousand years. They were off by 988.

At the start of this millennium, nothing resembling an accurate map of any continent existed. Now a hand-held Global Positioning System satellite receiver can pinpoint its owner's location anywhere on the face of the globe. Trade and enterprise have expanded beyond all reckoning. More volumes are printed each year than existed in the year 1000. The last 10 centuries have also seen global deforestation, a steep falling off in spoken languages and mass extinction on a scale beyond anything since the Cretaceous.

Any search for the millennium's most important concept already dooms itself to myopia. Consider the candidates that spring to mind: parliamentary democracy, the nation–state, free markets, due process, the limited liability corporation, insurance, the university, mandatory formal education, abolition, socialism, the emancipation of women, universal suffrage, universal human rights. The scope of the upheaval in social institutions suggests some corresponding revolution in underlying thought almost too large to isolate.

Line up the usual intellectual suspects: the theory of evolution, relativity, the mapping of the unconscious. As cataclysmic as each has been for our own era, they are 11th-hour arrivals, the latter-day consequences of ideas much larger and longer in motion. Push backward to Boyle's Law, Newton's $F = ma$ or the Copernican Revolution, and you begin to close in on that fundamental leap in human conception.

The notion of progress, the invention of the future, might itself be a leading candidate for the most influential idea of the millennium. But the belief in transformation and advancement, in a constantly increasing control over the material world, is still just a symptom of a wider conceptual revolution that lies at the heart of what has happened to the world in these last 1,000 years: the rise of the experimental method.

Say, then, that the most important idea of this millennium was set in motion by a man named Abu Ali al-Hasan Ibn al-Haytham, born around the year 965 in Basra, in what is now Iraq. Even by his Western name, Alhazen, he remains a little-known figure in the history of thought. But the idea that Ibn al-Haytham championed is so ingrained in us that we don't even think of it as an innovation, let alone one that has appeared so late in the human day.

Ibn al-Haytham resolved a scientific dispute that had remained deadlocked for more than 800 years. Two inimical theories vied to explain the mystery of vision. Euclid, Ptolemy and other mathematicians demonstrated that light necessarily traveled from the eye to the observed object. Aristotle and the atomists assumed the reverse. Both theories were complete and internally consistent, with no way to arbitrate between them.

Then Ibn al-Haytham made several remarkable observations. His most remarkable was also the simplest. He invited observers to stare at the sun, which proved the point: when you looked at a sufficiently bright object, it burned the eye. He made no appeal to geometry or theoretical necessity. Instead, he demolished a whole mountain of systematic theory with a single appeal to data. Light started outside the eye and reflected into it. No other explanation was consistent with the evidence.

Ptolemy had appealed to math and reason: Aristotle's position had been mere conjecture. The world, however, answered to neither reason nor conjecture. What argument required was something more than theory, something that would hold up in the court of controlled looking. This empirical insistence lay at the heart of Ibn al-Haytham's real revolution, and while he did not upend the world single-handedly, his influence has spread without limits.

T he shift from authority to observation seems small, self-evident, almost inevitable. In reality, it is none of these. Over the course of 1,000 years, the conceptual shift would grow catastrophic, and its consequences would transform every aspect of existence.

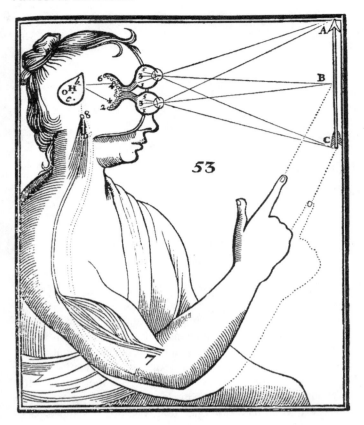

Figure 1 For René Descartes in the mid-1600's, seeing was believing, as underscored by this diagram in one of the mathematician and philosopher's books.

Ibn al-Haytham made numerous other experimental contributions to optics and physics, part of a surge of Arab science at a time when Europe possessed little science to speak of. His contemporaries, investigators like Ibn Ahmad al-Biruni, Ibn Rushd (Averroes) and Ibn Sina (Avicenna), revived and extended Greek thought, unhindered by Augustine's insistence that the world was an inscrutable riddle invented by God to lead us toward contemplation of a universe beyond this one. While none of these men can be called an experimental scientist in the modern sense, each helped to open up the possibility that the world can be known through its particulars and that direct observation was the best way to know it.

When the Arab cities in southern Spain began to fall in the late 11th century, the contents of their great libraries flooded into Christian Europe. Ibn al-Haytham's works on optics were at last translated into Latin late in the 12th century, enlightening the proto-empiricist Roger Bacon (c. 1220–1292).

Bacon—Dr. Mirabilis, as he came to be known—was a bizarre mixture of old and new mind. Both a philosophical Franciscan and an anti-philosophical experimentalist, he fought to introduce science into university curriculums and became the first European to write down the recipe for gunpowder. He proposed ideas for airplanes, power-driven ships and automobiles. Ibn al-Haytham's optics, which included the invention of a primitive camera obscura, led Bacon to many optical insights.

But optics formed just the visible surface of what Bacon took away from Ibn al-Haytham. "Argument," he asserted in his

"Opus Majus" (1267), ". . . does not remove doubt, so that the mind may rest in the sure knowledge of the truth, unless it finds it by the method of experiment. . . . For if any man who never saw fire proved by satisfactory arguments that fire burns . . . his hearer's mind would never be satisfied, nor would he avoid the fire until he put his hand in it . . . that he might learn by experiment what argument taught."

The world was not a vaporous trap but a collection of things with heft and substance, worth the closest scrutiny and palpation. Aristotle failed to see the value of controlled experiment, believing that nature could only be understood whole. With Bacon, through Ibn al-Haytham, there arises the idea of testing for truth through isolated particulars. Bacon's was also the moment in Western sculpture when Mary stops holding her child out in front of her like a pillar of stone and starts to straddle her grasping boy over one load-bearing, sensual hip.

Another three centuries passed before science emerged from its roots in natural philosophy. But the idea of looking had begun to shake the foundations of authority at the base of thought.

Light did not come from the eye, but rather fell into it. The world could be grasped in its particulars.

William of Ockham (c. 1285–c. 1347) bolstered empiricism with his own Law of Parsimony, or Ockham's Razor: when multiple ways exist to explain a datum, go with the one that requires the fewest theoretical assumptions. Jan van Eyck (c. 1395–c. 1441) took the zeal for nominal reality to such heights that his Ghent altarpiece depicts more than 40 identifiable plant species. Ibn al-Haytham's empirical optics traveled down yet another path to trouble the medieval mind into early modernism. If light entered the eye from the outside, then the eye sat at the tip of a visual cone, where the perpendicular ray dominated over all oblique ones. This implied a geometry of seeing, described by Ibn al-Haytham and elaborated on by Witelo (d. after 1281), a Pole connected with the papal court. Through Witelo, the idea of visual perspective spread in Italy.

The new depth of seeing worked its spell on Giotto (c. 1267–1337). The solid spaces hinted at in his frescoes were said to reduce viewers to alarm and ecstasy. The eye of Europe turned itself inside out. Ibn al-Haytham's camera obscura, improved upon by Bacon, set painters loose on the pursuit of light and its reflection off real surfaces.

But only when Brunelleschi, Masaccio and Uccello got wind of the new optical mathematics through their compatriot, the geographer-mathematician Paolo Toscanelli (b. 1397), did Western Europe achieve full liftoff into rectilinear reality. Using the techniques of deep perspective, with its ability to measure the relative size of objects at any distance, Toscanelli assembled a chart that wound up leading Columbus to the New World. The deep spaces of the new painting opened up even deeper spaces on the map, terra incognita that the Age of Exploration rushed to fill in.

Ibn al-Haytham's inexorable idea derives its power from a radical overthrow of what constitutes acceptable demonstration. Nothing, finally, can gainsay the data. Wholeness, harmony and radiance must give way to verifiability and repeatability. With the invention of printing, experimental data could proliferate without limit. Fueled by and fueling the Protestant Reformation, with its universal priesthood of man, skepticism's challenge to received wisdom spread into all quarters.

It lies beyond all reasonable doubt that no single idea has had a more profound or ubiquitous impact on what the human race has become, or what it has worked upon the face of the planet, than the vesting of authority in experiment.

So did Ibn al-Haytham's optics. His work on refraction and lenses led to the development of the telescope and microscope. Once these devices threw open their portals onto the invisible, there was no looking back. Van Leeuwenhoek's (1632–1723) "tiny animalcules" revealed the living world to be stranger than any natural philosopher could have guessed.

The Lutheran Kepler (1571–1630), in his "Supplement to Witelo," solved the problem of atmospheric refraction and built Ibn al-Haytham's foundation into a full account of vision. Freed up to cast his glance into the heavens, Kepler explained magnification and laid out the laws of planetary motion. And Galileo, the true prototype of the modern skeptical empiricist, looking at the light that fell into his telescope tube and reporting what he saw, defying all theory and common sense, moved the world against the world's wishes. Rising to his feet after recanting to the authorities, as legend has it, he muttered the words that would form the credo of triumphant science: "But it does move." In short order, measurement laid out the calculus behind its every wobble.

"And new philosophy calls all in doubt," John Donne wrote in his poem "An Anatomy of the World: the First Anniversary" (1611). And doubt itself became the engine of the new creation.

Francis Bacon (1561–1626) wrote the user's manual for the new scientific instrument of thought. He banished the "idols of the mind," those habits of reason that blinded you to the evidence. Knowledge depended on suspending belief in anything except the most indifferent measurement. In "The Advancement of Learning" (1605), he wrote, "If a man will begin with certainties, he shall end in doubts, but if he will be content to begin with doubts, he shall end in certainties."

With the Baconian method, knowledge did not stop at the curation and annotation of bygone ideas. Bacon was right: the revolution unleashed in Western Europe in the 17th century represents the sharpest break with the past in history. In the 300 years since the break commenced, modern science and its hand-maid, technology, have altered the globe beyond recognition or recall, revising the terms of material existence, not to mention the geopolitical ones. For politics, too, is born in experiment. The rise of a technological Europe produced an era of imperialism from which the continents have yet to recover.

"It is not *what* the man of science believes that distinguishes him," Bertrand Russell said, "but *how* and *why* he believes it. His beliefs are tentative, not dogmatic; they are based on evidence, not on authority or intuition." Out of that tentativeness have flowed the airplane, air pump, anesthesia, aniline dye, antiseptic surgery, aspirin, atomic energy, automobiles and on, ad infinitum.

The most adventurous mind from the year 1000—even Ibn al-Haytham himself—faced with the runaway results of the experimental method, would have no available mental response short of schizophrenia. Ibn al-Haytham's doubt of existing optical theory has led to the certainties of electron microscopy, retinal surgery and robotic vision. Millennial expectation has shifted away from the thousand-year reign of Christ toward the thousand-megahertz personal computer. The universe has progressed from an enigmatic metaphysical emblem to the accidental byproduct of superstrings. An orbiting telescope now extends the cone of vision out to the very edges of creation.

There is something paradoxical in claiming, as the greatest concept of the last millennium, the skeptical rejection of concept in favor of evidence. But there is something paradoxical in the idea of radical empiricism itself. At its purest, science strives to be neither logical nor reasonable, merely suspicious. It claims to begin in the abeyance of theory, but strives to produce a deeper, wider explanation of observable event. It pursues a relentless reductionism in order to erect a single, consistent material theory of everything from the unified cosmological force to the evolution of consciousness, a vastly more comprehensive blueprint than any City of God, yet still a theory, always tentative, and refutable at best.

In fact, in the most fundamental sense, skeptical empiricism may be a contradiction in terms. It has come under attack in recent years by a number of thinkers—from Ludwig Wittgenstein to Thomas Kuhn and beyond—who have no qualms about applying the same skepticism toward the scientific method that Francis Bacon advocated applying to any body of accepted lore. Their objections are many and varied: that fact and artifact may be closer than most empiricists are comfortable accepting. That even pure observation has an agenda. That great empiricists have rejected initial data on hunches, until their observations produced more acceptable numbers. That scientists need pre-existing theory and supposition even to ask the questions that will lead to data. That the shape of a question produces the data that answer it.

A new generation of cultural constructionists similarly maintains that Western science, whatever its technological triumphs, is the product of a certain cultural moment and represents no transcultural truths. But that notion, too, may beg the question of just which forces construct culture. You may well wonder whether any but a culture of high technology could have produced the theories of cultural construction.

Still, it lies beyond all reasonable doubt that no single idea has had a more profound or ubiquitous impact on what the human race has become, or what it has worked upon the face of the planet, than the vesting of authority in experiment. Anyone who looks can arrive at no other conclusion. More urgent, at this moment, is the question of what the greatest idea of the next thousand years will have to be if we are to survive the power unleashed by the last.

Many have noted, here at millennium's end, that our vast increase in technical ability has not been accompanied by a commensurate increase in our social or ethical maturity. A soul in the year 1000, from any region of the globe, knew more about its place in the grand scheme than a body in the year 2000 does. Francis Bacon was right: the program that began in doubt has produced certainties beyond a medieval mind's wildest dreams. But what was once a certainty now drifts in a gulf of doubt wider than the millennium itself.

The greatest idea of the last 1,000 years has granted us ascendance over matter by asking not how things ought to be but how things are. We have given ourselves to finding out not what we should do with the world, but what we can make the world do. The greatest idea of the next thousand years must make up the difference, returning subtlety and richness and morals and lightness of spirit to the long human experiment, if any part of it is to survive. Light falls into the eye, reflected from the object under observation. But something else, too, must go out from the eye to the things we observe.

RICHARD POWERS is the author of six novels, most recently "Gain."

In God's Place

With his discovery of gravity, Newton taught that understanding the cosmos is not confined to the divine.

ALAN LIGHTMAN

Giovanni di Paolo's 15th-century painting "The Creation of the World and the Expulsion From Paradise," which hangs in the Metropolitan Museum of Art in New York, offers an unexpected synthesis of Western art, religion and thought.

The picture has a split-level appearance. On the right is the title scene: a grove of fruit trees, the Garden of Eden and the frail, ashamed figures of Adam and Eve being shoved out by an angel. The left half is dominated by concentric spheres. At the middle is the earth, center of the universe, encircled by the planets and sun. An outermost sphere contains the stars, all straight out of Aristotle's "On the Heavens." Above this cosmic hierarchy floats a divine God, who gravely reaches down with an index finger to spin His heavenly spheres.

This painting presents a doubled portrait of the fierce boundary between human and divine. Aristotle made all terrestrial phenomena out of earth, air, water and fire. For the moon, the sun and the stars, however, he decided he needed to introduce a completely new kind of substance: the *divine* ether. Adam and Eve were banished from Eden for crossing a more local boundary and eating from the tree of knowledge, God's knowledge. As it turns out, the forbidding separations of substance and place in Aristotle's cosmology seem to resonate with the forbidden knowledge, transgression and guilt in Judeo-Christian theology. In both cases, and on both sides of di Paolo's painting, the proper domain of human existence and understanding is severely restricted.

Indeed, for centuries Western culture was ingrained with the notion that some areas of knowledge are inaccessible, or forbidden, to human possession. In this view, humankind is entitled to comprehend only what God deigns to reveal. Zeus chained Prometheus to a rock for giving fire, the secret of the gods and the wellspring of advanced civilization, to mortal man. St. Thomas Aquinas (1225–74) distinguished between scientific knowledge, discoverable by the human mind, and divine knowledge, "higher than man's knowledge." Divine knowledge could "not be sought by man through his reason, nevertheless, once . . . revealed by God [it] must be accepted by faith." When Dante asks the divine Beatrice about the mysteries of the moon,

she replies that "the opinion of mortals errs where the key of sense does not unlock." When Adam, in Milton's "Paradise Lost" (1667), questions the angel Raphael about celestial mechanics, Raphael offers some vague hints and then says that "the rest from Man or Angel the great Architect did wisely to conceal, and not divulge His secrets to be scann'd by them who ought rather admire."

The idea that there are limits to the rightful scope of human knowledge is, of course, partly a cultural belief. Surrounding it is an entire worldview, an understanding of how the cosmos is put together, spiritually and physically, and where we fit into the grand scheme. But the idea is also deeply psychological. It is an introspection, a state of mind that subtly imprisons individual thinkers as well as societies, and its effects and ramifications cannot possibly be weighed. No one can say how the history of civilization would have changed if God had never forbidden us to taste from that tree. However, a number of developments over the 16th and 17th centuries did succeed in introducing a new belief: that the entirety of the universe, at least its physical parts, was knowable and discoverable by human beings. This new belief, a belief in the unfettered entitlement to knowledge, was the most important intellectual development along the lengthy time line of the past millennium.

Perhaps the most glorious culmination of the new thinking was Isaac Newton's "Principia" (1687). This monumental treatise established fundamental ideas like inertia and force, articulated general laws of motion of bodies under general forces and proposed a specific law for the force of gravity. Newton's book was unprecedented in the history of science and played a pivotal role in the birth of modern science. But what was most important about Newton's work was not his particular law of gravity, great as it is, but the universality and unbounded application of that law. The same gravity that caused an apple to fall from a tree also caused the moon to orbit the earth, and these trajectories, and an infinity of others, could be mathematically calculated from equations that the English physicist and mathematician had discovered on his own. The heavenly bodies were, after all, physical things, like rocks—or inkwells tossed in frustration against a stone fireplace. The "Principia" dealt a mortal blow to Aristotle's strong division between earthly and cosmic phenomena.

Beneath Newton's idea of the universality of gravity, in turn, lay the implicit assumption that the physical universe was knowable by man. This was a new idea in the evolution of human self-awareness, a psychological turning point, a liberation, an empowerment. Without this idea we might never have had Newton. Nor would we have had the intellectual and scientific breakthroughs that followed: Lavoisier's discovery of oxygen and the beginnings of modern chemistry, Mendel's seminal work on genetics, Dalton's concept of the atom, Darwin and Wallace's theory of evolution and natural selection, Maxwell's formulation of the laws of electricity and magnetism, Einstein's relativity, Hubble's discovery of the expanding universe, Watson and Crick's unraveling of DNA and countless other scientific discoveries.

Even Newton's contemporaries realized that the great physicist had achieved something far deeper than his individual laws. Roger Cotes, in his introduction to the second edition of the "Principia," wrote that Newton had reached "discoveries of which the mind of man was thought incapable before. . . . The gates are now set open." Submersed in a scientific and technological culture as we are today—a culture that has been so totally shaped by telephones and microchips, daily reports on the genes of disease or the recession rate of galaxies—it is hard for us to conceive any limitations in knowledge. All things are our province. The universe is our oyster. We are mostly oblivious to the intellectual history that led us to this point. And we take for granted the active part being played by our own psyches.

What produced the new psychology found in Newton's "Principia"? Certainly, changes in religious thought played a role. Martin Luther's proclamations of 1517, which sparked the Protestant Reformation, helped diminish the authority of the church. Despite Luther's vicious anti-Semitism, his argument that every person should be able to read and interpret the Bible for herself, without lock-stepping with the priesthood, encouraged a certain freedom of mind. This religious freedom spread. For example, the subject matter of art turned from almost exclusively religious themes to landscapes, still lifes, interiors and other broad explorations of the secular and natural worlds. Compare Masaccio or Michelangelo with Rembrandt or Vermeer.

Science can push back the equations of modern cosmology to less than a nanosecond after the 'big bang,' but it cannot answer the question of why the universe came into being. Science can, in principle, explain all human behavior in terms of biochemical processes in the brain, but science can never determine what is ethical behavior.

There were scientific discoveries as well. On Nov. 11, 1572, soon after sunset, the Danish astronomer Tycho Brahe sighted an intensely bright object in the constellation Cassiopeia that he realized had not been there before. Brahe was the first person to prove that such novae lay beyond the orbit of the moon, within the celestial realm. Brahe had discovered an exploding star, and his discovery exploded the centuries-old belief that the stars were eternal and constant. The divine perfection of the heavens was further questioned when the Italian physicist Galileo turned his new telescope to the moon in 1610 and found the surface "to be not smooth, even, and perfectly spherical, as the great crowd of philosophers have believed about this and other heavenly bodies, but, on the contrary, to be uneven, rough and crowded with depressions and bulges."

Also of enormous influence, in the decades just preceding Newton, were the scientific and philosophical ideas of René Descartes. Most of the great thinkers throughout history have debated the kind of knowledge that is knowable by the human mind, but philosophers before Descartes assumed that at least some certain knowledge already existed. Descartes, for the first time, began a philosophical system by doubting everything, even his own existence. After convincing himself of his own reality ("I think, therefore I am"), he entered a long meditation that eventually established the existence of God.

Descartes helped us to question. He also prefigured Newton's idea of universality of physical law by proposing a universal mechanism himself, namely his "vortices," which swirled here and there through space, like whirlpools in an ocean, directing the motions of planets and other heavenly bodies. Although Descartes's vortices lacked quantitative description and proved finally unworkable, they had the psychological import of explaining and unifying a vast range of terrestrial and cosmic phenomena under one rational system.

One way of looking at these developments is that they altered and clarified the distinction between what one could call a physical universe and a spiritual universe. Little by little, the sacred geography of Aristotle was replaced by a more amorphous and subtle map of the world. In this map, there exists a material universe, which includes all matter and energy: electrons and atoms, light and heat, brains and stars and galaxies. This vast cosmos is subject to the inquiries of science and to rational mathematical laws that we can discover with our minds.

Coexisting with this physical universe is a spiritual one, not quantifiable, not located in space, not made of atoms and molecules but, to believers, pervasive nonetheless. Each universe poses an infinity of important questions. It is the physical universe, not the spiritual, that is the domain of science. Science has everything to say about the physical universe and nothing to say about its spiritual counterpart. Science can push back the equations of modern cosmology to less than a nanosecond after the "big bang," but science cannot answer the question of why the universe came into being in the first place or whether it has any purpose. Science can, in principle, explain all human behavior in terms of biochemical processes in the brain, but science can never determine what is ethical behavior.

These new perceptions did not happen quickly, neatly or with finality. Like all deep psychological seeds, the idea that some areas of knowledge are off-limits to human beings is not easily excised from our consciousness. The scientist in Mary Shelley's

"Frankenstein" (1818), a novel significantly subtitled "The Modern Prometheus," laments, "Learn from me . . . how dangerous is the acquirement of knowledge, and how much happier that man is who believes his native town to be the world, than he who aspires to become greater than his nature will allow." Some of the horror at the first test of the atom bomb in New Mexico was surely that we had unleashed forces greater than our nature. Soon after the Second World War, J. Robert Oppenheimer, the head of the Manhattan Project, told an audience that "we thought of the legend of Prometheus, of that deep sense of guilt in man's new powers." The troubled public reaction to Dolly, the first adult mammal to be cloned, shows that our fear remains. The sheep's human manipulators were described by The New York Times as having "suddenly pried open one of the most forbidden—and tantalizing—doors of modern life."

Most likely, each new door opened will continue to disturb us and play upon our guilt. We are advanced and we are primitive at the same time. We are Newton's flight of mind and we are Prometheus chained to a rock, we are Watson and Crick and we are Adam and Eve. All of it, all of the centuries of liberation and imprisonment, creation and dread, live together in one house. And each new door opened will disturb us. Yet we will keep opening the doors; we cannot be stopped.

ALAN LIGHTMAN, the author of "Einstein's Dreams," is Burchard Professor of Humanities and a senior lecturer in physics at M.I.T.

The Workshop of a New Society

The industrial revolution gave an utterly new shape to Britain's economy, its population, its cities and its society. But not quite as fast as is supposed

1670–1850

Britain's industrial revolution was more than that. In most senses, it was a revolution of society too. A mainland population of maybe 6m–7m in 1700 was put at 10.7m by the first official census in 1801, 20.9m in 1851 and 37.1m by 1901. A nation of countrymen went to town. Agriculture's share of male employment fell between 1700 and 1850 from about 60% to about 25%; industry's rose from under 20% to around 50%. And as industrialists built steam-powered factories near the markets, the one Briton in six living in town in 1700 became by 1850 one in two.

The industrial change, however, was neither as swift nor as complete as is often thought. Tradition describes a roaring take-off between 1770 and 1830, driven by a handful of technological innovations, such as textile machinery and James Watt's improved steam engines; and, hey presto, Britain is "the workshop of the world". In fact, the process had begun in the 17th century and was still incomplete in the 1830s, by when only a few industries—mining, metal-working, textiles, brewing—had taken to "factory" methods.

Technological change, important as it was, was not the be-all and end-all. Nor yet did it start with the machine-builders. They depended on earlier advances in iron technology that enabled that industry to produce, in quantity, better and cheaper iron goods such as components for the new machines or for structural use. And, from around 1670, other factors were at work.

One was the development of coal as a fuel, as the cost of wood rose. Next, the growth of thriving rural industries, supplementing farm incomes, which laid the basis for a skilled industrial workforce. Third, the increasing commercialisation of manufacturing, to meet rising demand for cheaper cloth and metal goods from the growing urban elites in Britain and mainland Europe, and from British colonies.

Britain was helped too by easy access to the sea, political stability and light regulation of trade, finance and industry. It also developed a highly specialised workforce, speeding up the development of new products and processes. Industrial output, according to one modern estimate, rose by 0.7% a year between 1700 and 1760, by 1.3% in the 1760s and 1770s, 2.0% in the 1780s and 1790s, and 2.8% between 1800 and 1830.

Work changed, and more than that, as manpower and water power gave way to steam and machines, and rural craftsmanship to urban factories manned by unskilled labour. For some, work vanished. Rural weavers put up a desperate fight for their jobs, marching, petitioning Parliament and burning mills and machinery such as Daniel Burton's textile factory in Middleton, Lancashire, in 1812, but all in vain.

The new factory workers who took their place were mostly unskilled, and earned less than the craftsmen had. Yet for the many men, women and children who flocked to the factory gate, the pay on offer was better than they had earned as farmhands or servants. And as one skill died, new ones were needed: those of tool- or machine-builders, or—almost a new class—foremen.

One aspect of factory life was universally hated by the workforce. Considerations of productivity and safety led employers to regulate all aspects of life in the factory: working hours, breaks and movement inside "the works". Many workers resisted what they saw as infringements of individual freedom, and some of the traditions of the small workshops survived for a while. Employers had to fight hard for the demise of "Saint Monday", when men went to the pub after work on Saturday and did not return until Tuesday morning, disrupting production in spite of (or by) their frantic efforts to catch up by the end of the week.

The clergy and the good-hearted middle classes worried much about their inferiors' morality, as men and women in the mass flocked into the new workplaces. Some industrialists tried to prevent workmen entering parts of the factory where women worked—without much success. In time, awkward-squad parts of the middle class began to worry about the employers' social morality too: Mrs Gaskell's "North and South" offers an early illustration.

Outside "the works" too, conditions altered greatly. Overcrowding, in jerry-built housing in the much-polluted new towns, brought ill-health; at its worst, the devastating cholera epidemics of 1831–32, 1848 and 1854–55. Despite efforts by some employers, charities and eventually local authorities, improvement was slow before the end of the 19th century. Yet a new, mass urban society was born, and not all of its life was the misery depicted by writers from Dickens to D.H. Lawrence. Our deprived Victorian ancestors were quite good at enjoying themselves.

The most obvious beneficiaries of the industrial revolution were the new "barons" such as the Whitbreads in brewing, the Guests in iron or the Strutts in the cotton industry. But the landed classes too profited, from mineral royalties, rises in urban land values and their own investment in industrial concerns. The greatest gainers, though, were the working class, whose living standards rose from 1820 onwards, after 70 years of stagnation. This rise accelerated between 1870 and 1900, when real wages, consumption and life expectancy all rose sharply.

Simultaneously, new forms of leisure emerged, which became synonymous with the British working class: football matches, social clubs, seaside resorts. By 1900, the ordinary Briton was better paid, fed, clothed, housed, educated, perhaps amused and certainly better represented in politics, than his forefathers could have dreamed of.

Not everyone was content. Lawrence was soon to pour out his ample bile on the machine world. In 1933, J.B. Priestley lamented that it was "as if the country had devoted a hundred years of its life to keeping gigantic sooty pigs. And the people who were choked by the reek of the sties did not get the bacon." Actually, they got quite a lot. Whether that was a fair share is a separate story.

The X Factor

A thousand years ago, China appeared to have assembled all the pieces for an industrial revolution. What happened?

MARK ELVIN

Early in the 11th century, Chinese government arsenals manufactured more than 16 million identical iron arrowheads a year. In other words, mass production. Rather later, in the 13th century, machines in northern China powered by belt transmissions off a waterwheel twisted a rough rope of hemp fibers into a finer yarn. The machine used 32 spinning heads rotating simultaneously in a technique that probably resembled modern ring-spinning. A similar device was used for doubling filaments of silk. In other words, mechanized production, in the sense that the actions of the human hand were replicated by units of wood and metal, and an array of these identical units was then set into motion by inanimate power.

Common sense thus suggests that the Chinese economy, early in the millennium just coming to a close, had already developed the two key elements of what we think of as the Industrial Revolution: mass production and mechanization. That, nonetheless, nothing much more happened in this direction during the next 600 or 700 years is also a matter of common knowledge. Even the spinning machine went out of use, and survived only in literature and ever less comprehensible copies of copies of diagrams made by artists who had never set eyes on the real thing.

Much later, from the middle of the 19th century on, China had to import, then service, adapt and even at times improve, mechanical engineering from the West. This was done with considerable flair, particularly by Chinese firms in Shanghai, a city which during treaty-port days turned into a nonstop international exhibition of machine building. So Chinese technical capability can hardly be said to have withered in the intervening centuries. But what went wrong the first time? Why did the first industrial revolution not take place in China, as it seems it should have?

Of course, there is much more to such a revolution than technology alone. It requires a large-scale market economy, and that presupposes cheap transport and communications, extensive commercialization, monetization and credit instruments. China during the Song dynasty (960–1279 A.D.) delivered all of these.

The Song enjoyed the results of an economic revolution that featured the rapid development of wet-field rice farming in the lower Yangtze valley, the burgeoning of a dense network of low-coasts, and a money supply increased by many means, including fiduciary money (some of it the world's first paper money) and credit. A proliferation of petty local markets supported three great market-regions in the north China plains, the lower Yangtze and Sichuan. Above these rose a nationwide market and an overseas commerce so vigorous that taxes on it were the main financial support of the Southern Song (1127–1279) government.

To these we may add a growing literacy, linked with woodblock printing, a growing numeracy and some of what were then the largest cities on the globe, in one or two cases with more than a million inhabitants. Many of these were now also producer cities, not just consumer cities living off administrative revenues. What could be called the "textbook package" of factors that we commonly assume produces an industrial revolution was all in place. And still there was no breakthrough. Why?

The disruption caused by the conquests of the Jurchen in the north during the 12th century, and then the Mongols in the whole of China during the 13th, is the most direct answer, and should not be discounted just because it is obvious. At a deeper level, the economic driving force provided by the expansion of production in the Yangtze valley had diminished. From the late 10th century until about 1100, the 26 prefectures of the lower Yangtze had maintained an average annual growth rate in population of more than 1%. For premodern times, this is impressive, approaching a tripling within a century.

But land fills up, and opportunities once taken cannot be taken again. The coherent pattern fell apart during the Southern Song and, with a few local exceptions, this sustained growth was not maintained. The climate also grew more variable and colder, dropping at times to two degrees Celsius below the annual average at the start of the medieval economic revolution.

Economic vitality returned in the later 16th and early 17th centuries. It was then disrupted again, by internal rebellions, the Manchu conquest, and one of the coldest periods of what in Europe at this time was called the "Little Ice Age." When growth picked up spectacularly in the warmer 18th century, it had distinctive characteristics.

First of all, it was more quantitative than qualitative. Some diffusion of technology that was new in China occurred, notably food crops, like sweet potatoes introduced from the New World, and some fine-tuning, notably of "intermediate" rices. There was no major innovation or invention. The pattern was more of the same, multiplied over and over again, and greater intensification, based on the input of more labour. Accounts of women working regularly in the fields become much more common at this time.

Second, the growth was environmentally destructive on an unprecedented scale. The stripping of vegetation cover of course had a long history in China. The Qing-period removal of original vegetation and forests, and exploitation of other resources like accessible coal and metallic ores, was on a new scale. China's population reached more than 400 million by 1850, about twice what it had been around the end of the 17th century. The literature is filled with a litany of woes about deforestation, shortage of construction timber and firewood, devastating erosion, loss of fertility in upland soils, salination of unsuitable lands opened for farming, and exhaustion of veins of copper and other materials. It was an ecosystem under a new intensity of attack.

Third, the general style of economic organization was to subcontract, employing commercial relationships instead of management. This can be seen in the production of cotton cloth. A legion of rural spinners bought raw cotton in local markets and sold their thread through intermediaries to another legion of weavers. A pyramid of lesser and greater brokers then purchased the cloth, putting it out to independent workshops for dyeing and, separately, calendering–hardening the cloth with pressure. The best of the cloth ended up with wholesalers who might have a turnover of a million bolts a year.

In one sense, this was an efficient system, based on pitting basic producers against each other in competition. On the other, it made technical innovation difficult, by separating marketing from production, and leaving producers with minimum reserves or incentives for experiment. Only in a few businesses, where there was a need for large-scale management was there much innovation. An example is some of the mountain timber-cutting organizations that pioneered more technically effective ways of getting timber out of difficult terrain, such as precursors of cable-skidder trackways that used overhead tow-lines to drag cut trunks along rough tracks.

Finally, the productivity of farming, both in per-hectare terms and seed-to-yield ratio (in better areas, about 1:35 for rice), was breathtakingly high in a comparative perspective. But success was beginning to block progress. Without modern science, and modern productive techniques, to draw on, there was a ceiling on further improvement. With usable land largely occupied, there were few if any easy ways to create the surges of extra demand that can have domino effects through an economy, and often prompt invention. And the Chinese economy was now too big for foreign trade to be able to deliver impulses of this sort on the required scale. This was the famous high-level equilibrium trap.

Was there, beyond this, still some "X factor" missing? Two possibilities are worth consideration. The first is that the analytical-experimental aspect of culture that crystallized in the West into modern science, but which often crucially affected technology, too, was much weaker in China. One can see this by comparing Chinese and Western analyses of water-pumping technology, a field located on the interface between science and technology (which it is an error in any case to distinguish too sharply). By the start of the 18th century, the French hydraulicist B.F. de Bélidor was already using formal geometry in his quest for the perfect trough-pump—which consists of a trough up which water is drawn by a continuous chain of pallets at a given slope. Chinese texts of this time merely noted empirically that effective high-angle and low-angle lifts needed trough–pumps with parts of differing dimensions.

The second possibility is democracy as a way of running public business. Jean Baechler at the Sorbonne has recently insisted that this is the aspect of the modern West for which premodern parallels in China are the weakest. The democratic style for safeguarding argument within a stable framework, and facilitating broadly acceptable change, may have helped the West develop new ways of thinking and new types of social organization. If we follow this line of thought, then the fifth modernization—to borrow Chinese dissident Wei Jing-sheng's phrase for democracy—appears as less of a luxury and more of an essential.

The late-imperial decline in inventiveness has also sometimes been ascribed to "Confucianism" or to the heavy hand of the Chinese state. This raises a difficulty. Weren't these exact features also associated in the Middle Ages with China's rise to economic world leadership? Can one rationally have it both ways? At best, these factors, suitably nuanced, might perhaps be included as part of a more complex analysis of the historically changing patterns in later times.

The riddle remains.

Mark Elvin is a research professor of Chinese history at the Australian National University.

Samurai, Shoguns & the Age of Steam

Ron Clough

In 1853 Commodore Matthew C. Perry of the U.S. Navy arrived with a small fleet in Tokyo Bay and coerced the Japanese into bringing to an end a period of 250 years of self-imposed seclusion. This seclusion had not been total, and knowledge of developments in other parts of the world had been brought to Japan via Dutch and Chinese traders who had been granted licenses to trade at Nagasaki, Japan's only official gateway to the outside world, and also from a few Japanese castaway sailors lucky enough to have avoided execution on their return—the almost invariable fate reserved for those feared to have been contaminated by contact with foreign lands.

The government of the Tokugawa shoguns, the military caste who controlled the Emperor, was therefore well aware of the ominous advance of Western power towards the East, and of the defeat of China, from which much of its culture derived, by superior European technology in the Opium War of 1841. In this way, even before Perry's arrival, the Japanese knew of the existence of railways. The first confirmed mention of railways appeared in 1846 in the Fusetsu-sho (regular reports of activities outside Japan presented by the Dutch to the shogunate), which referred to a French plan to build a railway across the Isthmus of Panama, and they were mentioned fairly regularly after that.

In 1851 Nakahima Manjiro, a returned shipwrecked sailor fortunate enough to have escaped the usual execution, gave an account of a railway journey he had made in America in his Narratives of a Castaway:

Usually when people go on trips they go by a fire burning vehicle known as a 'reirote' [railroad]. This device is shaped like a ship, water is boiled in a cauldron, and with the three of the hot water the device can run about 300 ri [1,200 kms] in a day. When you look outside the house-shaped object, it's as though you were a bird in flight, and there's no time to get a good look at things. They have iron laid along the vehicle's path.

On April 26th, 1860, the first samurai had cause to ride on a train. This was Muragaki Norimasa, who travelled by train between Panama and Colon while on a mission to exchange instruments of ratification of the Japan-U.S. Treaty of Friendship and Commerce. He was surprised that several people could ride together, his previous experience of passenger travel having presumably been limited to the palanquin:

It's as though a flock of birds was perched on one branch in such a way that the birds are jostling one another

An attendant on the same mission, Tamamushi Yasushige, made detailed technical notes of everything he saw: rolling stock, signals and track.

Once Japan had opened up there was an immediate influx of foreign officials and merchants who manoeuvred to further their interests with the shogunate, the stability of which became increasingly threatened by the shock of events. The government did not have the strength to resist the 'barbarians', as many reactionary samurai wanted, and was therefore seen as vacillating and ineffective. The slogan 'expel the barbarians' gradually gave way, in the cold light of experience, to the more practical 'enrich the country and strengthen the military', with the long-term aim of being able to stand up to the West after taking in its technology. This technology was seen as an important factor in bringing about a new era of 'civilisation and enlightenment'. The shogunate eventually collapsed after a brief civil war in 1867–68 in the face of opposition from the samurai of the western clans, who attached themselves to the cause of the Imperial family which had been cloistered in the old capital of Kyoto during the period of seclusion. A young British diplomat, Ernest Satow, had earlier predicted the likelihood of an Imperial victory over the shoguns and had advised his senior, Sir Harry Parkes, to favour the Imperial forces, whereas the French, also struggling to gain influence, had tended to side with the shogunate. Parkes' tireless lobbying of the new government paid off in the favouritism shown towards the British when it came to awarding contracts for technical advice. The first railways in Japan thus came to have a distinctly British flavour about them.

Notwithstanding the machinations of foreign diplomats, the first proposal for a railway had come from a samurai, Godai Tomoatsu of Satsuma, in 1865, for a line from Kyoto to Osaka, which was rejected. Given the upheavals of the period, it is not surprising that several proposed schemes came to nothing before work finally commenced. One application was accepted by the shogunate on January 17th, 1868, for a railway from Edo (now Tokyo) to Yokohama from the American A.L.C. Portman, but this was thwarted when the shogunate collapsed. In commercial terms the demise of this project was fortunate for Japan, as Portman had been guaranteed a full concession to build the railway, whereas the new Meiji government, rejecting the policy of allowing concessions to non-Japanese, ensured that Japan avoided China's fate of having its railways in hock to foreign interests.

In principle the new government was in favour of a railway and accepted the logic that the first route should link Tokyo with other important towns along the populous southern seaboard such as Yokohama, Nagoya, Kyoto, Osaka, and Kobe. This route, the section of which connecting Tokyo and Kyoto was known as the Tokaido, or Eastern Sea Route, was a logical first choice, and it followed that the first sections to be built should be those linking the treaty ports of Yokohama and Kobe to Tokyo and Osaka respectively. Raising capital for such expensive projects as railway construction was not an easy matter, however, particularly as the government wanted to keep foreign investment to a minimum. In the long run the Japanese managed to fund much of the construction themselves, but recourse to foreign loans was occasionally made. Such was the case for the Tokaido line, for which the decision to start building was finally taken in December 1869.

Before this government-sponsored scheme, Thomas Glover, a British merchant living in Nagasaki, laid down a short line along the dockside of that city. A locomotive named the 'Iron Duku' was imported to provide the power. This name was presumably a Japanicised form of the 'Iron Duke' of the Great Western Railway in England, of which it seems to have been a replica.

The Tokaido line project was to be carried out under the auspices of the newly-created Ministry of Works (Kobusho). Horatio Nelson Lay, an Englishman who had run the Chinese Customs service, was approached to negotiate a 1 million [pounds sterling] loan in London, with customs revenues as security. The Japanese, with a sketchy knowledge of British history, may have assumed a connection—wrongly—between Lay and his famous naval near-namesake, and thus considered him trustworthy. They were wrong on this point also. An American business rival, peeved at losing the contract, informed the Japanese government that Lay was fleecing them by charging twelve-and-a-half per cent interest on money which he had raised at nine-and-a-half per cent in London. His services were dispensed with and responsibility for the loan was passed to the Oriental Bank.

Not surprisingly, there was opposition to the project from traditionalists, and those who feared a heavier tax burden, from traders such as innkeepers along the route, and from hauliers who might feel the pinch of competition, as well as from nationalists who felt the country was being 'sold out' to foreign interests.

Nevertheless in 1870 Edmund Morell, an Englishman who had worked on railways in New Zealand, a country with similar terrain to that of Japan, arrived to take charge of construction. He decided on a 3'6" gauge. The narrow gauge was chosen in the expectation that there would not be a high demand for capacity. This mistaken decision was to bedevil the Japanese railways for years, and remains a problem to this day.

Cultural differences between the British advisers and the Japanese were not easily overcome. The British engineers constantly complained of obstruction by the officials and the inefficient methods of the workmen. E.G. Holtham, who supervised reconstruction of the Tokyo-Yokohama section in 1877, wrote:

My native assistants were some of them of a very dreamy temperament, and considered the first thing necessary in all calculations involving inches was to reduce every dimension into decimals of a foot, to six places of decimals at least, and then resorted to books of logarithms to throw some light upon their subject. In this way about a week was required to ascertain how many bricks went to a given-size wall.

Another bone of contention was the insistence of the samurai on wearing their swords, a jealously-guarded status symbol, while being instructed in the use of the surveying instruments. The steel in the swords affected the readings, and it was only after much argument that they were persuaded to discard them temporarily. Also, they found it demeaning to engage in manual labour, whereas the British engineers had no qualms in rolling up their sleeves to help out. For their part, the Japanese complained of the arrogance and overbearing attitude of the British. Evidence of this is found in a phrase-book of the Japanese language published shortly after the opening of the railway, which presumed that the following expressions would be necessary for travel in that country:

'You must put on another carriage'. 'I insist on another carriage being put on.'

'I will complain to the Chief of the Railroad Department if you don't put one on.'

Morell died in November 1871 of either pneumonia or tuberculosis, with work on the section only half-completed. Despite their differences, Morell's work was greatly valued by the Japanese, and a statue of him can now be seen at Sakuragicho Station in Yokohama.

The line was opened to passenger traffic on a single track from Shinagawa, in the southern suburbs of Tokyo, to Yokohama in July 1872. Goods traffic followed on September 15th, 1873. The official opening ceremony at Shinbashi, nearer to Tokyo's centre, took place on October 12th, 1872, with the Emperor himself presiding and many foreign and local dignitaries in attendance. The Emperor took a return trip to Yokohama. Thomas Hart, the British engine driver, was taken to task because, in his anxiety not to be late into Yokohama, he actually arrived early and caused embarrassment among waiting officials who were not ready to receive the Emperor. As an example of nineteenth-century culture shock, it is said that many Japanese stepped out of their shoes when boarding the train as if they were entering a house, and were mortified when the train drew out and the shoes were left behind on the platform.

The railway was largely British-staffed, from engineers and foremen-platelayers to drivers and ticket-collectors. The firemen were Japanese from the outset, however. One European was both ignorant and patronising when he said of the employment of Japanese drivers:

It would be all very well so long as the train was on a straight line, but I doubt if any Japs could be trusted to steer the engine round those curves!

The first Japanese, in fact, drove a train on the Tokyo-Yokohama section in April 1879.

In the peak years of employment of foreign labour in 1875–6, of foreign employees on the railways ninety-four were British, two American, two German and two Danish. The British were engaged not only as engineering advisers, but also as artisans such as stonemasons and blacksmiths. William Cargill, the Superintendent of Communications, received the highest regular salary: 2,000 [pounds sterling] a month, of any foreign worker in Japan in the Meiji era.

There were three classes of travel, referred to initially as upper, middle and lower, which were renamed first, second and third in 1897. Upper class passengers mainly comprised civil and military officials and foreigners. The middle class fare from Shinbashi to Yokohama was twice that of the lower, and the upper class three times. Despite the expense, the new form of transport proved popular with the paying public. Rates for carrying freight were very competitive. One estimate claims that freight costs between Tokyo and Yokohama were slashed to one-seventieth of the cost of previous methods of transport. In the first full year of freight operations 46,000 tons were carried by rail. By 1887 this had risen to 578,000 and by 1897 to 1,583,000.

In 1872 ten daily trains ran in each direction between Shinbashi and Yokohama, all scheduled to leave on the hour and to take forty-five minutes for the 29 km journey. Locomotive power was provided by ten tank engines made by the Vulcan foundry of Newton-le-Willows in England, which ran until 1930. One is now preserved in Tokyo's Transport Museum. Britain also provided all the passenger cars and goods wagons. These consisted of fifty-eight double-axle wooden passenger coaches divided into three classes, with eighteen seats for the upper, twenty-two for the middle and thirty for the lower class.

Opinions on the new railway were divided. The traveller Isabella Bird wrote in 1878:

> The Yokohama station is a handsome and suitable stone building with a spacious approach, ticket offices on our plan, roomy waiting rooms for different classes—uncarpeted, however, in consideration of Japanese clogs—and supplied with daily papers.

Henry Faulds wrote in 1874:

> The line, constructed by British engineers, is, on the testimony of a distinguished American railway constructor, 'as firm as a rock', the gauge is somewhat narrower than the usual British gauge; the engines are of British build, somewhat too light, perhaps, but effective and extremely elegant in appearance, while the carriages, with the exception of those in third class, have the seats arranged lengthwise, like our tramway cars.

More professional critics were not so effusive. The engineer E.G. Holtham, writing in 1877, said the railway was 'a model of how things should not be, from the rotting wooden drains to the ambitious terminal stations'. R.H. Brunton, another British engineer, was more caustic still:

> The construction of this line . . . was, perhaps not unnaturally, attended by a series of the most unfortunate mischances and mistakes—buildings were erected, pulled down, and re-erected in other places; numerous diversions were made; bridges were strengthened after completion; rails were twisted in every conceivable form and laid in such a way that it seemed impossible for a train to run over them . . . the main cause of this somewhat deplorable condition of affairs was that the European staff engaged to direct operations . . . supinely permitted interference of the native officials with their operations.

The Tokaido line was finally completed from Tokyo to Kobe in July 1889. British advisers and workers helped with construction at the western end throughout the 1870s, but it had always been envisaged that the employment of foreign labour would be a temporary expediency. After the peak year for foreign employment, 1876, the number of Britons working on the railways declined rapidly to just a handful by the early 1890s. One of these was Richard Trevithick, grandson of the man who designed the world's first steam locomotive. The younger Trevithick, in turn, designed the first steam locomotive to be built in Japan.

The opening of the Tokaido line made it possible to travel from Tokyo to Kobe in just over twenty hours. The speed, low cost and high capacity offered by the freight service was a major factor in the development of the industrial belt along the south coast of Japan, which today forms an almost continuous conurbation between Tokyo and Kobe.

Japan's railway network matured during the 1920s, by which time all major towns had been connected. After a speedy recovery from the chaos of the Second World War, Japan's railways were rapidly modernised and transformed into the highly efficient system much admired and studied by foreigners today. The student has become the teacher.

RON CLOUGH has lectured in Japanese at the University of Hertfordshire. He is the author of *Japanese Business Information: An Introduction.* (British Library, 1995).

The Transatlantic Telegraph Cable

Eighth Wonder of the World

Gillian Cookson describes how the first physical link across the Atlantic was finally achieved.

In 1858 a telegram of ninety-eight words from Queen Victoria to President James Buchanan of the United States opened a new era in global communication. The Queen's message of congratulation took sixteen and a half hours to transmit through the new transatlantic telegraph cable. After White House staff had satisfied themselves that it was not a hoax, the President sent a reply of 143 words in a relatively rapid ten hours. Without the cable, a despatch in one direction alone would have taken perhaps twelve days by the speediest combination of inland telegraph and fast steamer.

The Atlantic crossing had been achieved only at the third attempt, and until the first messages passed on August 17th, 1858, it was by no means certain that the project was technically feasible. Once its success had become clear, as far as the public was concerned all doubts melted away, to be replaced by huge enthusiasm. The impact of the first telegraphic communication between Europe and America is hard to appreciate now. *The Times* enthused:

> More was done yesterday for the consolidation of our Empire than the wisdom of our statesmen, the liberality of our Legislature, or the loyalty of our colonists could ever have effected. Distance between Canada and England is annihilated.

The United States celebrated its new closeness to Europe. City Hall in New York was alight with candles and fireworks. On September 1st, a procession filled Broadway and led to the largest ever fete in Union Square. On both sides of the ocean, songs were written, souvenir editions of newspapers published, sermons preached about the unity of mankind. Cyrus Field, the New York businessman whose vision had driven the project forward against great odds, became a national hero.

But even as the celebrations continued, the line was breaking down. In all, 271 messages, increasingly fragmentary and incomprehensible, passed down the cable before it finally failed on September 18th. The Atlantic Telegraph Company's total investment of around £500,000 on the three attempts was a complete loss. The failure was blamed on manufacturing faults in the copper core and insulation, and on poor electrical management. The company's chief electrician, Wildman Whitehouse, a former surgeon from Brighton, had hastened the cable's end by increasing the voltage as the cable deteriorated.

The sceptics, those who had criticised the Atlantic projectors for being over-ambitious and underqualified for such an enterprise, began to re-emerge. The criticisms had some justification. Yet although it is now clear that Whitehouse was incompetent, at the time there were few engineers with practical experience of electricity, fewer still with a sound understanding of the subject, and no easy means of telling who was best qualified to supervise such a project. Electrical science was in its infancy, and the associated technology for submarine telegraphs—including cable construction, cable laying, and the design of instruments to send and receive signals—was still in the process of development. Field trials were central to this, each expedition experimental, the Atlantic ocean a laboratory from which a new understanding of electricity was growing. Those who were to be leading practitioners of submarine telegraphy during the 1860s, including Charles Bright and William Thomson (later Lord Kelvin), learned their trade by experience through trial and error during the unsuccessful attempts on the Atlantic in 1857 and 1858.

In retrospect, the Atlantic expeditions during the 1850s do appear to have been over-ambitious. The scheme had been launched less than twenty years after Wheatstone's first experimental telegraph, which opened in 1837 between Euston and Camden. While overland telegraphs had become well-established by the 1850s, submarine lines were technically much more difficult. The first working submarine cable had been laid in 1851 between Dover and Calais. Its design formed the basis of future cables: a copper conductor, the cable's core, was insulated with gutta percha, a kind of latex from Malaya which had been found preferable to India rubber for underwater use. The cable was armoured with iron wire, thicker at the shore ends where extra protection from anchors and tidal chafing was needed. Although this basic technology was in place, there was a world of difference between a cross-Channel line of less than twenty-five miles and a cable capable of spanning the Atlantic, crossing the 1,660 nautical miles between Valentia, on the west coast of Ireland, and Newfoundland in depths of up to two miles. There were difficulties of scale, and also of electrical management. In long submarine cables, received signals were extremely feeble as there was no way of amplifying or relaying them in mid-ocean; there was also a phenomenon of 'smearing', where the sharpness of transmitted signals was lost.

An elaborate procedure had to be worked out to rendezvous and splice the line in mid-ocean.

The scale of the enterprise brought more obvious problems. There was no ship in the world large enough to stow the full length of cable. An elaborate procedure had to be worked out to rendezvous and splice the line in mid-ocean, for while the cable-laying vessel could communicate with the shore, ships out of sight could not communicate with each other. Cables could be laid only during a short summer season, so that cable production was rushed. Quality control was inadequate and other preparations carried out in haste. And even in summer the Atlantic could be cruel. On the 1857 and 1858 expeditions, the ships used were naval sailing vessels. Contemporary engravings of HMS *Agamemnon* and the US frigate *Niagara* at work laying the cable show scenes which rather evoke Tudor sea battles than suggest the dawning of a new age of electrical engineering. The first, unsuccessful, expedition of 1858 almost ended in outright disaster when one of the worst storms ever recorded came close to wrecking the *Agamemnon*.

Given the complexity of the problems, it was a great achievement to have completed a working line in the 1850s, and hardly surprising that it soon failed. Once the cable had expired, many of the public, including some who had suffered large losses, turned against the scheme. It was even suggested that the whole episode had been a confidence trick designed to extract money from gullible investors. Yet while many saw it only as a financial disaster, those closer to events took confidence from the experience. The small group which could be described as fledgling electrical engineers saw that amidst all the faults and difficulties there was the basis of a viable project. These men—such as Thomson, Bright, Fleeming Jenkin and Latimer Clark, who, like the telegraph companies and most others involved, were British—saw the expeditions as a glorious opportunity to experiment on evolving technology. Although the 1858 failure had shown that there were still fundamental electrical questions to be answered, the engineers' optimism was undimmed and their confidence actually increasing.

While the electricians had been heartened about the technical possibilities, there were others who continued to back the scheme for its potential to transform transatlantic relations. In its short life the cable had carried market information, official despatches, and news which, whatever its content, was exciting for its immediacy. The British government had had a stark lesson in how useful the telegraph could be in ruling its scattered empire. One of the messages passing through the 1858 cable told the 62nd Regiment in Nova Scotia that they were no longer needed to help subdue the Indian mutiny, countermanding previous instructions

to embark for London. This nine-word communication alone, it was said, had saved the British government £50,000, the expense of a needless mobilisation.

The government, though, was unwilling to offer any direct support for further attempts on the Atlantic. Their reluctance did not stem simply from a prevailing economic creed which frowned on public money supporting private enterprises. In fact both the British and United States governments had given significant help to the expeditions of 1857 and 1858, carrying out advance ocean surveys, and providing ships and personnel during the laying. Later, in 1868, all British inland cables were nationalised under Post Office control. So there was not an inflexible principle against public involvement in telegraphy. The real reason for the government's unwillingness to invest directly in a transatlantic cable lay in a calamity they had suffered with a projected telegraph to India.

The first British government venture into submarine cables had been encouraging. During the Crimean War in 1855 a temporary, unarmoured cable was laid between Bulgaria and Balaklava, financed, owned and operated by Britain. It served its purpose, functioning until the end of the war the following year. During the next major foreign crisis, the Indian Mutiny of 1857, an emergency request for reinforcements took forty days to reach London from the besieged British community in the city of Lucknow. As a direct consequence Lord Derby's government agreed to underwrite a privately promoted Red Sea cable. The existing arrangements, using an overland route across the Ottoman empire, were unsatisfactory even in times of peace. Telegraphers who did not understand English transcribed Morse code messages at far-flung relay stations, making so many errors that telegrams, delivered days or weeks late, were often impossible to decipher. There was additional anxiety about security when confidential messages passed over foreign territory. An advantage of submarine cables is that they are almost impossible to eavesdrop—which is why they continued to be used in preference to radio for classified despatches during the Second World War. A Red Sea line would solve these problems of reliability and security. Derby's government entered the Red Sea agreement despite the failure of the 1858 Atlantic cable, for public opinion strongly supported a secure line to India under British control. In any case the government's role was to encourage investors by giving only a guarantee, that shareholders would receive a minimum 4.5 per cent return on their investment providing the line tested well for a month after laying. The theory was that if the line were a technical failure, there would be no call on public funds; if it worked, it should make at least some profit and the government would at worst be subsidising a cable which was of great strategic benefit to the British Empire. In fact the result was the greatest possible financial disaster for the government—and it fell upon Derby's successor as prime minister, Palmerston, and Gladstone, his Chancellor of the Exchequer. The Red Sea cable, in six sections totalling 3,500 miles and connecting Egypt with the west coast of India, was completed in February 1860. No telegram ever passed its entire length, but crucially for the guarantors each section tested successfully before failing. The government was therefore bound to pay Red Sea investors £36,000 a year for fifty years, an eventual cost to the Exchequer of £1.8 million. After this there could be no further question of direct public support of long-distance cables.

The government still believed that there was a pressing need for long-distance deep-sea cables to link the outposts of the British Empire. Its next action was arguably of much greater value to the submarine telegraph industry than any number of financial guarantees. An inquiry into the technical aspects of long-distance telegraphy was set up, under the auspices of the Board of Trade and the Atlantic Telegraph Company. The committee was chaired by a respected Board of Trade technical expert, Captain Douglas Galton. It met during 1859 and 1860, taking evidence from every significant electrical engineer with submarine cable experience. In this new industry, some of these experts were still in their twenties: Charles Bright had been chief engineer on the 1858 expedition at the age of twenty-six, Jenkin was a year younger. Thomson, already a towering figure in the field, was not yet forty.

Galton's report, published in 1861, included detailed recommendations on cable construction, laying and operating. His committee summarised best practice and also suggested further definition and standardisation of electrical units. A number of electrical engineers, most notably Thomson and Jenkin, were already working to develop much more delicate and sensitive instruments to send and receive messages, and for cable testing. The British Association quickly formed its own committee, under the direction of Fleeming Jenkin, to deal with the matter of electrical units. The work of Galton, and of those responding to his challenges, proved decisive in the future of long-distance submarine telegraphs.

The period between Galton's report and the next attempt to lay a cable across the Atlantic, in 1865, coincides exactly with the duration of the Civil War in the United States. This is not to say that war directly delayed the project, although some of the US Navy officers who had been involved in the Atlantic cable scheme found themselves fighting on opposing sides. In fact the war strengthened the desire for a transatlantic cable. There was a clamour for news of a conflict whose effects were widely felt in Britain. The Reuter news agency even built its own telegraph line in 1863, covering the 80 miles from Cork to Crookhaven in the far south-west of Ireland, where incoming steamships from Newfoundland could be intercepted and the most urgent news from America despatched to London ahead of Reuters' rivals. The need for faster and more reliable communications was underlined by events during the war, particularly the *Trent* incident, which almost drew the United Kingdom into the American conflict. Cyrus Field, an Anglophile and firm supporter of the Union, worked tirelessly to sustain the Atlantic project while the war raged around him. Appealing to meetings of American businessmen for funds, Field argued the cable's benefits to commerce while also emphasising it could improve international understanding.

The American Civil War strengthened the desire for a transatlantic cable.

Above all, it was problems attracting new funds which led to the delay after 1861. While each successive disappointment brought nearer the prospect of technical success, the public did not distinguish between degrees of failure, so that with each renewed attempt it became harder to raise money from increasingly sceptical investors. The Civil War may also have made potential backers in Britain wary of supporting an Anglo-American scheme. Some leading promotors of the 1850s cables had suffered heavy losses which made them unable or unwilling to continue, and they were replaced as directors of the Atlantic Telegraph Company by a new breed of wealthy entrepreneur.

The financial arrangements and company structures in place for the next attempt on the Atlantic, in 1865, were every bit as innovative as the technology. There was a marked change in approach from the 1850s. It had been necessary to bring in city financiers and men with experience of large-scale business, in place of the regional merchants who had dominated the earlier company. Cyrus Field, his idealism and optimism intact, retained a central role. A distinctly more cynical group gathered around him, among them Daniel Gooch, best known for his work as engineer and manager of the Great Western Railway; Thomas Brassey, one of Britain's leading railway promoters, who invested £60,000 in the new project; and John Pender, with wealth founded in Manchester textiles and a long-standing interest in submarine telegraphs.

Even with Brassey and other substantial backers, there was a shortfall. The £700,000 required was raised partly through new fund-raising devices, made possible by a change in company laws in 1856 and 1862. The introduction of limited liability allowed a restructuring of the cable-making and laying industry. By merging the main submarine cable contractors with the company which made cable cores, Pender created the Telegraph Construction and Maintenance Company Ltd. (Telcon) in 1864. Telcon subscribed half the capital required, partly through deferred payments and also by accepting telegraph company stock in place of cash. Control of the Atlantic Telegraph Company and of Telcon had fallen to a small and close-knit group of large-scale investors.

Along with this streamlined organisation and the technical improvements—a cable manufactured with care in line with Galton's recommendations, improved instruments, more sensitive laying equipment, a profounder understanding of electricity—the 1865 expedition enjoyed another great advantage over previous attempts: there was at last a ship large enough to store the entire cable. Brunel's *Great Eastern,* the biggest ship in the world, launched in 1860 as a passenger liner, had proved a white elephant and bankrupted previous owners. She was laid up in 1863 and offered at auction. Gooch bought her for a knock-down price, stripped out the fittings, converted the holds to cable tanks, and chartered the ship to Telcon. Weighing 19,000 tons and powered by 11,500 h.p. steam engines, the *Great Eastern* offered manoeuvrability as well as size. All seemed set fair for the 1865 expedition.

But like its predecessors, the attempt, which began off the west coast of Ireland in June 1865, ended in failure. After a number of minor problems had been overcome during the early stages, the *Great Eastern* had laid 1,200 miles of the line and was only two days away from its destination at Heart's Content, Newfoundland, when the cable again snapped. Usually it was possible to grapple for broken cables, splice them and continue, but this time the weather made retrieval impossible. The spot was marked with a buoy and the attempt abandoned.

Success had once again eluded the scheme's backers. There was frustration and disappointment, but tinged with a belief that the objective was close to being achieved. This had been a setback, not a catastrophe. The projectors immediately began to organise another attempt for the following summer. New problems had arisen. A major and sudden obstacle was the discovery that the Atlantic Telegraph Company, which had been established under an Act of Parliament in 1856, was acting outside its powers in trying to raise its capital by a further £600,000 to finance the 1866 expedition. There was no parliamentary time to amend the company's charter. To avoid another year's delay, Gooch and Pender established a new limited liability company, the Anglo-American Telegraph Company Ltd., to take over the project. Ultimately this solution led to other difficulties, for the relationship between the Anglo and Atlantic companies was troubled and ill-defined, and the arrangements led to further rifts between old and new investors. But for 1866, Gooch and Pender's actions saved the scheme. The balance of funds needed was secured through Telcon and the merchant bank of Morgan and Co., only days before a stock market crash which might have ended any hopes of laying a cable that summer.

The 1866 expedition achieved everything that had been hoped for. In July, the *Great Eastern* landed a new cable in Newfoundland only two weeks after embarking from Valentia. By the beginning of September the 1865 line had been retrieved and repaired, and two Atlantic cables were in operation. Queen Victoria again exchanged congratulations with her American counterpart, President Andrew Johnson. Gooch received a baronetcy, Thomson and others involved were knighted. The celebrations were muted in comparison with those of 1858, especially in the United States, where war had recently ended and the new Atlantic telegraph, much more than on previous expeditions, was seen as a product of British work and capital.

John Pender was vexed not to have been honoured. His contribution to the Atlantic venture, especially after 1862, had been substantial, and ultimately he risked everything he owned on the 1866 attempt. Experience with the Atlantic line had shown Pender that intercontinental cables were no longer a gamble, that technical improvements had reduced them to an acceptable risk. Moreover they could be exceptionally profitable. This encouraged him to continue promoting long-distance telegraphs, and the companies he launched during the following years laid cables to the Far East, Australasia and South America. Once a line was established, he followed a pattern of consolidating it into his parent company. Pender made another fortune, and was finally rewarded with his knighthood in 1888. The global

communications empire which he had founded eventually became Cable & Wireless Ltd.

Perhaps the most exciting aspect of the new cable to the general public was the novelty of fresh news from across the Atlantic.

In contrast with Pender's hard-nosed pragmatism, Cyrus Field was driven by a higher vision. Yet Field was no innocent in business; he too had risked everything and then gained considerably from the Atlantic cable. His ideals were themselves business-oriented: world peace was advantageous to commerce. Whether the telegraph did improve international relations is questionable, for faster communications do not necessarily lead to better understanding. For Britain, the cable network certainly eased the task of ruling a far-flung empire. It also brought the benefits to commerce which Field had foreseen and transformed the financial markets of the world, bringing them into one global system. Not least, and perhaps the most exciting aspect of the new cable to the general public, was the novelty of fresh news from across the Atlantic, whetting an enduring appetite for more. It was here, rather than through diplomacy and politicians, that the cultures of two continents began to converge.

Although the successful cable of 1866 did not generate the same instant elation as the short-lived effort of 1858, its impact was far-reaching. Achieving the Atlantic crossing marked a turning point in long-distance telegraphy. Deep-sea cables, no longer an heroic struggle against the elements, had become instead a mature technology and a serious business.

For Further Reading

Gillian Cookson and Colin A. Hempstead, *A Victorian Scientist and Engineer: Fleeming Jenkin and the Birth of Electrical Engineering* (Ashgate, 2000); Hugh Barty-King, *Girdle round the Earth: the story of Cable and Wireless* (Heinemann, 1979); Charles Bright, *Submarine Cables: their history, construction and working* (Arno, New York, 1974 [1898]); B. S. Finn, *Submarine Telegraphy: the Grand Victorian Technology* (Science Museum, 1973); Daniel R. Headrick, *The Invisible Weapon: Telecommunications and International Politics, 1851–1945* (Oxford University Press, 1991); Donald Read, *The Power of News: the History of Reuters, 1849–1989* (Oxford University Press, 1999).

DR. GILLIAN COOKSON, Editor of the *Victoria County History of Durham,* is based in the History Department, University of Durham. She is grateful to the Leverhulme Trust for supporting the research on which this article is based.

This article first appeared in *History Today,* March 2000, pp. 44–51. Copyright © 2000 by History Today, Ltd. Reprinted by permission.

A Tale of Two Reputations

Jared Diamond

We scientists have fantasies of being uniquely qualified to make great discoveries. Alas, reality is cruel: most of us are replaceable. For the vast majority of scientific contributions, if scientist X hadn't achieved it that year, scientist Y would have achieved the same result or something very similar soon thereafter. In modern molecular biology, most famous discoveries emerged as multiple teams raced toward the finish line, with the "loser" only a few months behind the "winner." For instance, if James Watson and Francis Crick hadn't published the correct structure of DNA on April 25, 1953, Linus Pauling, who was working on the same problem and had just published an incorrect structure, would surely have arrived at the correct answer within a short time.

Have any individuals really made a major, lasting difference to the course of science? More specifically, would their discoveries or conceptualizations have eluded other scientists until decades later if these individuals had not been born, and did their contributions have a unique impact that persisted long afterward? By those two criteria, I think that only two scientists within the last two centuries clearly qualify as irreplaceable: Charles Darwin and Sigmund Freud. (I feel unsure whether Albert Einstein's impact was as far-reaching.) A comparison of Darwin and Freud proves interesting. What made them irreplaceable, what exactly did they get right, what did they get wrong, how similar were their personalities and their peer relations, and how do their reputations compare today?

To begin with, Darwin and Freud were both multifaceted geniuses with many talents in common. Both were great observers, attuned to perceiving in familiar phenomena a significance that had escaped almost everyone else. Searching with insatiable curiosity for underlying explanations, both did far more than discover new facts or solve circumscribed problems, such as the structure of DNA: they synthesized knowledge from a wide range of fields and created new conceptual frameworks, large parts of which are still accepted today. Both were prolific writers and forceful communicators who eventually converted many or most of their contemporaries to their positions. (In this, they were unlike Gregor Mendel, the founder of genetics, who within his lifetime convinced nobody of the significance of his discoveries.)

Both made their contributions as a result of new insights, not as a result of inventing a new instrument or technology. In fact, both used little more than their eyes and ears. One must therefore pause to wonder why Darwin's views on evolution, and Freud's on the human mind, had not already been formulated by Aristotle and the ancient Greeks. The answer is that the views of both depended on the enormous amount of knowledge that had accumulated over the two millennia since Aristotle's time—not only discoveries about natural history and the human mind but also a developing framework of concepts and questions (what historians describe by the German word Fragestellung).

Darwin's contributions came at a time when almost everyone (including scientists) believed in the divine and independent creation of species, and when scientists were recognizing patterns in the burgeoning discoveries about fossils, taxonomy, and biogeography but still lacked explanations for those patterns. Today Darwin is best known for establishing the fact of evolution and for recognizing the major role of natural selection in driving it. Actually, he achieved far more than those two most famous of his contributions. He also recognized sexual selection as an additional evolutionary driving force, laid the foundation for today's understanding of animal behavior, published a major work on the behavior and physiology of insectivorous plants, and provided the correct explanation for hierarchically branched taxonomies as well as for the origins of biogeographic regions, coral reefs, volcanic rocks, and soils. Underlying Darwin's contributions were his very broad technical competencies in anatomy, botany, embryology, geology, paleontology, taxonomy, and zoology, as well as his threefold methodological brilliance as an observer, experimentalist, and theoretician.

In his mastery and synthesis of many types of information and his ability to utilize diverse approaches, Darwin was unique. No biologist then or since has come even close to matching him, and that's why no one else made his contributions. While it is true that Alfred Russel Wallace and Darwin independently came up with the idea of natural selection and evolution, the reasons that Darwin, not Wallace, is regarded as the irreplaceable genius are instructive. Wallace's reasoning about natural selection, and the initial evidence he based it on, were essentially the same as Darwin's. But the papers about natural selection by Wallace and Darwin that the Linnean Society published side by side in its journal in 1858 were ignored. The world did not begin to be convinced of natural selection until Darwin published the Origin of Species a year later, making an overwhelming case by amassing evidence from many fields. Because Wallace lacked depth in many of the disciplines and approaches mastered by Darwin, Wallace could never have made the overwhelming case that Darwin did, and he frequently acknowledged Darwin's greatness thereafter.

Freud's contributions came at a time when interest in mental illness and its classification was growing but its etiology was virtually unknown and treatments were mostly ineffective—in part because clinicians and researchers were still focused on conscious, cognitive processes. Freud's status is unique because he recognized an entirely different mental realm, and many of his concepts—pioneering and radical in their time—are so familiar today that they have entered the daily vocabulary of the general public. These include the idea of the unconscious, the significance of dreams, the lingering importance of early childhood experience, the Oedipus complex, motivational conflict, and defenses such as denial, rationalization, and repression. For some mental conditions, Freud also devised therapies based on the "talking cure" rather than just on the then-prevalent treatments of electric shock, hypnosis, or institutionalization. He also developed a unifying theory of the normal personality, recognized transference and countertransference in the patient/therapist relationship, and explored the broader social consequences of individual psychopathology.

Freud searched constantly for the underlying causes of mental disorders, and he developed techniques such as free association and the study of dreams to probe the unconscious. As with Darwin, Freud's immense contributions arose from the breadth of his competence—in anatomy, neurology, pharmacology, philosophy, physiology, and psychology. More than just a psychologist who wanted to understand what makes people tick, Freud also had the therapeutic goals of a physician who wanted to help people. Like Darwin, he had no contemporaries whose contributions approached his in scope and originality; there was not even the equivalent of a Wallace to be mentioned and explained away.

Those are some of Darwin's and Freud's successes. What about their omissions and failures? Given their achievements, it may seem absurd even to bring up the issue. This question reminds me of a cartoon of some cavemen pointing to another caveman and asking, "What's that guy done since he invented fire?" Of course they were limited by the technology of their time: one can hardly fault Darwin for not anticipating by a century the recognition of DNA as the genetic material, or Freud for not determining chemical structures and the role of neurotransmitters.

Nevertheless, we still can't help wondering about some things that Darwin and Freud might have recognized or might have gotten right but didn't. Darwin's foremost omission was his failure to progress in elucidating the principles of genetics. Such progress potentially lay within his grasp, because he designed and executed brilliant experiments with plants and published a whole book on cross-pollination and self-pollination. Similarly, the results of his many experiments in pigeon breeding might readily have suggested to him the concept of recessive and dominant traits. Yet Darwin failed to extract the fundamental genetic insights that Gregor Mendel extracted by planting peas during the years just before and after Darwin was writing the Origin of Species.

Darwin also got some big things wrong. He shared the then-widespread belief in "soft inheritance" the assumption that the environment could cause adaptive changes in the hereditary material, but his younger contemporary August Weismann showed that this could not be so. Darwin accepted the postulate of "blending inheritance" (the fusion of a mother's and father's characteristics in their offspring), even though his own experiments on pigeons refuted it. Much more surprising are two other errors: he eventually failed to acknowledge the reality of species as non-interbreeding sets of populations, and hence he also eventually failed to accept that new species originate predominantly through geographic isolation, although that precise issue underlies the title of his most famous book. What makes the latter two errors so striking is that Darwin had previously formulated both ideas correctly but then abandoned his formulations in later editions of the Origin. These mistakes had long-lasting consequences, because they were not rectified by other biologists until about eighty years later and because a significant minority of biologists persist in those errors today.

Freud also made some disconcerting omissions and errors. He was a man of his time in some of his views of women; he believed, for example, that a woman's main and appropriate role was that of wife and mother. Rooted in an era that tabooed discussions of sex, he rebounded to the opposite extreme and exaggerated the roles of sex and sexual conflict in the development of the psyche. He gave insufficient credence to some patients' reports of being sexually abused as children. His emphasis on a death wish is now viewed as wrong or greatly exaggerated. At least in part because his driving motivation was to help and to cure people, not just to understand them intellectually, he was not scientifically rigorous. And as a therapist, Freud could be faulted for not departing from his focus on individuals to develop therapy for couples, families, or groups.

Today we seem much more inclined to castigate Freud for his omissions and errors than Darwin for his. I suspect that there are two reasons for our differing attitudes toward these two pioneers. One is that Freud's failures, unlike Darwin's, have had a direct impact on the lives of individual human beings. Most of us don't suffer as a result of Darwin's having eventually attributed too much scope to the process termed sympatric speciation than it actually deserves. But a powerful man's mistaken ideas about women have certainly caused suffering, just as victims of child abuse have been made to suffer when the reality of their trauma has been denied.

The other reason we are inclined to judge Freud more harshly than Darwin is that these two scientists were near opposites in their relations with peers. In this regard, we find much to admire in Darwin and much to deplore in Freud. Darwin was outstandingly generous in crediting others—including, most notably, Wallace—for their work. While Darwin came in for severe criticism from other scientists and in turn often expressed his disagreement with their views, he responded courteously, used scientific arguments, and completely avoided personalizing disputes. I can think of no one about whom he expressed hatred or said nasty things, and no one whom he tried to impede professionally. Freud, on the other hand, was outstandingly ungenerous: he denied credit to others, was intolerant of rivals, hated many people, and surrounded himself with unquestioningly loyal admirers. Freud's fallings-out with his famous psychoanalytic contemporaries Alfred Adler, Josef Breuer, Carl Jung, and Otto Rank are merely the most notorious examples. A legacy of this aspect of Freud's personality has been the ugly tendency among psychotherapists, especially those closest to the Freudian tradition, to personalize disputes and to break into factions.

Both Darwin and Freud have had their detractors, and the ideas of both men initially faced fierce opposition. Today very few scientists hold low opinions of Darwin, either as a person or as a scientist. The overwhelming majority of those who fundamentally disagree with Darwin's findings today are not scientists at all, but creationists, who do not engage seriously with the facts of biology. Virtually no contemporary scientists believe that Darwin was basically wrong. Since Darwin's time, we have of course discovered masses of new facts, formulated new concepts, and advanced beyond many of his specific interpretations, but modern biologists still consider themselves to be Darwin's intellectual descendants, working within his tradition.

By contrast, Freud's detractors remain numerous, even though they take for granted many of his concepts and contributions. Just consider how the Library of Congress's 1998–99 exhibition on Freud in Washington, D.C. (which has since traveled to major museums worldwide) triggered demands by serious thinkers that negative views of Freud be represented. There were protests that Freud was unworthy of even being honored by an exhibition. A corresponding exhibition on Darwin would have been protested only by creationists. I acknowledge a legitimate moral base underlying such Freudbashing: the human consequences of his scientific errors, and his often ugly interpersonal relations.

But there are two other types of Freud-bashing that are not defensible. One consists of pointing out all the new things learned and all the new therapies devised since Freud, as if these represent his failures or demonstrate the uselessness of his work. Yes, we now know much more about how people think and how to help them than we did in Freud's day. But just as with Darwin, that subsequent progress began with Freud's insights and would have been unthinkable without them.

The other type of Freud-bashing—much more damaging because it hurts patients—comes from a too-narrow focus on biological psychiatry. I fully accept the importance of biological psychiatry, having devoted some of my own research to problems in that area (neurotransmitters and manic-depressive illness). It has now become clear, as it could not have been in Freud's day, that some major thought and mood disorders have a biological basis, even though the details of that basis in the most widespread syndromes (depression, manic-depressive illness, schizophrenia, autism) remain elusive.

Many medical-school psychiatry departments were once bastions of Freudian psychoanalysis, whose practitioners resisted biological studies. But now the pendulum has swung to the opposite extreme: psychiatry departments have become bastions of molecular biology, at which much more time is devoted to studying and teaching psychopharmacology than to what are called talk therapies. Outside academia, however—among clinical psychologists, social workers, and lay analysts—those therapies are a growth industry. Among the many reasons for academe's imbalance are its reductionist bias and its professional reward system: many Nobel Prizes and National Institutes of Health grants are available for biochemical research, but many fewer NIH grants and nary a Nobel Prize for talk therapies. Other considerations are that contemporary Western societies tend to seek technological fixes, and health insurance companies are more willing to reimburse claims for drugs than for talk therapy. Certainly, it would be less painful for both therapists and patients if our problems could be solved by taking pills rather than accepting responsibility for our suffering and then learning new ways of interacting with others. Not only that, but the stigma of "mental illness" and the challenges of moral responsibility would be diminished if one's problems arose from chemical processes beyond one's control (as is true in some cases) rather than from voluntary actions.

To my mind, academe's swing away from talk therapies is tragic. Major advances are still being made in this field—for instance, in crisis counseling and in child and family therapy. Almost all of us face stress in our jobs, our health, our personal relationships, and our own aspirations. Almost all of us carry emotional and cognitive baggage from our early lives that leaves us with some inappropriate responses in our lives as adults. Some of those problems can be dealt with by talking with friends. But some problems require professional distance, experience, and skills—the skills in which a talk therapist is trained and that are far beyond the capacity of a friend to deliver.

Even specialists in biological psychiatry need thorough training in talk therapies, because it can be difficult to figure out whether a patient's problems have a primarily biological or a primarily nonbiological basis. Even clients whose problems are probably fundamentally biological (such as in manic-depressive illness) tend to have associated psychological issues that need attention. Physicians who rely heavily on prescribing drugs often don't take time to establish a relationship with a patient, regularly forget that the patient and physician are locked in an emotionally charged relationship, and then are surprised at how often patients fail to take the drugs prescribed for them. Understanding that unique two-way relationship was one of the many deep and far-reaching insights that put Freud right up there with Darwin.

JARED DIAMOND is a professor of physiology at the UCLA School of Medicine and a research associate in ornithology at the American Museum of Natural History.

The 20th-Century Scientific-Technical Revolution

Mikulas Teich looks at the impact of scientific transformations since 1900, and how these changes have produced a new world culture and global organisation.

MIKULAS TEICH

Just before the radical political changes of 1989/90, the renowned *Times Literary Supplement* asked fifteen historians to describe the books or project they would most like to see undertaken. In the context of my long-standing historical interest in the social relations of science (going back to the early 1940s), I found Eric Hobsbawm's contribution of particular relevance.

Briefly, Hobsbawm wished to see the history of the world written since the Second World War and, in particular, focusing on the third quarter of the twentieth century. He gave two reasons for putting forward this suggestion. First, he regarded this phase 'as the most revolutionary era in the recorded history of the glove', adding 'To the best of my knowledge there has not been another period when human society has been so profoundly transformed in a matter of decades'. His second reason was that contemporaries, including politicians, have failed to comprehend just what was happening. Thus many able observers, in his view, believe honestly but erroneously, that world peace since 1945 has been maintained only by reason of nuclear deterrence.

Underlying the questions this raises is the complex relationship between science, technology and society in history in general, and in the twentieth century in particular. Here I intend to discuss these issues briefly with respect to the Scientific Revolution in the sixteenth and seventeenth centuries, the Industrial Revolution in the eighteenth and nineteenth centuries and, more extensively, to look at the Scientific-Technical Revolution of the twentieth century. These terms have themselves come under question, not least because of recurring doubts about how we identify clear self-contained periods in the evolution of science(s), technology and the economy that people can agree with. According to this view (which I do not share) the concept 'revolution' is a historiographical construction which does not reflect historical reality. All the same, the question of wherein lies the revolutionariness of the Scientific, Industrial and Scientific-Technical Revolutions

merits consideration if only to avoid the danger of over-inflating, and thus putting on a pedestal, innumerable past and contemporary scientific-technical, agricultural and industrial innovations by repeatedly calling these revolutions.

The theoretical and practical directions in which Copernicus, Galileo, Kepler and Newton developed astronomy and mechanics are denoted as the commonly defined Scientific Revolution. Some are perplexed that this phase of scientific history can be declared 'revolutionary' when it lasted 150 years. Others dwell on the fact that these protagonists in the revolutionary transformation of astronomy and mechanics did not fully divest themselves of traditional ancient and medieval ideas. But neither the duration of the process, nor the blurred line that separates the old and the new in Copernicus' or Newton's thought is the problem.

Is there any point, then, in speaking of a Scientific Revolution in the sixteenth and seventeenth centuries? I believe there is. Its distinctive feature has to be sought after in its methodology. It was the maturation of a consolidated system of inquiry that distinguishes the investigations into natural phenomena during the sixteenth and seventeenth centuries from those of earlier times. Partial hallmarks, such as observation, classification, systematisation and theorising were already developed in Classical antiquity, but it was during the sixteenth and seventeenth centuries that these procedures, decisively extended by systemic experimentation and quantification, and the formulation of laws of nature, began to be institutionalised, giving rise to science as is still practised today. Its birth was intricately linked to the emergence of bourgeois society and formation of the capitalist system, defined and moulded by social, economic, political, religious and cultural forces which were pushing for change.

The social dynamics of the eighteenth and nineteenth centuries received substantial impetus from the expansion and establishment of the capitalist system of industrial production in parts of Europe and America, in the train of what is termed the Industrial Revolution. It is not particularly illuminating, as I have already said, to populate history with unlimited numbers of Industrial Revolutions on the basis of technical breakthroughs perceived to be 'revolutionary'. Such an approach relies on the view that, whereas the First Industrial Revolution centred on steam, at the heart of the Second was electric power, while the Third turns—currently—on microelectronics. In both the most general and specific senses, the Industrial Revolution is about the changeover from economies based on agriculture to ones based upon industry. It concerns a many-sided process encompassing not only technology (techniques) but also other spheres such as social others. Between approximately 1750 and 1850, it preceded in Britain homologous and to this day unconcluded transitions to industrial economies in other countries under not identical social conditions.

It is the historical experience of the atomic bomb, microelectronics or genetic engineering, rather than analysis, that lies behind the virtually undisputed view that, in comparison with the nineteenth century, a qualitative change in the relations between science and technology has taken place in the twentieth. This has found expression in terms such as 'science-based technology' or 'science-related technology' which, however, do not do justice to the fundamental transformation that has taken place in the complex relationships between scientific discovery, technological development, practical application and social factors. Following the lead of the physicist, J.D. Bernal (1901–71), let us refer to this twentieth-century phenomenon as the Scientific-Technical Revolution. Coining the phrase in 1957, Bernal wished to underline 'that only in our time has science come to dominate industry and agriculture'. It was the Great War, the economic crisis of the Thirties, and the advent of Fascism which impelled Bernal, a highly creative thinker in matters of scientific and social evolution, to examine critically the function of science in society in the first place, leading to the publication in 1939, on the eve of the Second World War, of his seminal and highly relevant book *The Social Function of Science*. In this work, Bernal devotes a whole chapter to assessing the application of scientific knowledge to war; explaining that the close historical links between science and warfare are due not to any mystical affinity between the two, but because the urgency of war needs are greater than that of civil needs, and that in war, novelty is at a premium.

The Great War, according to Bernal, profoundly altered the situation because, in his words, 'scientists found themselves for the first time not a luxury but a necessity to their respective Governments'. At the same time, he points out, this conflation of science and war created problems. For one, there were millions who came to blame scientific developments for the sufferings they experienced during the Great War and therefore went on to reject the idea that science was intrinsically beneficial to mankind. One consequence of this was that among the younger generation of scientists there were several who began to question an involvement in military research as something entirely alien to the spirit of science.

As a Marxist, Bernal placed history firmly at the centre of his analysis of what science is about. 'To see the function of science as a whole', he wrote, 'it is necessary to look at it against the widest possible background of history.' He went on to identify three major changes which mankind has experienced since its relatively late emergence on earth. The first and second changes, the foundation of human society and civilisation respectively, occurred before the dawn of recorded history. The third change he described as 'that scientific transformation of society which is now taking place and for which we have as yet no name.' Bernal traced its origins to the related processes of the rise of capitalism and the birth of modern science in about the middle of the fifteenth century, arguing:

> Though capitalism was essential to the early development of science, giving it for the first time, a practical value, the human importance of science transcends in every way that of capitalism, and, indeed, the full development of science in the service of humanity is incompatible with the continuance of capitalism.

In effect Bernal divided world history into three stages of humanity, stressing that the third stage had still to be achieved. The following passage from the concluding chapter of the book, published more than a half-century ago, may help bring Bernal a measure of recognition for his significance as one of the twentieth-century's most creative thinkers about society, man and nature:

> We must realize that we are in the middle of one of the major transition periods of human history. Our most immediate problem is to ensure that the transition is accomplished as rapidly as possible, with the minimum of materials, human and cultural destruction . . . belonging to an age of transition we are primarily concerned with its tasks, and here science is but one factor in a complex of economic and political forces.

There is no way to get to grips with the important issues raised by Eric Hobsbawm without going back to the chain of scientific and technical developments set in motion since the turn of this century. Take, for example, the radical rethinking about the structure of matter and space-time (as defined by the Curies, Rutherford, Einstein and others) the origins of which stem from this period. From here events coupled with military demands, economic expectations, technological feasibilities, political interests and other interlinked factors led to developments such as radar, the atomic and hydrogen bombs, electronic computers, automation and space navigation.

The penetration into the micro and macrocosmos has provided mankind with the means, in the context of nuclear and space warfare, to destroy itself. Alternatively, it has provided impetus for governments of the USA and USSR, irrespective of their different social systems, to look for non-military solutions to international problems. Having been made aware of the real danger of self-annihilation through the use of nuclear weapons both sides stepped back. Does this not suggest that the impact of nuclear weapons on the maintenance of peace merits a thorough historical analysis in its own right? It is not without historical interest that the early history of electronic computing intertwines with radar and atomic bomb development during the Second World War. The first electronic computer, built for the United

States army, went into operation in 1946. It became known under the acronym ENIAC (Electronic Numerical Integrator and Computer). The computer set up in connection with the construction of the hydrogen bomb received the name MANIAC reflecting, it is said, the opinion of some of the participants about the whole project. ENIAC contained 18,000 electronic valves, it weighed 30 tons and consumed 50,000 watts. Forty years later a computer containing a 25 mm. microchip and performing similarly, was 100 times quicker and 10,000 times more reliable, but used up only 1 watt of electrical energy.

This was the consequence of the discovery of the transistor in the Bell Laboratories in the USA (1947–48). It ushered in a development regarded by many as the greatest revolution in the history of technology. Certainly, the alterations in manufacturing techniques by employing microelectronic devices go far beyond the consequences of novel production technologies, introduced and developed during the Industrial Revolution. In a penetrating article Simon Head (writing for The New York Review, February 29th, 1996) argued that, in comparison with the situation during the Industrial Revolution, a much broader variety of middle-income workers in manufacturing and service occupations is threatened by the application of information technology. The following extract underlines the point clearly:

In manufacturing there has been the advent of 'lean production,' the techniques of mass production originating mostly in Japan and now diffused throughout the industrialized world. In industries such as automobiles, electronics and machine tools, lean production has three main requirements: products must be easy to assemble ('manufacturability'); workers must be less specialized in their skills ('flexibility of labour'); and stocks of inventory must be less costly to maintain (components arrive at the assembly plant 'just in time,' and so save on both warehousing and financing costs).

The second big change has been in service industries such as banking, communications, and insurance, where 'reengineering' has transformed the work of many employees, costing large numbers of them their jobs. Just as Henry Ford once found a substitute for skilled craftsmen in rows of machines arranged along an assembly line, so the experts called reengineers have combined the skills of specialist clerks and middle managers into software packages that are attached to desktop computers.

As far as I know, it was in Czechoslovakia, from 1965 onwards, that the most searching endeavor to investigate the Scientific-Technical Revolution as a social and historical phenomenon was undertaken on an interdisciplinary basis by a team formally attached to the Institute of Philosophy of the Czechoslovak Academy of Sciences. Headed by the philosopher, Radovan Richta, the team eventually included sixty men and women active, not only in philosophy, but also in the fields of economics, sociology, psychology, political science, history, medicine, the theory of architecture and environment and encompassing several branches of science and technology.

By the spring of 1968 the material embodying the results of their collective labours was assembled and appeared in print in July of that year. What is impressive is that over 50,000 copies of the Czech and Slovak editions were sold out immediately, demonstrating the broad and intense degree of concern in the country for the issues explored in the book. Recognised abroad as a significant contribution to the literature on the social and human dimensions of twentieth-century scientific and technological developments, the volume of findings was translated into several foreign languages.

In order to acquaint the foreign reader with the climate in which the book came about, a short explanatory section was added to the introduction from which the following extract is taken:

The work was conceived in an atmosphere of critical, radical searching and intensive discussion on the way forward for a society that has reached industrial maturity while passing through a phase of far-reaching socialist transformation. In the light of theoretical enquiries, we saw an image of all modern civilization. The choice advanced in our hypothesis emerged as a practical problem.

These sentences may appear rather remote, so perhaps, a brief comment is in order. To say that the team was somehow consciously participating in the preparation of the events that are known as the 'Prague Spring of 1968' would be misleading. Nevertheless, its work constitutes an integral part of the latter's history (as yet to be written), in the sense that the analysis produced regarding the social and human scientific and technological development also led to poignant critical questions about the Czechoslovak social environment and the perspective of building Socialism and Communism in Czechoslovakia respectively. Moreover, it especially emphasised the need to take into account the fullness of man's inner life.

Hitherto individual socialist endeavor has tended to be put at a disadvantage . . . individual initiative has been curbed by a mass of directives . . . An urgent task in this field, in which scientific and technological advance can make an especially hopeful contribution, is to bring into operation a variety of ways by which the individual can share in directing all controllable processes of contemporary civilization and to do away with some of the restricting, dehumanizing effects of the traditional industrial system.

The changed political climate, following the entry into Czechoslovakia of Soviet military units (and from Poland, Hungary, GDR and Bulgaria) on August 20th, 1968, put paid to this promising, organised approach to the historical process in which science and technology, under capitalism as well as socialism, had become cardinal.

As to enquiries by scholars in the West into the nature of the scientific-technical progress in the twentieth century, they are valuable and much information may be gleaned from them. But the reality is that, despite the unfolding of social science policy studies since the 1960s, critical contributions to the problem of how to define and assess the Scientific-Technical Revolution failed to appear. Possibly this has something to do with Thomas Kuhn's influential The Structure of Scientific Revolutions (1962,

1970) which, to all intents and purposes, paid no attention to the socio-historical context.

Let us take the Internet, presently much talked about for its signally pervading impact on a variety of social, economic, political and cultural activities. To a historian it is, or should be, of interest that its origins go back to the US government's concern, following the launching of the Sputnik (1957), to safeguard its communications system revolving around a few isolated supercomputers. Writing in the *Guardian* recently, Martin Woollacott, respected writer on economic affairs, notes 'the extraordinary hope invested in the Internet which is acquiring a curiously religious connotation' and continues:

It is new, it is all-pervasive. It is, like the Holy Ghost, insubstantial and yet present everywhere. It transports its users weightlessly and effortlessly around its virtual geography. In the beginning was the Web? Somehow, it is hinted, this new form of communication will produce the explosion of growth, the expansion of knowledge, and the means of global democracy that the world requires. Yet the promise of the Web is vague, and the reality of hardship today, and perhaps of worse tomorrow, is clear.

Then there is the Human Genome Project (HGP) which impinges on legal, commercial, ethical and a host of other matters. Here too, as in the case of the Internet, the post-1945 involvement of an American government agency—the Department of Energy—in human genetics is of historical interest. Asking questions about genetic effects of radiation in the wake of the bombing of Hiroshima and Nagasaki eventually evolved into the multi-partite and multi-stage project which is to establish, by 2005, the sequence and comprehensive analysis of an estimated 3 billion base pairs in the human DNA

HGP's representative figures maintain grandiloquently that it will lead to 'the understanding of the essence of man' and of the 'determining force behind historical events'. They are less keen on examining what one among them, Robert A. Weinberg—a professor of biology at Massachusetts Institute of Technology and a member of the Whitehead Institute for Biomedical Research—has said. Weinberg points to the danger of misusing genetic information by insurance companies and government agencies threatening persons who are looking for employment or indeed planning to marry. He concludes gloomily:

As a biologist I find this prospect a bitter pill. The biological revolution of the past decades has proven extraordinarily exciting and endlessly fascinating, and it will, without doubt, spawn enormous benefit. But as with most new technologies, we will pay a price unless we anticipate the Human Genome Project's dark side. We need to craft an ethic that cherishes our human ability to transcend biology, that enshrines our spontaneity, unpredictability, and individual uniqueness. At the moment, I find myself and those around me ill-equipped to respond to the challenge.

In a similar way to the Scientific Revolution in the sixteenth and seventeenth centuries and to the Industrial Revolution in the eighteenth and nineteenth centuries, the Scientific-Technical Revolution in the twentieth century is both a factor and a product of social change. The radical difference with the latter lies in the unprecedented global influence of the chain of scientific and technical developments since the turn of the century on society worldwide. The effect on human and social conditions are further underlined by the positive as well as negative experiences following ventures into the nucleus of the atom and the cell.

At the same time and related to it has been the growth of various, private and public, forms of economic socialisation. After the collapse of the Soviet-type of societies, it shows most visibly in the commanding position in the world economy of transnational (multinational) companies. In the early 1990s, according to a United Nations study, these accounted for one-third of global output. But as Martin Woollacott observes, pointing to recent behaviour of Shell in Nigeria, the multinationals are in a moral crisis:

Multinationals are insisting not only that they take an absolutely neutral line on the politics of the countries in which they invest and trade, but they must 'work with' local standards of ethics and morality . . . The worst suspicion is that corporations have gone beyond any supposed neutrality over political conditions to develop an attachment to a particular level of bad government: not so bad as to create chaotic conditions for business, but tough enough on its citizens to ensure a combination of public order, cheap labour, and low environmental and safety costs.

In his lecture at the Salzburg Festival in 1994 George Steiner, a critical commentator on contemporary cultural life, censured the barrenness of European culture at the end of the millennium by stressing, among others, that the landings on the Moon have not inspired the creation of a single great poem, picture or metaphor. Not known for being an advocate of radical social transformation, Steiner exclaims desparingly:

The only manifest energies are those of money. Money has never smelt more sharply, it has never cried more loudly in our public and private concerns. . . there are at present fewer and fewer voices which articulate a philosophy, a political or social theory, an aesthetic which would be both in the European heritage and of world relevance.

The twentieth-century Scientific-Technical Revolution, in order to come into its full human and humane heritage, calls for a type of society very different from forms of social organisation known so far, and in that lies its revolutionariness.

MIKULAS TEICH is Emeritus Professor of Robinson College, Cambridge and Honorary Professor of the Technical University of Vienna. He is the co-author with Dorothy Needham of a Documentary History of Biochemistry 1770–1940 (Leicester University Press, 1992).

This article first appeared in *History Today*, November 11, 1996, pp. 27–34. Copyright © 1996 by History Today, Ltd. Reprinted by permission.

UNIT 4

The Twentieth Century to 1950

Unit Selections

Key Points to Consider

- What was most remarkable about Japan's rapid industrialization in the late 19th century? What signs did Japan display to prove it had become a world power?

- Why should the exhumation and reburial of the remains of Russia's last Tsarist family have been a gesture of national healing? What conspired to work against this?

- What contributions did Gandhi and Nehru make to the creation of Indian nationhood? How well has India today lived up to those ideals?

- What circumstances contributed to Chinese xenophobic attitude toward the West? How does that influence today's diplomacy?

- Evaluate Neville Chamberlain's work at the 1938 Munich Conference. Does he deserve to be called an appeaser?

- How did the Nazi Party in Germany show contempt for German women? In spite of this, why did German women continue to give it support?

- How extensive were the atrocities committed by Japanese armed forces in Nanking? What circumstances conspired to "cover up" these atrocities?

- What was Churchill's finest hour? Does he deserve to be called a hero?

- What was new and revolutionary about the Nuremberg War Crimes Trials? What legacy did Nuremberg usher to posterity?

Student Web Site

www.mhcls.com/online

Internet References

Further information regarding these Web sites may be found in this book's preface or online.

U.S. Holocaust Memorial Museum
   http://www.ushmm.org/
World War (1914–1918)
   http://www.pitt.edu/~pugachev/greatwar/ww1.html
World War II on the Web
   http://www.geocities.com/Athens/Oracle/2691/welcome.htm

At the beginning of the twentieth century, the British Empire spread around the world. Britain's navy ruled the seas and Britain acted as the world's policeman. Britain's financial strength was equally unsurpassed, and the pound sterling was the money standard for world markets. Still, other nations—notably, Germany, Japan, and the United States—were rising in prestige and power. Japan, for example, after being forced to open its ports to Matthew Perry in the 1850s, embarked upon a successful program of national unity and industrialization called the Meiji Restoration. By 1900, its efforts to meld Western industry with traditional culture were complete. In the Russo-Japanese War, 1904–1905, Japan flexed its military muscle and became the first non-European power to defeat a European nation in modern warfare.

At the same time, the prestige and power of the West was diminishing, as the twentieth century brought World War I, the Great Depression, World War II, and the Cold War. The first World War left 10 million dead and a heritage of cynicism caused by the barbarism of trench warfare. Great Britain emerged exhausted, the great debtor nation of the world; and the Soviet Russians began their long experiment with communism by executing Nicholas II, the last czar of Russia. Only after the fall of the Soviet Union in 1989 was it possible to identify and rebury the remains of the czar and his family. The rumor that Anastasia, the czar's daughter, had survived was finally laid to rest.

In the 1930s, the Great Depression undermined the financial strength of the West and raised questions about the stability of the capitalist economic system. Fascism fed on this economic misery, and Adolf Hitler began his demagogic career. The Nazis attempted to form a perfect society, in part by eliminating Jews, Gypsies, and other so-called undesirable people. Women in the Third Reich were assigned the role of producing children to replace fallen warriors.

In Western Europe forces refused to challenge aggression from Fascist Italy and Nazi Germany in the 1930s. Appeasement was the "dirty word" used to describe such actions. The Munich Conference of 1936 marked appeasement's apogee, as Britain's Neville Chamberlain gave Hitler part of Czechoslovakia in exchange for a promise of peace that Hitler never kept. Nevertheless, some historians now question whether the vilification that Chamberlain has received is justified.

Fighting in World War II began first in Asia, with the Japanese invasion of China in 1937. The Japanese conquest of Nanking was marked by its brutality, which included torture, rape, and murder. Although this event was long known, historians have written about it only recently. After a four-year-long struggle, the war in the Pacific came to an end when the United States dropped two atomic bombs on the Japanese cities of Hiroshima and Nagasaki. The Japanese surrendered.

As allied armies captured various portions of Germany in the European theater of war, they found death camps. Barbarism on this scale was deeply shocking and the horrors of the holocaust demanded a rethinking of human morality. When the rule of law was reasserted, German leaders, not the German people, were to be held accountable. The Nuremberg trials set a precedent for subsequent war crimes trials. After Japan's surrender, the Allied powers also conducted war crimes trials in Tokyo for the Japanese leaders of the Pacific portion of the war.

In addition to the great drama of the two world wars, the first half of the twentieth century also witnessed struggles for national independence. In India, Gandhi and Nehru combined moral and political leadership to achieve their shared goal of home rule in India. Long independent, India today is divided by provincial and religious strife. The shared vision of Gandhi and Nehru might again have relevance as Hindus and Muslims clash over disputed areas in Kashmir.

And, in China, Mao-tse-tung's communist-inspired revolution turned China into a world power. Today, China is an economic and nuclear giant. However, after a century of what it sees as national humiliations inflicted by foreign powers, China appears xenophobic to the West. Nationalism, which inspired the unsuccessful Boxer Rebellion a century ago, remains a potent force in contemporary Chinese politics. As the remaining superpower, the United States is perceived by China as a threatening foreign power.

On the Turn—Japan, 1900

From isolation to Great Power status—Richard Perren explains how a mania for Westernisation primed the pump of Japan's transformation at the turn of the century.

RICHARD PERREN

Following the Meiji Restoration in 1868, when rule by the emperor replaced the government of Japan by the Tokugawa shogun, the country embarked on a process of modernisation. In the next thirty years Western experts were imported to train the Japanese at home, selected Japanese were sent abroad to learn from the West, and Japan's new leaders embarked on a programme of radical reform. By these means they aimed at transforming a country that was weak and backward into a strong modern industrial nation. This new Japan would be capable of dealing with Western powers on equal terms and of throwing off the humiliating 'unequal treaties' they had imposed between 1858 and 1869.

When the Emperor Meiji died in 1912, control was concentrated in a highly centralized state whose functions were carried out through Western-style political, administrative and judicial institutions operating in the name of the emperor. Western-style armed forces upheld the position of the Japanese state at home and abroad. A modern and efficient education system served the aims of the state. Western-style economic and business institutions were in place, and factory-based industry firmly established. Japan had already been victorious in two major wars, against China in 1894–95 and Russia in 1904–5. She had not only achieved the much desired revision of the unequal treaties, but was a world power with an alliance with Britain, and a possessor of colonies. Yet the country still retained many traditional features, and had only adopted those characteristics of the West that were absolutely necessary to achieve its desired aims.

How far had the transformation process gone by 1900, and can the decade of the 1890s be described as a 'turning point'? To answer this we need to judge when Japan passed beyond that point in time when her modernisation could not have been reversed. Because the whole process of Japanese modernisation involved a complex interaction of social, economic, and political change it is not possible to ascribe a precise date to its completion. Nevertheless, there are a number of factors to suggest that by 1900 it had reached a stage where it was unlikely to be reversed.

It was the authorities that had to provide the necessary pump-priming and make strategic decisions about which areas of Japanese life needed to be transformed. It had become a traditional habit of the Japanese to look to officialdom for example and direction in almost everything, and this habit naturally asserted itself when it became necessary to assimilate a foreign civilisation which for nearly three centuries had been an object of national repugnance. This required the education of the nation as a whole and the task of instruction was divided among foreigners of different nations. The Meiji government imported around 300 experts or *yatoi*—a Japanese term meaning 'live machines'—into the country to help upgrade its industry, infrastructure and institutions. Before the Franco-Prussian War, Frenchmen were employed in teaching strategy and tactics to the army and in revising the criminal code. The building of railways, installing telegraphs and lighthouses, and training the new navy was done by Englishmen. Americans were employed in forming a postal service, agricultural development, and in planning colonisation and an educational system. In an attempt to introduce Occidental ideas of art, Italian painters and sculptors were brought to Japan. German experts were asked to develop a system of local government, train Japanese doctors and, after the Franco-Prussian War, to educate army officers. A number of Western observers believed that such wholesale adoption of an alien civilisation was impossible and feared that it would produce a violent reaction.

Although this did not occur, many early innovations were not really necessary to modernisation but merely imitations of Western customs. At that time the distinction between the fundamental features of modern technology and mere Occidental peculiarities was by no means clear. If it was necessary to use Western weapons there might also be a virtue in wearing Western clothes or shaking hands in the Occidental manner. Moreover, Meiji Japan had good reason to adopt even the more superficial aspects of Western culture. The international world of the nineteenth century was completely dominated by the Occident, and in view of the Western assumption of cultural superiority, the Japanese were probably correct in judging that they could not be regarded as even quasi-equals until they possessed not only modern technology but also many of the superficial aspects of Western culture. The resulting attempts in the 1870s and 1880s to borrow almost anything and everything Western may now seem to us to be amusingly indiscriminate, but it is perfectly understandable.

As the object of modernisation was to obtain equal treatment by the West many of the cultural innovations, besides being more than outward forms to the Japanese themselves, had an important psychological influence on Western diplomats and politicians. Under the shogun, members of the first Japanese delegation to the United States in 1860 wore traditional samurai dress with shaved pate and long side hair tied in a bun and carried swords. Under the emperor, Western-style haircuts were a major symbol of Westernisation. Soldiers and civilian functionaries wore Western-style uniforms, and politicians often adopted Western clothes and even full beards. In 1872 Western dress was prescribed for all court and official ceremonies. Meat eating, previously frowned on because of Buddhist attitudes, was encouraged, and the beef dish of *sukiyaki* was developed at this time. Western art and architecture were adopted, producing an array of official portraits of leading statesmen as well as an incongruous Victorian veneer in the commercial and government districts of the cities and some rather depressing interiors in the mansions of the wealthy.

Though the pace of change was hectic at first, and the adoption of Western forms seemed indiscriminate, it soon slowed as the Japanese became more selective about which aspects of their society they wanted to transform. Their adaptability meant the contracts of most Western experts and instructors only needed to be short-term, the average length of service being five years, and *yatoi* were less in evidence by the 1890s. The craze for Westernisation reached its height in the 1880s, but thereafter there was a reaction against unnecessary imitations and many of its more superficial features, like ballroom dancing, were dropped. Other social innovations subsequently abandoned were the prohibition of prostitution and mixed bathing, both of which were initially enforced to placate the prejudice of Western missionaries.

In reforming the legal system, Western concepts of individual rather than family ownership of property were adopted. But for purposes of formal registration of the population the law continued to recognise the old extended family or 'house', known in Japanese as the *ie*. This consisted of a patriarch and those of his descendants and collateral relatives who had not yet established a new *ie*. Within this structure the position of women was one of obedient subservience. In the 1870s the theme of liberation of women from their traditional Confucianist bondage was taken up by a number of Japanese intellectuals, influenced by Western writers on the subject. At the same time a number of women activists publicly engaged in politics. As both movements lacked public appeal they waned in the 1880s. In 1887 the Peace Preservation Ordinance, which remained in force to 1922, banned women from political parties and meetings. Women under the Civil Code of 1898 had no independent legal status and all legal agreements were concluded on a woman's behalf by the male to whom she was subordinate—either father, husband, or son. Women had no free choice of spouse or domicile and while they could in theory protest against this situation, they could do so only in a non-political manner. Such action posed a

challenge to the whole social orthodoxy on which the Japanese state was founded, so in practice few women protested.

One Western institution whose adoption would have made a very favourable impression on the West, but which made next to no headway in Japan, was Christianity. Like the women's movement it had some impact among Japanese intellectuals, but prejudices against it ran too deep. In 1889 less than a quarter of one per cent of Japanese were Christians. The only religion that did flourish was Shinto which was one of the traditional faiths of Japan. Revived interest in it had been a key element in the intellectual trends that led to the imperial restoration. But there was little deep interest in religion among Japan's new leaders. Though the government continued to control and support the main Shinto shrines, the many cults that made up the faith lapsed into a traditional passive state forming no more than a ceremonial background to the life of the Japanese people.

There was great enthusiasm for Westernisation over the matter of constitutional reform, and this dated back to the early 1870s when Meiji rulers realised change here was necessary to gain international respect. In the next decade the major tasks for building a modern political constitution were undertaken. In 1882 the statesman Ito Hirobumi led a study mission to several European capitals to investigate the theories and practices he believed were most appropriate for Japan. Before his departure he decided not to slavishly reproduce any Western system but that whatever example was taken as a model would be adapted to Japan's special needs. Most of his time was spent in Berlin and Vienna, and after his return to Japan work on the new constitution began in the spring of 1884. A new peerage was created, in December 1885 a cabinet type government was introduced, and to support it, a modern civil service with entry by examination was established. The Meiji constitution which took effect from November 1890 was essentially a cautious, conservative document which served to reinforce the influence of the more traditionally-minded elements in Japan's ruling class. While distinctively Japanese, it compared most closely with the German model of the monarchy.

This constitution, though nominally democratic, retained power in the hands of a small ruling élite with minimal interference from or responsibility to, the majority of the population. There was to be a bicameral parliament, called, in English, the Diet. The House of Peers was mostly made up from the ranks of the new nobility and the lower house chosen by an electorate limited to adult males paying taxes of fifteen yen or more. In 1890 this was limited to 450,000 persons or 5 per cent of adult males. Even when the taxation qualification was reduced to ten yen in 1902 it only increased the electorate to 1,700,000 males. The constitution's architects hoped that the provisions for democratic government it contained would be counterbalanced by other safeguarding provisions. Most important of these was the position of the emperor, who was accorded a position of primacy in the state. The imperial family were said to rule over Japan in perpetuity, and under the constitution the emperor was the repository of absolute and inviolable sovereignty. This was underlined by making cabinet and armed forces responsible not to political party, nor to the Diet, or the Japanese people, but to the emperor alone.

The emperor as an individual had little personal influence on events, and was not strong enough to unify the various factions that vied for political power. This was only possible by reference to pre-existing traditions of Japanese culture. These were invoked to stress the duties of loyalty and obedience to the sovereign, and through him to the state. As early as October 1890 the Imperial Rescript on Education, often seen as the basic tool for inculcating the orthodox philosophy of the state, showed the strong influence of the Confucian view that the state was essentially a moral order. This edict made only passing reference to education itself, but showed the revived influence of Confucian ideology in its stress on harmony and loyalty to the throne. Its central concept of mass indoctrination through formal education was an entirely modern emphasis. Intensive drilling of Japanese children with lessons in patriotism became possible when funds were available for universal compulsory education. In 1885 only 46 per cent of children of statutory school age were in school, though by 1905 this had risen to 95 per cent.

The purpose of educational reform, at its most basic level, was to turn out efficient recruits for the army, factory, and farm. This was because political and military modernisation, as well as industrialisation, depended on new skills, new attitudes and broader knowledge. Japan's leaders realised from the 1870s that social and intellectual modernisation was a prerequisite to success in other fields. But in the social and intellectual areas, as in economics, the responsiveness of thousands of individuals was more important than the exhortations of authority.

While political and social reform and cultural change were limited in extent and selective in their nature by the end of the 1890s, the same picture emerges in economic life. Industrial modernisation took two forms—the reorganisation of traditional industries, and the transplantation of new industries from the West. Some traditional industries, like cotton-spinning, experienced radical change and the introduction of factory production, while others made slower progress. Japan was an important exporter of raw silk but that industry was not dependent upon elaborate or expensive machinery. The production of cocoons was a labour-intensive industry, already carried out as a by-employment in peasant households. Gradually small factories equipped with improved but relatively simple and inexpensive power-driven machines were introduced. The investment in this industry was thus spread thinly over a great number of producers. Where large investments of capital were absolutely necessary, as with Japan's strategic heavy industries like iron and steel, armaments, and shipbuilding, the initial investment was made by the government. But even here success was not immediate and these early concerns were sold off to Japanese businessmen at low prices in the 1880s. In some of the new industries success came sooner than in others. In 1897–1906, 90 per cent of railways rolling stock was built in Japan but 94 per cent of locomotives were still imported, mainly from England and Germany. It was not until after 1900 that the basis of heavy industry in Japan was firmly established.

Indeed, the whole of Japanese economic and social life in 1900 was still firmly rooted in traditional forms with quite a small modern superstructure. But for Japan the term 'traditional' needs qualification because it does not necessarily mean that pre-modern Japanese economy and society was antagonistic to change. In spite of Japan's decision to isolate itself for almost 300 years, features evolved that could be built upon once the country was forced to accept Western influence. The growing volume of research on the period before 1868, in the form of local and regional studies, has reinforced the view that Japan was a relatively advanced pre-industrial economy. For an underdeveloped country it was already well provided with a basic infrastructure by the time the process of modernisation began in earnest. Agricultural output per head of the population was quite high and premodern Japan possessed a substantial degree of commerce. In the more backward northern regions, on the island of Hokkaido, and also parts of the extreme southern island of Kyushu, medieval forms of social and economic organisation persisted until quite late. But on the more advanced regions of the main island of Hunshu, especially the Kanto Plain around Edo—the old name for Tokyo—and Osaka, there was a thriving urban-centred commercial economy. Merchants and traders supplied the wants of the towns of the region and production for exchange, and not just subsistence, was carried on in the countryside.

Much of Japan's growth after 1868 was built upon the foundations of its pre-modern economy. Partly under the protection and encouragement of government most of the capital-intensive investments went into railways, steamships, and mechanised heavy industrial plants. But just as important in promoting development at that time were a vast number of small improvements and minor capital undertakings. Before 1940 the majority of roads were of unsurfaced dirt and bridges were simple wooden structures. Agricultural construction, represented primarily by irrigation works, changed little from Tokugawa times. Only after the turn of the century did most Japanese make Western products a part of their daily lives, and they were adapted to a traditionally Japanese life-style. In Tokyo in 1910 most of the dwellings were made of wood and only about an eighth used brick, stone, or plaster. Within the houses most furniture was still the traditional kind and most of the food eaten was of a traditional type. This meant that there was still an enormous market to be supplied by peasant farmers, village entrepreneurs, small businesses and traditional craftsmen. In 1890 nearly 70 per cent of Japanese investment was in the traditional sector and it still accounted for 45 per cent, fifteen years later.

But the success of Japan's modernisation efforts needs to be judged not only by what happened within the economy itself, or by the changes within Japanese society. Reform was undertaken as a means to an end and that end was recognition as an equal by the West. This was necessary before there was any chance of removing the unequal treaties of the 1850s and 1860s and contained two major restrictions on Japanese sovereignty. Firstly, there was the provision of 'extra-territorial jurisdiction'. Under this Westerners accused of crimes were not tried by Japanese courts, but by consular courts within the foreign settlements of the seaports of Japan set out in the treaties. The other restriction was the loss of tariff autonomy. Eager for markets, the Western powers placed severe limits on Japanese import and export duties. These measures were the usual way for nineteenth-century Western powers to regulate diplomatic and commercial relations with Oriental countries, the model being the treaties imposed on China after the Opium War of the 1840s. For Japan the actual consequences of the treaties were not particularly damaging. No great market for opium was developed, and the opening of Japanese industry to competition from the West forced the pace of economic change instead of allowing inefficient industries to shelter behind protective tariffs. Foreigners resident in Japan were restricted to the treaty ports and needed official permits to travel outside so were never a great intrusion into Japanese life. And the justice dispensed in the consular courts was generally fair to both Japanese and Westerners.

Nevertheless, the fact of these treaties' existence was rightly regarded as a great humiliation as they usurped functions which are the proper preserve of a fully independent state. They came up for renewal periodically and from 1871 onwards Japan asked for their revision. In that year refusal was a foregone conclusion, as even the Japanese could see that the conditions originally necessitating extra-territorial jurisdiction had not undergone any change justifying its abolition. In later years Western nations were reluctant to allow their citizens to come under the power of a legal system that was still not fully reformed, despite the abolition of torture as an accepted legal practice in 1876 and the introduction of a Code of Criminal Procedure, framed in accordance with Western ideas, in 1882. But this was the start of what the West wanted and when negotiations were reopened in 1883, Japan included as compensation for the abolition of consular jurisdiction a promise to remove all restrictions on trade, travel, and residence for foreigners within the country. These and subsequent discussions in the 1880s reached no definite conclusion, mainly because the Japanese refused to grant foreigners living in the country the right to own freehold property. It was not until 1894 that a final settlement of the consular question became a real possibility when Britain agreed to abolish consular jurisdiction by 1899.

The five year delay was for two reasons. Before the new treaty came into force Japan had to fully implement a new legal code. The thorough recodification of the law this required was a slow and difficult task as most legal reforms were introduced piecemeal. This area is probably the strongest example of direct Western pressure being applied to change a fundamental feature of Japanese life. Drafts drawn up, largely under French influence, were submitted in 1881 and again in 1888, but a completely revised legal code only went into effect in 1896, removing the final impediment to ending extra-territorial jurisdiction in 1899.

The other cause for delay was to allow Japan to renegotiate the rest of its treaties—of which there were over fifteen—with other Western powers, so that all nations were on an equal footing. This aspect was undoubtedly made possible by the successful outcome with Britain. Tariff autonomy was not finally restored to Japan until twelve years after 1899, but up to 1911 she was allowed to increase import and export duties.

The successful negotiations in 1894 were important as a turning point for the Japanese and for the West. The greatest opponents of the loss of extra-territorial jurisdiction were the few hundred foreign merchants and businessmen who lived and worked in the treaty ports. But for Japan this was a national political question that had provoked fierce debates in the Diet and in the press. The first treaties between Japan and the West were signed when the nation was still in a state of torpor from its long slumber of seclusion, and under circumstances of duress. The redemption of her judicial and fiscal authority had been, for thirty years, the dream of Japanese national aspiration, and both domestic and foreign policies had been shaped with this one end in view. For Japan's rulers, innovation after innovation, often involving sacrifices of traditional sentiments, were introduced for the purpose of assimilating the country and its institutions to the standard of Western civilisation. By 1900 Japan was still not regarded as a full equal by Western nations, but she was now accorded greater respect. In the next decade this was built upon with the Anglo-Japanese Alliance in 1902, the defeat of Russia in 1905, and the annexation of Korea in 1910. By 1912 there was no doubt that Japan had achieved 'Great Power' status.

For Further Reading

H. J. Jones, *Live Machines,* (Vancouver, 1980); J. P. Lehnann, *The Roots of Modern Japan,* (Macmillan, 1982); H. Wray and H. Conroy, eds., *Perspectives on Modern Japanese History,* (Honolulu, 1983); J. Hunter, *The Emergence of Modern Japan,* (Longman, 1989); O. Checkland, *Britain's Encounter With Meiji Japan, 1868–1912,* (Macmillan, 1989); E. O. Reischauer and A. M. Craig, *Japan: Tradition and Transformation,* (Allen & Unwin, 1989).

RICHARD PERREN is Senior Lecturer in Economic History at the Department of History, University of Aberdeen and author of *Japanese Studies from Earliest Times to 1990: A Bibliographic Guide* (Manchester University Press, 1992).

Home at Last

Finally, the murdered Romanovs will be laid to rest. Their deaths were the real beginning of the 20th century. Their controversial burial marks its close.

BILL POWELL AND OWEN MATTHEWS

The Romanovs will come home this week, their five three-and-a-half-foot wooden coffins borne through St. Petersburg to their final resting place in a dignified, if not quite grand, procession. For six years the remains of the last tsar, Nicholas II, head of one of Europe's most storied families, were kept in a setting that hardly evoked imperial grandeur: since being exhumed in 1991, his bones, along with those of his wife, Alexandra, three of their daughters and four servants, sat most of the time in polyethylene bags on a storeroom shelf in an old criminal morgue in Yekaterinburg. There lay the House of Romanov, the family that presided over imperial Russia for more than three centuries.

Vladimir Ilyich Lenin personally ordered the assassination, in 1918, of the tsar and his family. (The assassins also murdered the cook, maid, valet and family physician.) The authorities of the Soviet Union had wanted Nicholas II, Alexandra and their family out of sight and out of mind. But in that, as in so much else, they failed. Thanks in part to Russian monarchists in exile, but mainly to the mythmaking power of Hollywood, the Romanov legend (if not the reality of their grim demise) endured, both at home and abroad.

In 1991 President Boris Yeltsin invited Vladimir Kirillovich Romanov, father of Maria Romanov, the current pretender to the throne, to St. Petersburg. He was greeted by a crowd of 60,000. At the time, in the flush of the latest Russian revolution, a poll showed 18 percent of the population supported a restoration of the monarchy. Six years later the few Romanovs interested in restoration had failed to capitalize on the sentiment, and the Yeltsin government filled the vacuum. Reassured by the new polling, Yeltsin last year began serious preparations to give the country's last imperial rulers a decent burial. After four years of deliberation, a government commission concluded that the remains discovered near Yekaterinburg in the late 1970s were those of the Romanovs. Yeltsin appointed his deputy prime minister, Boris Nemtsov, to make the appropriate arrangements. And this week, 80 years to the day after their brutal murder in Ipatyev House (demolished in 1977 by an up-and-coming communist politician named Boris Yeltsin),

Russia was to engage in a simple and honorable act of national healing. Five Romanovs were to be laid to rest in the Peter and Paul Cathedral next to Peter and Catherine the Great.

The ceremony will go on as scheduled, but not, as the government had hoped, in a spirit of reconciliation or healing. This is Russia, after all, and in Russia—imperial, communist or even new—nothing ever comes easily, not least an attempt to come to terms with a turbulent, haunted history. Aleksi II, the politically powerful patriarch of the Russian Orthodox Church, the institution most closely allied with the legacy of the Russian imperials, decided last month not to preside at the interment. The church said it's still not sure the remains are authentic. That virtually no one else has similar doubts evidently doesn't matter.

AND THE REST IS HISTORY:

In an epochal act of murder, Tsar Nicholas II and his wife, Alexandra, were killed with their daughters, Maria, Tatiana, Olga and Anastasia and their son, Alexis. Five of the family skulls have been recovered: those of Maria and Alexis apparently were burned to ash.

Boris Yeltsin, with an eye toward his own historical legacy, had wanted to attend the Romanov burial. But once the church balked, Yeltsin decided he couldn't take the political risk of defying it. And though nearly 50 Romanov descendants will be there, at least three outspoken members of the family will not, saying that the relative modesty of the planned ceremony is beneath their erstwhile imperial dignity. (According to 75-year-old family head Nicholas, only one Romanov—Maria Vladimirovna, granddaughter of Nicholas II's first cousin— makes any claim to the throne.)

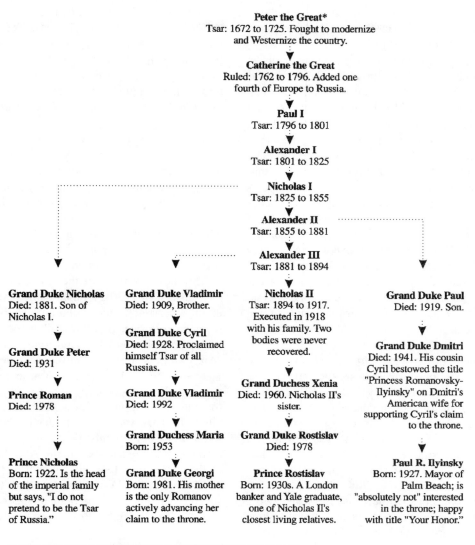

Peter the Great*
Tsar: 1672 to 1725. Fought to modernize
and Westernize the country.

Catherine the Great
Ruled: 1762 to 1796. Added one
fourth of Europe to Russia.

Paul I
Tsar: 1796 to 1801

Alexander I
Tsar: 1801 to 1825

Nicholas I
Tsar: 1825 to 1855

Alexander II
Tsar: 1855 to 1881

Alexander III
Tsar: 1881 to 1894

Nicholas II
Tsar: 1894 to 1917.
Executed in 1918
with his family. Two
bodies were never
recovered.

Grand Duke Nicholas
Died: 1881. Son of
Nicholas I.

Grand Duke Peter
Died: 1931

Prince Roman
Died: 1978

Prince Nicholas
Born: 1922. Is the head
of the imperial family
but says, "I do not
pretend to be the Tsar
of Russia."

Grand Duke Vladimir
Died: 1909, Brother.

Grand Duke Cyril
Died: 1928. Proclaimed
himself Tsar of all
Russias.

Grand Duke Vladimir
Died: 1992

Grand Duchess Maria
Born: 1953

Grand Duke Georgi
Born: 1981. His mother
is the only Romanov
actively advancing her
claim to the throne.

Grand Duchess Xenia
Died: 1960. Nicholas II's
sister.

Grand Duke Rostislav
Died: 1978

Prince Rostislav
Born: 1930s. A London
banker and Yale graduate,
one of Nicholas II's
closest living relatives.

Grand Duke Paul
Died: 1919. Son.

Grand Duke Dmitri
Died: 1941. His cousin
Cyril bestowed the title
"Princess Romanovsky-
Ilyinsky" on Dmitri's
American wife for
supporting Cyril's claim
to the throne.

Paul R. Ilyinsky
Born: 1927. Mayor of
Palm Beach; is
"absolutely not" interested
in the throne; happy
with title "Your Honor."

*THOSE WHO RULED BETWEEN PETER AND CATHERINE NOT SHOWN,
RESEARCH BY ANNA KUCHMENT, GRAPHIC BY KARL GUDE—NEWSWEEK

Figure 1   Family Ties: From Autocracy to Democracy.   The execution of Nicholas II,
his wife, Tsarina Alexandra, and their five children ended 300 years of uninterrupted
Romanov rule. It did not, however, prevent descendants from laying claim to the throne.
A look at the Romanovs before and after the last tsar.

A funeral that was to have been a step toward political maturity for a Russia emerging from 70 years of darkness has instead turned into the latest chapter of the ongoing Romanov tragedy. "The country had a chance to obliterate a large historical blemish—the massacre of this family that they concealed and lied about for years," says Harvard University historian Richard Pipes. "Instead, it's an opportunity missed."

It may have been naive to think it could have been otherwise. Most ordinary Russians, struggling to make ends meet as their nation's transition to capitalism now flags dangerously, couldn't care less about the disposition of Nicholas and Alexandra's bones. But for the political and religious establishments in Moscow, the burial was destined to be excruciatingly complicated. The abdication and subsequent assassination of Nicholas, and the revolution to which he was sacrificed, are among the 20th century's seminal events. From them flow the heinous Terror in Russia, the second world war and the cold war. Touch the Romanov bones and you touch a part of a century's central nervous system. A powerful reaction was inevitable.

The fall of the Romanovs is a study in brutality. Robert K. Massie, author of "Nicholas and Alexandra," reports that they were awakened after midnight and were sent from their bedrooms to the basement of Ipatyev House. Nicholas carried his 13-year-old-son, Alexis, who was crippled by hemophilia. Alexandra was next, followed by her daughters, Olga, 22, Tatiana, 21, Maria, 19, and Anastasia, 17. In the rear came the family physician, the cook, the maid and the valet. Two chairs were brought, and the mother and the boy sat down. The others, told that they were to be photographed, arranged themselves in two lines behind the chairs.

Suddenly, 11 men burst into the room. Each held a revolver; each had been assigned a specific victim. After the first round of bullets, the three younger sisters and the maid remained alive—thanks in part to corsets of hidden jewels that deflected the gunfire. The sisters, pressing against the walls, died in a second round. One of the executioners stepped up to the writhing boy lying on the floor and kicked him in the head. The chief executioner put the muzzle of his revolver directly into the boy's ear and fired two shots.

Only the maid was still alive. Rather than reload, the executioners took rifles from the next room and pursued her with bayonets. Running back and forth along the wall, screaming, she tried to fend off the bayonets with her hands. She fell, and her body was pierced more than 30 times. Rifle butts crushed the victims' faces to render them unrecognizable. The bleeding bodies were wrapped in bedsheets, loaded into a truck and taken into the forest. There they were stripped and thrown down a mine shaft. Lenin, sitting in the Kremlin, was informed that it was over.

The nine skeletons, burned with acid and gasoline, were discovered in 1979 in a wooded, swampy spot 12 miles northwest of Yekaterinburg. Confident they had found the burial spot of the imperial family, geologist Aleksandr Avdonin and Gely Ryabov, a famous Moscow filmmaker, were nonetheless petrified as they dug. As Massie writes in "The Romanovs, The Final Chapter," Avdonin said later, "All my life I had searched for this . . . and then, as we started to lift up the planking, I thought to myself, 'let me find nothing!' "

Fearful of the repercussions of their discovery, the two a year later returned the remains they'd unearthed to the same site. Then they vowed not to utter a word about their discovery until, Avdonin would later tell Massie, "the circumstances in our country changed." The bones of the tsar and his family remained buried in the woods for an additional 13 years, until, in 1991, they were officially exhumed from their shallow grave.

For the next six years, the remains were subjected to hundreds of forensic tests. Scientists compared the DNA with samples taken from Nicholas II's brother Georgy, who died in 1891 and is buried in the Peter and Paul Fortress. Prince Philip, Duke of Edinburgh and Alexandra's grandnephew, gave blood samples to be tested against the DNA of the skeleton thought to be Alexandra's. In both cases, laboratories in Russia, the United States and Britain confirmed the genetic match. The investigators also electronically superimposed the photographs of the skulls on archive photographs of the family. They compared the skeletons' measurements with clothing known to have belonged to the tsar and his daughters. They matched the platinum dental bridgework on one skull's jaw to the empress's dental records. Again, every test came up with exact correlations.

Only two slight mysteries remained. Two of the family's children's bodies were missing: Alexis and the second youngest daughter, Maria. Investigators concluded that they had been burned to ash by the executioners, who did not have time to destroy the rest of their victims. That notion matched the historical testimony of the chief executioner, Yakov Yurovsky, unearthed from a long-secret Moscow archive during *glasnost* in 1989.

The missing bodies have helped spawn a whole industry of Romanov rumor and myth. A variety of crackpots have turned up all over the world claiming either to be Romanovs who escaped execution or their direct descendants. In Moscow today Nikolai Dalsky parades around in an admiral's uniform convinced he's a direct descendant of Alexis, the tsarevich. Another man, Oleg Filatov, says he's also a direct descendant of the poor tsarevich—the hemophiliac who Filatov somehow believes survived several gunshot wounds.

The most powerful of the Romanov myths is, of course, Anastasia's. In 1920 a woman named Anna Anderson turned up in a Berlin hospital, claiming to be the heiress to the Romanova throne. In 1956 Hollywood got into the act with an Ingrid Bergman film. And today an animated version of "Anastasia" is attracting millions of young, impressionable viewers all over the world with an egregiously sweet story: that somehow the beautiful young princess survived to find romance and happiness. How many parents tell their children the truth? That Anastasia, after having been shot several times in the wee hours of July 17, 1918, quivered as she lay in her own blood in the dark basement. And that at some point, one of the 11 gunmen took his bayonet and stabbed that last bit of life out of her. As British historian Orlando Figes writes succinctly in his masterful book on the revolution, "it is inconceivable that any of the Romanovs survived this ordeal."

It is, in fact, the savagery of the "ordeal" that is its most important historical legacy. It presaged the Terror that was to come in Russia, the moment when, as historian Pipes has written, a government assigned itself "the power to kill its citizens not for what they had done but because their death 'was needed.' " That is a moment surely worth recognizing—and laying to rest—however belatedly. But as Yeltsin's government learned, in a country just seven years removed from Soviet communism, it is also obviously easier said than done—at least in so public a manner. One of the ironies about the controversy over the imperial interment is that Russia has actually made quiet progress in coming to terms with the revolutionary period. The more bitter irony is that it is the Russian Orthodox Church, to which the late tsar was so devoted, that has effectively tarnished what could have been a historic ceremony. The church remains a powerful but opaque institution in Russia, and its decision last month to undermine Yeltsin has triggered a fevered, but relatively uninformed, speculation that evokes Soviet-era Kremlinology.

The intrigue, circa 1998, cannot help but evoke, to some Russians, another era: "It's just like 1916," says Edvard Radzinsky, who wrote the first biography of Nicholas II using the primary materials first made available during *glasnost.* "A weak government, an invisible head of state, key issues blotted out by amazing, Byzantine intrigues . . . and a hypocritical church looking after its own interests instead of taking an opportunity to unite society." Amid it all, the Romanov cortege will trundle through St. Petersburg this week, finally laying the last tsar and his family to rest. At home at least, if not yet in peace.

Gandhi and Nehru: Frustrated Visionaries?

JUDITH BROWN

The observer of India in 1997 is rightly struck by the immense stability of this, the world's largest democracy, in contrast with her South Asian neighbours and many other new nation states which emerged out of the former British Empire. But equally striking is the great dichotomy between the reality of India at the end of the century and the vision of the new nation offered by its two greatest leaders at the time of independence, Mahatma Gandhi and Jawaharlal Nehru.

From 1920 at least, India's growing nationalist movement had stressed through its main organisation, the Indian National Congress, the meaning of independence for the poor and disadvantaged. There was to be a new and more egalitarian society, where the state would have a moral obligation to help the poor and under-privileged and provide opportunities to those who for centuries had been despised and deprived. These ideals were enshrined in the new constitution of 1950, whose preamble committed India to securing for all its citizens justice, liberty, equality and fraternity, and were spelt out in the sections of Fundamental Rights and Directive Principles of state policy.

Gandhi and Nehru had, in their different ways, spoken constantly of the moral, social and political regeneration of the country as the true heart of swaraj, or self-rule. But despite the seminal role of these two leaders, amongst the greatest visionaries of the post-colonial world, after fifty years of democratic government and economic development, there is still widespread and desperate poverty in India. With inequalities of status, consumption and opportunity as great as any in the world, the economy, having teetered on the edge of international bankruptcy at the start of this decade, now moves towards an open market policy with little ideological framework to distinguish it from Western economies. Moreover, this secular state has at times been rent by sectarian loyalties and violence, and India's religious minorities remain fearful and often profoundly disadvantaged. Why has this happened in place of the Mahatma's spiritual vision, and despite Nehru's eloquent pledge at the moment of independence that India would keep her 'tryst with destiny'?

Gandhi and the younger Nehru were, of course, very different as people and also in their vision of the new India to be created as imperial rule ended. A generation separated them, as did social origin and political experience. The older man came from a far more provincial and less privileged background, had reached professional competence as a lawyer by strict personal discipline and a regime of self-denial and hard work: and he had spent twenty formative years in South Africa, where exposure to a wide range of cultural influences and the experience of racial discrimination refined both his political skills and his religious sensibility.

The younger man had been brought up with everything that money could buy, educated at Harrow and Trinity College, Cambridge, and inducted with ease into the world of Indian public life by a father who was one of India's most successful and respected lawyers. With an effortless sense of superiority and no experience of hardship or personal challenge, he had no religious beliefs worth the name, and little knowledge of the India of the vast majority of his compatriots. It was little wonder that his father, Motilal, greatly feared what would befall his cosseted son, in personal and material terms, as he came under the influence of the homespun Mahatma.

Yet Gandhi and the somewhat aimless Jawaharlal formed a strong attachment and political partnership which was to last for almost three decades, until Gandhi's assassination in 1948. The attachment was partly personal, founded on mutual attraction between two strong and idiosyncratic personalities. It was partly forged out of mutual need, as both needed the other to further their public aims. To Gandhi, Nehru was the symbol of the younger generation, the heart and touchstone of a younger India whom he needed to weld into the nationalist movement. To Nehru, Gandhi was unique in his ability to sense the mind and mood of the vast numbers of uneducated Indians, and thus essential for the forging of a broad-based nationalist movement to oust the British. But far beyond mutual need the two shared a passionate conviction that India must change radically as independence was won. This was central to the commitment of each man to a public role, and far more than populist rhetoric. Sensing this core of visionary commitment in the other drew them together in a unique way.

Gandhi first worked out his vision of a new India in a small pamphlet published in 1909, entitled Hind Swaraj (Indian Home Rule). Here he made plain his belief that true self-rule was far more than mere political independence, or an inheritance of imperial structures of control, but manned by Indians. True Swaraj would be founded on a moral revolution of the individual upwards through society as a whole, changing both the pattern of the economy and the nature of political authority. What was needed was a society based on moral individuals who cared for each other and followed spiritual goals, rather than false standards of gain and wealth, imported from the West, along with the means of large-scale production and their potential for the increase of inequality and of violent relations between individuals and groups. After his final return to India in 1915, he never disavowed this early work with its ruthless denunciation of 'modern civilisation' and of Western educated Indians who accepted its values. He persisted in defining swaraj in moral and social, rather than political language, affirming that its hallmarks would be a more equal society, mutual tolerance between different religious groups, and a commitment to small-scale economic arrangements which put people before gain.

Above all, the hallmark of new Indians would be a commitment to non-violence in all public and private relationships, as the only moral means of achieving true change. For Gandhi non-violence was the only way to follow after what one perceived as truth without endangering the perception of truth held by others: by its very presence and working it would transform attitudes and relationships, and so begin the process of change at the roots of the individuals who formed the bedrock of society. In this vision a modern state had little role to play. Gandhi was deeply distrustful of the power of the state, and felt that individual self-control was the only true regulatory power which could change society. At the end of his life he advised Congressmen to disband their party, turn their backs on political power and engage in grass-roots social service.

Gandhi drew his inspiration from aspects of Hindu and other religious traditions, and from a wide range of dissenting voices in Western culture who feared for the spiritual and social implications of industrialisation in Western society. Nehru's vision, by contrast, was generated by his contacts with several variants of Western socialist thinking during his years of education in England and later during his European travels (including a visit to the Soviet Union in 1927), and through his wide reading. Despite his 'alliance' with Gandhi, he made plain the differences in their hopes for India's future, for example, in a series of press articles republished as a pamphlet entitled Whither India? (1933) and in his subsequent longer writings, including An Autobiography (1936). As he wrote in the former:

> India's immediate goal can . . . only be considered in terms of the ending of exploitation of her people. Politically, it must mean independence and the severance of the British connection . . . economically and socially it must mean the ending of all special class privileges and vested interests. . . . The real question before us . . . is one of fundamental change of regime, politically, economically, socially.

The means to this end was first a powerful and broadly-based nationalist movement to oust the imperial ruler; and second, a powerful modern state to redistribute resources more equitably and to manage a modern economy. Nehru had little time for Gandhi's commitments to non-violence and to individual moral 'change of heart' as the route to truly radical change; and he had no sympathy with the Mahatma's religious language and priorities, aiming instead, in more straightforward political terms, for both a secular state and society.

After India's independence the visions of both men were soon dashed on the rocks of reality. In Gandhi's case this was less surprising. He had always known that few Congressmen had shared his very particular moral viewpoint or sympathised with his broad-ranging plans for the reformation of Indians, their society and polity. When Congressmen had begun to gain significant power at provincial level under successive constitutional reforms, he had lamented that they were behaving like their imperial predecessors; and he spoke with sad realism of the way they left his 'constructive programme' lying littered on the floor at party gatherings.

Gandhi never held high office in Congress either after the Second World War, when it was clear that independence was imminent, or, later, in the new nation state; he recognised that political power was in the hands of those, like Nehru, who believed in the need for a strong state, both to serve their political ambitions and also to fulfil their genuine hopes for India's economic and social development. After his assassination he was greatly revered: but the only ways in which his vision was even partially enacted was in the legal abolition of the status and practice of untouchability, a gross form of social and ritual discrimination practised against those at the base of Hindu society, and in the encouragement of 'cottage industries' alongside large-scale industrialisation.

Nehru, on the other hand, was India's prime minister without a break from independence until his death in 1964. Yet even his socialist dreams remained unfulfilled. Despite attempts at far-reaching social legislation, he was unable to achieve genuinely radical reform of landholdings on any scale, which would have been a prerequisite for extensive redistribution of resources and abolition of vested interests. He was unable to push through a uniform civil code which would have done much to ameliorate the legal position of women and reduce the entrenched differences between various religious groups. Although there was significant economic development, particularly large-scale industry, planned and partly managed by the state, there was little change in agricultural practices and production, and the incidence of life-threatening poverty, malnutrition and disease remained widespread, making a mockery of the directive principles of the constitution.

Furthermore, India continued to be governed by Nehru in ways which were remarkably similar to those of his imperial predecessors, both in the structure of the state itself, despite the universal adult franchise, and in the style of the administrative services which he had once denounced as anti-national and requiring drastic reform. At the end of his life he was, like Gandhi, frustrated at his inability to achieve so much of his life's dreams. On his desk he kept the words of the poet, Robert Frost:

> But I have promises to keep,
> And miles to go before I sleep

The reasons for the frustrations of these great visionary leaders lay in part in their different, but unique, pathways into Indian political life. Both were to an extent 'apart from' the ordinary world of Indian professional and business life, or that of the nationalist politician. Gandhi had failed as a lawyer in his native Western India and had achieved professional success and personal maturity in another continent, working among the Indian migrant community. Nehru had been insulated, indeed isolated, by the great wealth of his family and by his prolonged period of education in England. Back home in Allahabad with his family he saw for himself no clear role either in politics or in the profession of the law, for which he was destined. On their return to India both found that they had few natural connections with the world of Indian politics, and no groups of allies or supporters with whom to make their mark.

Perhaps more importantly, their exposure to the world beyond India had created in each of them a distinctive and idiosyncratic vision of the meaning and nature of 'nationalism' and the Indian nation as they thought it should become. By contrast most of their contemporaries who saw themselves as nationalists thought primarily in terms either of ameliorating British rule and making more room for Indians within the imperial structures of power, or of removing the British altogether. But few thought beyond independence or had visions of radical change grounded in religious belief or a powerful secular ideology as did Gandhi and Nehru.

Their eruption into the politics of nationalism was therefore unpredictable. Gandhi emerged in 1920 as a leader within the Congress because he offered the party a mode of non-violent protest against the British Raj, at a specific juncture in nationalist politics when constitutional politics seemed to have achieved little and when few were willing to resort to the opposite tactic, namely that of violent protest. In the euphoria which followed, Nehru willingly became involved in politics for the first time, sensing that in Gandhi he had met a leader who would address real social and political problems, would lead Indians in fearless resistance to the imperial ruler, and would do away with the parlour politics of an older generation he had so despised. As he wrote in his autobiography of the heady experience of participating in Gandhi's first nation-wide campaign of non-violent non-co-operation with the Raj:

> Many of us who worked for the Congress programme lived in a kind of intoxication during the year 1921. We were full of excitement and optimism and a buoyant enthusiasm. We sensed the happiness of a person crusading for a cause . . . Above all, we had a sense of freedom and a pride in that freedom. The old feeling of oppression and frustration was completely gone.

However, the Congress party was never transformed into a band of moral Gandhian enthusiasts, committed to the Mahatma's constructive campaign for the renewal of the nation. Although many Congressmen and many more outside the Party's ranks were attracted by his fearlessness, by his personality and by his Indianness, few accepted his religious vision of man and society, and few were converted to his belief in the rightness and transformative nature of non-violence.

The Congress remained what it had become over the forty years since its inception—a loosely organised association of groups of local men (and a few women), many of high educational and professional background, who were politically active on a full or part-time basis, who wished to gain access to the decision-making and executive power of the state which the imperial authority was creating, and who knew that their hands and arguments would be strengthened by an all-India alliance under the umbrella of the national Congress. It had little full-time and effective party organisation, and depended largely on the co-operative stance of local individuals and groups who used its name—a fact which Gandhi and Nehru both recognised and sought to remedy, because they realised how it reduced the Congress's political effectiveness as a party of direct action or of long-term change.

A further consequence was that Congress had little in the way of a defining and driving ideology, apart from its anti-imperial stance. Ideological compromise was more often the cement which held its members together; particularly as so many of them were comparatively privileged and had social and economic interests to safeguard in the future. Consequently those of its declarations which had a socialist ring were generally little more than vote-catching rhetoric.

In this party Gandhi and Nehru were in their own ways unique, and that uniqueness was both their strength and a long-term weakness in terms of their ability to galvanise Congress into action in pursuit of visionary goals. Gandhi was never a 'leader' in any Western sense of the word. His role from 1920 to the 1940s was more that of an 'expert' on non-violence who could be welcomed and to an extent used by Congress when they felt his particular non-violent strategy of opposition and profoundly moral stance and style suited their purposes; to achieve compromises between different groups within Congress when its internal divisions threatened to rend it apart and destroy the vital unity of the nationalist movement.

Nehru's role was similarly not that of a leader with a natural power base in a locality or in a group of like-minded allies. His 'ticket' in Congress was that of Gandhi's protege and later heir, a fact which at times caused him embarrassment and distress. In the later 1930s his ideological position was so antipathetical to many of the more conservative in Congress that the latter would have made his position in the party impossible if it had not been for Gandhi's presence and watchful eye on the internal dynamics.

As independence became imminent after the end of the Second World War, Congress activists recognised Nehru's skills as a negotiator with the imperial authorities—in part because he spoke their language and had inhabited so much of their mental and political world. But even though he became leader of the transitional government which saw the transfer of power to Indian hands, and subsequently prime minister, Nehru was not secure as the party's undisputed leader and ideologue until some years later.

Although Gandhi lived for a brief period in an independent India, it was Nehru who had to wrestle with the problem of trying to enact his vision of change under the new circumstances—when Congress had become the party of government rather than of nationalist rhetoric and protest, and when he was constrained by the structure of the state and the ability of the administration.

For him there were a range of seemingly insurmountable barriers to the achievement of radical change. One continuing example was the nature of the Congress party. Even though he was from the early 1950s its undisputed leader, and though it paid lip service to his vision of a socialist transformation of society, it was now a party which even more than before independence represented the interests of those who had no wish for radical social and economic change. Its very success as a nationalist party had attracted into it many who needed access to power. Increasingly it became the party of the businessman, the prosperous farmer and the professional, those with a stake in the India inherited from the raj and being made more prosperous for those with resources by the actions of an independent government anxious to boost the economy. This rootedness in groups of locally influential people was its great strength at election time, but its weakness as an instrument of change. This Nehru learned the hard way when it came to attempts at land reform and social legislation for the benefit of the deprived.

Moreover, the very structure of the state inhibited change. Just as in imperial India the country had been administered through provinces, often the size of small European countries, now these became the basis of the States within the Indian Union, bound together in a federation. Consequently on many issues legislation had to pass through the legislatures of the States rather than through the Lok Sabha in New Delhi. As in the case of the abolition of great landlords and the redistribution of land into moderate holdings below a certain 'ceiling', those with vested interests could either get themselves into the State legislature where they could modify or delay reforming measures, or could use the months while legislation was being passed to hire lawyers and so equip themselves to avoid the law. Or in the case of agricultural improvement and the dire need to grow more food, policy implementation was in the hands of the agricultural ministries of the States: and Nehru found it impossible to chivvy them in the way he would have wished. Added to this, the actual tools of government were frustratingly weak and slow.

Independent India inherited an administration structured on an immensely slow bureaucracy, which had made a specialty of generating endless files and pushing them from one level to another with agonising slowness. It was a system where those at lower levels were neither trained nor accustomed to take responsibility and make decisions. At the top it was manned by elite generalists who, though highly educated, were essentially trained to conserve the status quo, to enable the collection of adequate revenue, but not to innovate or manage a social revolution. Nehru as a young nationalist had distrusted and criticised the elite Indian Civil Service, although over half of them were Indian by 1947. He spoke of the need for a total overhaul of the administration and the evolution of a new people-oriented class of administrators. But no administrative revolution occurred, and he found himself increasingly having to rely on the heirs of the service he had castigated, who remained in ethos, background and modes of operation so like their imperial predecessors. It was little wonder that he became increasingly frustrated, and at times bad-tempered, at his inability to 'get things done', despite his own vision and frenetic energy.

The frustrations of the idealisms of India's greatest nationalists, and the pragmatism of the Congress Party, created a profound ideological vacuum in independent India. Into this vacuum have emerged a host of parties in place of the once-great and embracing party which led the country to independence. Many are regional in origin and orientation, fostering the interests of specific areas within the subcontinent. But they have proved incapable of making a national appeal or providing the base for a stable all-India coalition. Perhaps the one party which has been able to construct a national vision is the revivalist Hindu Party, the BJP, which has emerged as a highly significant political force over the past decade. But this vision of the nation itself endangers the unity of a nation with many religious minorities and cultural diversities, which Gandhi sought to safeguard with his ethical religion and tolerance, and which Nehru hoped to cement and strengthen with a vision of modern secularism and socialism.

India's politicians need to dream dreams and see visions of a tolerant and compassionate India as their nation's fiftieth birthday is celebrated, for their electorate is telling them sober truths about the lack of repute in which they are held, and their need for integrity and a commitment to real change as the country's expanding population grows increasingly sophisticated and aware of the nature of the political system and its departure from the hopes so manifest in 1947. Gandhi and Nehru may have been frustrated in their hopes for India: but they laid down a marker and a standard by which subsequent leaders and aspirant leaders are judged.

The Roots of Chinese Xenophobia

During most of the twentieth century, Chinese schools taught history as a series of *guo chi*, or national humiliations caused by foreign powers.

DENNIS VAN VRANKEN HICKEY

In 1900, the American public reacted with horror to newspaper accounts describing a siege of hundreds of foreign diplomats and civilians who were trapped inside a diplomatic compound in Peking, China. The atrocities committed by some members of the Chinese population—in this instance instigated by a group known as the Boxers—seemed incomprehensible and barbaric to many in the international community.

Almost one century later—in 1999 to be exact—the American public once again expressed surprise and bewilderment as news stories depicted Chinese mobs attacking the U.S. Embassy in Beijing. In both cases, strong evidence suggested that the Chinese government tacitly condoned the sieges. At the same time, however, it appeared that the assaults enjoyed widespread popular approval.

When seeking to explain these and other ugly incidents, Western news reports traditionally dismissed them as symbols of Chinese irrationality and xenophobia. More recently, they are ascribed simply to a particularly virulent and nasty brand of nationalism. Unfortunately, little effort is directed toward uncovering the reasons *why* the Chinese sometimes seem xenophobic, angry, or irrational.

The Chinese Paradigm

The concept of paradigms is borrowed from Thomas Kuhn, who employed them to describe advances in science. A paradigm may be defined as a basic assumption in a field of science. The acceptance of these assumptions is shared by practitioners in a given field and usually is not subject to widespread discussion or debate. Over time, paradigms may shift, but this change often comes very slowly.

Some scholars have suggested that the concept may be applied to the orientation of a nation and its population. A country's foreign policy paradigm is shaped by critical events. For example, the Japanese sneak attack on Pearl Harbor in 1941 culminated in a paradigm shift in American policy. Following the attack, the United States abandoned isolationism and adopted an interventionist and internationalist approach to foreign policy—an approach that many believe remains intact today.

A series of cataclysmic events led China to adopt a distinctly different outlook. Beijing eyes much of the global community with deep suspicion and distrust—particularly the most powerful states in the international system. When provided the opportunity, it believes, these governments will use their power to bully, dismember, and humiliate China.

The Chinese also suspect that many of the problems confronting their country—particularly troubles relating to territorial sovereignty and economic development—may be traced to the actions of foreign powers. It is noteworthy that the central tenets of this paradigm were shared by the governing elites in both the Republican and communist eras of China's modern history.

Why do the Chinese hold such a dark view of international politics? Why does the population sometimes appear xenophobic and paranoid to outside observers? Why does Beijing suspect that foreign powers work to keep the country divided and weak? This article seeks to address these questions.

The National Humiliations

During most of the twentieth century, Chinese schools taught history as a series of *guo chi,* or national humiliations. Consequently, the Chinese tend to see numerous events—ranging from the accidental American bombing of the Chinese Embassy in Belgrade to the midair collision between a Chinese warplane and an American spy plane near Hainan Island—as major embarrassments.

Less dramatic incidents—ranging from trade disputes to quarrels over the location of the Olympic Games—are also considered prime examples of guo chi. To the Chinese, it's simply a matter of history repeating itself. A review of some of their country's major defeats and humiliations at the hands of foreign governments may help readers understand this perspective.

China's humiliations began in the nineteenth century, when the Western powers and Japan forced imperial China open and began to dismember it. One of the earliest (and worst) episodes involved the British and their determination to peddle opium to the Chinese population. Outraged by the Chinese government's

A History of Foreign Intervention

China's humiliations began in the nineteenth century, when the Western powers and Japan forced it open and began to dismember it.

In 1898, Britain coerced China into leasing the New Territories—a large agricultural area that would help support Hong Kong—for 99 years.

Britain's encroachments encouraged other powers to follow its lead. France, Germany, Belgium, Sweden, Norway, Russia, and the United States all forced treaties on China that would provide their governments with special rights and privileges.

The actions of the foreign powers gave the Chinese ample reason to become xenophobic. These sentiments exploded in 1900 when a peasant movement known as the Boxer Rebellion sought to expel the imperialists from the country.

Throughout the first half of the twentieth century, foreigners continued to enjoy special privileges in China while the people suffered.

Matters took a dramatic turn for the worse when Japan occupied Manchuria and initiated a war that lasted from 1937 to 1945. According to some estimates, 13.5 million Chinese perished in the conflict.

For example, Germany obtained a 99-year lease on the tip of Shandong, France secured a 99-year lease on the Bay of Guanzhou, and Russia obtained a 25-year lease for a base in Dalian and Port Arthur. And after China's defeat in the Sino-Japanese War of 1895, the island province of Taiwan was formally incorporated into the Empire of Japan.

During the last years of the nineteenth century, some predicted that China, like Africa, might be carved up entirely by the world's most powerful imperialist powers. These fears prompted America to promote an "open door" policy, under which all countries would be permitted to trade in Chinese territories that were dominated by other powers. This was not an altruistic gesture. Rather, it was designed to prevent the weaker imperialist nations—like the United States—from being cut out of the lucrative China trade.

The actions of the foreign powers gave the Chinese ample reason to become xenophobic. These sentiments exploded in 1900 when a peasant movement known as the Boxer Rebellion sought to expel imperialists from the country. To many Chinese, the Boxers symbolized patriotism. To the imperialists, however, they were barbarians who unwittingly provided foreigners with another excuse to carve up China.

After the Boxers were defeated, the Chinese government was forced to pay massive indemnities to the victors and permit foreign troops to be stationed at key positions throughout the country. The defeat also served as a spark that helped fuel the flames of nationalism in China, paving the way for the overthrow of the Qing dynasty in 1911 and the establishment of the Republic of China.

Perhaps the most critical incident contributing to the rise of Chinese nationalism occurred after World War I. In 1919, the victorious Allied powers announced at the Paris Peace Conference that Germany's special rights in Shandong Province would be transferred to Japan. There was a strong feeling that China—which had supported the Allied cause during the war—had been betrayed. The news from Paris sparked massive student protests, widespread demonstrations, and a boycott of Japanese goods throughout the country.

The ensuing turmoil came to be known as the May Fourth Movement. It set the stage for the rise of both the Kuomintang (KMT) and the Chinese Communist Party (CCP) as mass movements dedicated to promoting nationalism, uniting the country, and ending the era of guo chi.

The May Fourth Movement did not put an immediate end to China's humiliations. Throughout the first half of the twentieth century, foreigners continued to enjoy special privileges while the Chinese people suffered. Matters took a dramatic turn for the worse when Japan occupied Manchuria in 1931. The war it initiated on July 7, 1937, would last until 1945. According to some estimates, 13.5 million Chinese perished in the conflict.

Following World War II, China descended into civil war. After several years of bitter fighting, the CCP emerged victorious and the KMT retreated to Taiwan (in keeping with wartime agreements, the island and other territories had been formally returned to China in 1945). When proclaiming the founding of the new People's Republic of China on October 1, 1949, Mao Zedong declared proudly that the Chinese people had finally

attempts to ban the drug and punish opium traders, Great Britain declared war on China and defeated it in the so-called Opium War (1839–42).

The results of this conflict were disastrous. Millions of Chinese became drug addicts, and the imperial government was forced to pay Great Britain for the costs it had incurred during the war. Moreover, the resulting Treaty of Nanking—the first in a series of unequal treaties—provided the British with the right to trade with the Chinese at five ports and ceded the island of Hong Kong to the United Kingdom "in perpetuity."

Great Britain was not satisfied with the gains that it secured during the Opium War. After emerging victorious in a second conflict in 1860, the British obtained more indemnities from the Chinese government, secured 10 more treaty ports, and occupied the Kowloon Peninsula.

This prime piece of real estate, located directly across from the island of Hong Kong, was also ceded to the British in perpetuity. Then, in 1898, Great Britain coerced China into leasing the New Territories—a large agricultural area that would help support Hong Kong—for 99 years.

Great Britain's encroachments encouraged other powers to follow its lead. France, Germany, Belgium, Sweden, Norway, Russia, and the United States all forced treaties on China that would provide their respective governments with special rights and privileges.

"stood up." The message was unmistakable: the era of guo chi would come to an end.

As Mao's troops swept into China's major cities, the foreigners abandoned their opulent enclaves. This time, the imperialist powers did not intervene. After expelling the imperialists, Mao set out to reassemble the Chinese empire that had crumbled during the waning years of the Qing dynasty.

Chinese authority was reestablished in the territories of Eastern Turkestan, Inner Mongolia, and Tibet. The fact that the minority populations occupying these regions had little, if anything, in common with Chinese culture meant nothing to the communist regime. The territories had once belonged to the Chinese empire, and they had been claimed by Chiang Kaishek's KMT. Consequently, they would now become part of the "New China."

Other territories proved more difficult to acquire. In 1954, Mao asked the Soviet Union to "return" Outer Mongolia, but Moscow refused. After years of prolonged negotiation, Deng Xiaoping, Mao's successor, engineered the return of the British colony of Hong Kong (all three parts of it) to China in 1997.

Shortly afterward, the Portuguese colony of Macao was returned. Most recently, Beijing's attention has shifted to Taiwan. China insists that the island, like all other "lost" or "stolen" territories, must be returned. The prospect of independence for Taiwan—a proposition embraced by a new generation of leadership in Taipei—is deemed out of the question. If Taiwan moves too close to de jure independence, Beijing has threatened to use force to unite it with the mainland.

Conclusion

The foreign treaty ports, gunboats, and colonies that humiliated China for over 100 years are now part of history. Even the physical traces of this past are beginning to disappear. Many of the Western buildings that once characterized the international settlement in Shanghai are gone. The Victorian-era structures have been replaced by modern skyscrapers and shopping centers. Nevertheless, the psychological scars and pains of the era of guo chi linger and continue to influence relations with the outside world.

At present, China confronts massive corruption, unemployment, and other wrenching dislocations associated with its transition to a market-style economy. To be sure, the government sometimes seeks to use nationalism to deflect attention from its failures and shore up support for the regime.

Many Chinese complain that the government is not forceful enough in the face of perceived foreign transgressions.

Nevertheless, it would be a mistake to assume that the population's nationalistic sentiment may be attributed solely to government propaganda or manipulation. In fact, many Chinese complain that the government is not forceful enough in the face of perceived foreign transgressions.

Nationalism has been a potent force in Chinese politics since the Boxer Rebellion. Increasingly, many Chinese at both the elite and popular levels perceive the United States as the sole remaining foreign power that is determined to keep the country divided, weak, and poor. This is a very troubling development. Ironically, however, America is still popular among many Chinese. It remains a chief destination for China's students, and its technology, business methods, and even political institutions are widely admired.

One of the greatest challenges for the United States will be to manage an increasingly complicated relationship with China. Given the unfortunate history of Beijing's ties with much of the international community, it is likely that this relationship will be characterized by a fairly consistent amount of tension. Consequently, both sides will have to work hard to promote harmony and avoid conflict.

DENNIS VAN VRANKEN HICKEY is professor in the political science department at Southwest Missouri State University.

The Dirty A-Word

Peter Neville says that Bush and Blair failed to draw the proper lessons from Munich 1938 when they raised the spectre of Chamberlain and appeasement to justify their war against Saddam.

PETER NEVILLE

On September 30th, 1938, Neville Chamberlain signed the Munich Agreement that gave Germany the Czech Sudetenland. The next morning he also persuaded Adolf Hitler to sign the Anglo-German Declaration (now on view in the Imperial War Museum) that supposedly demonstrated the determination of the British and German peoples 'never to go to war with one another again'. The British Ambassador in Berlin, Sir Nevile Henderson, writing to congratulate Chamberlain, said that 'Millions of mothers will be blessing your name tonight for having saved their sons from the horrors of war. Oceans of ink will flow hereafter in criticism.'

Henderson wrote more truly than he knew, for Munich has become a pejorative term for betrayal and Chamberlain's name today is synonymous with military tardiness, diplomatic feebleness and general lack of resolve. The destruction of Chamberlain's reputation was sedulously assisted by the publication of the first volume of Winston Churchill's war memoirs, The Gathering Storm, in 1948. Churchill quoted in the book from his speech in the parliamentary debate on Munich in October 1938. 'All is over,' he told his colleagues. 'Silent, mournful, abandoned, broken, Czechoslovakia recedes into the darkness.' Such words had an immediate appeal, as everyone sympathized with the wrecking of a small state's independence—or they would, once the spasm of hysterical relief created by the Munich Agreement was over. Events were to prove Churchill right. In the same debate he had warned that '1 [pounds sterling] was demanded at the pistol's point. When it was given, 2 [pounds sterling] were demanded at the pistol's point. Finally the Dictator consented to take 1 [pounds sterling] 17s 6d and the rest in promises of goodwill.' Just six months later, Hitler undermined the appeasement policy by occupying Bohemia and Moravia, in flagrant breach of the promise he had made at Munich not to seek further territorial expansion. War followed inevitably six months after that, despite valiant efforts by Chamberlain to avoid the catastrophe.

For nearly twenty years after the Second World War, the so-called Churchillian critique dominated attempts to analyse what happened at Munich. Then, in 1961, the tide began to turn when A.J.P. Taylor suggested, with heretical panache, that the Munich Settlement was 'a triumph for all that was best and most enlightened in British life'. This statement seemed to turn history on its head. Everyone knew, didn't they, that Munich was a byword for vacillation and cowardice, a wretched reaction by Britain and France to a challenge from a despotic and genocidal regime. At the time, Taylor's views, which included a worryingly unconventional analysis of the role of Hitler, were regarded as absurd, if not actually perverse.

Slowly thereafter the balance began to shift. The idea of 'imperial overstretch' gained favour with revisionist historians, who stressed the undoubted tact that Britain in the late thirties faced an unprecedented peril from three potentially hostile great powers. Clearly the vast British Empire could not be safely guarded against Germany, Italy and Japan, as the opening phases of the Second World War demonstrated all too vividly. American isolationism, Soviet untrustworthiness, Dominion unreadiness all began to receive more attention in British studies. As did the Cassandra-like role of the defence chiefs of staff, who—as newly-released documentation showed—warned constantly of the perils that war would bring to an outmatched Britain. Through the seventies and eighties, a more nuanced, less knee-jerk analysis both of Munich and the wider context of global appeasement thus appeared. Britain in 1938 could not ignore the Japanese threat in the Pacific that it had recognized (via its defence requirements committee) as far back as 1934, any more than it could dismiss the (admittedly overrated) threat from Mussolini in the Mediterranean. If there were still illusions about the Italian dictator's usefulness as a mediator at the time of Munich, they did not extend as far as assuming that the Duce's goodwill could be relied upon.

Historian Roy Douglas went as far as to query wily it was that the British had not left the French, Czechs and Germans to their own devices over the Sudeten question. It was, after all, flying in the teeth of Britain's foreign policy traditions for Chamberlain to involve himself so intimately with a crisis in Central Europe. When foreign secretary in the 1920s, his half brother, Austen, had famously pronounced that Eastern Europe on Czechoslovakia's doorstep (however much the Czechs thought of themselves as western Europeans) was not worth 'the bones of a British grenadier'.

Douglas's question resonates. Why should one state cast aside its national interest in the interests of another? De Gaulle famously said that the state is 'the coldest of cold monsters' and yet Britain and France were apparently prepared to go to war for Czechoslovakia after the Godesberg meeting with Hitler had failed just days before Munich, even though the status of the Czech Sudetenland in 1938 was plainly no more a vital British national interest than the Rhineland had been in 1936. Unlike the Rhineland, the Sudetenland was not Hitler's 'backyard', but it was, as President Benes of Czechoslovakia had the grace to recognize in 1938, a long way away from Britain and France. Tory MPs still spoke of 'Czechoslovenia' and a Daily Express headline demanded 'Where is Prague?'

In justifying their actions over Iraq, Bush, Blair, Straw and Rumsfeld constantly denied the option of military non-intervention to Chamberlain in 1938, just as they denied it to their American and British publics in 2003. Stuffed with half-baked historical hindsight, these politicians self-righteously condemned the appeasers, without any proper understanding of the context. The difference between Chamberlain in 1938 and Blair in 2003 was that Chamberlain's actions at Munich reflected public opinion, whereas Blair's over Iraq did not. Refusal to acknowledge public opinion's significance in a democracy when war looms must betoken hubris—the very fault blamed on Chamberlain for seeking accommodation in a vastly more difficult situation.

The major lesson of Munich should not be to laud demonstrations of military virility, but to warn politicians of the dangers of intemperate and reckless attempts to resolve conflict by force. This was most classically demonstrated in 1956 during the Suez Crisis when British Prime Minister Anthony Eden (a former appeaser himself) almost comically imagined that Gamal Abdul Nasser was a reincarnation of Hitler or Mussolini. Yet it is hard to believe that Eden would have acted with such folly had he been facing a conflict with a major power of the military calibre of Nazi Germany in 1938.

Munich therefore is about the appropriateness of using force and the likelihood of its being successful. It may be possible to argue that Chamberlain took the wrong option in September 1938, but it is foolish not to recognize that the balance between military intervention and non-intervention was a fine one. And the consequences of going to war were likely to be infinitely more terrible for Britain than those of backing up Bush's folly in Iraq in 2003.

The great tragedy of the 1930s, 'a low dishonest decade' as the poet W. H. Auden called it, was that the promise represented by the League of Nations was stillborn. At the time of Munich, the League was an irrelevance, a sad talking-shop in Geneva to which the dictators paid no heed. The League had notoriously failed to prevent Japanese aggression in Manchuria, and Italian aggression in Abyssinia. When the idea of imposing sanctions on Mussolini was aired, Chamberlain himself said that such action would be the 'very midsummer of madness'. The Munich statesmen rejected internationalism by excluding both

the Soviet Union and Czechoslovakia from their discussions. The ceding of the Sudetenland may not have appeared to be a nineteenth-century-style land grab, but it encapsulated Hitler's real ethnic imperative, which was not just about bringing Germans into the Reich but also about dominating and subjugating 'sub-human' Slavs. This emerged clearly six months later, but in September 1938 the issue was also about recognizing the rights of ethnic minorities, not just Sudeten Germans, but also Poles and Hungarians within the borders of the Czechoslovak Republic.

To a degree, the need for international cooperation under the auspices of the new United Nations was learnt after 1945. In 1990 for example, a UN-led international coalition that included regional Arab powers ended Saddam Hussein's illegal occupation of Kuwait. But such action (Korea is another example) was always highly selective. Cold War realities made it impossible to aid the beleaguered Hungarians in 1956, at the very same time that Eden was embarking on his adventure in Egypt. Even when working within the parameters of the more effective UN, the great powers maintained their own agendas, always in the knowledge that the nuclear bomb as Churchill noted made 'peace the sturdy child of terror'.

Did the end of the Cold War make the flaunting of military muscle more seductive? Recent evidence suggests that, where the United States has been concerned, it has. And, it might be added, the desire of the Blair-led British government to pull Britain into the American slipstream has resulted in UN authority being undermined and a war being embarked on in the teeth of international and domestic opinion.

The situation in 1938 was, of course, quite different where Anglo-American relations were concerned. Chamberlain was frankly distrustful of the Americans; he told his sister that they could be relied upon for nothing except words. He got two famous words at the time of Munich from Roosevelt: 'good man' implied US approval for the Munich Agreement, and at no point was there any suggestion that the United States would intervene in the Sudeten crisis. It is worth pointing out also that when, nearly a year before, in December 1937, the Imperial Japanese Army massacred 300,000 Chinese in Nanjing, no one in Europe or the United States seriously supported intervention on behalf of China. Forests of paper have been consumed (much of it on the other side of the Atlantic) in condemning Chamberlain's action at Munich, but very little on castigating Anglo-American statesmen for failing to prevent Japan's act of genocide.

Not only are the occasions chosen fur intervention in the international system highly selective, so is the criticism of such action. The same Western statesmen who had no problem coexisting with Franco, Marcos, Suharto, Pinochet and (lest it be forgot) Saddam Hussein, declaim endlessly about the evils of Munich and appeasement. It is, of course, possible to argue, as the Canadian scholar Sidney Aster did some years ago, that Munich was immoral because it involved detaching territory from a small nation under the threat of force if it did not agree. But when was morality ever a strong point of the international system, and haven't the difficulties of an 'ethical' British foreign policy been vividly demonstrated recently? The appeasers also thought they were being moral by recognizing the ethnic principle in Czechoslovakia.

Politicians are in any case ill-advised to hurl the word 'morality' around without due care. Over Iraq, Bush and Blair tried to pretend (after the event) that the invasion was about 'regime change', when it was in fact about a vain and unsuccessful search for weapons of mass destruction. Chamberlain's foreign secretary, Lord Halifax, did not fall into the trap of trying to justify Munich by moralizing about it. He wrote later that it was 'a horrible and wretched business but the lesser of two evils'. This was the language of sane and sanguine pragmatism, not of hyperbole about divinely assisted crusades against darkness.

Some of the parallels between Munich and Iraq, as far as Britain is concerned, are striking. In 1938, as in 2003, Britain had a prime minister who wanted to run foreign policy himself and distrusted the Foreign Office. If one is to believe Sir Christopher Meyer's recently published account (DC Confidential 2005), Blair and his entourage were even jealous of the very modest amount of influence the Washington Embassy had with the Bush White House. And while 'spin' had not been invented in 1938, Chamberlain's office was capable of trying to manipulate the news media in a manner now all too familiar. But there the parallels end. Chamberlain faced problems that were dauntingly more difficult than those facing Blair. Britain in 1938 was a real global power, not a satrap of the United States, sans empire and real influence. One of the delusions of the so-called 'Special Relationship' is the British belief that the Americans really listen to British views and modify their policies accordingly. Had Neville Chamberlain remained in office longer than he did, it is hard to imagine him suffering from such delusions, and even Churchill was forced to recognize the impotence of 'the British donkey' when it tried to deal with the Russian bear and the American eagle.

At Munich, Chamberlain not only attempted to preserve a British place in the world that was ultimately bound to be lost; he also sought to prevent the wholesale carnage of the First World War. He can hardly be criticized for that, and if the loss of life in Czechoslovakia was much lower than in Poland as a fortunate consequence of Munich and what followed, the Sudeten Germans paid the ultimate price. In 1945, they were expelled from the Czech Republic en masse, a solution to the Sudeten problem that had not been contemplated in 1938. Some might argue that it should have been, but in 1938 Britain and France were attempting, rightly or wrongly, to apply the principles of ethnic self-determination enshrined in the Versailles settlement of Europe. That they ever contemplated war for the Sudetenland should be a matter for surprise, particularly where Britain was concerned.

In 1914, Britain had gone to war to protect Belgian neutrality, not for 'tiresome Serbia' as Queen Mary called it. It would have done so without a qualm in 1938 because Belgium was part of the zone of vital British interests in Western Europe identified in the 1925 Treaty of Locarno. Czechoslovakia lay outside this sphere of interest, and Chamberlain understandably opted to follow Britain's foreign policy traditions (although in another sense, he departed from them with innovative summit diplomacy). For Czechoslovakia Munich was a tragedy, and its poet Frantisek Halas noted their sense of betrayal in the lines:

The bell of treason is tolling
Whose band made it swing?
Sweet France
Proud Albion
And we loved them.

But what Neville Chamberlain did at Munich was not treason. He believed, along with most of the British political and military establishment, that Britain could not justify shedding its citizens' blood for the Sudetenland and this decision, although still controversial, was an entirely rational one. Especially as Britain's major ally France showed little stomach for a fight even though it, unlike Britain, had a treaty commitment to the Czechs. And even in his moment of triumph, Chamberlain knew that Hitler might still break his word. He told his parliamentary personal secretary, Lord Dunglass (the future prime minister, Alec Douglas Hume), that the purpose of the Anglo-German Declaration was to show Hitler up in the eyes of international opinion if he dared to go back on his word. Neither did Chamberlain stint on the rearmament programme (with much accelerated production by 1939) contrary to later myth, or go for a snap victorious election. Munich then, was about a balance between rearmament and accommodation not craven defeatism.

This article first appeared in *History Today,* April 2006. Copyright © 2006 by History Today, Ltd. Reprinted by permission.

Women in the Third Reich

As a result of the second wave of the women's movement, it is now generally accepted that women are in the best position not only to study the social situation of contemporary women, but also to explain women's roles in the more distant past. Indeed, the writing of history always contributes to the defense or criticism of the dominant order. In this way, historians' neglect has further enforced in the minds of their descendants the marginal existence of women in past centuries.

Girls who attended school after World War II certainly never heard of Lilo Herrmann in their history classes. Herrmann was a young woman and mother who, on June 20, 1938, was one of the first killed because of her brave and steadfast resistance to fascism. Nor did they hear of Hanne Martens, an actress and antifascist, whose skull was crushed by an SS man when she refused to be hanged naked. Nor of Martha Gillesen, who was shot in the head by SS officers, after she, with the rest of her resistance group, was tied up with barbed wire and given an injection in the tongue, so that she could not scream. Nor of Kaete Larsch, tortured to death, when she would not betray others in the resistance. Nor of the resistance fighter Johanna Kirschner, who was sentenced in half an hour and condemned to death in June of 1944.

We could list thousands of women's names: those who resisted and were sentenced and condemned in the so-called people's court; or who were gassed, shot, abused to death, experimented on or starved to death in concentration camps, or who died doing hard labor. Only the memories of the abuse and other horrors people endured and a thorough mourning for the terrible suffering of so many innocent people will protect later generations from similar experiences.

What did Nazi ideology have to say about women? Reading national socialist writings, what stands out most clearly is an unbelievable contempt for women. In 1921, just two years after women got the vote, the Nazi party voted unanimously in their first general meeting that "a woman can not be accepted to the party leadership!" In fact, a woman was never nominated by the NSDAP to serve in local or provincial parliaments, or in the Reichstag. Joseph Goebbels, the State Minister for People's Enlightenment and Propaganda, explained the political disenfranchisement of women in the following way during his speech at the opening of the exhibit "Woman" in Berlin:

> The National Socialist movement is the only party that keeps women out of direct involvement in daily politics . . .
> We have not kept her out of parliamentary-democratic intrigues because of any disrespect toward women. It is

not because we see in her and her mission something less worthy, but rather that we see in her and her mission something quite different from the vocation which men have . . . Her first and foremost, and most appropriate place is in the family, and the most wonderful duty which she can take on is to give her country and her people children, children which carry on the success of the race and assure the immortality of the nation.

Another Nazi leader, party member number two and president of the Reich's Tourist Bureau Hermann Esser, instructed women in the following way: "Women belong at home in the kitchen and the bedroom, they belong at home and should be raising their children."

And Adolf Hitler, who was Fuehrer of the German nation for twelve years, announced:

> What a man contributes in hero's courage on the battlefield, a woman contributes in her eternally patient sacrifice, in her eternally patient suffering. Every child that she brings into the world is a battle which she undergoes for the existence of her people.

So it is not surprising that women who had no children were seen as "duds in population politics." Families with fewer than four children had not fulfilled their "duty to the people's preservation rate," and woman who had many children received a "mother's cross."

These are the symptoms of the boundlessly controlling behavior of the Nazis toward women. Why wasn't National Socialism widely rejected by women? The German women's movement had been active for twenty years; by that time there was a tradition of collective struggle for women's rights. Since many women had lost fathers, sons, or brothers and were alone, they were forced to live very difficult, independent lives.

Of course, women were not a homogenous group that acted and thought alike. Taking a close look at the many different ways in which women acted during the Third Reich, I generally differentiate four groups. First, there were women who sooner or later resisted the Nazis and their terrible deeds. Many had to pay with their lives. They are, however, unknown—the heroines of history.

Then there were their adversaries: women who allowed themselves to be the tools of other people's torture and who for their part abused and beat people, and killed them in terrible ways. These women were most often dumb, young, arrogant and lured by the relatively good standard of living provided by the party. Since they often came from broken, authoritarian families, they often misused the power that they had over defenseless victims.

Between these two groups of women, there were the ignorant and those who just went along with things. Of course these groups were also heterogeneous. In each group there were women from every social class.

Among the ignorant women I count those who were totally apolitical (they usually remained apolitical after the war; they did not learn anything). These were the women who only thought about keeping their families alive; it didn't matter what happened to their neighbors. Even today, the "complete mastery of potatoes and their characteristics" is praised in German society "the art of gourmet potato dumplings" is admired, and pages are devoted to the potato, and thus the "triumph of survival" is celebrated. When concentration camps are mentioned, it's in a pithy aside: The Americans "posted horrible pictures of concentration camps on the walls." Even today, such ignorance sends chills up your spine.

The "fellow travellers" included the so-called leaders of Nazi women's organizations, such as the blond-haired woman, leader of the *Reichs*-women and eleven-time mother, Gertrud Scholtz-Klink, and also the women who voted for Hitler and fit in one way or another. However, people's belief that women helped Hitler to power has no basis in fact.

In the presidential election of 1932, 51.6 percent of women voted for Hindenburg, 26.5 percent for Hitler. In the second vote, 56 percent were for Hindenburg and 33.6 percent for Hitler. In both votes the number of men's votes was about 2 percent greater than women's. Many voted conservatively, so that the misogynist Center Party got a large percentage of women's votes, but not the Nazis.

We should not forget that women had just been granted the active and passive vote, and thus were not practiced in political matters. They were not able to recognize their own interests and to represent them politically. Even for those who had started leaving the home hearth, there hadn't been enough time to overcome their dependent intellectual, social and economic status in the family or in their professions. In the first years of Nazi rule, they were driven back to their traditional domain, the family, and thus shut out of all social activities. Next the eradication of unemployment became women's burden, as many were fired from their posts and jobs. Married women who worked were denounced as "double earners."

Only a few women recognized that being shut out of the workplace and restricted to the home, with loans available only to those families where the mother didn't work, and the awarding of privileges to families with many children would serve only one purpose: the strengthening of "national manpower", in other words, the "production of human material." In 1932, there was an average of 59 births per 1,000 women, but by 1938 it was already 81 births. The slogan was: "Give the Fuehrer children."

The so-called "Fountain of Life" (Lebensborn), an organization founded in 1935 by the national leader of the SS, Heinrich Himmler, was concerned with this "strengthened propagation." There, "racially worthy" girls were at the service of SS men for the procreation of Aryan children; here antifeminism and racism were bound up in the most intricate way. The administrator of these breeding institutions said, in all openness, that the goal was the production of human material: "Thanks to the 'Fountain of Life', we'll have 600 more regiments in thirty years."

There are reasons why so many women were blind to the dangers of the misogynist and racist ideology of the Nazis. For one thing, National Socialism was not so different from the attitude, opinion and posture of the conservatives, the German nationalists and the populists of the Weimar Republic, who were also often misogynist. For hundreds of years, the German people had been accustomed to state elitism and authoritarian behavior. This is also one of the reasons why there was no violent wave of protest from women collectively when the countless women's unions were dissolved, or forced to dissolve themselves, or when the decision that only 10% of students at the university could be female was announced, or when women were forbidden to take up influential positions, such as that of judge or administrator.

In western history, the struggle for women's equality and recognition is very young. At that moment when the women's movement could have developed on a broader level, it was destroyed. The refined strategy of strengthening and praising women in their traditionally dictated roles of caring housewife and mother had a very strong effect on the unenlightened. Never before had women been so directly addressed; never before had their reproductive function received so much recognition. Surely we should try to understand what drove the "fellow travellers" and the ignorant women to accept the degrading roles assigned to them by men.

What came out of the ignorance and willing sacrifice of these women is only a part of our history. The other part is often hidden from us.

Immediately after the war, numerous books were published by women who told how the war affected them, of their terrible suffering, but also of their bravery and the courage of antifascist women. The books quickly sold and only a few of them got a second printing. Yet these books relate the horrifying details, without which our knowledge of the murder of millions of people would be very superficial. Nanda Herbermann, for example, describes in her book *The Blessed Abyss* (which has been out of print for years) what she experienced in an imprisonment that came about for no obvious reason:

> In complete darkness, I felt a stool which had been screwed into the floor. I heard the groaning and whimpering of the poor souls who were next to me, above and below, languishing in cell after cell in solitary confinement. Some of them had lost their sanity. No wonder! They raged and beat on the doors of their cells, sang crazy songs all through the night. Still others sang distorted old church songs in desperate voices, like animals, until one of the wardens came and beat them terribly—they even sometimes locked dogs in the cells, so that the trained animals could attack the victims. Among those detained were some out of whom dogs had bitten huge pieces of flesh; some had lost half an ear, others a piece of their

nose, or their hand or whatever. Still others in the cell block were found covered with blood hard as ice. In this house of death, it was always bitterly cold. There I sat, barefoot in the darkness, freezing in my deepest soul.

The horror that we read in these lines should not make us turn away helplessly. Rather, the knowledge of the suppressed crimes and the unspeakable suffering should give us the conviction, the anger and courage we need in the fight against Naziism, which even now survives in our democracy and threatens us. The danger of being mere objects of political processes still exists. The scorn and mockery of pacifism, for example, has a tradition. ("To be a pacifist shows a lack of character and disposition," said Adolf Hitler in 1923.)

In a world where they make the stationing of neutron bombs appealing by saying, "they reduce the chances that these or any other weapons will ever be used;" in a world where we speak of the "balance of terror" and the "spiral of atomic retribution," women resistance fighters can be role models. With clear consciences, the women resistance fighters of the Third Reich set themselves against an ideology that did not value human life; they fought bravely and confidently for the old revolutionary goals: equality, justice and above all, humanity. For this they were tortured and for the most part murdered. But our memories of them and their courageous deeds can help us to prevent similar events—in whatever form they take—from ever being repeated in the future.

From the series *Vitae*, by ANGELIKA KAUFMANN

Editor's Note: (Translated and excerpted from *"Frauen im Dritten Reich,"* by RENATE WIGGERSHAUS in Auf, Austrian feminist quarterly, No. 33, 1982.)

Exposing the Rape of Nanking

Exclusive excerpts from a Chinese-American author's unflinching re-examination of one of the most horrifying chapters of the second world war.

IRIS CHANG

The chronicle of humankind's cruelty is a long and sorry tale. But if it is true that even in such horror tales there are degrees of ruthlessness, then few atrocities can compare in intensity and scale to the rape of Nanking during World War II.

The broad details of the rape are, except among the Japanese, not in dispute. In November 1937, after their successful invasion of Shanghai, the Japanese launched a massive attack on the newly established capital of the Republic of China. When the city fell on December 13, 1937, Japanese soldiers began an orgy of cruelty seldom if ever matched in world history. Tens of thousands of young men were rounded up and herded to the outer areas of the city, where they were mowed down by machine guns, used for bayonet practice, or soaked with gasoline and burned alive. By the end of the massacre an estimated 260,000 to 350,000 Chinese had been killed. Between 20,000 and 80,000 Chinese women were raped—and many soldiers went beyond rape to disembowel women, slice off their breasts, nail them alive to walls. So brutal were the Japanese in Nanking that even the Nazis in the city were shocked. John Rabe, a German businessman who led the local Nazi party, joined other foreigners in working tirelessly to save the innocent from slaughter by creating a safety zone where some 250,000 civilians found shelter.

Yet the Rape of Nanking remains an obscure incident. Although the death toll exceeds the immediate number of deaths from the atomic bombings of Hiroshima and Nagasaki (140,000 and 70,000 respectively, by the end of 1945) and even the total civilian casualties for several European countries during the entire war (Great Britain lost 61,000 civilians, France 108,000, Belgium 101,000, and the Netherlands 242,000), the horrors of the Nanking massacre remain virtually unknown to people outside Asia. The Rape of Nanking did not penetrate the world consciousness in the same manner as the Jewish Holocaust or Hiroshima because the victims themselves remained silent. The custodian of the curtain of silence was politics. The People's Republic of China, Taiwan, and even the United States all contributed to the historical neglect of this event for reasons deeply rooted in the cold war. After the 1949 Communist revolution in China, neither the People's Republic of China nor Taiwan demanded wartime reparations from Japan (as Israel had from

Germany) because the two governments were competing for Japanese trade and political recognition. And even the United States, faced with the threat of communism in the Soviet Union and mainland China, sought to ensure the friendship and loyalty of its former enemy Japan. In this manner, cold-war tensions permitted Japan to escape much of the intense critical examination that its wartime ally was forced to undergo.

In trying to understand the actions of the Japanese, we must begin with a little history. To prepare for what it viewed as an inevitable war with China, Japan had spent decades training its men. The molding of young men to serve in the Japanese military began early: In the 1930s, toy shops became virtual shrines to war, selling arsenals of toy soldiers, tanks, rifles, antiaircraft guns, bugles, and howitzers. Japanese schools operated like miniature military units. Indeed, some of the teachers were military officers, who lectured students on their duty to help Japan fulfill its divine destiny of conquering Asia and being able to stand up to the world's nations as a people second to none. They taught young boys how to handle wooden models of guns, and older boys how to handle real ones. Textbooks became vehicles for military propaganda. Teachers also instilled in boys hatred and contempt for the Chinese people, preparing them psychologically for a future invasion of the Chinese mainland. One historian tells the story of a squeamish Japanese schoolboy in the 1930s who burst into tears when told to dissect a frog. His teacher slammed his knuckles against the boy's head and yelled, "Why are you crying about one lousy frog? When you grow up you'll have to kill one hundred, two hundred chinks!"

In the summer of 1937 Japan finally seized the opportunity to provoke a full-scale war with China. One night in July several shots were fired at members of a Japanese regiment, garrisoned by treaty in the Chinese city of Tientsin, and a Japanese soldier failed to appear during roll call after the maneuvers. Japanese troops advanced upon the nearby Chinese fort of Wanping and demanded that its gates be opened so that they could search for the soldier. When the Chinese commander refused, the Japanese shelled the fort. The confrontation escalated, and by August the Japanese had invaded Shanghai. Conquering China proved to be a more difficult task than the Japanese anticipated. In Shanghai alone Chinese forces outnumbered the Japanese marines ten to one, and Chiang Kai-shek, leader of the Nationalist government, had reserved his best troops for the battle. For months the Chinese defended the metropolis with extraordinary valor. To the chagrin of the Japanese, the battle of Shanghai proceeded slowly, street by street, barricade by barricade.

Little was spared on the path to Nanking. Japanese veterans remember raiding tiny farm communities, where they clubbed or bayoneted everyone in sight. Small villages were not the only casualties; entire cities were razed to the ground. Consider the example of Suchow, a city on the east bank of the Tai Hu Lake. One of the oldest cities of China, it was prized for its delicate silk embroidery, palaces, and temples. Its canals and ancient bridges had earned the city its Western nickname as "the Venice of China." On November 19, on a morning of pouring rain, a Japanese advance guard marched through the gates of Suchow, wearing hoods that prevented Chinese sentries from recognizing them. Once inside, the Japanese murdered and plundered the city for days, burning ancient landmarks, and abducting thousands of Chinese women for sexual slavery. The invasion, according to the China Weekly Review, caused the population of the city to drop from 250,000 to less than 500. By the time Japanese troops entered Nanking, an order to eliminate all Chinese captives had been not only committed to paper but distributed to lower-echelon officers. On December 13, 1937, the Japanese 66th Battalion received the following command:

"All prisoners of war are to be executed. Method of execution: divide the prisoners into groups of a dozen. Shoot to kill separately. Our intentions are absolutely not to be detected by the prisoners."

There was a ruthless logic to the order: the captives could not be fed, so they had to be destroyed. Killing them would not only eliminate the food problem but diminish the possibility of retaliation. Moreover, dead enemies could not form up into guerrilla forces.

'It would be disastrous if they were to make any trouble'

But executing the order was another matter. When the Japanese troops smashed through Nanking's walls in the early predawn hours of December 13, they entered a city in which they were vastly outnumbered. Historians later estimated that more than half a million civilians and ninety thousand Chinese troops were trapped in Nanking, compared with the fifty thousand Japanese soldiers who assaulted the city. General Kesago Nakajima knew that killing tens of thousands of Chinese captives was a formidable task: "To deal with crowds of a thousand, five thousand, or ten thousand, it is tremendously difficult even just to disarm them. . . . It would be disastrous if they were to make any trouble."

Because of their limited manpower, the Japanese relied heavily on deception. The strategy for mass butchery involved

several steps: promising the Chinese fair treatment in return for an end to resistance, coaxing them into surrendering themselves to their Japanese conquerors, dividing them into groups of one to two hundred men, and then luring them to different areas near Nanking to be killed. Nakajima hoped that faced with the impossibility of further resistance, most of the captives would lose heart and comply with whatever directions the Japanese gave them.

Even war correspondents recoiled at the violence

All this was easier to achieve than the Japanese had anticipated. Resistance was sporadic; indeed, it was practically nonexistent. Having thrown away their arms when attempting to flee the city as the Japanese closed in, many Chinese soldiers simply turned themselves in, hoping for better treatment. Once the men surrendered and permitted their hands to be bound, the rest was easy.

After the soldiers surrendered en masse, there was virtually no one left to protect the citizens of the city. Knowing this, the Japanese poured into Nanking, occupying government buildings, banks, and warehouses, shooting people randomly in the streets, many of them in the back as they ran away. As victims toppled to the ground, moaning and screaming, the streets, alleys, and ditches of the fallen capital ran rivers of blood. During the last ten days of December, Japanese motorcycle brigades patrolled Nanking while Japanese soldiers shouldering loaded rifles guarded the entrances to all the streets, avenues, and alleys. Troops went from door to door, demanding that they be opened to welcome the victorious armies. The moment the shopkeepers complied, the Japanese opened fire on them. The imperial army massacred thousands of people in this manner and then systematically looted the stores and burned whatever they had no use for.

'The killing went on nonstop, from morning until night'

These atrocities shocked many of the Japanese correspondents who had followed the troops to Nanking. Even seasoned war correspondents recoiled at the orgy of violence, and their exclamations found their way into print. From the Japanese military correspondent Yukio Omata, who saw Chinese prisoners brought to Hsiakwan and lined up along the river: "Those in the first row were beheaded, those in the second row were forced to dump the severed bodies into the river before they themselves were beheaded. The killing went on nonstop, from morning until night, but they were only able to kill 2,000 persons in this way. The next day, tired of killing in this fashion, they set up machine guns. Two of them raked a cross-fire at the lined-up prisoners. Rat-tat-tat-tat. Triggers were pulled. The prisoners fled into the water, but no one was able to make it to the other shore."

Next, the Japanese turned their attention to the women. The rape of Nanking is considered the worst mass rape of world history with the sole exception of the treatment of Bengali women by Pakistani soldiers in 1971. Kozo Takokoro, a former soldier in the 114th Division of the Japanese army in Nanking, recalled, "No matter how young or old, they all could not escape the fate of being raped. We sent out coal trucks from Hsiakwan to the city streets and villages to seize a lot of women. And then each of them was allocated to 15 to 20 soldiers for sexual intercourse and abuse."

Surviving Japanese veterans claim that the army had officially outlawed the rape of enemy women. But rape remained so deeply embedded in Japanese military culture and superstition that no one took the rule seriously. Many believed that raping virgins would make them more powerful in battle. Soldiers were even known to wear amulets made from the pubic hair of such victims, believing that they possessed magical powers against injury.

The military policy forbidding rape only encouraged soldiers to kill their victims afterwards. Kozo Takokoro was blunt about this. "After raping, we would also kill them," he recalled. "Those women would start to flee once we let them go. Then we would bang! shoot them in the back to finish them up." According to surviving veterans, many of the soldiers felt remarkably little guilt about this. "Perhaps when we were raping her, we looked at her as a woman," Shiro Azuma, a former soldier in Nanking, wrote, "but when we killed her, we just thought of her as something like a pig."

One of the most bizarre consequences of the wholesale rape that took place at Nanking was the response of the Japanese government. The Japanese high command made plans to create a giant underground system of military prostitution—one that would draw into its web hundreds of thousands of women across Asia. The plan was straightforward. By luring, purchasing, or kidnapping between eighty thousand and two hundred thousand women—most of them from the Japanese colony of Korea but many also from China, Taiwan, the Philippines, and Indonesia—the Japanese military hoped to reduce the incidence of random rape of local women (thereby diminishing the opportunity for international criticism), to contain sexually transmitted diseases through the use of condoms, and to reward soldiers for fighting on the battlefront for long stretches of time. Later, of course, when the world learned of this plan, the Japanese government refused to acknowledge responsibility, insisting for decades afterwards that private entrepreneurs, not the imperial government, ran the wartime military brothels. But in 1991 Yoshiaki Yoshimi unearthed from the Japanese Defense Agency's archives a document entitled "Regarding the Recruitment of Women for Military Brothels." The document bore the personal stamps of leaders from the Japanese high command and contained orders for the immediate construction of "facilities of sexual comfort" to stop troops from raping women in regions they controlled in China.

The first official comfort house opened near Nanking in 1938. To use the word *comfort* in regard to either the women or the "houses" in which they lived is ludicrous, for it conjures up spa images of beautiful geisha girls strumming lutes, washing men, and giving them shiatsu massages. In reality, the conditions of these brothels were sordid beyond the imagination of most civilized people. Untold numbers of these women (whom the Japanese called "public toilets") took their own lives when they learned their destiny; others died from disease or murder. Those who survived suffered a lifetime of shame and isolation, sterility, or ruined health.

In interview after interview, Japanese veterans from the Nanking massacre reported honestly that they experienced a complete lack of remorse or sense of wrongdoing, even when torturing helpless civilians. Hakudo Nagatomi spoke candidly about his emotions in the fallen capital: "I remember being driven in a truck along a path that had been cleared through piles of thousands and thousands of slaughtered bodies. Wild dogs were gnawing at the dead flesh as we stopped and pulled a group of Chinese prisoners out of the back. Then the Japanese officer proposed a test of my courage. He unsheathed his sword, spat on it, and with a sudden mighty swing he brought it down on the neck of a Chinese boy cowering before us. The head was cut clean off and tumbled away on the group as the body slumped forward, blood spurting in two great gushing fountains from the neck. The officer suggested I take the head home as a souvenir. I remember smiling proudly as I took his sword and began killing people."

After almost sixty years of soul-searching, Nagatomi is a changed man. A doctor in Japan, he has built a shrine of remorse in his waiting room. Patients can watch videotapes of his trial in Nanking and a full confession of his crimes. The gentle and hospitable demeanor of the doctor belies the horror of his past, making it almost impossible for one to imagine that he had once been a ruthless murderer. "Few know that soldiers impaled babies on bayonets and tossed them still alive into pots of boiling water," Nagatomi said. "They gang-raped women from the ages of twelve to eighty and then killed them when they could no longer satisfy sexual requirements. I beheaded people, starved them to death, burned them, and buried them alive, over two hundred in all. It is terrible that I could turn into an animal and do these things. There are really no words to explain what I was doing. I was truly a devil."

His Finest Hour

With courage and sheer will, Churchill rallied a nation and turned back Hitler's tyranny

JOHN KEEGAN

Sixty years ago this month, in May 1940, Western civilization was threatened with defeat. Liberty, the principle on which it rests, was menaced by a man who despised freedom. Adolf Hitler, the dictator of Nazi Germany, had conquered Western Europe. He challenged Britain, the last outpost of resistance, to submit. He believed Britain would, and with good reason. Its Army was beaten, its Navy and Air Force were under attack by the all-conquering German Luftwaffe. He believed no one would oppose his demands.

He was wrong. One man would and did. Winston Churchill, recently appointed prime minister, defied Hitler. He rejected surrender. He insisted that Britain could fight on. In a series of magnificent speeches, appealing to his people's courage and historic greatness, he carried Britain with him. The country rallied to his call, held steady under a concentrated air bombardment, manned the beaches Hitler planned to invade, and took strength in the struggle of "the Few," Britain's fighter pilots, in their eventually victorious battle against Hitler's air power. By the end of the year, by the narrowest of margins, Britain had survived. Hitler's war plan was flawed, never to recover, and the Western world lived to fight another day. Western civilization had found a new hero in crisis, whose example would lead it to eventual triumph.

Most of the 20th century's men of power were the antithesis of Churchill. They ruled by standards the opposite of those to which Churchill held. Churchill believed in liberty, the rule of law, and the rights of the individual. They rejected such standards. Lenin, Stalin, Hitler, Mao Zedong elevated power itself into a value in its own right. Truth, for Lenin, was a bourgeois concept, to be manipulated for revolutionary ends. Stalin despised truth, taking pleasure in forcing revolutionary idealists to deny their beliefs and confess to crimes of which they were not guilty. Hitler went further. He propagated the idea of the big lie that, if large enough, became undeniable. Mao encouraged a Cultural Revolution that vilified his civilization's historic culture and encouraged the ignorant to humiliate the learned and wise. In Bolshevik Russia, Nazi Germany, and Maoist China, civilization itself was threatened with death.

Two titans. Indeed, civilization might well have gone under in the years of the great dictators. That it did not was

because of its defenders, men of principle who were also men of courage. Foremost among them were two titans of the Anglo-Saxon world, Franklin Delano Roosevelt and Winston Churchill. That they were Anglo-Saxons was no coincidence. Both derived their moral purpose from the Anglo-Saxon tradition of respect for the rule of law and freedom of the individual. Each could champion that tradition because the sea protected his country from the landbound enemies of liberty. Roosevelt's America was protected by the vast expanse of the Atlantic Ocean, Churchill's England by the English Channel. The channel is a puny bastion by comparison with the Atlantic. It was Churchill's will, buttressed by the power of the Royal Navy and Royal Air Force, that made the channel an insurmountable obstacle to Hitler's attack on liberty.

In terms of moral stature, there is little to choose between the two men. Roosevelt was a great American, consistently true to the principles on which the great republic was founded. Churchill was a great Englishman, committed with an equivalent passion to the Anglo-Saxon idea of liberty that had inspired America's founding fathers. There was this difference. The challenge of dictatorship came later to the United States than to Britain. It also came as an indirect threat. Hitler could never have invaded America. He might, following his military triumph in northwest Europe in the summer of 1940, all too easily have invaded Britain. A weaker man than Churchill might have capitulated to the threat. His refusal to contemplate surrender elevates him to a status unique among champions of freedom. Churchill was the Western world's last great hero.

Who was Churchill? The son of a prominent parliamentarian, Lord Randolph Churchill, and his beautiful American wife, Jennie Jerome, daughter of the proprietor of the *New York Times,* Winston was born into the purple of British society. His grandfather was Duke of Marlborough, a title conferred on his great ancestor, victor of the 18th-century War of the Spanish Succession—Queen Anne's War to Americans—and the place of his birth, in 1874, was Blenheim Palace, given to the first duke by a grateful nation as a trophy of generalship.

The young Winston wanted for nothing by way of privilege and connections. Unfortunately, he wanted for money. His father, a younger son, was profligate with the wealth he inherited. Jennie was extravagant with her American income. After Lord Randolph's early death, Winston was left to make his way in the world. He yearned to follow his father into politics. Without money, however, a political career was closed to him.

He had, moreover, been a failure at school. Headstrong and wayward, careers with prospects—business, the law—were thus closed to him. He took the only option open to a penniless youth of his class. He joined the Army.

Not without difficulty. Even the comparatively simple Army exams defeated Winston at his first two attempts. He passed into the Royal Military College only on his third try, which would have been his last attempt. His grades qualified him only for the cavalry, which did not look for brains. In 1895, he joined the 4th Hussars. In 1896 he went with his regiment to India.

Soldiering may have been a career of last resort. Winston embraced it enthusiastically. He was deeply conscious of his descent from Queen Anne's great general. He also had a passionate and adventurous nature. While a junior lieutenant he used his leave to visit the fighting in Cuba between Spain and the rebels. In India he used his connections to go as a war correspondent to the Northwest Frontier; in 1898 he again went as a correspondent to the Sudan, which Britain was recapturing from the Mahdi, an inspirational Islamic leader; and in 1899 he went, again as a correspondent, to the Boer War in South Africa.

Along the way, Churchill discovered a talent. He could write. The gift did not come without effort. In his hot Indian barracks he had spent his afternoons reading the English classics—Gibbon, Macaulay—and imitating their style. It was an unusual occupation for a young cavalry officer, particularly one who enjoyed the practice of his profession. Churchill was bored by routine but loved action. He was physically fearless and had no hesitation in killing Queen Victoria's enemies. On the Northwest Frontier, he had clashed at close quarters with rival tribesmen. In the Sudan he had ridden in the British Army's last great cavalry charge. In South Africa he had fought in several battles and made a daring escape from Boer captivity.

But bravery in action did not, he early recognized, win cash returns. Vivid journalism did. By his 25th year he had made himself not only one of the most successful war correspondents of his age but also a bestselling author. His books on Indian tribal warfare, the recapture of the Sudan, and the Boer War sold in thousands, both in Britain and America, and he added to his literary income by well-paid lecturing. In 1900, with the money accumulated by writing, he was independent enough to stand for a parliamentary seat and win.

His literary success had not made him popular. Senior soldiers resented the way he had used family influence to escape from regimental duty. In the political world he was thought bumptious and self-promoting. Churchill did not care. He knew he was brave. Having proved that fact to his own satisfaction, he felt liberated to pursue his fundamental ambition, which was to achieve in politics the position he believed his father had been denied. Churchill adulated his father. The admiration was not returned. Lord Randolph regarded his son as a disappointment and often told him so. Despite the rebuffs suffered at his father's hands, Churchill took up Lord Randolph's pet cause—"Tory

Democracy," which sought to align the Conservative Party of property owners with the interests of the working man. At the outset of his parliamentary career, Churchill spoke of "taking up the banner he had found lying on a stricken field," and, as an act of piety, he later wrote his father's biography. But the banner of Tory Democracy found so few followers that Churchill soon despaired of his father's party. In 1904 he left the Conservatives and joined the Liberals. "Crossing the floor" was a foolhardy act for a young parliamentarian. He thereby made himself the enemy of all of his former colleagues without any certainty of finding new friends on the other side.

The reformer. Such were his gifts of oratory, however, that Churchill escaped the floor crosser's common lot. In 1905 he was promoted to ministerial rank, only an under secretaryship but at the Colonial Office, whose work interested him. In that office he returned self-government to the Boers, whom he greatly admired. In 1908 he made a real leap, joining the cabinet as president of the Board of Trade. His responsibilities included social policy, and he was able to introduce a series of measures that benefited the working man, including unemployment pay and the creation of a job placement service. By 1910, when he became home secretary (a cabinet-level position similar to minister of the interior), he made a reputation as a radical social reformer, doing in the Liberal Party what he had hoped to achieve as a Tory Democrat.

Had he been kept in the social ministries, he would have built on the reputation. In 1911, however, he was made first lord of the admiralty at the height of Britain's competition with Germany in a costly naval race. Churchill loved the Royal Navy and fought successfully to win it the funds it needed. When the crisis came in July 1914, the fleet greatly outnumbered Germany's and was ready for war. Churchill sought every chance to bring it into action, actually leading a division of sailors turned soldiers in the defense of Antwerp during the German advance into Belgium. Soon afterward came the opportunity to use the Navy's battleships in the sort of decisive campaign he craved to direct. With the war in France stalemated, Churchill successfully argued that a diversionary effort should be made against Turkey, Germany's ally, by seizing the Dardanelles, the sea route from the Mediterranean to the Black Sea.

The campaign proved a failure from the start. The fleet was repulsed in March 1915, when it tried to bombard its way through the Dardanelles. When troops were landed the following month, they were quickly confined to shallow footholds on the Gallipoli Peninsula. By the year's end, casualties had risen to hundreds of thousands, and no progress had been made. In January 1916 Gallipoli was evacuated. By then Churchill was a discredited man. He had resigned political office and rejoined the Army in a junior rank, commanding a battalion in the trenches.

The reactionary. He was the only politician of his stature to serve in the trenches, and the gesture—which put him often in great danger—restored something of his reputation. In 1917 he became minister of munitions, in 1919 war minister. In the war's aftermath his responsibilities involved him in the Allied intervention against Russian Bolsheviks and in the negotiations of Irish independence. In none of his posts could he show himself at his best, however, and his political career in the 1920s took a downward path. In 1924 he fell out with the Liberal leadership over economic policy and returned to the Conservatives. As chancellor of the exchequer in 1925 he helped to precipitate the general strike of 1926 against the resulting financial stringency. He was henceforth regarded as a social reactionary by the working man he had championed when a young Liberal. He soon after acquired a reactionary name in imperial policy also. The freedom he had been eager to grant the Boers he thought inapplicable in India, and over that issue he left the Conservatives' upper ranks. By 1932 he was a lonely man. Hated by the Liberals and the new Labor Party, isolated in his own Conservative Party, he sat on the back benches of the House of Commons, frustrated and increasingly embittered.

He had consolations. His wife, the former Clementine Hozier, was one. She was a woman of strong character whom Churchill had married in 1908. Clemmie never lost faith in him. Their children also brought much pleasure. Writing, above all, filled the gap left by the collapse of his political career. Ever short of money, Churchill worked hard as a journalist to cover the costs of his ample way of life. He also found time out of office to complete his most substantial literary work, a life of his great ancestor, the first Duke of Marlborough.

Even as he brooded on the back benches, however, Churchill was identifying a new cause. He had thus far had four lives, as a soldier, as an author, as a social reformer, and as a minister at the center of events. He now embarked on a fifth, as a Cassandra of Britain's present danger. Russian Communism had outraged his libertarian beliefs in the early Bolshevik years. In Hitler, whose rise to power began in 1933, he recognized a new enemy of liberty and one whose policies directly menaced his own country. The foreign policy of the government from which he stood aloof was one of appeasement. Anxious to protect Britain's fragile economy in the aftermath of the Great Depression, it preferred to palliate Hitler's demands rather than spend money on the rearmament that would have allowed it to oppose them. Year after year, between 1933 and 1938, Churchill warned of Germany's growing military might. He found support among experts in government who surreptitiously supplied him with the facts to authenticate his warnings. Official government persisted in denying their truth.

War is declared. Then, in 1938, the facts could no longer be denied. Hitler browbeat Czechoslovakia into surrendering much of its territory. He peremptorily incorporated Austria into Greater Germany. Neville Chamberlain's administration accepted that rearmament must now take precedence over sound economic management. France, too, bit the bullet of preparation for war, if war should come. When Hitler's aggressive diplomacy was directed against Poland, Britain and France issued guarantees to protect its integrity. Hitler chose to disbelieve their worth. He deluded himself. Two days after the Wehrmacht invaded Polish territory on Sept. 1, 1939, Britain and France declared hostilities against Germany. The Second World War had begun.

The Second World War was to be the consummation of Churchill's lifelong preparation for heroic leadership. He had proved his abilities as a soldier, as an administrator, as a publicist, as a statesman, as a master of the written and spoken word, and as a philosopher of democracy. In the circumstances of

climactic conflict between the principles of good and evil, all the difficulties of his eventful life were to be overlaid by a magnificent display of command in national crisis.

Hitler almost won the Second World War. By July 1940 he had conquered Poland, Belgium, the Netherlands, and France, beaten their armies, and expelled the British Army from the Continent. He stood poised to conquer Britain also. On his strategic agenda, once Britain was invaded, stood the conquest of the Balkans and then the Soviet Union. He looked forward to being the master of Europe, perhaps of the world.

So certain was Hitler of victory that, during September 1940, he delayed the invasion of Britain in the expectation of Churchill's suing for peace. His expectation was false. There had been a moment, in late May, when Churchill was tempted to negotiate. Once it became clear that the Royal Navy could rescue the Army from Dunkirk he put that temptation behind him. Britain would fight. Its Army might be in ruins, but its Navy was intact, and so was its Air Force. To invade Britain, Hitler must first destroy the Royal Air Force so that he could sink the Royal Navy. Only then could his invasion fleet cross the English Channel. Churchill convinced himself that his Air Force would defeat the Germans in a Battle of Britain. In midsummer 1940 he set out to convince the British people also.

As war leader, Churchill was to display vital qualities: courage, boldness, intellect, cunning, and charisma all founded on deep moral purpose. His courage, and the charisma his courage created, were shown first in the series of great speeches he made to Parliament and the people in the invasion summer of 1940. On May 19, just over a week after Chamberlain resigned, Churchill broadcast to the nation: "I speak to you for the first time as prime minister," he began. He went on to describe how the Allied front was collapsing before the German attack, calling the moment "a solemn hour for the life of our country, of our empire, of our Allies, and, above all, of the cause of freedom." Further details of the crisis followed. He concluded, "We have differed and quarreled in the past, but now one bond unites us all—to wage war until victory is won, and never to surrender ourselves to servitude and shame, whatever the cost and agony may be. . . . Conquer we must—conquer we shall."

On May 13 he had already told the House of Commons that he could offer only "blood, toil, tears, and sweat" but went on, "You ask: What is our aim? I can answer in one word: Victory. It is victory. Victory at all costs. Victory in spite of all terror, victory, however long and hard the road may be." On June 4 he made to the Commons the same declaration in words that were to become the most famous he ever uttered.

"We shall not flag or fail," he said. "We shall go on to the end. . . . We shall defend our island, whatever the cost may be. We shall fight on the landing-grounds; we shall fight in the fields and in the streets. . . . We shall never surrender." The effect was electrifying. A taut and anxious House put aside its fears and rose to cheer him to the rafters. His words, soon transmitted to the people, also electrified them. They caught a mood of popular disbelief that so great a nation should stand in such sudden danger and transformed it into one of dogged defiance. It was from this moment that began what philosopher Isaiah Berlin identified as the imposition of Churchill's "will and imagination on his countrymen" so that they "approached his ideals, and began to see themselves as he saw them."

There had always been a strong element of the populist in Churchill. From his father he had inherited the watchword "Trust the people," and it was because of his democratic ideals that he had, as a young statesman, thrown himself so enthusiastically into legislating for the welfare of the working man. In his later posts it was the welfare of his country as a whole that had come to concern him, and his fellow politicians' laxity of purpose in defending its interests that had dispirited him and alienated him from government. Now, in the supreme crisis of his country's life, he found the voice once more to speak to his people's hearts, to encourage and to inspire. In another great speech to the Commons on June 18, the day of the French capitulation to Hitler, he appealed directly to their sense of greatness. "If we can stand up to Hitler, all Europe may be free, and the life of the world may move forward into broad, sun-lit uplands. But if we fail, then the whole world, including the United States, including all that we have known and cared for, will sink into the abyss of a new Dark Age. Let us therefore brace ourselves to our duties and so bear ourselves that if Britain and its Commonwealth last for a thousand years, many will say, 'This was their finest hour.' "

Britain's year of 1940 would have been the finest hour of any nation. The British, under the threat of invasion and starvation by the U-boats too, heavily bombed in their cities, without allies, without any prospect of salvation at all, wholly exemplified how a finest hour should be lived. They dug the dead and the living from the rubble, manned their beaches, tightened their belts, and watched spellbound the aerobatics overhead of Fighter Command's fighting—and eventually winning—the Battle of Britain. Above all, they lent their ears to Churchill's great oratory. Speech by speech, they were taught by him to shrug off danger, glory in "standing alone," and determine to wait out isolation until the turn of events brought hope of better days.

Churchill's courage, and the charisma he won by it, was matched by his extraordinary boldness in adversity. A lesser man would have husbanded every resource to defend his homeland under the threat of invasion. Under such threat, Churchill nevertheless sought means to strike back. Identifying Hitler's ally, the Italian dictator, Benito Mussolini, as a weak link in the Axis system, Churchill stripped the home islands of troops to reinforce Britain's Army in the Middle East, where, in December 1940, it inflicted a humiliating defeat on the garrison of Italy's overseas empire. The setback caused Hitler to send Field Marshal Erwin Rommel to Mussolini's aid and, when Churchill next detached troops to aid Greece as well, to complicate his plans for the invasion of Russia by launching an offensive into the Balkans. Hitler's Russian timetable never recovered.

Churchill's boldness, based on the weakest of capabilities, thus won huge advantages. His real strategic priority, throughout the months of "standing alone," had, however, been to bring the United States into the war against Hitler on Britain's side. America was indeed Britain's last best hope. In June 1941, Hitler attacked the Soviet Union but, in a few weeks, Stalin's lot was even worse than Churchill's. German troops stood deep inside Russian territory, and the Red Army was falling to pieces. Churchill had offered Stalin a British alliance, but it was aid from the weak to the weak. Only America could reverse the balance for either.

Churchill's intellect had told him so from the inception of the disaster of 1940. A master of strategic analysis, he saw that Britain's numerical and economic inferiority to Hitler's Fortress Europe could only be offset by massive American assistance. He was also aware that an America at peace, barely recovering from the depths of the Great Depression, could be brought to intervene only step by step. It was there his cunning showed. Half American as he was, and long intimate with his mother's homeland, he recognized the strength of American suspicions of Britain's imperial position. He understood that President Roosevelt's profession of commitment to common democratic ideals and repugnance of European dictatorship was balanced by calculations of national interest and domestic policy. Where a less subtle man might have blustered and demanded, Churchill cajoled and flattered. All his efforts at establishing a "special relationship" were made by indirect appeal, through artistry and symbolism.

Five pledges. At Argentia Bay in August 1941, where Roosevelt arrived on the USS Augusta and Churchill on the HMS Prince of Wales—to be sunk five months later off Malaya by the Japanese—the prime minister extracted from the president five pledges: to give "massive aid" to Russia; to enlarge American convoys to Britain; to strengthen convoy escorts; to send American bombers to join the Royal Air Force; and to patrol the western Atlantic against U-boats. The two statesmen also agreed on a commitment to world democracy later to be known as the Atlantic Charter. It was a heartening encounter, of which Churchill made the most at home. The results still fell short of what Britain needed: a full-blooded American alliance.

That was brought him in the weeks after Dec. 7, 1941, when the Japanese Combined Fleet attacked Pearl Harbor. "So we have won after all," Churchill confided to himself that evening. His hopes ran ahead of events. Pearl Harbor merely opened a Japanese-American war. It was Hitler's megalomaniacal decision on December 11 to declare war on the United States that made America Britain's ally. Even then Churchill had much careful diplomacy to complete before he could be sure that the weight of the American war effort would be concentrated in Europe rather than in the Pacific. In the opening months of 1942 the American people's ire was directed against Japan, not Germany. Even though Roosevelt shared Churchill's judgment that Germany was the more dangerous enemy, America's generals and admirals had to be convinced of the correctness of "Germany first" as a strategy. The admirals never fully accepted it. The generals were brought to do so only by reasoned argument. Then, paradoxically, they had to be restrained. George Marshall, Roosevelt's great chief of staff, and Dwight Eisenhower, future supreme Allied commander and president, pushed in mid-1942 for an attack on Hitler's Fortress Europe at the earliest possible moment. Their impetuosity aroused Churchill's caution. Strong though his gambling instinct was, his memory of the Dardanelles disaster, the greatest setback of his career, remained with him. He was terrified by the prospect of a beaten Allied army falling back into the sea. His relief at Marshall's and Eisenhower's recognition of the prematurity of their plans was evident to all.

His caution would persist throughout 1943. It is from that year that the waning of his powers of leadership dates. He was approaching his 70th year and failing in health. He suffered a mild heart attack and other illnesses. He was confronted by a vote of confidence in the Commons, where sufficient of his old enemies remained to reproach him for the military disasters at Singapore and Tobruk. Roosevelt stood by him. "What can we do to help?" the president had asked after the fall of Tobruk in June 1942. Other Americans were less patient. They pressed for action from which Churchill increasingly appeared to shrink. The Russians were even more exigent.

Left out. Stalin took to deriding British half-heartedness, eventually to mocking Churchill to his face. At the three-power Tehran conference of November 1943, Stalin taunted Churchill to declare a final date for the invasion of Europe. Roosevelt lent Churchill no support. It was the beginning of a new, Russo-American special relationship, from which Churchill felt excluded. He was becoming an old man. His glory days were over.

There was to be a recovery. On May 8, 1945, the day of Germany's surrender, he made a speech to the London crowds in which he found his old voice and repaid the people for all he had asked of them in the dark days of 1940. "God bless you all," he trumpeted. "This is your victory. Everyone, man or woman, has done their best. Neither the long years nor the dangers, nor the fierce attacks of the enemy, have in any way weakened the independent resolve of the British nation. God bless you all." He, however, was not to be repaid for his lionlike wartime courage. His reputation as a young social reformer was long forgotten. The reputation given him by his Liberal and Labor opponents as a reactionary was not. In July 1945 the electorate voted against the Conservatives by a landslide. Churchill ceased to be prime minister, not to return to office for six years.

When he did resume the premiership in 1951, his powers had left him and his administration of government was an embarrassment. His resignation, forced by illness in 1955, was greeted with relief even by his closest friends and family. Yet the years since 1945 had not been without achievement. He had written a great history of the Second World War, which won him the Nobel Prize for Literature. He had become a European statesman, welcomed and honored in all the European countries that, in 1940, he had promised to liberate from Nazi tyranny and lived to see free again. He had become a hero in the United States, his mother's homeland, where he remains today the object of a cult status he does not enjoy in his own country. He had, above all, become the standard-bearer of a new crusade against a new tyranny, that of Stalinism. At Fulton, Mo., on March 5, 1946, he had warned against the descent of an "Iron Curtain" cutting off Eastern and Central Europe from the free world. The development reminded him, he said, of the appeasement years of the '30s, and he urged America and his own country not to become "divided and falter in their duty" lest "catastrophe overwhelm us all."

The Fulton speech, now so celebrated, aroused strong hostility at the time, both in America and Britain. It nevertheless laid the basis for the West's democratic resistance to the spread of communist dictatorship that, culminating in the fall of the Berlin Wall in 1989, at last restored the world to the condition of freedom that had been Churchill's central ideal and for which he had struggled all his life. "I asked," he answered his critics after the Fulton speech, "for fraternal association—free, voluntary. I have no doubt it will come to pass, as surely as the sun will rise tomorrow."

Churchill's sun, at the beginning of the third millennium, has risen and, if it should seem to shine fitfully at times and places, is nevertheless the light of the world. No other citizen of the last century of the second millennium, the worst in history, deserved better to be recognized as a hero to mankind.

SIR JOHN KEEGAN, defense editor of the *Daily Telegraph* and a contributing editor of *U.S. News,* is author of 20 books of military history. He is at work on a biography of Churchill for Viking Press.

From *U.S. News & World Report,* May 29, 2000, pp. 50–57. Copyright © 2000 by John Keegan. Reprinted by permission of the author.

Judgment at Nuremberg

Fifty years ago the trial of Nazi war criminals ended: the world had witnessed the rule of law invoked to punish unspeakable atrocities

ROBERT SHNAYERSON

I n the war-shattered city of Nuremberg, 51 years ago, an eloquent American prosecutor named Robert H. Jackson opened what he called "the first trial in history for crimes against the peace of the world." The setting was the once lovely Bavarian city's hastily refurbished Palace of Justice, an SS prison only eight months before. In the dock were 21 captured Nazi leaders, notably the fat, cunning drug addict Hermann Göring.

Their alleged crimes, the ultimate in 20th-century depravity, included the mass murders of some six million Jews and millions of other human beings deemed "undesirable" by Adolf Hitler. "The wrongs which we seek to condemn and punish," said Robert Jackson, "have been so calculated, so malignant and so devastating, that civilization cannot tolerate their being ignored because it cannot survive their being repeated."

Here were satanic men like Ernst Kaltenbrunner, the scar-faced functionary second only to Heinrich Himmler in overseeing the death camps and the Nazi police apparatus; Alfred Rosenberg, cofounder of the Nazi Party and chief theorist of anti-Semitism; and Hans Frank, the vicious and venal Nazi proconsul in Poland. At the time, many asked why such messengers of evil were to be allowed even one day in court, much less the 403 sessions they were about to undergo. It was a question that Jackson, on leave from his job as a Justice of the U.S. Supreme Court to prosecute this case, quickly addressed in his opening statement.

With the kind of moral clarity that marked American idealism at the time, Jackson declared, "That four great nations, flushed with victory and stung with injury stay the hand of vengeance and voluntarily submit their captive enemies to the judgment of the law is one of the most significant tributes that Power ever has paid to Reason. . . . The real complaining party at your bar is Civilization. . . . [It] asks whether law is so laggard as to be utterly helpless to deal with crimes of this magnitude."

So began, in November 1945, the century's most heroic attempt to achieve justice without vengeance—heroic because the victors of World War II had every reason to destroy the vanquished without pity. Heroic because they ultimately resisted the temptation to impose on the Germans what the Nazis had imposed on their victims—collective guilt. Instead, they granted their captives a presumption of innocence and conducted a ten-month trial to determine their personal responsibility.

Locked up in solitary cells each night, constantly guarded by American M.P.'s mindful of recent suicides among high-ranking Nazis, the defendants spent their days in a giant courtroom built for 400 spectators, listening to evidence drawn from 300,000 affidavits and meticulous German documents so voluminous they filled six freight cars. Nearly all were ready to acknowledge the horrific facts while cravenly assigning blame to others. (Göring, who died unrepentant, was the exception.) When it was all over in October 1946, and ten defendants had been hanged messily in the Palace of Justice's gymnasium, this first Nuremberg trial stood as the judicial Everest of those who hoped, as Jackson did, that the rule of law could punish, if not prevent, the atrocities of war.

The exercise of justice at Nuremberg reverberates across this century. And next month, on November 13 and 14, scholars will ponder the lessons of history at an international conference on the trials, sponsored by the Library of Congress and the U.S. Holocaust Memorial Museum.

How this trial, and the 12 that followed, came to be held is a story in itself. In April 1944, two Jews who escaped the Auschwitz death camp described its horrors to the world. They detailed Germany's technology of genocide, such as the camp's four new gas-and-burn machines, each designed to kill 2,000 prisoners at a time. They pinpointed a huge slave-labor operation at nearby Birkenau, run by Germany's fine old industrial names (I. G. Farben and Siemens among others), where Allied prisoners and kidnapped foreign laborers were fed so little and worked so hard that as many as one-third died every week. Their testimony paved the way to Nuremberg.

The Allied leaders had little trouble agreeing that German war crimes must be punished. But punished how? Treasury Secretary Henry Morgenthau Jr. urged that all captured Nazi leaders be shot immediately, without trial, and that Germany be reduced to the status of an agricultural backwater. Secretary of War Henry Stimson thought dooming all Germans to a kind of national execution would not do. It violated the Allied (if not Soviet) belief in the rule of law. It would deny postwar Germany a working economy and perhaps, ultimately, breed another war.

Roosevelt, who wanted to bring G.I.'s (and their votes) home promptly, sought a compromise between Morgenthau and Stimson. The man asked to find it was Murray Bernays, a 51-year-old lawyer turned wartime Army colonel in the Pentagon.

Immediately, a basic but legally complex question rose to the fore—what is a war crime, anyway? At the end of the 19th century, the increased killing power of modern weapons led to the various Hague and Geneva conventions, binding most great powers to treat civilians humanely, shun the killing of unarmed prisoners and avoid ultimate weapons, such as germ warfare, "calculated to cause unnecessary suffering." Such "laws of war" are quite frequently applied. They have saved thousands of lives. In combat the basic distinction between legitimate warfare and atrocities occurs when acts of violence exceed "military necessity."

Before Nuremberg, jurisdiction over war crimes was limited to each country's military courts. After World War I, when the victors accused 896 Germans of serious war crimes, demanding their surrender to Allied military courts, the Germans insisted on trying them and accepted a mere 12 cases. Three defendants never showed up; charges against three others were dropped; the remaining six got trivial sentences.

Bernays envisioned a different scenario: an international court that held individuals liable for crimes the world deemed crimes, even if their nation had approved or required those actions. The accused could not plead obedience to superiors. They would be held personally responsible.

Other big questions remained. One was how an international court trying war crimes could legally deal with crimes committed by the Nazis before the war. Another involved the sheer volume of guilt. The dreaded Schutzstaffel, or SS (in charge of intelligence, security and the extermination of undesirables), and other large Nazi organizations included hundreds of thousands of alleged war criminals. How could they possibly be tried individually? Bernays suggested putting Nazism and the entire Hitler era on trial as a giant criminal conspiracy. In a single stroke, this would create a kind of unified field theory of Nazi depravity, eliminating time constraints, allowing prosecution of war crimes and prewar crimes as well. He also suggested picking a handful of top Nazi defendants as representatives of key Nazi organizations like the SS. If the leaders were convicted, members of their organizations would automatically be deemed guilty. Result: few trials, many convictions and a devastating exposé of Nazi crimes.

Roosevelt promptly endorsed the plan, with one addition. The Nazis would be charged with the crime of waging "aggressive" war, or what the eventual indictments called "crimes against peace"—the first such charge in legal history.

Nobody was more enthusiastic about the strategy than Robert Jackson. Then 53, Jackson was a small-town lawyer from western New York with a gift for language. He had served in various posts in New Deal Washington before Roosevelt elevated him to the Supreme Court in 1941. By July 21, 1945, barely two months after Germany surrendered, Jackson had won President Truman's approval for a four-power International Military Tribunal and had persuaded the Allies to conduct it in Nuremberg.

A master list of 122 war criminals was put together, headed by Hermann Göring, the ranking Nazi survivor. (Hitler, Himmler and Goebbels were dead by their own hand. Martin Bormann, Hitler's secretary, had vanished, never to be found.) Reichsmarschall Göring, a daring World War I ace, had not allowed defeat to tarnish his reputation for candor, cunning and gluttony. He had turned himself in at a weight of 264 pounds (he was 5 feet 6 inches tall). His entourage included a nurse, four aides, two chauffeurs and five cooks. His fingernails and toenails were painted bright red. His 16 monogrammed suitcases contained rare jewels, a red hatbox, frilly nightclothes and 20,000 paracodeine pills, a painkiller he had taken at the rate of about 40 pills a day. He managed to charm some of his captors to the point of almost forgetting his diabolism.

On August 8, 1945, the Charter of the International Military Tribunal (IMT, unveiled by the victorious Allies in London, declared aggressive war and international crime. The IMT charter was grounded in the idea that Nazism was a 26-year-long criminal conspiracy. Its aim: to build a war machine, satisfy Hitler's psychopathic hatred of Jews and turn Europe into a German empire. Judges representing the four powers (the United States, Great Britain, France and the Soviet Union), plus four alternates, were named. They were to take jurisdiction over high-ranking Nazis deemed personally guilty of war crimes, conspiracy to commit war crimes, crimes against peace and crimes against humanity.

The 24 men named in the original indictment represented a wide spectrum of Germany's political-military-industrial complex. With Martin Bormann (tried in absentia), the list of those actually presented for trial was further reduced by two surprise events. Robert Ley, the alcoholic, Jew-baiting boss of the German Labor Front, which had governed the lives of 30 million German workers, hanged himself in his cell on the night of October 25. And, at the last moment, the prosecutors realized their key industrial defendant, the weapons maker Alfried Krupp, had not personally run his family's slave-labor factories until after the war began, giving him an easy defense against the prewar conspiracy charge. (Krupp was later sentenced to 12 years for war crimes, but he was released from prison in 1951.)

The trial of the remaining defendants began on the morning of November 20, 1945. In the refurbished courtroom, floodlights warmed the new green curtains and crimson chairs, illuminating the two rows of once fearsome Nazis sitting in the dock guarded by young American soldiers. Göring had shed 60 pounds during his six months of confinement, acquiring what novelist John Dos Passos, reporting for Life, called "that wizened look of a leaky balloon of a fat man who has lost a great deal of weight." Next to him in the front row were the ghostly Rudolf Hess, feigning amnesia; Joachim von Ribbentrop, Hitler's foreign minister; and Field Marshal Wilhelm Keitel, the Führer's Wehrmacht chief. Next in order of indictment came Ernst Kaltenbrunner (ill and absent for the first three weeks), Alfred Rosenberg and Hans Frank, who somehow thought his captors would spare his life when he handed over one of the trial's most damning documents—his 38-volume journal. (He would be sentenced to hang.)

Throughout that first day, as black-robed American, British and French judges and their two uniformed Soviet colleagues peered somberly from the bench, listening via earphones to translations in four languages, the prosecutors droned an almost boring litany of sickening crimes—shooting, torture, starvation, hanging—to which, in descending tones of indignation, from Göring downward, the accused each pleaded not guilty.

The next morning, Robert Jackson opened the prosecution case on Count One, conspiracy to commit war crimes. "This war did not just happen," Jackson told the judges. The defendants' seizure of the German state, he continued, "their subjugation of the German people, their terrorism and extermination of dissident elements, their planning and waging of war . . . , their deliberate and planned criminality toward conquered peoples—all these are ends for which they acted in concert."

"We will not ask you to convict these men on the testimony of their foes," Jackson told the court. There was no need. Allied agents had found 47 crates of Alfred Rosenberg's files hidden in a 16th-century castle, 485 tons of diplomatic papers secreted in the Harz Mountains, and Göring's art loot and Luftwaffe records stashed in a salt mine in Obersalzberg.

One especially incriminating find—indispensable to the conspiracy theory—was the notes of Hitler aide Col. Friedrich Hossbach from a meeting between Hitler, Göring and other Nazis in Berlin on November 5, 1937. Hossbach quoted Hitler insisting that, as Europe's racially "purest" stock, the Germans were entitled to "more living space" in neighboring countries, which he planned to seize, he said, "no later than 1943–45."

During the opening weeks, the pace of the trial was slow. Most of the American prosecution team neither read nor understood German. What with translation gaffes, repetitions and monotone readings, the documentary evidence—reams of it—at times had judges yawning and the defendants themselves dozing off.

Of course, the banality of overdocumented evil did not soften the prosecution's gruesome narrative. And a month into the recitation of Hitler's prewar aggressions from the Rhineland to Austria to Czechoslovakia, the Americans suddenly animated the documents by showing films of Nazi horrors. One German soldier's home movie depicted his comrades in Warsaw, clubbing and kicking naked Jews. In one scene, an officer helped a battered young woman to her feet so that she could be knocked down again.

An American movie documented the liberation of concentration camps at Bergen-Belson, Dachau and Buchenwald, filling the darkened courtroom with ghastly images of skeletal survivors, stacked cadavers and bulldozers shoveling victims into mass graves. In his cell that night, Hans Frank burst out: "To think we lived like kings and believed in that beast!" Göring was merely rueful. "It was such a good afternoon, too—" he said, "and then they showed that awful film, and it just spoiled everything."

Even when badly translated, Jackson's documents made a mesmerizing record of Hitler's appalling acts on the road to Armageddon. They revisited his rise to power as the people's choice in the depression year 1932. Billing himself as Germany's economic savior, the Führer immediately began spending so much on weapons that in six years, the treasury was almost empty. A diversion was called for.

Thrilling his admirers—millions of still worshipful Germans—Hitler bullied British and French leaders into selling out Czechoslovakia at the pusillanimous Munich conference in 1938 (SMITHSONIAN, October 1988). Next, Nazi thugs were unleashed on *Kristallnacht,* the "Night of Broken Glass" (November 9)—a nationwide campaign of anti-Semitic violence. Huge chunks of Jewish wealth wound up in Nazi pockets. Göring, the biggest thief, further demeaned his victims by ordering German Jews to pay the regime a "fine" of one billion marks ($400 million). As he explained it, "The Jew being ejected from the economy transfers his property to the state."

Hjalmar Schacht, then head of the Reichsbank, warned Hitler in January 1939 that his arms race was fueling runaway inflation. Hitler immediately fired Schacht and ordered new currency, largely backed by stolen Jewish property. Schacht, long a Hitler apologist, then began working secretly for U.S. intelligence and wound up at Dachau. Now, to his disgust, he sat in the Nuremberg dock.

According to trial documents, Hitler's profligacy helped propel his aggressions. By 1941, Hitler had made his suicidal decision to renege on the nonaggression pact signed with Stalin in 1939 and invade the Soviet Union. "What one does not have, but needs," he said, "one must conquer."

It began well, on June 22, 1941, and ended badly. By late 1942, with German casualties soaring at Stalingrad, Hitler had lost so many soldiers in Russia that he had to keep drafting German workers into the army, replacing them with foreign laborers, mainly French and Russian prisoners. In early 1943, with more than five million industrial slaves already toiling in Germany, the surrender at Stalingrad forced Hitler's manpower boss, Nuremberg defendant Fritz Sauckel, to kidnap 10,000 Russian civilians per day for work in Germany. Few survived longer than 18 months—a powerful incentive for Russians still at home to flee the kidnappers and join Soviet guerrillas in killing German troops.

Hitler's campaign to "Aryanize" Germany began before the war with the deliberate poisoning of incurably sick people and retarded children—labeled "garbage children." The regime's contempt for non-Aryan life conditioned millions of Germans to turn a blind eye to more and more epidemic evils—the death camps, the ghastly medical experiments, the relentless massacres of those Hitler called "Jews, Poles, and similar trash."

Listening to the facts, the almost incomprehensible facts, even the defendants longed for some answer to the overpowering question—why? Why did one of the world's most advanced nations descend to such acts so easily? So swiftly? The trial provided few answers. Hitler's truly diabolic achievement, French prosecutor François de Menthon observed, was to revive "all the instincts of barbarism, repressed by centuries of civilization, but always present in men's innermost nature."

For weeks, the prosecution cited such acts as the use of Jewish prisoners as guinea pigs in military medical experiments to determine the limits of high-altitude flying by locking them in pressure chambers, slowly rupturing their lungs and skulls. How long downed German pilots could last in the ocean was determined by submerging prisoners in icy water until they died. To develop a blood-clotting chemical, the doctors shot and dismembered live prisoners to simulate battlefield injuries. Death did not end this abuse. A Czech doctor who spent four years imprisoned at Dachau, where he performed some 12,000 autopsies, told investigators that he was ordered to strip the skin off bodies. "It was cut into various sizes for use as saddles, riding breeches, gloves, house slippers, and ladies handbags. Tattooed skin was especially valued by SS men."

The scale of Hitler's madness was almost beyond imagination. The documents showed that after conquering Poland in 1939, he ordered the expulsion of nearly nine million Poles and Jews from Polish areas he annexed for his promised Nordic empire. The incoming colonists were "racially pure" ethnic Germans imported from places like the Italian Tirol. The SS duly began herding the exiles from their homes toward ethnic quarantine in a 39,000-square-mile cul-de-sac near Warsaw. Opposition grew; progress slowed. In righteous rage, the SS unleashed hundreds of *Einsatzgruppen*—killer packs assigned to spread terror by looting, shooting and slaughtering without restraint. Thereafter, the SS action groups murdered and plundered behind the German Army as it advanced eastward.

By January 1946, prosecutor Jackson was at last animating his documents with live witnesses. The first was a stunner. Otto Ohlendorf, blond and short, looked like the choirboy next door. In fact he was 38, a fanatic anti-Semite and the former commander of Einsatzgruppe D, the scourge of southern Russia. He testified with icy candor and not an iota of remorse.

How many persons were killed under your direction? asked Jackson. From June 1941 to June 1942, Ohlendorf flatly replied, "90,000 people."

Q. "Did that include men, women, and children?"

A. "Yes."

Rather proudly, Ohlendorf asserted that his 500-man unit killed civilians "in a military manner by firing squads under command." Asked if he had "scruples" about these murders, he said, "Yes, of course."

Q. "And how is it they were carried out regardless of these scruples?"

A. "Because to me it is inconceivable that a subordinate leader should not carry out orders given by the leaders of the state."

The prosecution rested after three months, capped off by another movie distilling still more Nazi horror, and displays of macabre human-skin lampshades and shrunken Jewish heads submitted as evidence.

German defense lawyers then spent five months trying to cope with major handicaps. Most had grown to abhor their clients. All were unfamiliar with adversarial cross-examinations used in the United States and Britain, to say nothing of key documents that the Americans tended to withhold before springing them in court.

They managed to outflank the court's ban on tu quoque evidence (meaning, "If I am guilty, you are, too")—a stricture aimed at keeping Allied excesses, notably the mass bombing of German cities, out of the trial. In the dock was Adm. Karl Dönitz, accused of ordering U-boats to sink merchantmen without warning and let the crews drown whenever a rescue attempt might jeopardize the Germans. Dönitz never denied the charge. Instead, his lawyer produced an affidavit from Adm. Chester Nimitz, commander of the wartime U.S. Pacific fleet, stating that American submariners had followed the same policy against Japanese ships. (In the end, he was sentenced to ten years; upon release in 1956, he lived 24 more years, to age 88.)

The prosecution had depicted a vast conspiracy to wage war and commit atrocities. But in choosing representative Nazis as defendants, it wound up with 21 men who, though all pleaded ignorance or powerlessness, were otherwise so different that many hated one another. Each tried to save himself by accusing others. As a result, the defense naturally failed to muster a united front, and the prosecution's conspiracy theory steadily unraveled.

The trial's highlight was the star turn of its one wholly unabashed defendant, Hermann Göring. In three days of direct examination, Göring sailed through an insider's history of Nazism, defending Germany's right to rearm and reoccupy territory lost by the Versailles treaty. He laughed off the notion that his fellow defendants were ever close enough to Hitler to be called conspirators. "At best," he said, "only the Führer and I could have conspired."

Jackson's cross-examination was a disaster. Göring understood English well; while questions were translated into German, he had time to improvise his answers. At one point, Jackson prodded Göring to admit that the Nazis' plan to occupy the Rhineland, enacted without warning in 1936, was a Nazi secret, hidden from other countries. Göring smoothly answered, "I do not believe I can recall reading beforehand the publication of the mobilization preparations of the United States."

Jackson conducted a bizarre cross-examination of Albert Speer, Hitler's personal architect of gigantic edifices and stage manager of the Nuremberg rallies. Smart, suave, handsome, not yet 40, the wellborn Speer ranked high among Hitler's few confidants and was chief of all Nazi war production for the regime's last three years. He oversaw 14 million workers; he could hardly claim ignorance of their condition or how they were recruited. In the spring of 1944, for example, he ordered 100,000 Jewish slave workers from Hungary as casually as if they were bags of cement.

On the witness stand, Speer said he had become totally disillusioned with Hitler when the Führer responded to Germany's inevitable defeat by ordering a nationwide scorched-earth policy: the total destruction of everything in the path of the

Allied armies. Rejecting Hitler's monomania, which he called a betrayal of ordinary Germans, Speer told the court, "It is my unquestionable duty to assume my share of responsibility for the disaster of the German people." And he revealed—offering no proof—that in February 1945 he had set out to assassinate Hitler by dropping poison gas through an air shaft in the Führer's bunker, only to find the shaft sealed off.

Speer, the most attractive defendant at Nuremberg, had been debriefed by interrogators avid for his special knowledge of how German war factories managed to keep humming despite immense Allied bombing. Some saw him as just the kind of man needed to rehabilitate postwar Germany. Under cross-examination, he got mostly easy questions, typically prefaced by Jackson's disclaimer, "I am not attempting to say that you were personally responsible for these conditions."

That Speer actually received a 20-year sentence seems remarkable, given his adroit performance. That his equally (or perhaps less) culpable colleague, Fritz Sauckel—brutal, low-born, ill spoken—was sentenced to death, seems as legally unfair as it was morally deserved.

After Robert Jackson's powerful summation of the trial's "mad and melancholy record," the case went to the trial judges, from whom no appeal was permitted. The great unspoken issue at Nuremberg was the question of collective guilt, and hindsight clarifies the extraordinary dilemma those eight judges faced 50 years ago. Collective guilt had tainted the Versailles treaty and helped ignite the Holocaust. It is the fuel of human barbarism, currently on display from Rwanda to Serbia. And though the Nuremberg judges were given every reason to savage the Nazi tyranny, they came to believe that justice could be served only by asserting the principle of individual responsibility. Justice required, in fact, a virtual rejection of the United States' whole grand conspiracy concept.

The Nazi Party founders had been charged with conspiring for 26 years (1919–45) to launch World War II and related atrocities. All 22 defendants (including Bormann) stood accused of planning aggressive war; 18 were charged with wartime crimes and crimes against humanity, such as genocide. If the court approved, seven Nazi organizations would also be convicted, rendering all their thousands of members guilty without trial.

The problem was that conspiracy is a crime of joint participation. Conviction required proof that two or more people knowingly agreed at a specific time and place to use criminal means to achieve criminal ends. But the distinguished French judge, Donnedieu de Vabres, urged his colleagues to observe that the defendants had seemed to act less in cahoots with, than in bondage to, a megalomaniac. Jackson's documents showed the "Führer Principle" in practice—the madness of Hitler's erratic orders, executed by lackeys too blind, venal or terrified to disobey. The evidence seemingly proved chaos, not organized conspiracy.

The judges, risking a backlash from Europe's Nazi victims by sharply limiting their verdicts to the hard evidence, ruled that the war conspiracy began not in 1919 but on November 5, 1937, at the "Hossbach conference" in which Hitler's aides heard his schemes for conquering Germany's neighbors.

The conspiracy charge (Count One) was restricted to eight defendants (led by Göring) who knowingly carried out Hitler's war plans from 1938 onward. In effect, the defendants were liable only for actual wartime crimes beginning September 1, 1939—a dizzying number of crimes but one that eliminated perhaps a third of the prosecution's evidence and produced three acquittals, including that of Schacht.

Under such an approach, guilt for simply belonging to the Nazi organizations was impossible. The court held that only the SS, the Gestapo-SD and the top Nazi leadership had been proved "criminal," meaning that their members had voluntarily joined in committing war crimes after 1939. That left several million potential defendants for lower courts to handle. But since the Nuremberg judges ruled them all innocent until proven guilty, relatively few were ever tried—the prosecutorial job was too formidable.

The trial removed 11 of the most despicable Nazis from life itself. In the early morning hours of Wednesday, October 16, 1946, ten men died in the courthouse gymnasium in a botched hanging that left several strangling to death for as long as 25 minutes. Ribbentrop departed with dignity, saying, "God protect Germany." Göring had cheated the hangman 2 1/2 hours earlier. He killed himself in his cell, using a cyanide capsule he had managed to hide until then. In one of four suicide notes, he wrote, "I would have consented anytime to be shot. But the Reichsmarschall of Germany cannot be hanged."

The Nuremberg trial never remotely enabled the world to outlaw war. By 1991, the wars of the 20th century had killed more than 107 million people. And given Nuremberg's uniqueness—winners in total control of losers—the court of 1945 may seem irrelevant to the wars of the 1990s, in which ethnic killers, such as Gen. Ratko Mladic, the Bosnian Serb implicated in the mass murder of unarmed prisoners, manage to avoid justice.

Yet the United Nations' seven "Nuremberg Principles" hold that no accused war criminal in any place or position is above the law. What the Nuremberg judges really achieved, in fact, has never been more relevant. By rejecting group guilt and mass purges, the 1945 judges defied hatred and struck a blow for peace that may yet, half a century later, help temper the madness of war.

The author, formerly editor of *Harper's,* has written extensively on the U.S. Supreme Court and on legal matters.

UNIT 5

The Era of the Cold War, 1950–1990

Unit Selections

Key Points to Consider

- Was the Marshall Plan an act of altruism or political realism? Make a case for both arguments.

- What circumstances produced the Korean War? What resulted from it?

- Why has Japan refused to come to terms with its war crimes past? What has resulted from this refusal?

- How has the last century been a troubling one for Iraq? Does it have any relationship to what is happening there today?

- What circumstances occurred which led the United States into the war in Vietnam? Can anything or anyone be held responsible for this?

- What resulted from the Spanish-American War and our subjugation of the Philippines? Do these actions have any influence on our present-day diplomacy?

Student Web Site

www.mhcls.com/online

Internet References

Further information regarding these Web sites may be found in this book's preface or online.

The Chornobyl Nuclear Accident
http://www.infoukes.com/history/chornobyl

The Marshall Plan
http://www.marshallfoundation.org

Russia on the Web
http://www.valley.net/~transnat/

Vietnam Online
http://www.pbs.org/wgbh/amex/vietnam

WWW Virtual Library: Russian and East European Studies
http://www.ucis.pitt.edu/reesweb/

Since the end of World War II Japan has, for the most part, refused to accept responsibility for aggressive actions against its Asian neighbors that many have labeled war crimes. With public attention on the "Rape of Nanking" and the use of Korean women as sex slaves, some in Japan have urged their country to own up to its wartime atrocities. Thus far, steps in this direction have been minimal.

Following World War II, Western leaders realized that they would have to confront the power of the Soviet Union. In 1946, Winston Churchill, the wartime prime minister of Great Britain, described the descent of an iron curtain across central Europe and warned about the spread of communism. United States leaders calculated that the economic distress of war-torn Europe would provide fertile ground for communism. Congress, and Secretary of State George Marshall, sponsored an aid program to enable Western Europe to rebuild and restore its economic foundations. The Marshall Plan worked and is considered an unprecedented act of generosity.

Although the major struggle of the Cold War involved competition between two superpowers—the United States and the Soviet Union—there were other troublesome events in the world. In 1951, China annexed Tibet and began to assimilate its unique culture into that of China. And, the United Nations created the state of Israel in 1947 as a refuge for the world's Jewish peoples. This enraged Muslims of the region, displaced from their land, and has engendered a series of Arab-Israeli wars, as well as various schemes to divide Jerusalem, a city sacred to Judaism and Islam (as well as Christianity).

In the struggle between the United States and the Soviet Union, the competition remained "cold," never resulting in direct conflict that heated up into open warfare. With the Cold War in the background, however, the United States fought against presumed communist aggression in both Korea and Vietnam, while the Soviet Union fought in Afghanistan. In Korea, the attempt by the North to subdue the South was blocked by a United Nations army, consisting mainly of U.S. troops. For the United States, which had prided itself on never having lost a war, the conflict ended frustratingly where it began, along the 38th parallel line. It was a limited war that resulted in an unstable conclusion.

Four consecutive U.S. presidents committed the country to the containment of communism. By the time Lyndon Johnson became president, after the assassination of John F. Kennedy in 1963, there were a half million U.S. troops in Vietnam. After a decade, the U.S. withdrew. Defeat was bitter, and the war became a cautionary tale about the dangers of waging war against an elusive enemy. Some are beginning to call the U.S. war in Iraq a "quagmire," the same phrase used to describe Vietnam. Iraq began as a British protectorate, when European powers carved up the Middle East, after the first World War. Saddam Hussein's dictatorship began in 1979. The question today is whether the U.S.-sponsored war in Iraq will have liberated the country to unleash deadly factional violence.

Some Americans have found the roots of their country's interventions in Afghanistan and Iraq in the U.S.'s forceful subjugation of the Philippine Islands after the Spanish-American War. The jingoism, patriotism and egocentrism that fueled that action seem to some a parallel with the attitudes that have created an Iraq quagmire today.

The Plan and the Man

High vision and low politics: how George Marshall and a few good men led America to an extraordinary act of strategic generosity.

EVAN THOMAS

During the winter of 1946–47, the worst in memory, Europe seemed on the verge of collapse. For the victors in World War II, there were no spoils. In London, coal shortages left only enough fuel to heat and light homes for a few hours a day. In Berlin, the vanquished were freezing and starving to death. On the walls of the bombed-out Reichstag, someone scrawled "Blessed are the dead, for their hands do not freeze." European cities were seas of rubble—500 million cubic yards of it in Germany alone. Bridges were broken, canals were choked, rails were twisted. Across the Continent, darkness was rising.

Americans, for the most part, were not paying much attention. Having won World War II, "most Americans just wanted to go to the movies and drink Coca-Cola," said Averell Harriman, who had been FDR's special envoy to London and Moscow during the second world war. But in Washington and New York, a small group of men feared the worst. Most of them were, like Harriman, Wall Street bankers and diplomats with close ties to Europe and a long view of America's role in the world. They suspected that in the Kremlin, Soviet dictator Joseph Stalin was waiting like a vulture. Only the United States, they believed, could save Europe from chaos and communism.

With sureness of purpose, some luck and not a little finagling, these men persuaded Congress to help rescue Europe with $13.3 billion in economic assistance over three years. That sum—more than $100 billion in today's dollars, or about six times what America now spends annually on foreign aid—seems unthinkable today. Announced 50 years ago next week, the European Recovery Program, better known as the Marshall Plan, was an extraordinary act of strategic generosity. How a few policymakers persuaded their countrymen to pony up for the sake of others is a tale of low politics and high vision.

Yet their achievement is recalled by many scholars as a historical blip, a moment of virtue before the cold war really locked in. A truer, if more grandiloquent, assessment was made by Winston Churchill. The Marshall Plan, and England's war leader from his retirement, was "the most unsordid act in history."

It was, at the time, a very hard sell. The men who wanted to save Europe—Harriman, Under Secretary of State Dean Acheson, diplomats like George Kennan—were unelected and for the most part unknown. They needed a hero, a brand name respected by ordinary Americans. They turned to George C. Marshall.

His name would bring blank stares from schoolchildren today, but Marshall, the army's highest-ranking general in World War II, was widely regarded then as the Organizer of Victory. "He is the great one of the age," said President Harry Truman, who made Marshall secretary of state in January 1947. Upright, cool to the point of asperity ("I have no feelings," he said, "except those I reserve for Mrs. Marshall"), Marshall made worshipers of his followers. Dean Acheson described his boss walking into a room: "Everyone felt his presence. It was a striking and communicated force. His figure conveyed intensity, which his voice, low, staccato and incisive, reinforced. It compelled respect. It spread a sense of authority and calm." Though self-effacing and not prone to speechifying, Marshall used a few basic maxims. One was "Don't fight the problem. Decide it."

Without hesitation, Marshall gave his name and authority to the plan to rescue Europe. His only advice to the policymakers: "Avoid trivia." The unveiling came in a commencement speech at Harvard on June 5, 1947. Wearing a plain business suit amid the colorful academic robes, Marshall was typically plain-spoken and direct: "Our policy," he said, "is not directed against any country or doctrine, but against hunger, poverty, desperation and chaos."

The response in the American press was tepid, but the leaders of Europe were electrified. Listening to the address on the BBC, British Foreign Minister Ernest Bevin regarded Marshall's speech as a "lifeline to a sinking man." Bevin immediately headed for Paris to urge the French to join him in grabbing the rope.

Marshall did not want Washington to appear to be dictating to its allies. "The initiative, I think, must come from Europe," he had said at Harvard. But the Europeans fell to squabbling. The French, in particular, were wary of reviving Germany. "The Plan? There is no plan," grumbled George Kennan, the diplomat sent to Paris that summer of 1947 to monitor the talks. The Europeans were able to write shopping lists, but nothing resembling an overall program. In a cable to Marshall, Kennan predicted that the United States would listen, "but in the end, we would not *ask* them, we would just *tell* them what they would get."

First, however, Marshall's men had to persuade Congress to provide the money. In October, President Truman tried to appeal to America's sense of sacrifice, urging Americans to eat less chicken and fewer eggs so there would be food for starving Europeans. Urged to "waste not," some schoolchildren formed "clean-plate clubs," but that was about as far as the sacrificial zeal went. Members of Congress were profoundly wary. Bob Lovett, another Wall Streeter who replaced Acheson in the summer of 1947 as under secretary, managed to win over Senate Foreign Relations Committee chairman Arthur Vandenberg, mostly by feeding him top-secret cables over martinis at cocktails every night. But many lawmakers regarded foreign aid as "Operation Rathole," and viewed the rescue plan slowly taking shape at the State Department as a "socialist blueprint." Said Charles Halleck, the Republican leader in the House: "I've been out on the hustings, and I know, the people don't like it."

Clearly appealing to good will was not going to suffice. It was necessary, then, to scare the voters and their elected representatives. As it happened, Russia growled at just the right moment. In the winter of 1948, Moscow cracked down on its new satellite state of Czechoslovakia. Jan Masaryk, the pro-Western foreign minister, fell—or was pushed—to his death from his office window in Prague. At the Pentagon, the generals worried that Soviet tanks could begin to roll into Western Europe at any moment. The atmosphere in Washington, wrote Joseph and Stewart Alsop, the hawkish establishment columnists, was no longer "post-war." It was now "pre-war."

In fact, the fears of Soviet invasion were exaggerated. We now know that after World War II the Red Army began tearing up railroad tracks in Eastern Europe because Stalin feared an attack by the West against the Soviet Union. Exhausted by a war that cost the lives of 20 million Russians, the Kremlin was not ready to wage another. Because of poor intelligence, Washington did not fully appreciate Russia's weakness. Top policymakers were aware, however, that the hysteria was exaggerated, that war was unlikely. Even so, they were not above using scare tactics in a good cause—like winning congressional approval of the Marshall Plan. Sometimes, said Acheson, "it is necessary to make things clearer than the truth."

Frightened by the talk of war, urged to recall that isolationism after World War I succeeded only in producing World War II, Congress waved through the European Recovery Plan that spring. In April the SS John H. Quick sailed from Galveston, Texas, with 19,000 tons of wheat. Before long, there were 150 ships every day carrying food and fuel to Europe. There were new nets for the fishermen of Norway, wheat for French bakers, tractors for Belgian farmers, a thousand baby chicks for the children of Vienna from 4-H Club members in America.

Politics, needless to say, sometimes interfered with altruism. Some congressmen tried to turn the Marshall Plan into a giant pork barrel, voting to send Europeans the fruits of their districts,

needed or not. From Kentucky and North Carolina poured millions of cigarettes; from the Midwest arrived thousands of pounds of canned spaghetti, delivered to gagging Italians. In London drawing rooms, there was some resentment of the heavy American hand. "Our Uncle, who art in America, Sam be thy name/Thy Navy come, they will be done," went one ditty. In Paris, fearful for the purity of the culture (and the sale of wine), the French National Assembly banned the sale, manufacture and import of Coca-Cola.

American aid had a darker side. The Marshall Plan provided the CIA with a handy slush fund. To keep communists from taking over Italy (a genuine threat in 1948), the CIA began handing out money to Italian politicians. At first, the agency had so little money that America's gentlemen spooks had to pass the hat in New York men's clubs to raise cash for bribes. But with the Marshall Plan, there was suddenly plenty of "candy," as CIA official E. Howard Hunt called it, to tempt European politicians and labor leaders.

The CIA's meddling looks sinister in retrospect (though it seemed essential in 1948, when policymakers feared Stalin could start a revolution in Italy and France "just by picking up the phone"). The actual impact of the aid is also a source of dispute. Some economists have argued that the plan played only a superficial role in Europe's recovery. They point to Europe's pent-up innovation and restorative will. But the fact is that from 1938 to 1947 the standard of living in Europe had been declining by about 8 percent a year. After the arrival of the first Marshall aid, the arrows all turned up. Europe's per capita GNP rose by a third between 1948 and 1951. American technicians brought know-how to Europe and reaped enormous good will.

Perhaps America's best export was hope. The Marshall Plan arrived at a time of despondency as well as hardship. Forced to work together, Europeans overcame some historic enmities while America shed its tradition of peacetime isolationism. Ties strengthened by the Marshall Plan evolved into the Western Alliance that stood fast until communism crumbled of its own weight in the Soviet Union. Some of the men who made the Marshall Plan possible saw the romantic and epic quality of their task. It was "one of the greatest and most honorable adventures in history," wrote Dean Acheson. His friend and successor at State, Bob Lovett, had a more practical view: the Marshall Plan was that rare government program that came in on budget, accomplished its goal—and then ended.

The men who made the Marshall Plan were practical, and their motivations can be regarded coldly as a matter of economics and power. But they also wanted to act because they believed that saving Europe was the right and only thing to do. They achieved that rarity among nations—a bold act by one that benefited all.

Newsweek Assistant Managing Editor **Evan Thomas** is coauthor of "The Wise Men," a history of six friends who shaped postwar American foreign policy.

Korea: Echoes of a War

After 50 years, is it time for real peace?

Steven Butler

Big anniversaries rarely coincide with genuinely important events. Yet this week, the leaders of North and South Korea will meet for the first time ever, 50 years to the month after North Korean troops opened a massive artillery barrage and then stormed across the 38th parallel in a drive that nearly obliterated South Korea. The meeting is more than symbolic. For decades, North Korea refused to talk directly to South Korea because the Seoul government never signed the armistice that halted fighting between belligerents—United Nations forces led by the United States on one side, North Korean and Chinese forces on the other. When North Korean leader Kim Jong Il meets as an equal with South Korean President Kim Dae Jung, it will be an admission of sorts that war is finally over and that South Korea is a reality that can't be wished away.

Even so, 50 years of combat and military stalemate have left unsolved the main issue of the Korean War: how to restore unity to an ancient nation that was divided as a tragic afterthought at the end of World War II. As Japan prepared to surrender in August 1945, two American Army colonels, Dean Rusk (later President Kennedy's secretary of state) and Charles H. Bonesteel, were ordered to find a place to divide the Korean Peninsula. Within 30 minutes, they chose the 38th parallel as the spot where Soviet troops, coming south to accept the surrender of Japanese troops, would meet the American troops moving north. No one imagined it would become a permanent border. The Soviets helped establish a Stalinist-style dictatorship in Pyongyang under the leadership of Kim Il Sung.

Meanwhile, America struggled with only partial success to establish a democracy under Syngman Rhee in half a nation whose civil infrastructure and society were torn apart by 35 years of harsh Japanese colonial rule. In fact, America gave up the job as hopeless. America withdrew its occupation troops in 1949, and public and private statements by Secretary of State Acheson and military leaders suggested that the United States had resigned itself to watching all of Korea fall under Soviet influence. Who would have dreamed that a civil war launched by North Korea to reunify its homeland would have

brought a massive response involving at its peak almost a quarter of a million U.S. troops and contributions from 19 other United Nations members? Certainly not Kim Il Sung nor Soviet dictator Joseph Stalin, who hesitantly gave the nod to Kim's war plans.

Collision course. America assumed—erroneously, historians say—that the invasion launched on June 25, 1950, was part of a communist master plan involving eventual expansion of communist China and a Soviet move into Western Europe. As a result, with little consideration for the consequences, President Truman ordered the 7th Fleet into the Taiwan Strait. That thwarted plans by Chinese communists to end the Chinese civil war by launching an amphibious assault against Taiwan, where remnants of Chiang Kai-shek's Nationalist Army had taken refuge. And it put China and America on a collision course from which they have yet to veer.

Of course, Truman also ordered U.S. troops into Korea, with approval from the U.N. Security Council after the Soviet delegate foolishly boycotted the proceedings. Inexperienced soldiers on soft duty in Japan were airlifted to Pusan, from where they formed Task Force Smith and raced north to block the southern advance of North Korean troops. They failed to halt the unexpectedly disciplined and well-equipped North Korean Army, and were forced into a chaotic retreat, sometimes dropping equipment on the run.

Yet Task Force Smith slowed the enemy's advance, giving America crucial extra days to move supplies and men through the port of Pusan. A wide defensive perimeter around the city held against repeated assaults from North Korean troops. Full relief came on September 15, when Gen. Douglas MacArthur launched a risky but technically brilliant assault at the port of Inchon, near Seoul, where tides as high as 30 feet seemed to make a big amphibious landing impossible. Military historians still debate whether the Inchon landing was actually necessary from a military standpoint or whether it was instead another example of MacArthurian showboating. But American troops succeeded in cutting supply and retreat lines of the overextended North Korean Army and broke the back of the invasion.

View from Moscow

Why Stalin thought the U.S. would stay out

The Korean War might never have happened—or might have turned out quite differently—if the Soviet Union and the West had accurately gauged each other's intentions.

President Truman and his advisers reacted to the North Korean invasion on June 25, 1950, as a direct challenge to the United States by Joseph Stalin. But in the post-Soviet 1990s, archives revealed that the push actually came from North Korean President Kim Il Sung, who pestered Stalin with 48 telegrams seeking approval for an attack. Stalin refused many times, then finally gave his assent in January 1950.

But why did he change his mind? Since the Soviet dictator didn't have to explain himself to anyone, historians could only guess. Now they know for sure: Stalin, who wanted anything but a head-on confrontation with Washington, believed the United States would not respond. "According to information coming from the United States, it is really so," he told Kim, during an April 1950 meeting in Moscow, where the plan took shape. "The prevailing mood is not to interfere." The U.S. mood was reinforced, Stalin said, by the Soviet Union's successful A-bomb test the previous August. One can only imagine what might have happened if Washington had warned in advance it would resist a thrust into South Korea, says historian Kathryn Weathersby, who has studied the new evidence for the Woodrow Wilson Center's Cold War International History Project.

Miscalculation. The summary of the critical Stalin-Kim talks, contained in documents from Moscow's tightly guarded Presidential Archive, may refuel an old controversy. Secretary of State Dean Acheson notably excluded South Korea from the U.S. "defense perimeter" in a National Press Club speech on Jan. 12, 1950. Redbaiters later accused him of helping precipitate the invasion. But Acheson was merely citing Truman's policy. And the "information" Stalin alluded to was apparently the U.S. Asia policy document itself, NSC 48. Moscow would have known about it thanks to British spy Donald Maclean. Stalin cited another reason why Korea could be unified by force: the Chinese Communists' victory over the Nationalists. It was a sign of Western weakness and freed Mao's revolutionaries to help in Korea if need be.

Stalin made another major blunder. The original war plan called for an advance on the Ongjin Peninsula, which would bring a response from the South. Claiming it had been attacked first, the North would then launch the full invasion. "The war should be quick. . . . Southerners and Americans should not have time to come to their senses," Stalin told Kim. The U.S.S.R. would not participate directly, he said. But on June 21, four days before the war was to start, Stalin received a telegram from his ambassador in Pyongyang, warning that the South had learned of the plan. Stalin replied the same day, agreeing to Kim's proposal for an all-out attack across the 38th parallel. The World War II-style blitzkrieg virtually ensured that the West would respond, Weathersby says. Respond it did. While that's history, it may hold a lesson for dealing with tomorrow's dictators.

—*Warren P. Strobel*

It was MacArthur's last triumph. The overconfident general sent U.S. troops north of the 38th parallel toward the Chinese border, despite warnings from China that it would enter the war on the North's side. And he blundered tactically by allowing his forces to become separated by the mountain range running down the spine of Korea. Chinese "volunteers" began infiltrating the border in late October and moved down the center of the peninsula before launching a massive counterattack in November, forcing U.S. troops into yet another disorderly retreat at a huge cost of men and equipment. It was the longest U.S. military retreat in history.

"American Caesar." In less than six months, the city of Seoul had changed hands no less than three times. U.N. forces regrouped and charged north again, but on reaching the 38th parallel, few were willing to risk going farther north again. Few, that is, except MacArthur, who threatened China with attack in public defiance of Truman's policies. Truman fired MacArthur for insubordination, causing a political uproar at home, where MacArthur was revered as a World War II hero, an "American Caesar," as biographer William Manchester called him. The war ground on—World War I style—with huge, bloody battles from entrenched positions over relatively small tactical objectives, places dubbed Heartbreak Ridge and Pork Chop Hill.

Failure to bring the war to an early close may have cost the Democrats the presidential election in 1952, and President-elect Eisenhower made good his pledge to visit Korea. Eisenhower hinted he might expand the war, perhaps even using atomic weapons. Then Stalin died, and negotiators at last settled the final issue that had held up armistice for several years: whether prisoners of war could choose repatriation or not. A committee from neutral nations screened POWs, with 23 Americans and 14,704 Chinese choosing not to go home.

Americans were anxious to forget the war and to enjoy the long economic boom of the 1950s. Yet the war changed the world, and America, in ways that few people appreciate today. For one, it was America's first taste of military defeat, and its first experience of limited warfare, where outright victory was deemed too costly an objective. The wartime demand helped restore Japan's economy, devastated by its defeat in World War II, and made the former enemy into a strategic partner in Asia. It was the first of many military interventions under the United Nations flag. It also was the event that first turned the Cold War hot, swiftly reversing the cuts in U.S. military spending that had left U.S. forces unprepared to fight. An enormous military buildup followed: Military spending nearly quadrupled in three years, and the ranks of the armed forces more than doubled from 1.5 million to 3.5 million.

And yet, the war really settled nothing—36,516 Americans and millions of Koreans and Chinese dead just to agree on an existing demarcation line. North Korea survives as perhaps the most repressive government in the world, a lone Stalinist state that embraces central planning, threatening the world with long-range missiles while its own people starve in a horrendous famine. South Korea evolved tortuously into a proud and prosperous democracy. And Korea is still divided, with over a million heavily armed men on both sides of the 38th parallel. Taiwan, too, remains dangerously estranged from China. This week's Korean summit could prove a modest step to resolving a Cold War that has ended almost everywhere else in a victory for democracy and free-market capitalism.

Coming to Terms with the Past

Rikki Kersten extols the example of an unlikely hero, the historian Ienaga Saburo, who singlehandedly challenged Japan's official view of responsibility for its behaviour in the Second World War.

RIKKI KERSTEN

In Japan since the Second World War, the battle over history and memory concerning Japan's war experience has largely been fought in the arena of junior and senior high school history textbooks. Since Japan's defeat in 1945, questions of war responsibility, imperial accountability and the cultural roots of Japan's expansionist adventure into Asia and the Pacific between 1931 and 1945 have festered in the popular and academic imagination. In fundamental ways, the issues of the Second World War in postwar Japan remain unresolved, thus opening the way for opportunistic readings of the past in the present, and tot history to be used for political purposes. The history textbook lawsuits waged against the Japanese government by Professor Ienaga Saburo have reflected and sustained this divided discourse on the war in contemporary Japan.

Academics are unlikely heroes. In the case of Japanese historian Ienaga Saburo, one could be forgiven for deeming this a self-evident truth. Painfully thin, bald and bespectacled, Ienaga reminded one more of an elongated sparrow than of a champion; he was so demonstrably feeble in his youth that he was declared unfit for military service, and the closest he got to any kind of action was an inglorious stint in the Army Reserve in the last desperate days of the Second World War.

Ienaga passed away on November 29th, 2002, at the ripe old age of 98. Whatever judgement awaits us in the next life, death invariably forces us to judge the sum of achievements in this one. In a spirit of tribute but also of critical assessment, I would like to examine the legacy of Ienaga Saburo in terms of his impact on how postwar Japan has read and remembered its wartime past.

The last four decades of Ienaga's life were the ones that defined his image in the minds of his contemporaries. In the final years of his long life, Ienaga achieved the status of hero and crusader in radical and popular circles. For this bookish university professor single-handedly challenged the Japanese state over a thirty-two-year period in a series of lawsuits over the alleged censorship of his history textbooks. The crux of these lawsuits, and of Ienaga's fame, was his conviction that the unpleasant details of Japan's crimes and abhorrent behaviour during the war ought to be included in school history textbooks. The non-combatant of wartime became the combative conscience of postwar Japan, even though none of his three lawsuits ended in total success.

In contemporary Japan the 'revisionists' and conservatives hold centre-stage in the ongoing controversy over the teaching of the Second World War in Japanese schools. Since 1997, the so-called 'Liberal School of History' and their activist wing, the Society for the Creation of New History Textbooks, has swept through the best-seller lists with their own versions of Japan's war. Apologist, aggressively patriotic and cheap, their mass market books prepared the way for the production of a new textbook intended for use in Japanese junior high schools. The very existence of this movement seems to condemn any notion of an Ienaga legacy to the status of an historical curiosity at best.

The Society's New History of Japan, having undergone 137 mandatory revisions at the insistence of the same official entity that had provoked Ienaga to go to court, has been available as an approved text for use in schools from April 2002. This occurred despite the extraordinary uproar caused when the results of a vetting by the Ministry of Education were released in March 2001: the Korean ambassador was withdrawn, and formal protests and demands for numerous revisions came from both Korea and China. Eight prominent Japanese historians subsequently published an itemised list of fifty-one factual errors that they say remain in the revised text.

The conservative turn in contemporary Japanese politics further discourages any notion of Ienaga's impact. Japan in 2003 had an ultra-conservative prime minister who felt emboldened by his initially high popularity ratings to visit Yasukuni Shrine (where Japan's war dead—including war criminals—are worshipped) to commemorate the August 15th anniversary of defeat, without the fig-leaf of doing so in a 'private capacity' as his predecessors had felt obliged to do. A continuous parade of lawsuits lodged in Japan's court system in the 1990s by (mainly foreign) war victims claiming apologies and compensation were invariably dismissed, using the pretext that in international law all of these issues have been settled in state-to-state treaties following the war.

Today, Japan's historians are sometimes cartoonists (like Kobayashi Yoshinori, for example), so that the complexities of war and memory are scribbled into balloons emanating from the mouths of heroes in the pages of manga comic books. Yet lightning-rod issues such as the despatch of troops on UN Peacekeeping activities, that in the early 1990s provoked fierce public controversy and anger, pass through parliament in the pre-9/11 era with barely a murmur. Revision of the pacifist clause in Japan's postwar constitution, Article 9, seems only a matter of time.

So where is Ienaga's legacy? In spite of the light and heat emanating from the ascendant 'revisionist' movement, Ienaga has nonetheless substantially changed the landscape of Japanese historiography. In a real sense, the vehemence of 'revisionists' engaged in passionate denial of a negative past to contemporary Japan is in direct proportion to the impact Ienaga has made on postwar Japanese intellectual life. Without Ienaga, there would be no Kobayashi Yoshinori. Cartoon history is enormously popular and influential amongst the younger postwar generation in Japan, but it exists on a terrain that has been shaped and sign-posted by a sickly scholar who never saw a battlefield.

Born in Nagoya in 1913, Ienaga fell into academe almost by default, or at least he would have it that way. Being of a weak disposition, he stated that most alternative avenues of activity were not open to him. What he did not stress was his obvious intelligence, yet even here there is evidence of timidity improbably tinged with pragmatism. He really wanted to study philosophy, but saw no future career there. History, he decided, was the path to take.

He had entered high school in 1931, the year when Japan embarked on its imperial adventure in Manchuria, and bowed to the Imperial portrait along with his classmates. By the time he had graduated from university in 1937, the Manchurian Incident had developed into full-scale war with China. The reality of imperial Japan was impressed upon him when his attempt to publish part of his graduation thesis was thwarted by fellow scholars and journal editors. His topic was considered too dangerous, as it touched on the subject of the Imperial foundation myth. Ienaga writes, 'This manuscript, my first scholarly essay to be set in print, died and was buried at the galley-proof stage, and until the defeat I had no choice but to keep it under lock and key.'

The autobiographical narrative takes a curious turn when he describes his subsequent career as a high school teacher in the early 1940s. He vividly describes the map on the noticeboard in the staff-room, with little pink flags tracking the glorious military successes of Japan in battlefields stretching from China to Australia and the Pacific. He depicts his predicament as a teacher of history in a time of authoritarian control and thought police as "fumie no sekai", equating his situation with that of the Japanese Christians in sixteenth-century Japan who were forced to tread on a portrait of Jesus to prove their contempt for the foreign ideology.

This is a tantalising association. At this stage in his life, Ienaga had no belief system other than that of meticulous scholarship. In other words, he implies that he felt he was being forced to betray the discipline of history itself. Eventually, Ienaga intertwined the distortion and emasculation of history with the causes of the war: 'the vast majority of the people were educated from youth into a frame of mind in which they could not criticise state policies independently but had to follow them, mistaken though they were. Education since 1868 carries heavy responsibility for bringing on that tragedy.'

Unlike many of his peers, Ienaga's personal example in postwar Japan tolerated no notional 'year zero' in personal responsibility. Rather, his postwar activism was an organic outgrowth of his failure to resist in wartime. In his own version of his story, Ienaga describes his activities as a kind of 'postwar responsibility', a personal crusade of atonement for failing to resist the militarism of the wartime Japanese state. Worse, in Ienaga's own eyes, he was a passive collaborator in that he taught the 'history' of the Emperor System and its foundation myths to the youth of the 1940s. He is scathing about his own active part in wartime Japan, when he 'taught propaganda'. Through his postwar activism, he demonstrated that wartime impotence also entailed some responsibility on the part of passive collaborators. 'In the classroom I had to jump through the hoops: that fact damaged my very soul'.

Ienaga was involved in the formulation of Japan's first postwar textbook, and began drafting his own texts for the Ministry of Education in the 1950s. Around the same time, he became increasingly radicalised by the Cold War turn in Occupation policies towards Japan, particularly as it concerned education. As Japan's conservative politicians encroached further on the content of education following independence in 1959, he voluntarily became embroiled in a series of textbook lawsuits where he spoke as a witness for the defendants.

Finally, in 1965, Ienaga felt compelled to put the Japanese authorities on the defensive through lodging his own case, this time against the Ministry of Education itself. Provoked beyond tolerance by a succession of critical vettings of his draft high school textbooks by Education authorities, and incensed by the reasons given for their revisions, he embarked on the journey that would inspire countless ordinary folk, and generations of lawyers and scholars in his lifetime.

Ienaga's legendary court cases did indeed inspire and radicalise postwar generations from diverse walks of life, through identifying freedom of thought as an ongoing concern in a postwar Japan that had grown complacent about its democratic legitimacy as a Cold War ally and 'economic miracle' nation. But the significance of his personal example, and of the cases themselves, resonates more deeply.

Ienaga's fight for history exposed a bigger issue, namely that of how Japan had failed to reconcile its Second World War history with the substance of its postwar democracy. Telling the history of war and embracing war guilt has, through the textbook trials, attained the status of a litmus test for democracy in postwar Japan.

The legal thrust of the textbook trials was quite simple: that the process of screening school textbooks represented a denial of freedom of education to the point of censorship, and thus was unconstitutional. Furthermore, screening violated the spirit of the 1947 Fundamental Law on Education, a law designed by the American occupiers to mobilise education as an instrument of democratic indoctrination. Over time, as repeated rulings against Ienaga created a cycle of inevitable failure through the establishment of legal precedent, he shifted his ground to focus on the validity of the screening process, asserting that the Minister had exceeded his authority in his rulings over textbook content.

Basic democratic rights seemed to be the fulcrum of these cases, and indeed they were. But the cases were also about whether or not postwar generations should be taught about Japanese war crimes, and this fact teased observers and participants alike into confronting more than abstract philosophies of democratic legitimacy.

In their screenings of Ienaga's texts, the Textbook Authorisation Council exposed its conviction that the purpose of history education was to create patriotic citizens. In 1957 the Council criticised Ienaga for 'excessive fervour to encourage soul-searching rather than historical accuracy about the past', and for straying 'from the goals of teaching Japanese history . . . [namely] to recognise the efforts of ancestors, to heighten one's consciousness of being Japanese, and to instil a rich love of the race'. In 1964, he was asked to make over 300 revisions for similar reasons.

The flavour and tone of screening was consistent with this desire for a past that was not only usable but that would provide a positive foundation for the present. Commenting on the Rape of Nanjing, one screening committee declared that 'the violation of women is something that has happened on every battlefield in every era of human history. This is not an issue that needs to be taken up with respect to the Japanese Army in particular'. And referring to Ienaga's inclusion of pictures of maimed Japanese soldiers in his draft textbooks, it was decided that 'this conveys an excessively" negative impression of war'. Ienaga's purpose had been to warn future generations that a state inclined towards war did not have the interests of its citizens at heart. For the Ministry of Education, this was the crux of the matter. Attitudes towards history in general, and towards the Second World War in particular, were not compatible with the official self-image of the postwar Japanese state. Through sanitising the actions of the state and its relationship to society in the past, Japanese education

officials were attempting to realise their ideal vision of this relationship in the future.

The trials have also had profound implications on the discipline of history. In their screenings of Ienaga's draft textbooks, the Ministry of Education revealed its implicit belief that history ought to be the product of consensus. Unit 731, a Japanese military unit which conducted experiments in bacteriological warfare on human subjects, could not be mentioned, they argued, because 'no credible scholarly research exists concerning Unit 731'. Their references to the need for 'commonly held' or 'correct' views of events represent nothing less than a formula for an official, politically correct, view of history.

Furthermore, through the textbook trials, we see orthodox history being determined not by historians but by lawyers and bureaucrats. Rulings on whether certain sections are allowable are tantamount to a 'seal of approval' for one interpretation of history. The exclusion of a section similarly dismisses the legitimacy not only of the interpretation of an event, but its very existence. If we do not know all of the facts, can we say that the Rape of Nanjing really happened?

Finally; as Nagahara Kenji poignantly indicates, by identifying the creation of patriotic citizens as the goal of history education, the Ministry of Education effectively divorced research and scholarship from education. In the twenty-first century, the line between education and propaganda in Japan appears to be gossamer-thin.

Yet the hundreds of historians who appeared as witnesses for Ienaga over the years took away a very different kind of lesson. They had seen that it was indeed possible to combine morality and social responsibility with the study of history, particularly regarding the research and writing of Japan's history during the Second World War. For many of these scholars, passive collaboration would no longer be an option.

As a direct result of Ienaga's lawsuits, 'comfort women', the Rape of Nanjing, and Unit 731 can now be mentioned in school history texts in Japan. The appearance of 'comfort women' in all junior high school texts from April 1997 was the major catalyst for the furious reaction from 'revisionist' quarters that continues to this day, notably in the form of the Society for the Creation of New History Textbooks. This crowd have had some successes too. Feeling the pressure of their ire, textbook publishers are increasingly engaging in self-censorship before submitting their textbooks for the mandatory screening and approval process. In April 2001, five out of eight textbook publishers chose not to mention 'comfort women' at all.

Far from symbolising the smothering of Ienaga's legacy, the very intensity of the revisionist backlash demonstrates that Ienaga has made a powerful impact on Japan's historical consciousness. Japan's 'revisionists' are in essence reactionaries: clearly, Ienaga gave them something to react against.

In 1978 Ienaga described his motivation to write the truth about Japan's war: 'To be told to write nice things about the war again, to whip Japan up once again to war, this time in subjection to the United States—I had to resist such education policies, otherwise on my deathbed I would relive the remorse I felt then: once again, back then, why didn't I act?'

Ienaga's multifaceted legacy begins with the legacy of resistance. Partly through his example, resistance has become the indicator of democratic legitimacy in a nation where democracy exists mainly in the space that divides society from the state. In the Yokohama court system, Professor Takashima is continuing the textbook lawsuit tradition. To date, very few local prefectural school boards have chosen the Society's New History of Japan as their preferred textbook.

The discipline and profession of history in Japan have been the major beneficiaries of Ienaga's lawsuits. Perhaps one day, the children of Japan will likewise be allowed to benefit from the titanic struggles of one mighty fighter for a history that is not merely compatible with democracy, but inhabits its very core.

Iraq's Unruly Century

Ever since Britain carved the nation out of the Ottoman Empire after World War I, the land long known as Mesopotamia has been wracked by instability.

JONATHAN KANDELL

As summer temperatures headed toward 105 degrees on the morning of August 23, 1921, some 1,500 dignitaries assembled in the courtyard of a government building on the banks on the Tigris River for a coronation. British Army officers and colonial administrators mingled with Shiite Arabs from Basra near the Persian Gulf, Kurds from Mosul near Turkey, and Sunni Arabs from Baghdad to witness the installation of a foreign prince, Faisal, as the first king of the newly created nation. "It was an amazing thing to see all Iraq, from North to South, gathered together," wrote Gertrude Bell, a British colonial official who had recommended Faisal to her government and would be his staunchest supporter. "It is the first time it has happened in history."

Faisal's subjects had no anthem, so a band struck up "God Save the King." The selection aptly symbolized Britain's role not only in inventing the Iraqi government—complete with a figurehead king and soon a new parliament and constitution—but also in orchestrating it for years to come.

On a July morning in Baghdad in 1958, Iraq's constitutional monarchy came to a brutal end when an army faction led by Iraqi Gen. Abdul Karim Qassem stormed the royal palace. In the courtyard, rebel troops killed King Faisal II, the 23-year-old grandson of the first monarch, and a score of men, women and children. Faisal's body was removed to a secret burial place. But no such respect was accorded his uncle and former regent, Abdul Ilah, whom the plotters blamed for the monarchy's pro-British slant; his corpse was thrown to a mob outside the palace gates, dragged around the city and displayed for two days in a public square.

The 1958 coup d'état was not the first upheaval in Iraq's modern political history, which has been marked by nationalist fervor, ethnic uprisings, tribal conflicts, palace treacheries, warfare and deadly oppression. In the monarchy's 37 years, the government cabinet was shuffled more than 50 times. Scholars have offered a catalog of reasons why antiquity's "cradle of civilization" has been so unstable. Some blame geography, pointing out that Iraq, which covers some 168,000 square miles, has a mere 12 miles of shoreline, on the Persian Gulf, making it the most landlocked—and culturally isolated—nation in the Middle East. Others tie Iraq's "bloody history," as many have described it, to the preponderance of groups vying for power. The rivalry goes deeper than Arab versus British, however, or Sunni versus Shiite versus Kurd. As the Kurdish analyst Siyamend Othman said this

past November, the "history of Iraq has been conditioned, if not determined, by the conflict between city and countryside," meaning the conflict between an emerging educated class around major urban areas and the old semiliterate rural sheikhdoms.

Britain's experiment in nation-building failed partly because it did not unify the disparate factions, says Charles Tripp, a British citizen and author of the 2000 book, *A History of Iraq.* Instead, Britain seeded unrest by relying on the Sunni minority to run the military and civil service and also by subordinating the northern, Kurdish territory. In addition, he says, Britain's decision to allow tribal sheikhs to maintain order in rural areas heightened tensions by "treating Iraqi society as a collection of groups rather than individuals."

But Adeed Dawisha, an Iraq-born historian and author of *Arab Nationalism in the Twentieth Century,* suggests that Britain failed mainly because it granted Iraq too little autonomy. "From the establishment of the constitutional monarchy in 1921 all the way to its fall in 1958," Dawisha says, "it was very clear that none of the Iraqi governments could carry out any policy against British opposition. And I would put oil [policies] at the top of the list. Oil sales served the interests of Britain, not Iraq."

It was at the start of World War I that Britain first occupied Mesopotamia, then part of the Ottoman Empire. The Ottomans had allied with Germany, and Britain justified its 1914 invasion as a move to protect its oil fields in neighboring Iran and its access to Persian Gulf shipping lanes to India. Many Iraqis welcomed the British troops with open arms. The 1916–1918 Arab Revolt against the Ottoman Turks, encouraged by the British military liaison officer T. E. Lawrence (better known as Lawrence of Arabia), raised nationalist Arab expectations in the region. And to court Arabs throughout the Middle East, the British vowed to end three centuries of Ottoman rule, which had grown corrupt, repressive and economically stifling. "Our armies do not come into your cities and lands as conquerors or enemies but as liberators," proclaimed Gen. Stanley Maude, commander of the British forces, as his troops marched into Baghdad in 1917.

In 1920, the newly formed League of Nations granted Britain a "mandate" over Iraq—a kind of pre-independence trusteeship. It gave Britain the right to raise and spend revenues, to appoint officials and to make and enforce laws. (Britain was also mandated to govern Palestine. Another mandate put Syria and Lebanon under French jurisdiction.) Though the mandate approach was flawed, says historian David Fromkin, it appealed to League members because it gave the Allied powers control over territories without endorsing imperialism outright. "The mandate system responded to people who were idealistic and anti-imperialistic and others who felt it was a useful disguise to maintain the old colonial system in place," says Fromkin, author of *A Peace to End All Peace*.

In the end, the boundaries of the new Iraq—a seventhcentury name meaning "well-rooted country"—largely mirrored the boundaries of three Ottoman provinces, though that was not the original plan. In 1915 the British had wanted the northernmost province around Mosul to go to France, to serve as a buffer between British holdings and possible Russian expansion. But Britain changed its stance in 1918 in part because of growing appreciation for the importance of oil, believed to be abundant in the Mosul area. (So it is. A well first struck oil in Kirkuk in 1927.) As for Kuwait, it had been virtually a separate British protectorate since 1899 and by World War I was already splitting from the Ottoman province of Basra that would become part of Iraq.

By the time of the 1920 mandate, Iraqi nationalism outweighed pro-British feeling. British officials differed over how to deal with the threat. "There were people like Gertrude Bell," says Phebe Marr, a Washington, D.C.-based historian, "who came to believe in the need for some sort of self-government as soon as possible, and conservatives like Arnold Wilson [Bell's chief], who thought that the local folk weren't capable of running their own show and had to be tutored for a long time."

For a while, Wilson's arguments held sway—to the frustration of Bell and most Iraqis. When an Iraqi delegation met with Wilson, a forceful imperialist then in his 30s, he brushed them off as "ungrateful politicians." He proceeded to turn Iraq into a virtual appendage of Britain's colonial rule in India, bringing troops and administrators over from the subcontinent. Nationalist protests increased, and in the summer of 1920, one leader, Imam Shirazi of Karbala, issued a fatwa, or religious decree, that British rule violated Islamic law. He called for a jihad, or holy war, against the British—and for once Sunnis, Shiites and rival sheikhdoms united in a common cause. The armed rebellion spread from Karbala and Najaf, in the center, to the south of the country, with uprisings by Kurds in the north as well.

Wilson came down hard, ordering aerial bombardments, the machine-gunning of rebels and the destruction of whole towns. "The British overreaction made things much worse," says Janet Wallach, author of a biography of Bell, *Desert Queen*. An aghast Bell wrote to her mother, "We have underestimated the fact that this country is really an inchoate mass of tribes which can't as yet be reduced to any system. The Turks didn't govern and we have tried to govern—and failed." Some 6,000 Iraqis and 500 British and Indian soldiers perished before the revolt was finally put down in October. By then, the British press and public had turned against Colonial Office plans to run Iraq. As *The Times* of London had put it three months earlier, "How much longer are valuable lives to be sacrificed in the vain endeavour to impose upon the Arab population an elaborate and expensive administration which they never asked for and do not want?"

The following year, a conference in Cairo presided over by Winston Churchill, then colonial secretary for Iraq affairs, determined that a constitutional monarchy was the surest path toward a stable, prosperous Iraq. At first glance, Faisal seemed an unlikely choice as ruler. The 35-year-old prince, son of the Sharif Hussein of Mecca (now part of Saudi Arabia), had never set foot in Iraq and spoke an Arabic dialect that was barely intelligible to many of his future subjects. "He had no knowledge of the Iraqi tribes, no friendships with their sheikhs, no familiarity with the terrain—the marshes in the south, the mountains in the north, the grain fields, the river life—and no sense of connection with its ancient past," Wallach writes.

But Bell and other Arabists in the Colonial Office believed that Faisal, who had fought with Lawrence against the Turks, had the charisma to hold the new country together. Also, he traced his lineage to Muhammad, and to emphasize that claim he set out for his new kingdom from Mecca, birthplace of the Prophet. Along his route, chieftains tried to rally crowds—"For the sake of Allah, cheer!"—but most spectators remained unmoved. In a national referendum on his monarchy, Faisal was officially declared to have won 96 percent of the vote, prompting charges that the election was rigged. Still, a relieved Bell wrote in another letter: "We've got our King crowned."

The Oxford-educated Bell served as Faisal's adviser and confidante. During afternoon teas at the palace, she reeled out her vision of a progressive Iraq that could become a beacon for the Middle East. "When we have made Mesopotamia a model state, there is not an Arab of Syria and Palestine who wouldn't want to be part of it," she told the king, adding that she hoped to see Faisal "ruling from the Persian frontier to the Mediterranean."

But Faisal wasn't looking beyond his borders. Ruling his subjects—divided by ethnicity, religion and geography—was trouble enough. Like the Ottomans before them, the British and Faisal, himself a Sunni, found it expedient to favor the more pro-Western Sunni Arabs of Baghdad and the central region, though they accounted for barely 20 percent of the population. More than half of Iraqis were Shiite Arabs, concentrated in the south. Close to 20 percent were Kurds, living mostly in the north. The remainder included Jews, Assyrians and other minorities. "The British turned to the same educated elite—mostly Sunni—who had been trained and used by the Ottomans," says historian Marr. "But a number of them soon proved to be ornery and nationalistic."

It was left to Faisal to deal with the Iraqi nationalists. The British-designed constitution gave him the power to select the prime minister, dissolve parliament and issue decrees when parliament wasn't in session. And no law could be passed without his assent. But Faisal struggled to balance British and Iraqi demands. One moment, he was beseeching British officials not to withdraw from Iraq. Days later, he was refusing to suppress anti-British demonstrations in Baghdad and Basra. "There's always this problem of needing the support of the West and at the same time bowing to the will of the people for independence," says Wallach.

The most insistent issue that the king faced was a new Anglo-Iraq treaty, which would provide for the maintenance of British military bases, give British officials a veto over legislation and perpetuate British influence over financial and international matters for 20 years. Faisal equivocated. In private, he assured Bell that he favored the treaty. But in public speeches, he criticized it for stopping short of removing the mandate. "Gertrude was livid at his double-dealing," Wallach writes. A special Iraqi assembly ratified the treaty in 1924, with Faisal's tacit support. But he had demonstrated that the British could not take him for granted.

Faisal ruled long enough to see the mandate end, in 1932, when Iraq was admitted to the League of Nations as an independent state. (Though Britain's direct participation in local government ended in 1930, pro-British elements would exercise influence until 1958.) Faisal died of a heart attack at age 48 in 1933 while seeing physicians in Switzerland. "He made himself a buffer between Iraqi nationalists and the British," says Tripp, the British historian. "Before he died, he reached out beyond that small Sunni circle he had inherited from the Ottomans and built ties with the Shiites and Kurds."

Today, scholars debate the extent of British influence on Iraq after the mandate. "If Faisal had lived ten more years, the history of Iraq would have been very different," says Edmund Ghareeb, an Iraq-born historian at Georgetown University. "After his death, the British were able to undermine the government and the monarchy by constantly putting pressure on them to serve Britain's interests—involving oil, foreign affairs in the gulf region and other issues."

But Reeva S. Simon, a Columbia University historian, says Iraq achieved a measure of independence: "It joined the League of Nations. It had a press that was open and critical of the British. In foreign policy, it did not simply follow the British lead but showed itself to be increasingly pro-German during the 1930s, and invited to Baghdad people who opposed British rule in the Middle East."

In any event, Marr says, Britain's imprint was profound. "Even after the mandate ended, the British presence focused Iraqis constantly on independence. Not on developing the country, not on how to make the constitutional system work better, not on how to integrate Kurds, Shiites and Sunnis. Instead, the question that was always asked was, how can we get rid of the British? As a result, there is even to this day an obsession that there be no foreign control." As Fromkin says, "We tend to overlook a basic rule: that people prefer bad rule by their own kind to good rule by somebody else."

An unusual and perceptive Western chronicler of Iraq in that critical era was Freya Stark, 36, an English adventuress and journalist, who arrived in Baghdad in the fall of 1929 with ten pounds in her pocket and a conviction that "the most interesting things in the world were likely to happen in the neighborhood of oil." She was excited by Iraq's ancient glories, writes her biographer, Jane Fletcher Geniesse. Those included Babylon, 50 miles south of Baghdad; the ruins of Ur, where Abraham was born, and of Uruk, not far from the banks of the Eurphrates; and the Assyrian cities of Khorsabad and Nineveh.

In Baghdad itself, Stark sought out traces of the eighth-century caliphate that had turned the city into an extraordinary intellectual and artistic center—at a time when Europe plunged into its dark ages. "What you first see of the Caliphs' city is a most sordid aspect," she wrote in a dispatch to the Baghdad Times. "The crowd looks unhealthy and sallow, the children are pitiful, the shops are ineffective compromises with Europe; and the dust is wicked." But Stark wasn't put off. At dawn, she walked the narrow, winding alleys under latticed balconies. She strolled through the bazaars where Muslims, Indians, Jews and Armenians hawked silks, velvets, indigo and spices.

Fluent in Arabic, she interviewed the women of the harems. She studied the Koran and, veiled from head to foot, slipped into a Muslim shrine. Shunning the suburban bungalows of the Western community, Stark initially settled across the Tigris in a slum—the prostitutes' quarter, it turned out, to her amusement. An English acquaintance accused her of "lowering the prestige of British womanhood."

Most important, Stark witnessed Iraq's mounting rebellion. In the 1930s, the Baghdad press railed against overbearing British advisers in government and the Royal Air Force's control of bases around Baghdad and Basra. The British found few defenders even among the Iraqi elite who owed the British their status and prosperity. "To be anti-British made you successful either as a lawyer, a politician or a journalist," wrote Stark.

It also boosted the king, Ghazi, Faisal's son, who assumed the throne in 1933 at age 21. Ghazi had neither his father's diplomatic skills nor his work ethic. He liked partygoing more than governing. Still, his ability to rally subjects with incendiary speeches broadcast over the palace radio station troubled British functionaries. They worried about his repeated denunciations of British control over Kuwait—which Ghazi clamed was a province of Iraq—and his attacks on the Kuwaiti ruling family. But the rhetoric thrilled young Iraqis.

Six years after becoming king, Ghazi crashed his sports car into a utility pole in Baghdad after an evening of drinking. His two British physicians summoned an Iraqi colleague to the scene of the mortally wounded king. "I was fearful lest, if no Iraqi doctor was in attendance, Anglophobic mischief-makers might originate canards to the effect that [we] were responsible for the king's demise," Dr. Harry C. Sinderson, the monarch's chief physician, wrote in his memoirs. Even so, violent street demonstrations erupted in Baghdad the next day. In Mosul, a mob killed the British consul. For years, many Iraqis insisted that Ghazi was killed by the British and their allies. He was succeeded by his son Faisal II.

The conspiracy theories also stirred foment in the Iraqi Army, though the British largely missed the warning signs. "For all their many advisers in the Iraqi government, the British didn't show much interest in military affairs," says Simon. "Certainly, they didn't imagine that army officers would interfere directly in politics.

Britain's presence in Iraq was not the only thing that aroused Iraqi anger. By the 1930s, Arab leaders were also angered by the growing numbers of European Jews migrating to Palestine, a British mandate until 1948. When the British suppressed a revolt by Palestinian Arabs in 1939, Iraqi Army officers invited the defeated leader, the Mufti of Jerusalem, to live in Baghdad. Then, as World War II began, Iraqi antipathy to Britain turned into support for Hitler. "It was widely acknowledged that most of the junior officers in the Iraqi army are pro-German and anti-British," Paul Knabenshue, a U.S. diplomat in Baghdad, wrote in May 1940. Iraq attempted to ally itself with Germany and in 1941 threatened to fire on British planes at an airfield near Baghdad.

In April 1941, Rashid Ali, a civilian figurehead for an Iraqi Army faction led by four colonels staged a coup d'état. British Royal Air Force troops stationed on the outskirts of Baghdad held the Iraqi Army at bay while British reinforcements from India landed in Basra and marched north.

In Baghdad, some 400 British nationals and their Iraqi sympathizers sought refuge in the British Embassy. The last person admitted into the compound was Freya Stark. Previously disdained by many compatriots, she was now hailed as a savior. "With her fluent local Arabic and her aplomb and bonhomie, she became our most useful contact at our gates with the Iraqi police posted here, and helped us to buy fresh meat and vegetables to leaven our Spartan fare," one observer recalled. Her good relations with the guards may have saved the embassy from mobs. "We could see the crowds from the upper town, incited by speeches of the Mufti and their own radio, advancing with banners and drums and dancing figures silhouetted against the sky, towards our gates," Stark wrote.

By early June, British forces had taken control of Baghdad. Rashid Ali's two-month rule ended when he fled to Berlin. The four Iraqi colonels behind his coup were captured and hanged. In retaliation, outraged Iraqi mobs stormed the Jewish quarter, presumed to be pro-British, and killed 179 men, women and children, injuring hundreds more.

Saddam Hussein, a child at the time, would later say that Rashid Ali's rise and fall affected him deeply because the uncle who raised him was an army officer whose career ended when the coup was crushed.

Anti-British passions were further inflamed by the outbreak, in 1948, of war in Palestine, where Iraqi troops fought on the Arab side against the Israelis, whose ultimate victory, most Iraqis believed, could not have been achieved without British (and American) assistance. They were inflamed again in 1956 by the British role in wresting the Suez Canal back from Egyptian president Gamal Abdel Nasser. Then, the Qassem coup d'état in 1958 destroyed the monarchy once and for all. Ilah, the former regent, and Prime Minister Nuri Said were killed because they were felt to have been too eager to please the British by executing the plotters of Rashid Ali's coup 17 years earlier.

The massacre of the Iraqi royal family left two major legacies of Great Britain's four-decades-long involvement in Iraq: the nation retained essentially the same boundaries that Britain had traced in the early 1920s, and the Sunni minority held on to power.

The monarchy's collapse was followed by a decade of even greater instability, ending with a coup in 1968 by army officers linked to the Baathists, a pan-Arab socialist movement that opponents have described as neo-Fascist. A jubilant Saddam Hussein, 31, rode through Baghdad atop a tank. His kinsman, Gen. Ahmad Hassan al-Bakr, had led the coup and became president. Like Bakr, Hussein was from Tikrit, a Sunni town north of Baghdad that historically had fielded a disproportionate share of army officers. But Hussein did not come up through the military ranks in the usual way. After high school in Baghdad, he earned a living as a street tough for politicians, organizing gangs that disrupted opponents' political rallies and beating up shopkeepers whose stores remained open during strikes. Hussein graduated to assassin and spent almost two years in prison and in exile for political murders or attempted killings.

But his ferocity and cunning had impressed General Bakr, who, as president, appointed him to run the national security apparatus. In that capacity he set out to eliminate his main rivals, and he placed relatives and fellow Tikritis in positions of power and influence in the Baath Party, the armed forces and the government. As Bakr's power broker, Hussein nationalized foreign oil holdings in 1972, then accepted acclaim as Iraq's annual oil revenues rose eight-fold, to $8 million over the next three years, then tripled over the next five. Hussein then oversaw state investments in education, health, transportation, agriculture and industry, drawing praise as a model for the Middle East.

When, in 1979, Hussein became president following Bakr's "resignation"—Hussein almost certainly engineered it—many Iraqis thought he would lead them into prosperity. (Bakr died in 1982.) Instead, Hussein, after having his rivals killed, ruled despotically for nearly a quarter of a century, waging war on Iran (with American backing) and killing many thousands of Iraqis, including thousands of Kurds killed by chemical weapons. Hussein dragged his oil-rich, once-ascendent nation into poverty, and his pursuit of weapons of mass destruction put him on a collision course with the world's lone superpower.

JONATHAN KANDELL, a former foreign correspondent for the *New York Times,* wrote last for these pages about "Boss" Tweed.

The USA in Vietnam

America's allies kept out and President Johnson wanted to concentrate on reform at home. So why did America let itself get sucked into an agonising war it could not win?

Kevin Ruane

The USA was involved in two major wars in Asia during the Cold War. The first, the Korean War, saw America respond to a single blatant act of aggression. The second, the Vietnam War, was different. In 1965, the US decision to try and save South Vietnam from communism was the culmination of 15 years of gradual and deepening involvement in the affairs of that country.

Ironically, it is the US experience of Korea between 1950 and 1953 that helps explain the hesitancy with which America approached the problem of Vietnam. To US policymakers in the early 1950s, the 'lesson' of Korea was that land wars in Asia could soak up money and life almost endlessly. In future, they determined, the local non-communist governments would have to take primary responsibility for the containment of communism in Asia. The USA should offer military advice and support but not troops.

For 12 years after the Korean War ended this lesson was heeded in Washington. In 1965, however, President Lyndon B. Johnson finally jettisoned the Korean precedent in authorising the [dispatch] of hundreds of thousands of US combat troops to South Vietnam to preserve that country from communism.

Unlike President Truman's decision to go to war in Korea in 1950, Johnson's Vietnam decision proved disastrous for America. The war in Vietnam would last longer than Korea (1965–73) and involve even greater loss of life (58,000 American deaths compared to more than 36,000 in Korea). The Vietnam War also proved to be the most politically divisive domestic issue in the United States since the civil war of the nineteenth century. Korea, in contrast, generated no comparable domestic criticism, mainly because the soldiers who fought in that conflict were predominantly professionals for whom war was an occupational hazard, not conscripted civilians as was the case in Vietnam.

There were other important differences between Korea and Vietnam. In Korea, the USA fought as part of a United Nations (UN) coalition, whereas Vietnam was an American rather than a UN undertaking. By 1965, the UN had expanded its membership as a consequence of decolinisation, and many of the new countries were highly critical of what they saw as American interference in the affairs of less economically developed countries. The UN, in short, could no longer be considered a reliable instrument of US foreign policy.

The USA also had to deal with something in Vietnam that it had avoided in Korea—defeat. Although by the time North Vietnam conquered South Vietnam in 1975 all US troops had been removed, the outcome of the war was still a tremendous humiliation for America. All its earlier sacrifices had been undertaken to preserve an independent South Vietnam. In April 1975, South Vietnam ceased to exist.

Truman and Vietnam

Why, then, did Johnson commit American troops to a 'new' Korea? In seeking an answer to this question it is necessary to look first at Johnson's three immediate predecessors as president. The reason for this is that the choice Johnson faced in 1965 between war or the abandonment of South Vietnam was the inevitable consequence of decisions taken by US governments over the previous 15 years.

The first crucial step on the slippery slope to full US involvement came in 1950, when President Truman authorised a military aid programme for France to help with the war it was fighting in Vietnam, one of its colonies, against a communist-led independence movement, the Vietminh.

In April 1950, Truman had approved a new version of the US Cold War strategy of containment, known simply as NSC-68 (National Security Council document number 68). According to NSC-68, communism had to be strictly contained everywhere. Conversely, any failure of containment threatened to set in motion the domino theory, with incalculable consequences for American national security and for the Western position in the Cold War.

A month later, in May 1950, America began providing military assistance to France. This was a Cold War decision in keeping with the reasoning of NSC-68. Vietnam was now regarded as the trigger domino of southeast Asia, and US policymakers feared that its loss could lead to neighbouring Laos and Cambodia turning communist, followed by Thailand, Burma, Malaya, Indonesia and Japan. Looking further westward, India, the middle east and even Europe could be threatened.

The lasting consequence of Truman's decision was that, from 1950 onwards, victory or defeat in Vietnam was no longer a matter of just French concern but was also a vital American interest. The scale of subsequent US military aid to France serves to illustrate this point: by 1954, America was paying for almost 80% of the financial cost of the French war effort.

Eisenhower and Vietnam

To Washington's consternation, however, it was the Vietminh, itself supported by Chinese military aid, that was winning the war. In the spring of 1954, the Eisenhower administration explored the possibility of military intervention to shore up the crumbling French position. But the memory and lessons of Korea were too recent and too vivid to permit unilateral US action. At the same time, relying upon the UN, as in 1950, was impracticable, given the Soviet Union's power of veto in the Security Council.

As a compromise solution, the USA attempted to create a coalition of like-minded powers to intervene in support of France, but America's principal allies were reluctant to become involved in Vietnam in case communist China entered the war in support of the Vietminh and transformed the conflict into a potential catalyst for a Third World War.

Unable to influence events, the US government could only look on as a war-weary France negotiated a peace settlement with the Vietminh at the Geneva Accords, April–July 1954. Under its terms, Vietnam was temporarily partitioned, with the Vietminh occupying the area north of the 17th parallel and the French regrouping south of that line. Nationwide elections were scheduled for July 1956, after which it was intended that a single indigenous government would rule over a reunified and independent Vietnam.

The elections would never be held. The Eisenhower administration had publicly distanced itself from what it had deemed to be the 'appeasement' of the Geneva agreement, but in private US policymakers were relieved that at least the southern half of the trigger domino of southeast Asia had been preserved. Thereafter, the US set itself the task of 'nation-building' in southern Vietnam—the construction of a separate anti-communist state. But American plans meant ignoring the Geneva agreement on nationwide elections, which most impartial observers believed would be won by the Vietminh. Thus the temporary division of Vietnam took on an air of permanence.

During the rest of the 1950s, the Eisenhower administration provided South Vietnam—or the Republic of Vietnam, as it was officially known—with billions of dollars in economic and military aid. But Eisenhower always drew the line at committing US troops, despite a mounting communist guerrilla threat to the US-backed government in Saigon from 1959 onwards.

Kennedy, Johnson and Vietnam

In January 1961, a new US president, John F. Kennedy, took office, but there was no lessening in the American commitment to South Vietnam. To counter the rising Vietcong danger, the Kennedy administration sent 16,000 US 'advisers' (MAAG) to South Vietnam, ostensibly to instruct the native army in how to use the sophisticated military equipment that the USA was supplying in ever-increasing quantities. In practice, however, US Special Forces—the Green Berets—became involved in combat, although officially the US government insisted that it was not an active participant in the war.

It was only in 1965, 15 years after President Truman first accorded Vietnam the status of a vital American interest, that the USA became directly and fully committed to the defence of South Vietnam. The man who led America into war, Lyndon Johnson, has often been portrayed as a 'hawk', a gung-ho Texan who was determined from the outset to break with his predecessors' preferences and employ full US military power to destroy both the Vietcong and its North Vietnamese ally.

This crude and simplistic assessment is no longer valid in the light of recent scholarship. Far from being the hawk of legend, historians now tend to see Johnson as a man wracked with uncertainty about which direction to take on Vietnam. Johnson, it is argued, was especially worried that American escalation would produce Chinese counter-intervention on the Korean model and lead to a wider and more dangerous conflict.

It is also evident that the war Johnson really wanted to fight was not in Vietnam at all but in America, a war against poverty and social injustice. Johnson wanted to build a 'great society' in the USA. The 'great society' was a catch-all term for his commitment to civil rights, the eradication of poverty, increased access to education and health care, and a cleaner environment. In consequence, Johnson fretted constantly lest a major war in Vietnam divert public attention and money away from his domestic priorities.

Johnson's War?

For these reasons, as well as because of the lesson of Korea, Johnson hesitated to go to war in Vietnam. Yet, in the end, his Cold War orthodoxy won through. Johnson believed in containment. Johnson also feared the consequences of the domino theory. These two considerations ultimately conditioned his decision on Vietnam. But it is also clear that Johnson had very little room in which to manoeuvre by 1965, thanks to earlier and very public assertions by Eisenhower and Kennedy of how vital South Vietnam was to US national security.

It was Johnson's misfortune that he, rather than either of his predecessors, was in office when the situation in Vietnam reached crisis point and when, thanks to previous presidential decisions, he was confronted by just two choices. One was war. The other, as he put it, was 'bugging out'. Johnson chose war.

Vietnam was not, as critics would later charge, Johnson's war. It was America's war. It was a war in support of an American ally, and an American creation, the state of South Vietnam, and a war to make good a commitment to South Vietnam entered into by earlier American Cold War presidents, both Republican and Democrat.

From *Modern History Review*, April 2003. Copyright © 2003 by Philip Allan Updates. Reprinted by permission.

Article 40

The Common Currents of Imperialism

GREGORY SHAFER

"We are there to reach out to love them and to save them, and as a Christian I do this in the name of Jesus Christ."—Franklin Graham

"There was nothing left for us to do but to take them all and to educate the Filipinos, and uplift and civilize, and Christianize them. . . ."—President McKinley

Imperialism is a pesky thing. No matter how ardently one tries to adorn it in the garb of democracy and liberation, it seems always to look the same. One hundred years ago, the United States fought Spain with the pretense of liberating the Philippines and other "possessions" from subjugation. "A splendid little war," mused John Hay, the U.S. ambassador to England, in pondering the windfall it would mean for U.S. citizens. For the Filipino people, however, the occupation of their nation was anything but splendid. As a subjugated people, they fought the U.S. oppressors and their exploitive plans as heroically as they had the Spanish. While Mark Twain and others castigated American icons like President Theodore Roosevelt for their genocidal cleansing of the Filipino people, too many others remained mute, unwilling or unaware of how the United States had used the ruse of liberty and democracy to establish a pacific base in the Philippines.

Much of the same has also occurred in Iraq, where searches for weapons of mass destruction have been overshadowed by a growing Iraqi chorus for U.S. troops to leave their country. Whether President George W. Bush ever had any desire to do anything but give contracts to his favorite oil companies is questionable, but one thing is rather clear: the Iraqi people, both Shiite and Sunni, don't want Americans in their country and have asked them to leave in daily protests and orchestrated demonstrations: through marches, through civil disobedience, and in talks with U.S. officials. "Iraq cannot be ruled except by Iraqis," said Sheikh Hussein Sadr, dean of the Islamic Council in London, on April 28, 2003, as reported by *USA Today.* Just two days alter a disquieting *60 Minutes* special revealed the sweetheart deals that were going to Haliburton—Dick Cheney's former oil company—Bush tried to remind the nation that the mission in Iraq was noble. "America has no intention of imposing our form of government or our culture," *USA Today* quoted Bush in a speech to Iraqi-Americans in Michigan on April 28. Interestingly, Bush omitted any discussion about intentions to develop the reservoir of Iraqi oil or the contracts that had been doled out to U.S. companies with ties to the White House.

Not surprisingly, many also wondered about the people who weren't being invited to talk about the rebuilding of Iraq. Many were concerned about the exclusion of certain Iraqi groups that might want U.S. troops expelled and an end to U.S. rapacity in their nation. Others wondered why nobody was finding connections to terrorism or weapons of mass destruction, as that was the pretext for invading the country in the first place. As an American student asked, "Can someone remind me why we invaded Iraq? If it was to rid the world of a deluded and dangerous dictator, shouldn't we have pursued Kim Jong in North Korea? Is this about freedom or Americanization?"

Actually, the phrase often used for this kind of colonialism is *benevolent assimilation,* an insidious process in which the aggressor nation prostrates the victim nation and then begins to absorb it by plundering its resources and inculcating its people to believe that the usurpation was all done to liberate them and extricate them from an evil force. This lesson of imperialism, as has been played out in Iraq, amazingly and horrifyingly parallels the actions in the Philippines one century earlier.

When the United States first occupied the Philippines, the same mantra of liberating the people and bringing civilization to the land was espoused. Roosevelt referred to the Filipino people as childlike and suggested that they were too barbaric, too savage, to be left to their own devices. This eruption of manifest destiny seemed to justify the carnage, the plundering, and the abject disregard for human rights. In writing about the terror in his piece, "The Philippine-American War: Friendship and Forgetting," Reynaldo Ileto reminds us that the United States had an Axis of Evil one century ago as well, where one was either an American or an official villain. In trying to conquer the Filipino rebels, the U.S. military resorted to a policy that abandoned "amigo warfare" for an approach that was eerily similar to Bush's "shock and awe." "Henceforth," announced General Franklin Bell, in dealing with incorrigible Filipinoes, "no one will be permitted to be neutral. . . . The towns of Tiaong, Dolores, and Candelaria will probably be destroyed unless the insurgents who take refuge in them are destroyed."

It was the absorption of one country by another that was more powerful— replete with domination, occupation, and propaganda.

Colonel Cornelius Gardener, the first governor of Tayabas, recalled the irony of the violence. The United States was supposed to be the emancipator, but instead it simply lorded over a people for whom it had little regard. In speaking of the U.S. troops and their actions, Gardener lamented, "Of course the best houses in every town were occupied by them and every hidden place ransacked in hope of the booty of Eastern lands, so often read of in novels."

Mark Twain, the celebrated author and humorist, was never deluded by the patriotic fervor. In his essay "To the Person Sitting in the Darkness," he refers to the deception and perfidy of the American cause:

> We knew they supposed we were also fighting in their worthy cause—just as we had helped the Cubans fight for Cuban independence—and we allowed them to go on thinking so. Until Manila was ours and we could get along without them.

In the process, thousands of Filipino people were killed and dispossessed. It was all trumpeted as a crusade to emancipate. In reality, it was the absorption of one country by another that was more powerful—replete with domination, occupation, and propaganda.

April 27, 2003, presented the world with some of the first rumblings of what occupation is like in Iraq and how uneasy the relationship is between colonizer and colonized. After an acrimonious demonstration against U.S. presence in the area, sixteen Iraqi citizens were gunned down by U.S. soldiers, and seventy-five more were injured. According to the *Detroit Free Press*, Dr. Ahmed Ghanim al-Ali, director of the Fallujah General Hospital, reported that three of the thirteen dead were boys no older than ten. And he added later that his "medical crews were shot at when they went to retrieve the injured, which he said numbered 75 people."

May 1, 2003, brought more of the same. The *Detroit Free Press* reported that U.S. soldiers fired on anti-American demonstrators massed outside a U.S. compound—killing two and wounding eighteen—when unidentified attackers lobbed two grenades into the compound. Such escalating violence—the daily ritual of challenging U.S. presence on Iraqi soil—is emblematic of the imperialist's struggle. With citizens ardently opposed to a cultural interloper, and with the taste of real freedom resonating through their systems, they have little patience for the invading force.

And so the real conflict begins. With former Iraqi President Saddam Hussein—the designated villain—removed from power, Bush is continually forced to dance around the prickly issue of imperialism. Much like the situation in the Philippines, the Iraqi situation is no longer about amigo warfare but the subjugation of an intractable people—people who refuse to let the United States absorb their culture and appropriate their resources. Indeed, if Iraqi autonomy were the goal, wouldn't it be good for the United States to abdicate power to a United Nations team, so that questions about the surreptitious interests of the United States wouldn't be raised? If democracy and self-government were the endeavor, wouldn't it be wise to step to the side and permit Iraqis—in conjunction with an international team—to construct a democracy from the rubble of another U.S. attack?

In late June the United Nations called for the establishment of a representative Iraqi interim authority to help in rebuilding the country that was ravaged by U.S. bombs. "A fundamental precursor to any process is the establishment of a representative Iraqi interim administration to lead the reconstruction process," said Ramiro Lopez da Silva, the UN humanitarian coordinator for Iraq in speaking to the Associated Press. To this end, an inaugural meeting of the Iraqi governing council met for the first time on July 13 in order to delegate more responsibility to Iraqi officials over local municipalities.

Curiously, the nation with only "altruistic designs" gave contracts to oil companies six months before the war even started.

Such questions were made more provocative by the enduring and rather shadowy place of oil companies in Iraq. Curiously, the nation with only "altruistic designs" gave contracts to oil companies six months before the war even started. Even more unsettling, Haliburton, the oil company once directed by Dick Cheney, was chosen to develop this energy, which will generate incredible profits. Again, imperialism suggests that one nation exploit a less powerful nation for its human and natural resources, perceiving its people as inferior and unable to govern itself. The dominating nation sees its role as paternalistic, as charitable to a population incapable of self-rule. It exploits its superior status to take what it wants under the presumption that it is doing the victim nation a favor.

"The Bush administration is marinated in oil," argued consumer advocate Ralph Nader while speaking on a February 26, 2003, National Public Radio program.

> Forty-one of the top administration officials were on boards of directors, including Condoleezza Rice, of course Cheney was head of Haliburton, George Bush came out of Harken Energy. There are enormous ties.

Added Arianna Huffington in a revealing March 19 essay entitled "Corporate America Divvies Up the Post-Saddam Spoils":

> The Bush Administration is currently in the process of doling out over $1.5 billion in government contracts to American companies lining up to cash in on the rebuilding of postwar Iraq. So bombs away. The more the better—at least for the lucky few in the rebuilding business.

Imperialism is founded in media distortion and national fear. Because the aggression is clearly unjustified, the imperialist must weave a fabric of accusations, persuading its citizens that attacking and subjugating the victim nation is in their self-interest. In 2003 this was accomplished with the assistance of the events of September 11, 2001. With many U.S. citizens reeling from the unforgettable carnage, the soil was fertile for action—action that would make easy scapegoats of any country the president already wanted to attack. From that point it was easy. The goal of the Bush team—which had long eyed the untapped oil fields of Iraq—was to make a case for terrorism. With Osama bin Laden seemingly on an extended vacation, why not pursue the world's second largest oil fields? Within weeks after the 9/11 terrorist attacks, the White House was whipping up fear and blending it with hatred—all in hopes of justifying aggression against oil-rich Iraq. Nobody liked Hussein anyway, and his use as a puppet of the United States had long since passed. The temptation was just too great, and the frenzy of fear was an irresistible tonic for violence.

And so the political machine went into action. While no credible evidence linked Hussein to 9/11, the administration fomented a string of provocative allegations, sending Secretary of Defense Donald Rumsfeld and Secretary of State Colin Powell around the country with dire predictions for U.S. safety. By fall 2002, the Pew Research Center reported that two-thirds of the U.S. citizenry believed that Hussein "helped the terrorists in the September 11 attacks." Fascinatingly, this was despite the fact that, according to Norman Solomon in his book *Target Iraq,* there was unanimous agreement among U.S. spy agencies that "evidence linking Baghdad with the September 11 attacks, or any attacks against Western targets since 1993, is simply non-existent." Middle East correspondent Robert Fisk was laconic in adding, "Iraq had absolutely nothing to do with 11 September. If the United States attacks Iraq, we should remember that."

In Iraq the mantra has been along the same racist and Eurocentric lines and has included talk of the inherently violent character of Islamic people.

In the Philippines and the larger war with Spain, the propaganda war was also predicated upon lust for expansion and driven by a compliant media. Indeed, journalist William Randolph Hearst clearly wanted war and used his *New York Journal* to generate turbulence whenever he could. As in Iraq, war was simply good business. As Howard Zinn's *A People's History of the United States* reveals, Roosevelt wrote to a friend in 1897, "In strict confidence, I should welcome almost any war, for I think this country needs one." On the eve of the Spanish American War, the *Washington Post* wrote:

A new consciousness seems to have come upon us—the consciousness of strength—and with it a new appetite, the yearning to show our strength. . . . Ambition, interest, land hunger, pride, the mere joy of fighting, whatever it may be, we are animated by a new sensation. We are face to face with a strange destiny. The taste of the Empire is

in the mouth of the people even as the taste of blood in the jungle.

Today, many only know of a Spanish-American war in which the Philippines was extricated from imperialistic Spain. We hear quixotic tales about rough riders and intrepid marches. Few schools in either the Philippines or the United States discuss the disquieting details of how U.S. troops blazed a trail of destruction, killing women and children and labeling the casualties uncivilized niggers. Zinn recounts that a volunteer soldier from the state of Washington wrote, "our fighting blood was up, and we all wanted to kill niggers . . . This shooting human beings beats rabbit hunting all to pieces."

What do the words of imperialism sound like? Consider the excerpts from Senator Albert Beveridge in January 1900. In recalling the carnage of Filipinos and the laments from some that the war was rapacious and cruel, Beveridge reveals the hubris of a people who are inebriated on nationalistic fervor—a people who believe, like Bush, that Americanization is synonymous with civilization:

My own belief is that there are not 100 men among them who comprehend what Anglo-Saxon self-government even means, and there are over 5,000,000 people to be governed. It has been charged that our conduct of the war has been cruel. Senators, it has been the reverse. . . . Senators must remember that we are not dealing with Americans or Europeans. We are dealing with Orientals.

In Iraq the mantra has been along the same racist and Eurocentric lines and has included talk of the inherently violent character of Islamic people. As Bush supposedly tries to placate critics and assure citizens of his altruistic mission, others wonder about his ties to conservative Christians who have spoken in monolithic terms about Islam. The Reverend Billy Graham's son Franklin is infamous for his depiction of Islam as intrinsically evil. The man who offered prayers at Bush's inauguration was quoted in the December 12, 2001, issue of *Christian Century* depicting Islam as "wicked, violent, and not of the same God." He continued, "It wasn't Methodists flying into those buildings, and it wasn't Lutherans."

And of course, conservatives have been unabashed in their agenda to develop the oil fields that make Iraq a treasured conquest. In 1899, the United States sought the coal, sugar, coffee, hemp, and tobacco of the Philippines. Earlier it had opened the natural resources of Cuba and annexed Guam as a base for meddling in the affairs of Japan. Why not plunder the nation you are civilizing? Iraq has oil—lots of it. What better solution for a nation that drives gas-guzzling SUVs and thrives under the assumption that it has a celestial mission to bring capitalism and increased opportunity so as to benefit its corporate friends.

In the end, imperialism has a very distinctive look: it is arrayed in corporate money, driven by jingoism, and sprinkled with whiffs of patriotism and egocentrism. It looks the same today as it did a century ago—and smells just as bad.

From The Humanist, September/October 2003, pp. 22–25. Copyright © 2003 by Gregory Shafer. Reprinted by permission of the author.

UNIT 6

Global Problems, Global Interdependence

Unit Selections

Key Points to Consider

- To what extent is population growth a serious problem today? Will the situation worsen or improve in the future?

- Is global warming a problem? Is there any historical precedent that is informative?

- Are weapons of mass destruction a serious threat to world peace? If so, what could be done to remove those fears?

- How serious is Africa's AIDS crisis today? What will be its impact on human history?

- What were the similarities and differences between the Rwandan genocide of 1994 and the Nazi-inspired Jewish Holocaust of World War II? What role did religion play in both atrocities?

- How is today's terrorism different from those of the past? What role does religion play in the current one.

- How will the Middle East's future be shaped by its present generation? What impact might they have on peace in the region?

Student Web Site

www.mhcls.com/online

Internet References

Further information regarding these Websites may be found in this book's preface or online.

Africa News Web Site: Crisis in the Great Lakes Region
http://www.africanews.org/greatlakes.html
Africa Notes
http://www.csis.org/html/2africa.html
Amnesty International
http://www.amnesty.org/
Population Awareness
http://www.overpopulation.org/nav.html
Reliefweb
http://www.reliefweb.int/
Target America
http://www.pbs.org/wgbh/pages/frontline/shows/target

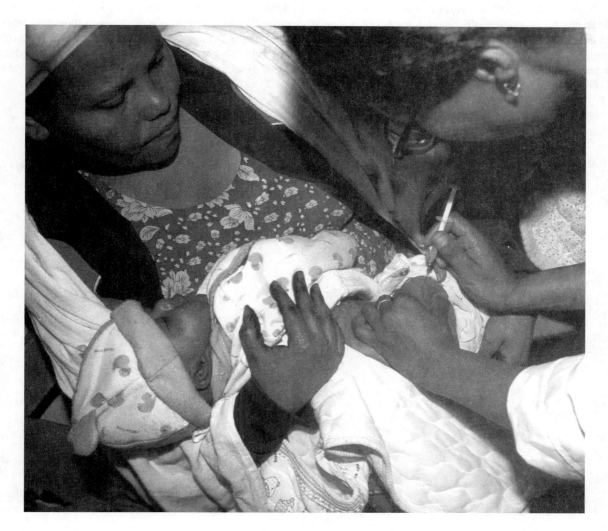

The cold war and its aftermath left many unresolved problems for a world in which every nation is linked with the welfare of others. As the Soviet Union collapsed, the landscape was revealed as an environmental shambles, with polluted air, food, and water. The countries abandoned by the former Soviet bloc are too poor to repair the damage and their recovery will probably take decades. There has also been a proliferation of knowledge about methods of mass destruction, not only nuclear weapons, but also poison gasses and infectious diseases. Almost any determined nation can manufacture these weapons, as recent threats from Iraq, Iran, and North Korea confirm. Ironically, we may look back on the cold war, when two superpowers controlled most of the weaponry, as a time of desirable simplicity.

In the background of contemporary concerns is a rapidly-increasing world population that will soon reach 6.5 billion people. Will the planet be able to sustain the projected population of 9 billion in 2050? The population of democratic India is projected to surpass that of communist China in the near future—mainly because China strictly enforces a one-child policy. Is China right to restrict its own population growth? No one knows the capacity of the planet, but shortages seem likely to occur in many areas as the world's population grows. It seems clear that all the world's peoples will share a common fate.

Population, moreover, is moving from the countryside to the cities and from farming into manufacturing and information technology. Air pollution has increased and scientists are in agreement that we are experiencing a rise in temperature that is known as global warming. Consequences are somewhat difficult to pinpoint, but the increase in violent storms as well as earthquakes and volcanic eruptions have many concerned.

Some ancient conflicts remain. One example is the Sudan, where civil war has raged for 20 years. In the Near east, terrorism keeps the flames of hatred going between Israelis and

Palestinians. In Central Africa, Uganda and Rwanda fell into warfare over which side to support in the Congo; tribal hatreds and ethnic cleansing have been the devastating results. Problems in Africa are compounded by disease, particularly HIV/AIDS, which has created more than 10 million orphans—an unprecedented humanitarian crisis.

Recent events suggest that the 21st century may be at least as challenging as the 20th century was. Some have compared the Rwandan genocide with the Nazi-perpetrated holocaust of the Jews. Large numbers of Christians were complicit in both genocides. Contemporary warfare is justified by evoking a cosmic struggle of good vs. evil, and some Islamist terrorism has its roots in an anti-secular, anti-globalism worldview that "satanizes" enemies and is willing to wait eons for the ultimate victory. While this kind of apocalyptic thinking threatens world peace, one hopeful sign is a new generation of Muslim children—half the total Islamic population—who have high economic and social expectations and may choose peace over terrorism.

Like Herrings in a Barrel

In 1,000 years, the human race has multiplied 20-fold. Today's 6 billion people may be 9 billion by 2050. Yet the increase has slowed; rich nations breed less

The power of population is so superior to the power of the earth to produce subsistence for man that premature death must in some shape or other visit the human race. The vices of mankind are active and able ministers of depopulation . . . but should they fail in this war of extermination, sickly seasons, epidemic, pestilence and plague advance in terrific array, and sweep off their thousands and ten thousands. Should success be still incomplete, gigantic, inevitable famine stalks in the rear, and with one mighty blow levels the population with the food of the world.

When Thomas Malthus, an English economist, in 1798 published his "Essay on the Principle of Population", quoted above, he caused a sensation. At the time the world's population was close to 1 billion, having risen slowly and erratically from maybe 300m at the start of the millennium; which in turn was probably not much, if at all, more than it had been in 1AD. And today? Give or take the odd 100m of us, 6 billion.

When Malthus wrote, there was no widespread sense that numbers were running out of control. The general mood was upbeat. Indeed, most thinkers considered a growing population a good thing: more people, more hands at work, more output.

A century earlier, a pioneer statistician, Gregory King, had predicted that the human race would double from its then total of around 650m in about 600 years' time, and ventured boldly:

If the world should continue to [16052AD], it might then have 6,500m.

In fact it will do so in about 2006.

By Malthus's time, a few prophets of doom had begun to give forth. Giammaria Ortes, an Italian economist, wrote in 1790 that no one wanted to see humanity grow

Not only beyond the number of persons that could breathe on the earth, but to such a number as could not be contained on all its surface, from lowest valley to highest mountain, crammed together like dried herrings in a barrel.

But Malthus's message was much more urgent than that. Some—probably unrepresentative—American figures gathered by Benjamin Franklin had persuaded him that, unless checked, most populations were likely to double every 25 years, increasing at a geometric rate (1,2,4,8,16 and so on), while food supplies

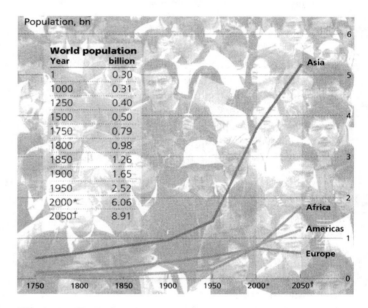

Figure 1 Exploding, but not so fast.

Sources: To 1500, J. D. Durand; from 1750, United Nations
*Forecast
†UN 'medium' forecast

World population	
Year	billion
1	0.30
1000	0.31
1250	0.40
1500	0.50
1750	0.79
1800	0.98
1850	1.26
1900	1.65
1950	2.52
2000*	6.06
2050†	8.91

would grow at only an arithmetic rate (1,2,3,4,5 and so on). Sooner or later the food was bound to run out.

Mankind had a choice: either let matters take their course, thus inviting "positive" checks—wars, plagues and famines—to reduce numbers to sustainable levels; or adopt "preventative" checks to ensure fewer children, for example by bridling passion and delaying marriage. Malthus was not optimistic that enough people would choose restraint. He himself tried to set an example by not marrying until he was 38 (and then had three children in quick succession).

Malthus was wrong in expecting populations to double every 25 years. But not far wrong: in the 200 years since he wrote, the time it takes mankind to double has shrunk from several centuries to 40 years. And he was clearly right to note that the earth's resources are finite, though he vastly underestimated man's ingenuity in utilising them more efficiently, and at making new inventions. Technology and innovation, speeded up by the industrial revolution, allowed food supplies to increase at a faster-than-arithmetical rate. Even during Malthus's lifetime, crop land was being expanded rapidly as forests were felled, and innovations such as crop rotation and selective breeding brought large increases in yields. These continue, through the "green revolution" of the 1950s to today's high-yielding, if unloved, genetically engineered crops.

What Malthus could not have predicted, since nothing like it had ever happened before and it was barely under way by his day, was something known now as the "demographic transition": the way societies alter as they get richer. First comes a decline in mortality, leading to a short population explosion; then, after an interval of variable length, a steep decline in the birth rate, which slows, halts or may even reverse the rise in numbers.

For most of human history, people had lots of children, of whom many died in infancy. If things were going well, and there were no serious wars, epidemics or famines, more would be born, more would survive longer, and populations would rise. From about 1000 to 1300, Europe enjoyed a spurt of economic growth. A lot of new land was taken into cultivation, and the number of cities multiplied. The population doubled or trebled.

Enter, in 1347, via the Mediterranean, the Black Death. Within a few years this plague had traversed the continent. By 1400 Europe's population had shrunk by maybe 25m, about one-third. Plague reappeared periodically over the next three centuries, the last big wave rolling over north-western Europe in the later 17th century, soon after the Thirty Years War, which had already slashed Germany's population. In the New World, smallpox brought by Spanish *conquistadors* and European settlers in the 16th century killed maybe 10m–20m of the native populations. Not even the 20th century has escaped such scourges: the worldwide flu of 1918–19 is thought to have caused 25m–40m deaths, far more than the first world war; and since 1980 AIDS has killed some 12m people, so far.

In pre-industrial Europe, frequent food crises also served as periodic population checks. When bad harvests pushed up the cost of grain, more people died and, while the trouble lasted, couples had fewer children. Figures from Tuscany (not alone) in the 16th–18th centuries show grain prices and mortality closely correlated. But by the 19th century the days of famine in Europe were largely over, except in Ireland, where the potato blight of 1846–47 and its side-effects may have killed a sixth of the 8m-odd people.

The Transition Begins

By the mid-19th century most of Europe was in the first stage of the demographic transition. Mortality had lessened, as wars, famines and epidemics had; local food shortages were rarer, thanks to better economic organisation and transport; public health, medical care (notably, midwifery) and the control of infectious diseases such as cholera and smallpox had improved. The population spurted, as Malthus had predicted. Between 1800 and 1900 Europe's population doubled, to over 400m, whereas that of Asia, further behind in the demographic transition, increased by less than 50%, to about 950m.

Europe by now was crowded, and most worthwhile land already under the plough. But there was space elsewhere. Thanks to a steady trickle of migration over the previous three centuries,

North and South America by 1800 each held about 4m people of European extraction. From around 1850 that trickle became a flood. Over the next 100 years or so, some 50m Europeans quit their continent, most going to North America, others to South America and the Antipodes. At the peak of this wave of emigration, Europe was exporting about a third of the natural increase in its population.

But something else was happening there that would have taken Malthus by surprise: as people came to expect to live longer, and better, they started to have fewer children. They realised they no longer needed several babies just to ensure that two or three would survive. And as they moved from country to town, they also found that children were no longer an economic asset that could be set to work at an early age, but a liability to be fed, housed and (some of them) educated, for years. Worse, with too many children, a mother would find it hard to take and keep a job, to add to the family income. Nor were offspring any longer a guarantee against a destitute old age: in the new industrial society, they were likelier to go their own way.

Thanks to Europe's new-found restraint, in the past 100 years or so its population has risen only 80%, to 730m, and most countries' birth rate is now so low that numbers are static or falling. But their composition is very different from the past: better living standards, health and health care are multiplying old heads, even as the number of young ones shrinks.

In contrast, Asia's population over the same time has nearly quadrupled, to more than 3.6 billion. North America's too has grown almost as fast, but largely thanks to immigration. Africa's has multiplied 5 1/2 times, and Latin America's nearly sevenfold.

Why these differences? From around 1950, mortality in developing countries also began to fall, and much faster than it ever had in Europe. The know-how needed to avoid premature death, especially of small children, travelled so readily that life expectancy in many poor countries is now not far behind the rich world's. But the attitudes and values that persuade people to have fewer children are taking longer to adjust.

Yet adjust they do. In China, the world's most populous country, with over 1.2 billion people, and still relatively poor, the demographic transition is already almost complete; not only has mortality come down faster than in other countries with similar income levels, but in recent decades a sometimes brutal population policy (now being relaxed a little) has restricted couples to one or two children. India's population rushed ahead for longer, and has just reached 1 billion, despite attempts to slow it, including a period in the 1970s when the government promoted large-scale sterilisation. The UN's "medium-variant" forecast is that by 2050 India's headcount may be over 1.5 billion, slightly ahead of China's. Yet in India too fertility has fallen fast. Only in Africa is population growth still rampant, though slowed by AIDS, which in some countries is killing a large proportion of the young adults.

Does More Mean Worse?

Demographers like to dramatise this recent population growth by asking a spooky question. Of all the people who have ever lived, how many are alive today? The answer requires a lot of

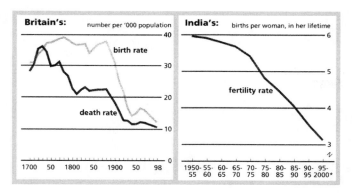

Figure 2 Birth follows death.

Sources: To 1800, various estimates; then, registrar at general. For India, United Nations.
*Forecast

guesswork, except for the very recent past; but a fair estimate for the number of people born throughout human history is 80 billion–100 billion. With mankind now numbering 6 billion, the astonishing answer must be: 6–7%. The figures are even more spectacular if you count man-years lived rather than people, because life for early man was usually short: at birth, he could expect 20 years of it in 10000BC, only 27 as late as 1750AD, and 58 today. On that reckoning, those alive today account for one-sixth of the time that humans collectively have spent on earth.

Is all this rise in numbers necessarily a bad thing? Economists have disputed endlessly: does it promote economic growth, by expanding the workforce, or, if it happens too quickly, choke growth off? Their answers seem to boil down to an unhelpful "It all depends." But then governments' population policies are not guided solely by economics. Prussia's Frederick the Great made

a sharp political point when he observed in the 18th century that "a country's wealth is the number of its men." Two centuries later, Mao Zedong insisted that "China's vast population should be viewed as a positive asset."

Of course, numbers are not the only measure. The United States, with its 275m people, has less than 5% of the planet's population, yet it dominates the other 95%. Still, in many rich countries the birth rate has now fallen so low that the population is actually shrinking; and in some their governments see this as a problem. Their main fear may be that soon there will be too few young workers around to pay for older ones' pensions. But at the back of their minds there may also be the thought that, say, a Japan of 105m people in 2050 (the UNC's medium forecast) might carry less clout than today's Japan of 125m.

Many say the globe is already overcrowded, risking environmental disasters such as global warming and pervasive pollution. Nonsense, say others: with careful management it could carry plenty more, say 10 billion. A few optimists, if that's the word, muse that, with a bit of squeezing and the astute use of technology, the figure might be several times that, maybe even 100 billion.

One thing is sure: even if from tomorrow every couple on earth practised Malthusian restraint and stopped at two children, the momentum built up by the huge population growth in developing countries since 1950 will keep numbers rising fast for decades to come; the UNC's medium forecast for 2050 is 8.9 billion people. But, fingers crossed, soon thereafter even the poorest countries may have lost their enthusiasm for large families, while couples in some richer countries may—may—have rediscovered that two children are, and have, more fun than one. A century or so from now, if mankind survives that long, its number may have reached a new (and surely better) steady state.

The Weather Turns Wild

Global warming could cause droughts, disease, and political upheaval

NANCY SHUTE

The people of Atlanta can be forgiven for not worrying about global warming as they shivered in the dark last January, their city crippled by a monster ice storm that hit just before the Super Bowl. So can the 15 families in Hilo, Hawaii, whose houses were washed away by the 27 inches of rain that fell in 24 hours last November. And the FBI agents who searched for evidence blown out of their downtown Fort Worth office building, which was destroyed by a tornado last March. Not to mention the baffled residents of Barrow, Alaska, who flooded the local weather office with calls on June 19, as rumbling black clouds descended—a rare Arctic thunderstorm.

But such bizarre weather could soon become more common, and the consequences far more dire, according to a United Nations scientific panel. Last week, the Intergovernmental Panel on Climate Change met in Shanghai and officially released the most definitive—and scary—report yet, declaring that global warming is not only real but man-made. The decade of the '90s was the warmest on record, and most of the rise was likely caused by the burning of oil, coal, and other fuels that release carbon dioxide, as well as other so-called greenhouse gases. What's more, future changes will be twice as severe as predicted just five years ago, the group says. Over the next 100 years, temperatures are projected to rise by 2.5 to 10.4 degrees worldwide, enough to spark floods, epidemics, and millions of "environmental refugees."

By midcentury, the chic Art Deco hotels that now line Miami's South Beach could stand waterlogged and abandoned. Malaria could be a public health threat in Vermont. Nebraska farmers could abandon their fields for lack of water. Outside the United States, the impact would be much more severe. Rising sea levels could contaminate the aquifers that supply drinking water for Caribbean islands, while entire Pacific island nations could simply disappear under the sea. Perhaps the hardest-hit country would be Bangladesh, where thousands of people already die from floods each year. Increased snowmelt in the Himalayas could combine with rising seas to make at least 10 percent of the country uninhabitable. The water level of most of Africa's largest rivers, including the Nile, could plunge, triggering widespread crop failure and idling hydroelectric plants. Higher temperatures and lower rainfall could stunt food production in Mexico and other parts of Latin America.

No more words. "The debate is over," says Peter Gleick, president of the Pacific Institute for Studies in Development, Environment, and Security, in Oakland, Calif. "No matter what we do to reduce greenhouse-gas emissions, we will not be able to avoid some impacts of climate change."

This newest global-warming forecast is backed by data from myriad satellites, weather balloons, ships at sea, and weather stations, and by immense computer models of the global climate system. As scientists have moved toward consensus on warming's inevitability, there has been growing movement to come up with realistic adaptations to blunt the expected effects. Instead of casting blame at polluting SUV drivers, environmentalists and businesses alike are working to create feasible solutions. These range from measures as complex as global carbon-dioxide-emissions taxes to ones as simple as caulking leaks in Russian and Chinese natural gas pipelines. The take-home message: Change is difficult but not impossible, and the sooner we start, the easier it will be. Civilization has adjusted to drastic weather changes in the past (see box, "Weathering the storms") and is well positioned to do so again. Indeed, while governments squabble over what is to be done, major corporations such as BP Amoco and DuPont are retooling operations to reduce greenhouse gases. "I am very, very optimistic," says Robert Watson, an atmospheric scientist, World Bank official, and leader of the IPCC panel that created the report.

Concern about greenhouse gases is hardly new; as early as the 1700s, scientists were wondering whether atmospheric gases could transmit light but trap heat, much like glass in a greenhouse. By 1860, Irish physicist John Tyndall (the first man to explain why the sky is blue) suggested that ice ages follow a decrease in carbon dioxide. In 1957, Roger Revelle, a researcher at the Scripps Institution of Oceanography in California, declared that human alteration of the climate amounted to a "large-scale geophysical experiment" with potentially vast consequences.

Such dire predictions had been made before and not come true, and this environmental hysteria emboldened skeptics. But by 1988, the evidence was hard to rebut; when NASA atmospheric scientist James Hansen told a congressional hearing

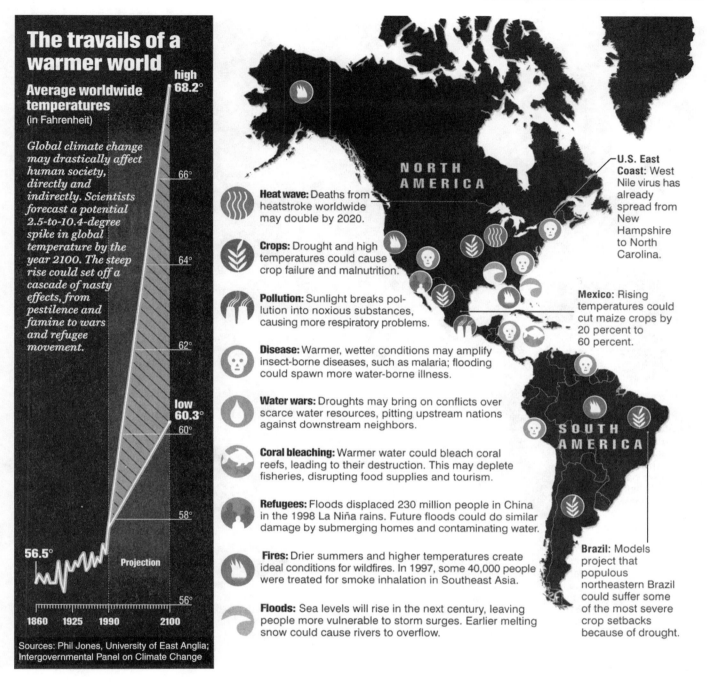

The travails of a warmer world

Average worldwide temperatures
(in Fahrenheit)

Global climate change may drastically affect human society, directly and indirectly. Scientists forecast a potential 2.5-to-10.4-degree spike in global temperature by the year 2100. The steep rise could set off a cascade of nasty effects, from pestilence and famine to wars and refugee movement.

high 68.2°

66°

64°

62°

low 60.3°
60°

58°

56.5°   Projection

56°

1860   1925   1990   2100

Sources: Phil Jones, University of East Anglia; Intergovernmental Panel on Climate Change

Heat wave: Deaths from heatstroke worldwide may double by 2020.

Crops: Drought and high temperatures could cause crop failure and malnutrition.

Pollution: Sunlight breaks pollution into noxious substances, causing more respiratory problems.

Disease: Warmer, wetter conditions may amplify insect-borne diseases, such as malaria; flooding could spawn more water-borne illness.

Water wars: Droughts may bring on conflicts over scarce water resources, pitting upstream nations against downstream neighbors.

Coral bleaching: Warmer water could bleach coral reefs, leading to their destruction. This may deplete fisheries, disrupting food supplies and tourism.

Refugees: Floods displaced 230 million people in China in the 1998 La Niña rains. Future floods could do similar damage by submerging homes and contaminating water.

Fires: Drier summers and higher temperatures create ideal conditions for wildfires. In 1997, some 40,000 people were treated for smoke inhalation in Southeast Asia.

Floods: Sea levels will rise in the next century, leaving people more vulnerable to storm surges. Earlier melting snow could cause rivers to overflow.

NORTH AMERICA

SOUTH AMERICA

U.S. East Coast: West Nile virus has already spread from New Hampshire to North Carolina.

Mexico: Rising temperatures could cut maize crops by 20 percent to 60 percent.

Brazil: Models project that populous northeastern Brazil could suffer some of the most severe crop setbacks because of drought.

Figure 1

(Graphic continued next page)

Reporting by Rachel K. Sobel and Kevin Whitelaw

Sources: National Center for Atmospheric Research, University of Virginia, Worldwatch Institute, National Climatic Data Center, World Meteorological Organization, and staff reports

Note: Rod Little, Rob Cady, and Stephen Rountree—*USN&WR*

---

that global warming had arrived, climate change became a hot political topic. At the 1992 Rio de Janeiro Earth Summit, 155 nations, including the United States, signed a treaty to control greenhouse emissions, which also include other gases such as methane. That accord led to the 1997 Kyoto protocol calling for reducing emissions of developed nations below 1990 levels but placing no emissions restrictions on China and other developing nations. In November, talks over the treaty broke down over the issue of how to measure nations' progress in reducing

emissions. They are set to resume by midyear, after the Bush administration has formulated its position.

Doubters remain. Some argue that climate is too chaotic and complex to trust to any computerized prediction, or that Earth's climate is too stable to be greatly upset by a little more CO_2. "I don't see how the IPCC can say it's going to warm for sure," says Craig Idso, a climatologist and vice president of the Center for the Study of Carbon Dioxide and Global Change in Tempe, Ariz. He calls predictions of drastic warming "a sheer guess"

Marshall Islands, Tuvalu, Kiribati: Swelling oceans could cover these islands, forcing residents to evacuate.

Nigeria: A 3-foot rise in sea level could displace almost 4 million people and leave parts of the capital city, Lagos, underwater.

Bangladesh: Faster melting snowpacks in the Himalayas, rising sea levels, and cholera outbreaks could force millions from their homes.

South Africa: Malaria may surge in areas previously too cold for mosquitoes to inhabit.

Zimbabwe: River flow along the Zambezi could fall steeply, disrupting crop production and possibly producing refugees.

Australia: The Great Barrier Reef could be ruined as a tourist attraction if the water temperature increases by a mere 3.6 degrees.

Figure 1 (continued)

and says that extra carbon dioxide "is going to be nothing but a boon for the biosphere. Plants will grow like gangbusters."

But these skeptics appear to be losing ground. "There are fewer and fewer of them every year," says William Kellogg, former president of the American Meteorological Society and a retired senior scientist at the National Center for Atmospheric Research. "There are very few people in the serious meteorological community who doubt that the warming is taking place."

If the majority view holds up and temperatures keep rising, over the next century global weather patterns will shift enough to affect everyday life on every continent. The effects would vary wildly from one place to the next; what might be good news for one region (warmer winters in Fairbanks, Alaska) would be

bad news for another (more avalanches in the Alps). Weather would become more unpredictable and violent, with thunderstorms sparking increased tornadoes and lightning, a major cause of fires. The effects of El Niño, the atmospheric oscillation that causes flooding and mudslides in California and the tropics, would become more severe. Natural disasters already cost plenty; in the 1990s the tab was $608 billion, more than the four previous decades combined, according to Worldwatch Institute. The IPCC will release its tally of anticipated effects on climate and societies on February 19 in Geneva. Key climate scientists say that major points include:

Death and pestilence. Cities in the Northern Hemisphere would very likely become hotter, prompting more deaths from

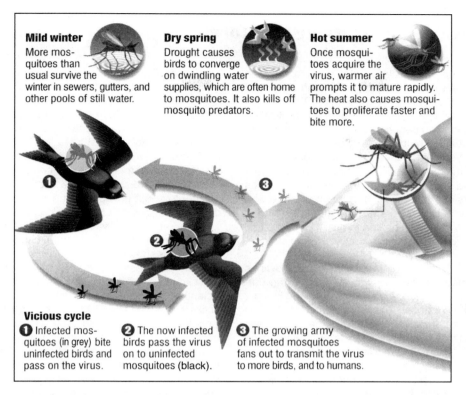

Mild winter
More mosquitoes than usual survive the winter in sewers, gutters, and other pools of still water.

Dry spring
Drought causes birds to converge on dwindling water supplies, which are often home to mosquitoes. It also kills off mosquito predators.

Hot summer
Once mosquitoes acquire the virus, warmer air prompts it to mature rapidly. The heat also causes mosquitoes to proliferate faster and bite more.

Vicious cycle
❶ Infected mosquitoes (in grey) bite uninfected birds and pass on the virus.

❷ The now infected birds pass the virus on to uninfected mosquitoes (black).

❸ The growing army of infected mosquitoes fans out to transmit the virus to more birds, and to humans.

Figure 2 Mercury rising: droughts and fevers. Cycles of extreme weather, likely caused by global warming, may have helped fuel the spread of West Nile virus in North America by boosting the mosquito population.

Source: Robert Kemp—*USN&WR*

heatstroke in cities such as Chicago and Shanghai. Deaths would also increase from natural disasters, and warmer weather would affect transmission of insect-borne diseases such as malaria and West Nile virus, which made a surprise arrival in the United States in 1999. "We don't know exactly how West Nile was introduced to the U.S., but we do know that drought, warm winter, and heat waves are the conditions that help amplify it," says Paul Epstein, a researcher at Harvard's School of Public Health (see box, "Mercury Rising").

Wildfires. Rising temperatures and declining rainfall would dry out vegetation, making wildfires like last summer's—which burned nearly 7 million acres in the West and cost $1.65 billion—more common, especially in California, New Mexico, and Florida.

Rain and flooding. Rain would become more frequent and intense in the Northern Hemisphere. Snow would melt faster and earlier in the Rockies and the Himalayas, exacerbating spring flooding and leaving summers drier. "This is the opposite of what we want," says Gleick. "We want to be able to save that water for dry periods."

Rising sea levels. Sea level worldwide has risen 9 inches in the last century, and 46 million people live at risk of flooding due to storm surges. That figure would double if oceans rise 20 inches. The IPCC predicts that seas will rise anywhere from 3.5 inches to 34.6 inches by 2010, largely because of "thermal expansion" (warmer water takes up more space), but also because of melting glaciers and ice caps. A 3-foot rise, at the

top range of the forecast, would swamp parts of major cities and islands, including the Marshall Islands in the South Pacific and the Florida Keys.

Water wars. Drought—and an accompanying lack of water—would be the most obvious consequence of warmer temperatures. By 2015, 3 billion people will be living in areas without enough water. The already water-starved Middle East could become the center of conflicts, even war, over water access. Turkey has already diverted water from the Tigris and Euphrates rivers with dams and irrigation systems, leaving downstream countries like Iraq and Syria complaining about low river levels. By 2050, such downstream nations could be left without enough water for drinking and irrigation.

Refugees. The United States is the single largest generator of greenhouse gases, contributing one quarter of the global total. But it, and other higher-latitude countries, would be affected less by climate change than would more tropical nations. The developing world will be hit hardest—and least able to cope. "Bangladesh has no prayer," says Stephen Schneider, a climatologist at Stanford University, noting that flooding there, and in Southeast Asia and China, could dislocate millions of people. "The rich will get richer, and the poor will get poorer. That's not a stable situation for the world."

Those daunted by this roster of afflictions will be cheered, a bit, by the United Nations group's report on how to fend off these perils, which will be released March 5 in Ghana. Not only is humanity not helpless in the face of global warming, but we

History Lessons: Weathering the storms

It was a pretty good run as societies go: over a millennium with all the material wealth, political organization, and advanced arts and learning that the word *society* implies. Then, at the dawn of the 10th century A.D., the Classic Maya civilization abruptly imploded, leaving deserted cities, trade routes, and pyramids throughout the southern Yucatán.

Three hundred years later, a very different story unfolded on California's Channel Islands. The Chumash people there rapidly transformed themselves from scattered populations of hunter-gatherers into a sophisticated trading culture with clear political leadership and an areawide monopoly on the production of trading beads. The connection? Both groups, climate reconstructions show, were confronted with sudden, dramatic, and long-lasting climate change.

It may be our fault this time around, but climate swings have always affected human societies. Writing in the current issue of the journal *Science*, Yale archaeologist Harvey Weiss cites more than a dozen examples of ancient cultures collapsing in the face of rapidly altered weather. Bad news for a society facing massive global change. But perhaps we can learn something from the Chumash, who, says University of California–Los Angeles archaeologist Jeanne Arnold, "came up with creative political and economic responses to their changing environment." Prospective survivors of climate upheaval, in other words, should be flexible and must be wary of leaders who are overly occupied with building monuments, getting re-elected, and other such trivialities.

Choices. "Different cultures have different philosophies about things like making changes," says Brian Fagan, a University of California–Santa Barbara archaeologist. In his forthcoming book, *The Little Ice Age,* Fagan details how various European nations dealt with that unusually cool period, which stretched from 1300 to 1850. The French endured famine, disease, and general wretchedness when cold, wet weather spoiled their traditional cereal crops year after year. The Dutch suffered the same miserable weather but were quicker to adopt new crops and intensive farming methods, perhaps, suggests Fagan, sparking the development of mature market economies.

Confronting massive climate change is never easy—excavations show evidence of dislocation and violence during the Chumash restructuring. But the record at least suggests that climate is not necessarily destiny. Fast-forward to 2001. Scientists tell us we have the technology to adapt, and unlike the Akkadians of Mesopotamia (done in by drought, circa 2290 B.C.) or the Peruvian Moche civilization (drought backed by floods some three millenniums later), we have advance notice that trouble's coming. All we need then is the flexibility of the Dutch and the political will of the Chumash. Will we find them? That's one for the historians in a couple of hundred years. If there are any of them left.

—Thomas Hayden

may not even have to give up all the trappings of a First World lifestyle in order to survive—and prosper.

The first question is whether it's possible to slow, or even halt, the rise in greenhouse gases in the atmosphere. Scientists and energy policy experts say yes, unequivocally. Much of the needed technology either has already been developed or is in the works. The first step is so simple it's known to every third grader: Conserve energy. Over the past few decades, innovations from higher gas mileage to more efficient refrigerators to compact fluorescent lights have saved billions of kilowatts of energy. The second step is to use less oil and coal, which produce greenhouse gases, and rely more on cleaner energy sources such as natural gas and wind, and later on, solar and hydrogen. In Denmark, 13 percent of electricity now comes from wind power, probably the most economical alternative source. In Britain, a company called Wavegen recently activated the first commercial ocean-wave-energy generator, making enough electricity to power about 400 homes.

Taxing ideas. But despite such promising experiments, fossil fuels remain far cheaper than the alternatives. To reduce this cost advantage, most Western European countries, including Sweden, Norway, the Netherlands, Austria, and Italy, have levied taxes on carbon emissions or fossil fuels. The taxes also are intended to nudge utilities toward technologies, like coal gasification, that burn fossil fuels more cleanly. In Germany, where "eco-taxes" are being phased in on most fossil fuels, a new carbon levy will add almost 11 cents to the price of a gallon of gasoline.

But the United States has always shunned a carbon tax. John Holdren, a professor of environmental policy at Harvard's Kennedy School of Government, says such a tax could stimulate economic growth and help position the United States as a leader in energy technology. "The energy technology sector is worth $300 billion a year, and it'll be $500 to $600 billion by 2010," Holdren says. "The companies and countries that get the biggest chunk of that will be the ones that deliver efficient, clean, inexpensive energy."

A growing number of companies have already figured that out. One of the most advanced large corporations is chemical giant DuPont, which first acknowledged the problem of climate change in 1991. Throughout the past decade, the company worked to cut its carbon dioxide emissions 45 percent from 1990 levels. Last year, it pledged to find at least 10 percent of its energy from renewable sources.

Even more surprising was the dramatic announcement by oil giant BP in 1997 agreeing that climate change was indeed occurring. Even with other oil firms protesting that the evidence was too thin, BP pledged to reduce its greenhouse-gas emissions by 10 percent from 1990 levels by 2010. At the same time, BP Amoco is pouring money into natural gas exploration and investing in renewable energy like solar power and hydrogen.

Even America's largest coal-burning utility company is experimenting. American Electric Power of Columbus, Ohio, is testing "carbon capture," which would separate out carbon dioxide emissions and dispose of them in deep underground saline aquifers, effectively creating carbon-emission-free coal power. Application is at least a decade away. "If we're able to find creative solutions, they're going to place us at a competitive advantage in our industry," says Dale Heydlauff, AEP's senior vice president for environmental affairs.

In automobile manufacturing, there is already a race on for alternatives to fossil fuels. Several automakers like Ford, DaimlerChrysler, and Volkswagen have developed prototypes of cars run by hydrogen fuel cells rather than gasoline. The performance is very similar to that of today's cars, but the cost remains, for now, prohibitive. Fuel-cell vehicles are unlikely to be mass-produced until after 2010, and even then, people will need a push to make the switch. "Climate change is too diffuse to focus people's attention," says C. E. Thomas, a vice president at Directed Technologies, an Arlington, Va., engineering firm working on fuel cells. "But if we have another war in the Middle East or gasoline lines, that will get their attention."

Even with these efforts, and many more, climatologists point out that turning the atmosphere around is much harder than turning a supertanker. Indeed, atmospheric changes already underway may take hundreds of years to change. As a result, some vulnerable countries are already taking preventive, if costly, measures. More than half of the Netherlands lies below sea level and would be threatened by increased storm surges. Last December, the Dutch government outlined an ambitious plan to bolster the sea defenses. Over the next decade, the Netherlands will spend more than $1 billion to build new dikes, bolster the natural sand dunes, and widen and deepen rivers enough to protect the country against a 3-foot rise in ocean levels.

Some of the most successful adaptations to climate change probably won't involve high-tech gizmos or global taxes. They'll be as simple as the strips of cloth distributed to women in Bangladesh, which they use to screen cholera-causing microbes from water. Villages where women strained water have reduced cholera cases by 50 percent.

"Society is more robust than we give it credit for," says Michael Glantz, a political scientist at the National Center for Atmospheric Research. Like farmers who gradually change to new crops as wells grow dry, people may learn to live comfortably in a new, warmer world.

With reporting by Thomas Hayden, Charles W. Petit, Rachel K. Sobel, Kevin Whitelaw, and David Whitman.

Bombs, Gas and Microbes

The Desperate Efforts to Block the Road to Doomsday

India and Pakistan have reawakened the world to the dangers of nuclear weapons. Chemical and biological ones may be just as hard to control

It did not need the nuclear tests conducted last month by India and Pakistan to show that the nuclear age, which has dominated the second half of this century, is destined for a longer half-life than many had begun to hope. Indeed, almost a decade since the cold war ended and the threat of nuclear Armageddon that had hung over the world for more than 40 years was supposedly lifted, fears about the spread of weapons of mass destruction—nuclear, chemical and biological weapons and the missiles to deliver them—have, if anything, intensified.

Such fears are not irrational. The collapse of the otherwise unlamented Soviet Union brought with it the danger that ex-Soviet weapons scientists might start to hawk their skills abroad—as some have. In any event, the secrets of building nuclear and chemical weapons are now decades old and increasingly hard to keep. Moreover, regional rivalries that used to be bottled up by America and the Soviet Union lest they led to a superpower confrontation are bottled up no longer. The rivalry between India and Pakistan had long driven a slow-motion arms race, in both missile and nuclear technology, before last month's tit-for-tat testing of bombs. Other potential flashpoints include the Korean peninsula and the Middle East, where tensions between Israel and its Arab neighbours are rising as hopes for peace collapse.

As India and Pakistan have proved, such regional pressures to proliferate should not be underestimated. Yet so far only a few countries have actually crossed the threshold to build weapons of mass destruction. One reason is general abhorrence of their use. The destruction visited on Hiroshima and Nagasaki in 1945 ensured that nuclear weapons were from then on held in reserve as a deterrent, rather than used as weapons for waging war. Similarly, most countries have ruled out the use of chemical weapons as too nasty for the battlefield (though Iraq has already proved one exception, both in its war with Iran and in its determination to suppress its own Kurdish population). Biological weapons—less useful in the heat of the battle, as their awful effects may take several days to appear—have likewise been stigmatised.

Restraint, however, has not rested entirely on moral injunctions. As important in halting the spread of the horrible new weapons have been arms-control regimes. These work by raising the technical barriers and the costs to would-be proliferators. The question raised by the decisions of India and Pakistan to step across the nuclear threshold, however, is whether such regimes can really work.

The most intensive efforts have gone into controlling nuclear weapons. The Nuclear Non-Proliferation Treaty (NPT), which came into force in 1970 and was extended indefinitely in 1995, divides the world into two groups: the five nuclear haves (America, Russia, China, Britain and France, which had tested a nuclear weapon before January 1st 1967) and the rest. The haves promise to work towards nuclear disarmament, as part of an effort towards general and complete disarmament, and the have-nots promise not to acquire nuclear weapons of their own, in return for help with their civilian nuclear industry.

Is it a fair bargain? It is certainly one freely entered into by the 186 states that have signed the treaty: only India, Pakistan, Israel, Brazil and Cuba still sit outside.

In its near-universality, the NPT is one of the most successful arms-control regimes on record. Its system of obligations and checks has persuaded many countries that could have built nuclear weapons not to do so. In the 1980s Argentina and Brazil used the monitoring help and methods of the International Atomic Energy Agency (IAEA), the NPT's watchdog, when they decided to roll back their competing nuclear-weapons programmes. In 1993 South Africa announced that it had built, then dismantled, six nuclear devices before it joined the NPT in 1991—and then invited the IAEA in to check its nuclear records.

Yet the NPT regime at one point nearly collapsed under the burden of its own complacency. After the Gulf war ended in 1991, it emerged that Iraq, which had signed the treaty, had secretly come within a year or two of building itself a bomb, despite regular IAEA inspections. Since the hardest part of building a bomb is getting hold of the highly enriched uranium or plutonium for its explosive core, the inspectors had been spending most of their time—at the behest of member governments—simply accounting for the nuclear material that was known to exist (because countries had declared they had made it). After Iraq had shown up the flaws in that cosy system of checking, and IAEA inspectors had caught North Korea telling lies about exactly how much plutonium it had produced, the

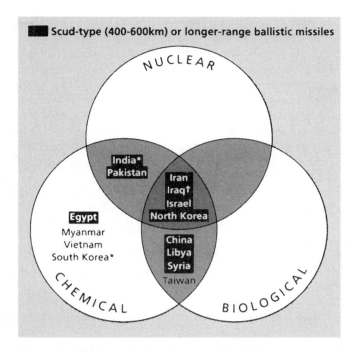

Figure 1 Circles of fear.   Asia and Middle East: suspected programmes of weapons of mass destruction.

Source: US Congress, updated by *The Economist*.

*Declared chemical weapons, subject to verification
†Subject to special UN inspection regime

agency was asked to devise a new, far more intrusive inspection system that would do more to deter cheats.

Under the new rules, inspectors have to be given much more information about nuclear activities and facilities in a country—and not just those where nuclear fuel is present; countries are also required to pass on more information about their trade in sensitive nuclear materials; and inspectors can use much more sophisticated equipment and sampling, including environmental monitoring, to ensure that no secret nuclear activity is taking place. The new protocol to the NPT incorporating the extra powers required came into force in 1997. It is not binding on a country unless that country has explicitly accepted it, and so far only a handful have.

Alongside the NPT and the work of the IAEA, there are two groups that seek to prohibit or control trade in sensitive nuclear technologies. The Zangger Committee is made up of 33 nuclear-exporting countries and provides a list to the IAEA of items which, if exported to an NPT member, should trigger the application of IAEA safeguards; the group also exchanges confidential information on exports to countries that are outside the treaty. The Nuclear Suppliers' Group has a slightly larger membership and operates a code that goes beyond strict NPT obligations, laying down rules about trade in nuclear exports, including any that could be used for either civilian or military purposes.

However, most recent efforts to control nuclear proliferation have concentrated on bringing into force the Comprehensive Test-Ban Treaty that was opened for signature in 1996, and on negotiating a new treaty to cut off the production of fissile material for bomb making. Both treaties are seen as crucial if support for the NPT among the non-nuclear states is not to waver. Yet neither will be easy to achieve.

Although 149 countries have put their signatures to a ban on tests, only 13 have fully ratified the treaty. Yet, to ensure that a test ban is truly comprehensive, the treaty cannot come fully into force until ratified at least by all 44 countries that have nuclear reactors on their territory. These include both India and Pakistan, neither of which has signed the test ban, but also other countries, such as Israel (which has signed but not ratified it) and North Korea (which shows no sign of doing either). Assuming the treaty is still in limbo, its members will meet next year to decide how to proceed. One possibility would be to try to bring the proposed monitoring and information-gathering system into effect, as a confidence-building step, before the treaty itself comes legally into force.

Neither a test ban nor a fissile-materials cut-off treaty (which has a lot of support but has been caught up in bickering at the United Nations Conference on Disarmament in Geneva) would actually oblige countries that have nuclear weapons to abandon them. However, each in its own way would help to cap the ability of those with nuclear weapons to keep building more such weapons and testing ever more sophisticated designs.

Confounded Chemicals

The guardians of the Chemical Weapons Convention (CWC), which came into force just over a year ago, have in many ways an even harder task. Whereas it takes a lot of deliberate and nowadays increasingly noticeable effort to build up a nuclear-weapons capability, many countries have sizeable chemicals industries. Moreover, many chemicals with humdrum civilian uses can be combined to make deadly weapons.

For many years, it was against international law to use chemical weapons, but not to manufacture or stockpile them. The CWC, by contrast, outlaws all chemical weapons and requires the destruction of all stockpiles. It also bans trade in some chemicals and restricts it in others (non-signatories will find it increasingly difficult to buy chemicals from CWC members). Within 30 days of signing the convention, governments must give an account of the chemicals industry on their territory, with declarations subject to inspection, including short-notice "anywhere, anytime" checks. And, unlike the NPT's rules, the CWC's apply equally to all.

Already the convention has had its successes. Among the handful of countries that declared a chemical-weapons stockpile, which must now be destroyed under the supervision of the Organisation for the Prohibition of Chemical Weapons (OPCW), were India and South Korea, neither of which had previously admitted to having a chemical-weapons programme. France and China, which had both previously had chemical-weapons programmes, said they destroyed their weapons shortly before signing the convention (those claims are subject to verification by OPCW inspectors). America and Russia, with the world's biggest stockpiles of chemical weapons (33,000 tonnes and 40,000 tonnes of them respectively), are destroying theirs, although Russia, which has only just started, is desperately short of funds for the job.

In their first year the OPCW's inspectors set a furious pace, with over 200 inspections in 25 countries, checking both on the destruction of weapons stocks and on the accuracy of industrial declarations. The danger, to some of the convention's critics, is that all this could prove ineffectively costly—with inspectors spending too much time on official declarations and too little ferreting out illicit activity.

The convention's chief deterrent power against cheats is the right to carry out short-notice challenge inspections, but none has yet been tried. That is in part because many countries are still in "technical non-compliance", taking an age to pass the national legislation and work through the bureaucratic procedures necessary to collect the industrial information that the convention demands. Governments with these problems are reluctant to challenge information supplied by others, however dubious it looks (Pakistan, Iran and some countries in the Balkans were thought to have chemical-weapons programmes but have not declared any), until they have their own house in order. But challenge inspections have to be shown to be possible if they are to have their intended deterrent effect. The real strength of the convention has therefore yet to be shown.

Other problems loom: barely noticed in the recent furore over the Indian and Pakistani nuclear testing, the American Senate last month attached amendments to enabling legislation that, if allowed to stand, would give the president the right to refuse challenge inspections. Many countries are uneasy about such inspections, which they fear might enable others to walk off with their commercial secrets. But for America to give itself the right to block them, contrary to the convention it has already ratified, sets a bad precedent that others might seek to exploit for sinister purposes.

Another big problem is the number of hold-outs. So far a gratifying 168 countries have signed and 110 have ratified the convention. But the CWC's most obvious bald spot, the Middle East, is also a region of serious concern about proliferation: though Israel and Jordan have signed the convention, they are still to ratify it, and so are not yet bound by the reporting and inspection regime. Meanwhile, most other Arab states, led by Egypt, have refused to sign, citing Israel's refusal to sign the NPT.

Devilish Brew

If searching out hidden chemical weapons is like looking for a needle in a haystack, trying to track a hidden biological-weapons programme is like looking for the eye of a needle in a haystack. In theory it takes only a tiny amount of a biological agent, such as botulinum, anthrax or plague, to spread destruction on a vast scale (making biological weapons closer to nuclear weapons in their potential effects). Luckily, turning biological agents into usable weapons is not always easy.

So far more than 130 countries have ratified the 1972 Biological and Toxins Weapons Convention (BWC), which prohibits development and production of such weapons (their use has been outlawed since 1925). But as yet the convention has no built-in checks. Groups of experts have been trying for several years to devise a new verification protocol, but it is difficult to strike a balance between useful checks and the need for biotech companies to preserve their legitimate commercial secrets.

Even more so than chemical inspections, biological ones would need to rely heavily on the right to carry out sudden searches to investigate suspicious activity or unusual outbreaks of disease.

But if the biological-weapons convention has survived this long without such weapons being used, why worry? One reason is that, like any other arms-control regime, unless it is seen to be enforced it will fall into disrepute. What is more, as other proliferation loopholes are plugged, biological weapons, which are easier to make than nuclear weapons and more destructive than chemical ones, may become the weapon of choice for rogue governments or terrorist groups.

In 1992 Russia, one of the sponsoring governments for the convention, admitted that in the past it had illegally built biological weapons. Although it now claims to have abandoned the programme, not everyone is convinced. Aum Shinrikyo, the Japanese sect that released a nerve gas, sarin, on the Tokyo metro in 1995, killing a dozen people, is now known to have experimented with biological agents too, which it attempted to spray from rooftops and trucks both in central Tokyo and near American military bases in Japan. None of the experiments appears to have worked.

But it was Iraq's industrial-sized biological-weapons programme, uncovered by UN inspectors after the Gulf war, that injected the new urgency into efforts to bolster the BWC. After repeated denials, Iraq eventually confessed to producing biological weapons. Some biological agents had even been loaded into missile warheads and artillery shells ready for use against American and allied troops. Although inspectors have since uncovered many of the details of the programme, Iraq has still failed to account for several tonnes of the medium used for growing microbes and other specialised materials. The fear is that Iraq could restart production of anthrax and other substances within weeks unless the inspectors are allowed to complete their job.

Iraq and other countries suspected of trying to develop biological weapons often got their start in the business by ordering toxic microbes from western germ banks, ostensibly for the development of vaccines and suchlike. This has added to calls for much tighter controls. At the moment trade in such substances is monitored only by the Australia Group, an informal body of more than 20 supplier countries formed in 1985 to harmonise export controls on chemicals that could be used to produce either chemical or biological weapons.

Range of Possibilities

But even if a verification protocol is eventually bolted on to the BWC, some governments are getting nervous about the threat from biological weapons, which can be distributed by anything from crop-spraying aircraft to aerosol canister. America is considering the stockpiling of vaccines for use in the event of a biological threat against civilians (vaccines are already available for American troops).

Usually, however, the quickest way to deliver a bomb, and the one that is hardest to defend against, is by missile. The Missile Technology Control Regime (MTCR) was set up in 1987 in an attempt to restrict the sales of equipment and technology for missiles with a range (300 kilometres, or 190 miles) and payload (500kg, or 1,100lb) that would enable them to carry nuclear warheads. Export guidelines were later extended to cover missiles capable of carrying any type of weapon of mass destruction. The MTCR now has some 30 members.

But the controls are far from perfect. Russia is a member of the MTCR, but Russian companies have long been accused of supplying technology and know-how to anyone who will pay for it, most recently Iran, which is thought to be trying to build a new missile with a range of up to 1,300km, capable of striking Israel, Saudi Arabia and Turkey. China, a major exporter of missile technology in the past, has said it will keep to the basic guidelines of the MTCR, but refuses to join it. It has been repeatedly criticised by America for providing missiles and know-how to others, including Pakistan. Other hard cases include Iraq (which is banned by UN rules from building missiles of more than 150km range but has been caught trying to circumvent the restrictions), Libya, Syria and North Korea.

Both Iran and Pakistan are thought to have benefited from North Korea's missile programme to develop longer-range missiles.

The spread of weapons technologies seems inexorable. The best protection is to persuade countries to forgo particularly dangerous technologies in their own interests. Both India and Pakistan may find that, once the euphoria over their demonstrated nuclear prowess has faded, their security is not improved, indeed may even be worsened, by having—and facing—powerful new weapons loaded on missiles that bring a hair-trigger instability to any future crisis.

In the end, getting at the roots of regional disputes is the only sure way to reduce the danger of a hideously lethal exchange. Arms-control regimes can help by building confidence that obligations not to build or to deploy certain deadly weapons are being kept. Yet such regimes are only as strong as the will of those whose task it is to enforce them. It is the hard cases that will test the world's resolve to prevent the further spread of nuclear, chemical or biological weapons. India and Pakistan are the latest of these. They will not be the last.

10 Million Orphans

For the children who have lost their parents to AIDS, grief is only the beginning of their troubles. The disease's lasting victims.

TOM MASLAND AND ROD NORDLAND

Even on the mean streets of Homa Bay, a fishing center of 750,000 on Lake Victoria, the children stand out: Kenya has 350,000 AIDS orphans, and 35,000 of them live here. Many of those who have not been forcibly removed to the orphanage are street children—pickpockets and beggars, prostitutes and thieves. To Hamis Otieno, 14, and his brother, Rashid Faraji, 10, the streets of Homa Bay were their last, best hope. Their father had died of AIDS in 1995; their mother turned to prostitution and abandoned them soon after. Relatives, unable to provide for the boys, cast them out. The brothers made their way by bus to Nairobi, 150 miles away, where they stole, begged and worked as drug couriers. But after a year, hungry and alone, the boys went home; hustling promised to be easier on the less competitive streets of Homa Bay. Soon after their arrival, however, they caught what in their world counts as a break: they were picked up and taken by force to an orphanage. There, every one of the children is an AIDS orphan. But then, that is hardly surprising: in Homa Bay, some 50 to 70 percent of the adults are HIV-positive. "So many have died," says Hamis, "so many."

In the nations south of the Sahara, almost two decades of AIDS deaths—2.2 million in 1998 alone, and a still untallied but certainly greater number in 1999—is leaving a sea of orphans in its wake. By the end of this year, 10.4 million of the children under 15 will have lost their mothers or both parents to AIDS. Before the current epidemic, the perennial cataclysms of war and famine orphaned 2 percent of the region's children; AIDS makes that figure look benign. A generation of orphans threatens to undermine economic development, for children without parents can seldom afford education. And many AIDS orphans end up "roaming the streets, prime targets for gangs [and] militia and creating more child armies like those that participated in massacres in West Africa," says Dr. Peter Piot, executive director of UNAIDS. But worse lies ahead. The number of AIDS orphans in the region is projected to double or triple by 2010.

It is not only the raw numbers that make this orphan crisis unlike any ever seen. The children, who have often watched their parents die alone and in pain, are left in a world where AIDS has unraveled such traditional safety nets as the extended family, and in households where not a single adult is able to earn a living. Josephine Ssenyonga, 69, lives on a small farm in the Rakai district of Uganda, where AIDS has been cutting through the population like a malevolent scythe for 14 years: 32 percent of the under-15 population, a total of 75,000 children, have been orphaned in Rakai. Of the four daughters and nine sons Ssenyonga raised, 11 are dead. Her son Joseph left her with eight children; Francis left four; Peter left three. "At first there were 22, living in that small hut over there," she says. "My children did not leave me any means to look after these young ones. All they had was sold to help treat them." Overwhelmed, she took the children to the hut one day. "I told them to shut the door so we could all starve to death inside and join the others," Ssenyonga says. She changed her mind when a daughter returned home to help, and World Vision provided a three-room house for them all.

Bernadette Nakayima, 70, lives in Uganda's Masaka district, where 110,000 of the 342,000 children are orphans. Nakayima lost every one of her 11 children to AIDS. "All these left me with 35 grandchildren to look after," she says. "I was a woman struck with sorrow beyond tears." But she is not alone: one out of every four families in Uganda is now caring for an AIDS orphan, says Pelucy Ntambirweki of the Ugandan Women's Effort to Save Orphans (UWESO).

When AIDS takes a parent, it usually takes a childhood, too, for if no other relative steps in, the oldest child becomes the head of a household. Yuda Sanyu Kitali was 10 in 1992 when his mother died of AIDS; the disease had killed his father in 1986. Sanyu had to drop out of school, of course, as did his younger brother, Emmanuel Kulabigwo, now 16, and sister, Margaret Nalubega, 15: when their parents died, so did any hope of affording academic fees. "No one came to claim us or to offer help," says Sanyu. A year after the children were orphaned, the grass-thatched house their father had built in the Rakai district collapsed in a heavy rain. "Since I was the oldest, I had to build another house," Sanyu says. He did his best with mud, poles, reeds and banana fiber. The children grew cassavas and greens on the land their parents left them, but they still went to sleep hungry many nights. As Sanyu tells his story Emmanuel nods silently. Margaret sits on a papyrus mat in the corner, staring at a wall and hiding a tear in her dirty brown dress.

"The number of people who have gone into the coffin-making business—that is something you can see without being an epidemiologist."

–G. SIKIPA, *UNAIDS*

Most orphans are taken in by their extended families, if they are taken in by anyone, but the sheer number of these lost children fills orphanages, too. Ethembeni House, run by the Salvation Army in downtown Johannesburg, has 38 children 5 or younger. All of them have tested HIV-positive. All were abandoned: a vagrant found the newborn Moses, now 3, in a dumpster; a woman handed days-old Simon, now 2, to a street vendor and never returned. The rooms in Ethembeni, lined with cribs, are clean and decorated with pictures of clowns and dolls. Other pictures, of children who died here, line the mantel. Moses points to one: "He's gone," he says. When a stranger enters the room, the children turn expectant faces to her: "Mama, mama," they cry.

In times past it was usually war or neglect or famine or poverty that brought abandoned or orphaned children to the Sanyu Babies Home in Kampala. Now the caseload of 26 is almost entirely AIDS orphans, many of whom have lost not only parents but all their other adult relatives, too. Patricia Namutebi, 3, was brought in as a 1-year-old by a thin, sickly man who said he was her neighbor and that her mother had died of AIDS. Patricia has been sick with one opportunistic infection after another; today she restlessly drags a chair to and fro and swings on the curtains, apart from the other children. Workers at the Babies Home suspect that the man was her father, but it hardly mattered. When they trace abandoned children back to their families, says Joyce Lolindya, administrator of the home, the survivors seem to feel that "it is hard to look after an AIDS victim, and then also the children of that victim, when you know they will all die." Especially when AIDS carries with it such a social stigma. Unless abandoned AIDS orphans reach an institution like hers, they risk getting sucked into what Godfrey Sikipa of UNAIDS calls "a vicious circle." He adds: "In many cases the orphans, unless we prevent them from going into deeper poverty, will become prostitutes." The fortunate ones become child brides, or the plaything of a sugar-daddy. They can only hope that the men will not be among the millions who believe that sex with a virgin cures AIDS.

When an extended family cannot afford to educate all the children in its care—virtually everywhere in Africa governments charge school fees—it is the orphan who is the likeliest dropout. In Zambia, a study cited by the UNAIDS report found, one third of urban children with parents enroll in school, but only one quarter of orphans do. "I wish I could go all the time," says Ben Sengazi, 13, one of Ssenyonga's grandsons. But when the family cannot scrape up the fees, the school turns him away.

Compared with children with parents, AIDS orphans are at far greater risk of malnutrition and of not receiving the health care they need. The little girl named Forget was 4 when her mother died of AIDS last November and she went to live with her grandmother in a village southeast of Harare. Her small body has recently developed ugly lesions, which she scratches constantly. Her grandmother says the causes of the plague are a mystery to her. Although she is doing what she can for Forget, the assumption by many caregivers is that the orphan, too, is infected with HIV, and that her illness is untreatable. Perhaps that explains one of the puzzles of the AIDS orphans. In 1995 Uganda had 1.2 million of them; based on the number of AIDS deaths and other factors, there should be 1.5 million now, but there are "only" 1.1 million. That is, Uganda is missing 400,000 AIDS orphans. "Either the babies were born [HIV-] positive, or they died from a lack of care," says UWESO's Ntambirweki.

Government and private programs do what they can for AIDS orphans. In Botswana, nongovernmental and community-based organizations provide services ranging from day care to food, clothing and bus fare to and from school. Villages in Malawi have organized communal gardens. Charity groups and orphanages teach the older children AIDS prevention, hoping that the cataclysm that befell the parents will not be visited on the children. World Vision built Sanyu's family a four-room house, paid for his sister and brother's schooling and trained Sanyu in bicycle repair. And after Harriett Namayanja, now 17, lost her parents to AIDS, a loan from a private agency saved her and her eight brothers and sisters. Harriett used the money for sisal grass, from which she weaves doormats. She sells them in Kampala, and with the money, she says, "I am able to look after my younger siblings" and even pay school fees for her brothers. But she and Sanyu are exceptions. Funding has not kept up with the needs of so many orphans, and institutions are stretched almost to the breaking point.

Some 6,000 men and women in sub-Saharan Africa will die of AIDS today. Six thousand more will die tomorrow, and the next day. For the children they leave behind, the tragedy is only beginning.

With **Simon Kaheru** in Kampala, **Lara Santoro** in Homa Bay, **Vera Haller** in Johannesburg and **Sharon Begley**

In God's Name: Genocide and Religion in the Twentieth Century

Stephen R. Haynes

I vividly remember riding in a car during the summer of 1994 and listening with rapt attention to an account of the tragedy in Rwanda. In just 100 days, following a government coup in early April, some 800,000 Rwandans were ruthlessly murdered by their countrymen. When I arrived home, I located Rwanda on a map. For several weeks I paid close attention to reports of the refugee crisis that followed the slaughter. But then the genocide and its aftermath were mentioned less and less frequently by the news media and, like most Westerners, I stopped thinking about it. Later, when Rwanda did enter my mind, I had difficulty remembering who had killed whom. Had Tutsis been the victims of Hutus? Or was it the other way around?

While popular interest in Rwanda has waned in the years since the genocide, the literature of description and analysis continues to grow. Mahmood Mamdani's *When Victims Become Killers* is a detailed account of the political conditions underlying the Rwandan tragedy. While it devotes little attention to the killing per se or to the individuals who committed it, it sheds a great deal of light on Rwandan history and political institutions—precolonial, colonial and revolutionary. One notable feature of Mamdani's analysis is his recurrent mention of parallels between Rwanda and the Holocaust.

In fact, most studies of the Rwandan slaughter refer to the Nazi Final Solution. Apparently, the landscape of contemporary genocide is so dominated by the Holocaust that other tragedies remain invisible unless they are compared to it. As arguments for the uniqueness of the Jewish experience have multiplied over the past decade, students of genocide in other places—in Armenia, the Americas, the Balkans—have combated that argument with attention to understudied cases of genocide.

Philip Gourevitch introduces his riveting account of the Rwandan crisis and its aftermath (*We Wish to Inform You . . .*) with the observation that "the dead of Rwanda accumulated at nearly three times the rate of Jewish dead during the Holocaust. It was the most efficient killing since the atomic bombings of Hiroshima and Nagasaki." One of the first books on the subject, Alain Destexhe's *Rwanda and Genocide in the Twentieth Century,* begins with a quote from Holocaust survivor Primo Levi: "It has happened once, and it could all happen again."

But references to the Holocaust reflect more than competition for the attention of atrocity-numbed readers. The two tragedies share quite a few formal similarities. There are analogous stories of unprovoked cruelty and betrayal, of rescue and gratuitous kindness, of hiding, passing and surviving. There are similar rationalizations on the part of perpetrators and by-standers—self-exculpating images of entrapment, of killers having no choice but to act as they did. There is similar evidence of complicit Christian leaders and institutions, evidence that poses a challenge to the credibility of faith.

There are the same pregenocidal legal persecutions used to identify and stigmatize an ethnic minority (including quotas and identity cards); the same essentializing of "race" that casts one group as a threat to the other's survival; the same mystification of a minority as a strangely powerful entity against whom the majority must defend itself; the same dehumanizing of the victims through images ("rats" in Germany; "cockroaches" in Rwanda) that makes elimination easier once the genocide begins. And there are the same painstaking attempts afterwards to discover why some people killed their neighbors while others protected them, along with the same amazement at the latter's refusal to consider their behavior extraordinary.

Like Nazi Germany, genocidal Rwanda is an exceedingly unattractive venue for Christian self-examination. Much of the evidence indicates that "blood" proved thicker than baptismal water, that faith was powerless to overcome the interests of class or ethnicity. And Rwanda has provided few stories designed to restore our trust in humankind or the role of faith in confronting evil. So far, we know of no Rwandan Bonhoeffers with whom mainline Protestants can identify; no Hutu Corrie ten Booms to sustain evangelicals' belief that God protects the righteous; no Catholic bishops who risked their lives to speak out against the violence; no Le Chambon-sur-Lignons where the persecuted were sheltered by simple Christians in a "conspiracy of goodness."

Yet precisely because so little good news can be gleaned from the Rwandan genocide, Christians must not ignore it. One pressing issue raised by Rwanda is human nature, what theologians have traditionally called anthropology. Although scholars of the genocide assiduously avoid theological questions,

Christians must ask what this and other episodes of mass killing reveal about the essence and extent of our fallenness.

Reinhold Niebuhr reportedly said that the doctrine of original sin is the only doctrine for which Christians have any empirical evidence. If Niebuhr is correct, certainly the most compelling evidence for original sin is to be found in the study of mass murder. Considering this evidence theologically does not require that we ignore the communal and systemic dimensions of evil highlighted by social scientists, but it does help explain how easily human beings become complicit in the destruction of others—through abhorrence of difference, self-deception and the idolatry of race and nation.

Even more than the Holocaust, Rwanda pushes us to ask what adaptations or situational factors exacerbate the genocidal tendencies in human nature. Because it was extraordinarily low-tech, the Rwandan genocide does not allow us to take refuge in impersonal categories such as "bureaucratization" or "modernity." The killing was perpetrated not anonymously in gas chambers, but face to face with machetes, knives, guns and grenades. It was carried out not by a class of professional killers "doing their duty," but by bands of ordinary people that included women and children.

Rwanda also presents us with a stark reminder of the narrowness of national interests and the hollowness of official commitments to moral actions when they conflict with those interests. Both Gourevitch's book and the television documentary "The Triumph of Evil" argue that the Rwandan genocide might well have been averted if the UN or its member nations had acted on information received in January 1994 from a UNAMIR (United Nations Mission in Rwanda) field commander.

An informant close to Hutu Power extremists in the Rwandan government revealed that the militias he was charged with training had been formed not for protection from the RPF (a guerrilla army of Rwandan exiles) but for the extermination of Tutsis. UNAMIR's message to New York detailed his account of the Rwandan government's plans: "He has been ordered to register all Tutsi in Kigali. He suspects it's for their extermination. Example he gave was that in 20 minutes his personnel could kill up to 1,000 Tutsis."

Since the Hutu informant revealed the location of arms to be used for this grisly task, the UNAMIR commander requested permission to seize the weapons and protect the informant and his family. The information and request were discussed by key members of the UN staff and then ignored. Motivated by the desire to avoid "another Somalia," the commander's superiors prohibited him from taking any action.

Three months later, events in Rwanda unfolded just as the informant had predicted. The morning after President Juvenal Habyarimana's plane was shot down under suspicious circumstances, ten Belgian peacekeepers were kidnapped, tortured and mutilated as a warning to the Western democracies. Then the genocide was on: roadblocks were set up and marauding death squads (interahamwe) took the streets, encouraged and directed by broadcasts on national radio; educated professionals massacred their colleagues in churches and hospitals; Tutsis and moderate Hutus attempted to flee or cowered in embassies and hotels protected by foreign interests; white citizens of Western nations were evacuated amid heart-wrenching pleas for help by desperate Africans; and UNAMIR troops ignominiously withdrew from their compounds, leaving those who had sought their protection to be hacked to death.

As corpses began to rot in the streets and clog the rivers, the Western response to this maelstrom of genocidal evil was precisely what Hutu Power extremists had hoped for. Under pressure from Belgium and the United States, the UN Security Council voted to terminate its mission in Rwanda. While American and UN representatives steadfastly refused to utter the word "genocide," the Czech Republic's ambassador to the UN spoke to the point: "When you come from Central Europe, [you have] a sense of what holocausts are about; you recognize one when you see one."

All of which leads to a troubling question: If one of the Nazi leaders present at the Wannsee Conference in Berlin in January 1942 had—in a fit of conscience—leaked plans for the "Final Solution of the Jewish Question in Europe" to the Allies, would this information have altered the fate of Jews under Nazi control?

The Western response to the genocidal crisis in Rwanda suggests that the answer is no. There is every reason to believe that Allied government officials would have treated a leaked Wannsee protocol as irrelevant to their strategic interests. And recall that in 1942 Western democracies had neither the experience of the Holocaust to reflect on nor a political obligation under the UN's Genocide Convention to prevent genocide.

Thus, while our consciousness of mass death and our use of the word "genocide" have been thoroughly conditioned by the Holocaust, it is not at all clear that Holocaust awareness has made Western democracies or their citizens more sensitive to mass death, or more committed to incurring personal risk to stop it. This despite the fact that "never again"—the ubiquitous mantra of Holocaust remembrance—indicates a commitment on the part of the powerful and morally aware "never again" to stand by while a nation destroys those it deems a threat to its survival.

As the documentary "The Triumph of Evil" so poignantly demonstrates, it was only a few months after ceremonies marking the opening of the U.S. Holocaust Memorial Museum—ceremonies at which President Clinton vowed on behalf of all Americans "to preserve this shared history of anguish, to keep it vivid and real so that evil can be combated and contained"—that warnings of the Rwandan tragedy reached the White House. In April 1994, just a few weeks after *Schindler's List* claimed the Oscar for best picture, Vice President Al Gore proclaimed that Washington's Holocaust memorial was needed "to remind those who make the agonizing decisions of foreign policy of the consequences of those decisions." Meanwhile, his government was rejecting State Department proposals to impede the genocide and worrying about whether its refusal to act might hurt the party in upcoming mid-term elections. It is difficult to imagine a more dramatic example of the yawning gap between rhetoric and reality in contemporary politics.

While our culture is awash in images of a genocide that ended over 50 years ago, we have trouble remembering the victims of a genocidal assault that occurred within the past decade. Is it simply the passage of time that fixes international tragedies in our consciousness? More likely it is a function of what Richard L. Rubenstein has identified as a fundamental dimension of the Holocaust's "uniqueness"—its resonance with the biblical and theological motifs that animate Judeo-Christian civilization.

Yet perhaps the failure of Rwanda's tragedy to penetrate the Western mind has to do with geography and race as well. Perhaps Westerners perceive the Holocaust not only through a religious grid, but through the prism of color. Ironically, given the explicit racial dimensions of Nazi ideology, both perpetrator and victim in the Holocaust are perceived as vaguely "white." Even in the Balkans, the difficult-to-pronounce names and unfamiliar traditions notwithstanding, we perceive victims who "look like us."

Rwanda, however, is a different story. The mental maps of most Americans simply do not include East Africa. The crises there—even when they reach the threshold of media consciousness—seem far away, the historical and political contexts unfamiliar, the "tribes" involved indistinguishable. Unless a conflict pits "white" against "black," as in South Africa or Zimbabwe, it does not hold our attention for long. Is it possible that we find it difficult to forge a connection with victims of genocide unless we can identify with them on the level of ethnicity, religious affiliation or color? If so, herein lies another grim lesson regarding human nature.

What can Christians who want to remember Rwanda learn from this genocide? Most scholarly analyses ignore the religious dimensions of the tragedy, portraying the Hutu extermination campaign as an indictment of European colonialism or a metaphor for the dilemmas of post-cold-war foreign policy. But there are important exceptions. For instance, Timothy Longman's contribution to *In God's Name: Genocide and Religion in the Twentieth Century* documents the active involvement of church personnel and institutions in the genocide: "Numerous priests, pastors, nuns, brothers, catechists, and Catholic and Protestant lay leaders supported, participated in, or helped to organize the killings," Longman writes. And he remarks that more people may have been killed in church buildings than anywhere else.

In the same volume, Charles de Lespinay charges the Rwandan clergy of being "propagators of false information tending to maintain a climate of fear, suspicion and hatred." Prominent clergy refused to condemn the killing (characterizing it as wartime self-defense or "double genocide"), and even excused the murders as a sort of delayed justice for past wrongs. In Rwanda, Lespinay concludes, "the exacerbation of past and present rivalries is entirely the fault of the missionary-educated intellectual 'elites.'"

But the religious lessons from Rwanda transcend the genocidal behavior of believers in one of Africa's most Christianized societies (90 percent Christian and 63 percent Roman Catholic, according to a 1991 census). Rwanda also reminds us of the way biblical myths of origin can exercise a pernicious influence in history. As almost every commentator on the genocide has noted, the antagonism between Hutu and Tutsi is based on presumed racial distinctions constructed from a quasi-biblical

ideology introduced by 19th-century white explorers and reiterated by European colonialists who benefited from inter-African antagonism.

The intellectual foundation for the construction of racial difference in Rwanda is John Hanning Speke's *Journal of the Discovery of the Source of the Nile* (1863, reprinted in 1996). Like other 19th-century Westerners, the English explorer assumed that Africans were descendants of "our poor elder brother Ham [who] was cursed by his father, and condemned to be the slave of both Shem and Japheth." Speke's contribution to white perceptions of Africa was a theory of ethnology "founded on the traditions of the several nations, as checked by [his] own observation of what [he] saw when passing through them."

The distinctive physical appearance of the Wahuma (Tutsis) led Speke to surmise that they were descended from "the semi-Shem-Hamitic of Ethiopia," cattle-herding "Asiatic" invaders who moved south, lost their original language and religion, and darkened through inter-marriage. According to his journal, Speke elaborated his ethnological theory for a Tutsi king using the Book of Genesis "to explain all [he] fancied [he] knew about the origin and present condition of the Wahuma branch of the Ethiopians, beginning with Adam, to show how it was the king had heard by tradition that at one time the people of his race were half white and half black."

In the western mind this so-called Hamitic Hypothesis evolved to become an explanation for the arrival of "civilization" in Africa. Inside Rwanda, it was adopted as the basis for colonial theories of Tutsi superiority, for missionary education that placed ethnic diversity in a European class perspective, and for the Hutu revolutionary image of Tutsis as nonindigenous invaders from the north. While this "biblical" dimension of Rwandan history is rarely reported, it was well known to both the perpetrators and the victims of the genocide.

Rwanda also presents us with compelling evidence for the ineptitude of Christian leaders and institutions in resisting genocidal evil. Even as we struggle to understand the failure of Christian witness and action during the Holocaust, Rwanda raises new specters: of churches becoming killing sites, of parishioners murdering each other, of pastors being sought as war criminals, and of priests denying or excusing mass murder.

As Longman argues, one reason Christians failed to resist the forces that led to genocide was the Rwandan church's close relationship with the Habyarimana government and the refusal of church leaders to support groups and individuals advocating reform. The church's commitment to preserving the status quo helps explain its "resounding silence" in the wake of sporadic persecutions during the early 1990s, and all-out genocide in 1994.

Stories from Rwanda—like so many stories from the Holocaust—force us to ask how we would have behaved in a similar situation, whether we are different from the perpetrators and bystanders who became agents of genocide. These questions are faced with disturbing honesty in James Waller's forthcoming book *Children of Cain: How Ordinary People Commit Extraordinary Evil*. The book's title is taken from Gourevitch's application of Genesis 4 to the Rwandan tragedy: "In the famous story, the older brother, Cain, was a cultivator, and Abel, the younger, was a herdsman. They made their offerings to God—Cain from his crops, Abel from his herds. Abel's portion won God's regard; Cain's did not. So Cain killed Abel." In offering a unified theory of perpetrator behavior, Waller discredits the various psychological mechanisms we rely upon to distance ourselves from those who commit or countenance genocide.

Finally, because it reveals how the world's leading democracy conspired to ignore and deny an ongoing genocide at the very moment when American consciousness of the Holocaust was at its height, Rwanda forces Christians to ask precisely how Holocaust awareness contributes to antigenocidal thought and action. When we say "never again," we must pledge to remember Rwanda.

STEPHEN R. HAYNES is associate professor of religious studies at Rhodes College and a member of the Church Relations Committee of the United States Holocaust Memorial Council.

From *The Christian Century,* February 27, 2002, pp. 30–35. Copyright © 2002 by Christian Century. Reprinted by permission of Christian Century via the Copyright Clearance Center.

Terror in the Name of God

Mark Juergensmeyer

Perhaps the first question that came to mind on September 11 when the horrific images of the aerial assaults on the World Trade Center and the Pentagon were conveyed around the world was: Why would anyone want to do such a thing? As the twin towers crumbled in clouds of dust and the identities and motives of the perpetrators began to emerge, a second question arose: Why would anyone want to do such a thing in the name of God?

These are the questions that have arisen frequently in the post–cold war world. Religion seems to be connected with violence everywhere—from the World Trade Center bombings to suicide attacks in Israel and the Palestinian Authority; assassinations in India, Israel, Egypt, and Algeria; nerve gas in Tokyo subways; unending battles in Northern Ireland; abortion-clinic killings in Florida; and the bombing of Oklahoma City's federal building.

Osama bin Laden is no more representative of Islam than Timothy McVeigh is of Christianity

What does religion have to do with this virtually global rise of religious violence? In one sense, very little. If the activists involved in the World Trade Center bombing are associated with Osama bin Laden's al Qaeda, they are a small network at the extreme end of a subculture of dissatisfied Muslims who are in turn a small minority within the world of Islam. Osama bin Laden is no more representative of Islam than Timothy McVeigh is of Christianity, or Japan's Shoko Asahara is of Buddhism.

Still, one cannot deny that the ideals and ideas of these vicious activists are permeated with religion. The authority of religion has given bin Laden's cadres what they believe is the moral standing to employ violence in their assault on the very symbol of global economic power. It has also provided the metaphor of cosmic war, an image of spiritual struggle that every religion has within its repository of symbols: the fight between good and bad, truth and evil. In this sense, the attack on the World Trade Center was very religious. It was meant to be catastrophic, an act of biblical proportions.

What is striking about the World Trade Center assault and many other recent acts of religious terrorism is that they have no obvious military goal. These are acts meant for television. They are a kind of perverse performance of power meant to ennoble the perpetrators' views of the world and to draw us into their notions of cosmic war.

The recent attacks in New York City and Washington, D.C.—although unusual in the scale of the assault—are remarkably similar to many other acts of religious terrorism around the world. In my recent comparative study of religious terrorism, *Terror in the Mind of God,* I have found a strikingly familiar pattern. In each case, concepts of cosmic war are accompanied by strong claims of moral justification and an enduring absolutism that transforms worldly struggles into sacred battles. It is not so much that religion has become politicized but that politics has become religionized. Worldly struggles have been lifted onto the high proscenium of sacred battle.

This is what makes religious terrorism so difficult to combat. Its enemies have become satanized: one cannot negotiate with them or easily compromise. The rewards for those who fight for the cause are transtemporal, and the time lines of their struggles are vast. Most social and political struggles look for conclusions within the lifetimes of their participants, but religious struggles can take generations to succeed. When I pointed out to political leaders of the Hamas movement in the Palestinian Authority that Israel's military force was such that a Palestinian military effort could never succeed, I was told that "Palestine was occupied before, for two hundred years." The Hamas official assured me that he and his Palestinian comrades "can wait again—at least that long," for the struggles of God can endure for eons. Ultimately, however, Hamas members "knew" they would succeed.

In such battles, waged in divine time and with heaven's rewards, there is no need to compromise one's goals. No need, also, to contend with society's laws and limitations when one is obeying a higher authority. In spiritualizing violence, religion gives terrorism a remarkable power.

Ironically, the reverse is also true: terrorism can give religion power as well. Although sporadic acts of terrorism do not lead to the establishment of new religious states, they make the political potency of religious ideology impossible to ignore. Terrorism not only gives individuals the illusion of empowerment, it also gives religious organizations and ideas a public attention and importance that they have not enjoyed for many years. In modern America and Europe it has given religion a prominence in public life that it has not held since before the Enlightenment over two centuries ago.

Empowering Religion

The radical religious movements that have emerged from cultures of violence around the world have three elements in common. First, they reject the compromises with liberal values and secular institutions that most mainstream religion has made, be it Christian, Muslim, Jewish, Hindu, Sikh, or Buddhist. Second, radical religious movements refuse to observe the boundaries that secular society has set around religion—keeping it private rather than allowing it to intrude into public spaces. And third, these radical movements try to create a new form of religiosity that rejects what they regard as weak, modern substitutes for the more vibrant and demanding forms of religion that they imagine to be essential to their religion's origins.

One of the men accused of bombing the World Trade Center in 1993 told me in a prison interview that the critical moment in his religious life came when he realized that he could not compromise his Islamic integrity with the easy vices offered by modern society. The convicted terrorist, Mahmud Abouhalima, claimed that the early part of his life was spent running away from himself. Although involved in radical Egyptian Islamic movements since his college years in Alexandria, he felt there was no place where he could settle down. He told me that the low point came when he was in Germany, trying to live the way that he imagined Europeans and Americans did: a life where the superficial comforts of sex and inebriates masked an internal emptiness and despair. Abouhalima said his return to Islam as the center of his life carried with it a renewed sense of obligation to make Islamic society truly Islamic—to "struggle against oppression and injustice" wherever it existed. What was now constant, Abouhalima said, was his family and his faith. Islam was both a "rock and a pillar of mercy." But it was not the Islam of liberal, modern Muslims—they, he felt, had compromised the tough and disciplined life the faith demanded.

In Abouhalima's case, he wanted his religion to be hard, not soft like the humiliating, mind-numbing comforts of secular modernity. Activists such as Abouhalima—and Osama bin Laden—imagine themselves defenders of ancient faiths. But in fact they have created new forms of religiosity: like many present-day religious leaders they have used the language of traditional religion to build bulwarks around aspects of modernity that have threatened them, and to suggest ways out of the mindless humiliation of modern life. Vital to their image of religion, however, was that it be perceived as ancient.

The need for religion—a "hard" religion as Abouhalima called it—was a response to the soft treachery they had observed in the new societies around them. The modern secular world that Abouhalima and the others inhabited was a chaotic and violent sea for which religion offered an anchor in a harbor of calm. At some deep and almost transcendent level of their consciousnesses, they sensed their lives slipping out of control, and they felt both responsible for the disarray and a victim of it. To be abandoned by religion in such a world would mean a loss of their own individual locations and identities. In fashioning a "traditional religion" of their own making, they exposed their concerns not so much with their religious, ethnic, or national communities, but with their own personal, perilous selves.

Assaults on Secularism

These intimate concerns have been prompted by the perceived failures of public institutions. As the French sociologists Pierre Bourdieu has observed, social structures never have a disembodied reality; they are always negotiated by individuals in their own strategies for maintaining self-identity and success in life. Such institutions are legitimized by the "symbolic capital" they accrue through the collective trust of many individuals. When that symbolic capital is devalued, when political and religious institutions undergo what German philosopher Jurgen Habermas has called a "crisis of legitimacy," the devaluation of authority is experienced not only as a political problem but as an intensively personal one, as a loss of agency.

This sense of a personal loss of power in the face of chaotic political and religious authorities is common, and I believe critical, to Osama bin Laden's al Qaeda group and most other movements for Christian, Muslim, Jewish, Sikh, Buddhist, and Hindu nationalism around the world. The syndrome begins with the perception that the public world has gone awry, and the suspicion that behind this social confusion lies a great spiritual and moral conflict, a cosmic battle between the forces of order and chaos, good and evil. Such a conflict is understandably violent, a violence that is often felt by the victimized activist as powerlessness, either individually or in association with others of his gender, race, or ethnicity. The government—already delegitimized—is perceived to be in league with the forces of chaos and evil.

One of the reasons why secular government is easily la[beled] as the enemy of religion is that to some degree it is. By its [nature] the secular state is opposed to the idea that religion sho[uld have] a role in public life. From the time that modern secul[ar ide]alism emerged in the eighteenth century as a prod[uct of the] European Enlightenment's political values, it did s[o with a dis]tinctly antireligious, or at least anticlerical, posture[. The ideas of] John Locke about the origins of a civil community [and the "social] contract" theories of Jean Jacques Rousseau re[quired little] commitment to religious belief. Although th[ey evoked a] divine order that made the rights of humans p[ossible, they] had the effect of taking religion—at leas[t church religion—] out of public life. At the time, religio[n of the] Enlightenment"—as the historian Darri[n McMahon calls] them in a new book with this title—pr[edicted its] demise. But their views were submerg[ed by the demands] for a new view of social order in whi[ch the nation was] thought to be virtually a natural law[, universal and] morally right.

Post-Enlightenment modernit[y proclaimed the death of reli]gion. Modernity signaled not o[nly the demise of the church's] institutional authority and cler[ical power, but the loosen]ing of religion's ideologica[l and intellectual grip on society.] Scientific reasoning and the [secular logic of the social] contract replaced theology [as the bases for moral order] and social identity. The re[sult was what Nietzsche called] a "general crisis of relig[ion."]

In countering this [modernist secularism, reli]gious activists have proclaim[ed]

dismissed the efforts of secular culture and its forms of nationalism to replace religion. They have challenged the idea that secular society and the modern nation-state are able to provide the moral fiber that unites national communities or give the ideological strength to sustain states buffeted by ethical, economic, and military failures. Their message has been easy to believe and has been widely received because the failures of the secular state have been so real.

Antiglobalism

The moral leadership of the secular state was increasingly challenged in the last decade of the twentieth century following the end of the cold war and the rise of a global economy. The cold war provided contesting models of moral politics—communism and democracy—that were replaced with a global market that weakened national sovereignty and was conspicuously devoid of political ideals. The global economy became controlled by transnational businesses accountable to no single governmental authority and with no clear ideological or moral standards of behavior. But while both Christian and Enlightenment values were left behind, transnational commerce transported aspects of westernized popular culture to the rest of the world. American European music, videos, and films were beamed across al boundaries, where they threatened to obliterate local tional forms of artistic expression.

o this social confusion were convulsive shifts in politi-
t followed the breakup of the Soviet Union and the
an economies at the end of the twentieth century.
of insecurity that came in the wake of these cat-
anges was felt not only in the societies of those
nomically devastated by them—especially
ers Soviet Union—but also in economically
that cieties. The United States, for example,
gove of disaffection with its political lead-
Is of right-wing religious movements
chang tion of the inherent immorality of
in indu
agenda. rism related to these global
United Ds associated with violence
group Den antimodernist political
Identity nan seligious rejection in the
Davidian merican anti-abortion
government litia and Christian
logy of the Kum ch as the Branch
with the Aum toward secular
tentious group s tionalist ideo-
the ability of se and in Japan
They identified States, con-
The global sh, ied about
movements have stinies.
Jawaharlal Nehru,
Riza Shah Pahlavi

nist
's

of

America—or a kind of cross between America and the Soviet Union—in their own countries. But new generations of leaders no longer believed in the Westernized visions of Nehru, Nasser, or the Shah. Rather, they were eager to complete the process of decolonization and build new, indigenous nationalisms.

When activists in Algeria who demonstrated against the crackdown against the Islamic Salvation Front in 1991 proclaimed that they were continuing the war of liberation against French colonialism, they had the ideological rather than political reach of European influence in mind. Religious activists such as the Algerian leaders; the Ayatollah Khomeini in Iran; Sheikh Ahmed Yassin in the Palestinian Authority; Maulana Abu al-Ala Mawdudi in Pakistan; Sayyid Qutb and his disciple, Sheik Omar Abdul Rahman, in Egypt; L. K. Advani in India; and Sant Jarnail Singh Bhindranwale in India's Punjab have asserted the legitimacy of a postcolonial national identity based on traditional culture.

The result of this disaffection with the values of the modern West has been what I described in my earlier book, *The New Cold War?*, as a "loss of faith" in the ideological form of that culture, secular nationalism. Although a few years ago it would have been a startling notion, the idea has now become virtually commonplace that secular nationalism—the idea that the nation is rooted in a secular compact rather than religious or ethnic identity—is in crisis. In many parts of the world it is seen as an alien cultural construction, once closely linked with what has been called the "project of modernity." In such cases, religious alternatives to secular ideologies have had extraordinary appeal.

This uncertainty about what constitutes a valid basis for national identity is a political form of post-modernism. In Iran it has resulted in the rejection of a modern Western political regime and the creation of a successful religious state. Increasingly, even secular scholars in the West have recognized that religious ideologies might offer an alternative to modernity in the political sphere. Yet, what lies beyond modernity is not necessarily a new form of political order, religious or not. In nations formerly under Soviet control, for example, the specter of the future beyond the socialist form of modernity has been one of cultural anarchism.

The al Qaeda network associated with Osama bin Laden takes religious violence to yet another level. The implicit attack on global economic and political systems that are leveled by religious nationalists from Algeria to Indonesia are made explicit: America is the enemy. Moreover, it is a war waged not on a national plane but a transnational one. Their agenda is not for any specific form of religious nation-state but an inchoate vision of a global rule of religious law. Rather than religious nationalists, transnational activists like bin Laden are guerrilla antiglobalists.

Postmodern Terror

Bin Laden and his vicious acts have a credibility in some quarters of the world because of the uncertainties of this moment of global history. Both violence and religion historically have appeared when authority is in question, since they are both ways of challenging and replacing authority. One gains its power from force, and the other from its claims to ultimate order. The combination of the two in acts of religious terrorism has been a potent assertion indeed.

Regardless of whether the perpetrators consciously intended them to be political acts, all public acts of violence have political consequences. Insofar as they are attempts to reshape the public order, they are examples of what the sociologist Jose Casanova has called the increasing "deprivatization" of religion. In various parts of the world where defenders of religion have attempted to reclaim the center of public attention and authority, religious terrorism is often the violent face of these attempts.

The postmodern religious rebels such as those who rally to the side of Osama bin Laden have therefore been neither anomalies nor anachronisms. From Algeria to Idaho, their small but potent groups of violent activists have represented masses of supporters, and they have exemplified currents of thinking and cultures of commitment that have risen to counter the prevailing modernism—the ideology of individualism and skepticism—that in the past three centuries emerged from the European Enlightenment and spread throughout the world. They have come to hate secular governments with an almost transcendent passion. They have dreamed of revolutionary changes that would establish a godly social order in the rubble of what the citizens of most secular societies have regarded as modern, egalitarian democracies. Their enemies have seemed to most people to be both benign and banal: symbols of prosperity and authority such as the World Trade Center. The logic of this kind of militant religiosity has therefore been difficult for many people to comprehend. Yet its challenge has been profound, for it has contained a fundamental critique of the world's post-Enlightenment secular culture and politics.

Acts of religious terrorism have thus been attempts to purchase public recognition of the legitimacy of religious world views with the currency of violence. Since religious authority can provide a ready-made replacement for secular leadership, it is no surprise that when secular authority has been deemed to be morally insufficient, the challenges to its legitimacy and the attempts to gain support for its rivals have been based in religion. When the proponents of religion have asserted their claims to be the moral force undergirding public order, they sometimes have done so with the kind of power that a confused society can graphically recognize: the force of terror.

MARK JUERGENSMEYER is the author of *Terror in the Mind of God: The Global Rise of Religious Violence* (Berkeley: University of California Press, 2000), from which portions of this essay have been adapted. He is a professor of sociology and director of global and international studies at the University of California at Santa Barbara.

Reprinted from *Current History,* November 2001, pp. 357–361. Copyright © 2001 by Current History, Inc. Reprinted with permission.

A New Generation in the Middle East

Elizabeth Warnock Fernea

Lubna is 15 years old and lives in Kuwait. She is a sophomore at a private high school where the classes are taught in English. Her father and mother, who work in banking and at Kuwait University respectively, feel strongly that she should also have a formal background in Arabic, the language of her heritage and her Islamic faith, so Lubna spends Fridays at home being tutored by a local teacher. Like middle-class Western teenagers, Lubna wears T-shirts, jeans and Dr. Martens; she has her own room and her own stereo in her parents' spacious house, where she listens not only to Fayrouz—still a beloved singer in the Arab world—but also to gen-x rockers No Doubt. She hopes to go on to the American University in Beirut, but she also thinks about studying in England or the United States.

Omar is 14; he lives in Cairo. His father died several years ago. Last year Omar had to drop out of his neighborhood public school and go to work to help support his family: his mother, his 16-year-old brother Gamal and four younger siblings. Fortunately, Gamal was already working in a small, privately owned factory, and the owner hired Omar on as well. Omar is proud to be contributing to the family income, he says, but he regrets having to leave school, since that means he will not be able to rise much beyond his present unskilled job. Most attractive jobs in Egypt these days—especially in the private sector, but in the public sector as well—require at least a high-school diploma. Omar wears jeans and T-shirts, too, but he shares a tiny room with his older brother and two of the younger children. Television is the family recreation, and Omar loves westerns, as well as pop-music programs both from the West and from the Arab world.

Nadia also lives in Cairo. She's 11, and she attends a private elementary school in well-heeled Zamalek, across the Nile from the city center. Both her parents work full-time: Her mother is a journalist and her father is in advertising. Thus Nadia and her eight-year-old sister Hala are escorted to and from school by the family nanny. On Fridays Nadia often goes to the Gezira Sporting Club, one of the city's oldest clubs, where she plays, swims and meets her friends. She, too, watches television, especially the Cairo-produced family-style soap operas popular in Egypt and beyond.

Abdul Hamid is 16 and lives in Morocco's capital, Rabat. The son of parents who are both lawyers, he is enrolled in a public school, but he receives special tutoring in mathematics. This tutoring, his parents hope, will help him score well on the national exams that determine whether or not Abdul Hamid will go on to a university. His goal is to go to medical school like his older brother Yehia, but competition for those places is keen. Abdul Hamid, too, prefers to dress in jeans and T-shirts, and he is proud of his new Nike shoes, which he received as a birthday present. On weekends he often helps his father, who has started an extensive organic garden in the family's country house just outside Rabat.

Driss, a friend of Abdul Hamid's from school, also wants to go to medical school, but his family cannot afford tutoring. Driss is the sixth of eight children, and lives with his mother and seven siblings in a small two-room apartment. His father is a "guest worker" in France and regularly sends money home, but Driss and his older brother still have to work part-time to help make ends meet. Abdul Hamid shares his tutoring notes with Driss. "He's smarter than I am," Abdul Hamid confides. Driss works hard and believes he might do well enough on the exams to get into medical school, or at least into the engineering school in Rabat. Those are realistic hopes: For students who place high on the exams, tuition is free, and the government guarantees their education. Driss's parents, who grew up when free public education was just beginning to reach every Moroccan citizen, are both illiterate; they are proud of their son's efforts, and do their best to support him.

Lubna, Omar, Nadia, Abdul Hamid and Driss are members of a new generation in the Middle East, and are very different from the children romanticized by both Western and Middle Eastern writers in the past. That small figure, photographed in a nomadic or rural landscape, so isolated from—and foreign to—the greater world the writers themselves inhabited, is gone. To begin with, more than half of all children in the Middle East today live in cities, not in the country or, rarer still, in desert oases. This shift from predominantly rural to predominantly urban life has taken place in just over 30 years.

The new generation is growing not only in age, but also in numbers and in interconnectedness. Demographers point out that half of the Arab world's total population today is under the age of 15. These young people are growing up in a world of wider horizons and shorter distances than their parents', thanks in no small part to the communications revolution. Lubna, in Kuwait, and Omar, in Cairo—despite the differences between their social and economic positions—watch many of the same television programs and listen to the same commercial messages offering designer jeans and jogging shoes, stereos and sports equipment.

This is a generation with high material expectations and occupational ambitions. Children in this generation see themselves as citizens of modern nation-states, and take for granted the right to free education, something that, in some of their countries, was once limited to the elite. This raising of hopes is dramatic: Driss would have been unable to think of medical school in Morocco 20 years ago, and at that time Omar's regret over leaving school would have been less, since he would have known that other choices were simply not available.

Lubna, Omar, Nadia, Abdul Hamid and Driss also are part of societies where traditional class systems are changing. A real middle class has emerged, recruited on the basis of merit and economic interest rather than lineage, and is playing an important role in social and business life. But in this middle class, it is increasingly common to find both parents working full-time, and so children end up spending time at home alone, another great change from the past. As women increasingly work outside the home and women's roles in the family are gradually renegotiated—a bit more here and a bit less there—this, too, affects children by changing the traditional family unit and the relationships within it. National leaders and opinion-makers have recently organized, both privately and publicly, to improve the lives of children across the region. An early pioneer in these efforts is Dr. Hasan Al-Ibrahim, who founded and continues to direct the Kuwait Society for the Advancement of Arab Children. In 1986, the situation of children across the Arab world was the subject of the first Conference on Arab Childhood and Development, held in Tunis, and jointly organized by the League of Arab States and the United Nations. Growing from an initiative of Prince Talal ibn 'Abd al-'Aziz al-Sa'ud of Saudi Arabia, this conference led to the organization of the Arab Council for Childhood and Development, a voluntary, non-governmental organization which, according to its founders, aims "to upgrade the standard of the Arab child, seeks to develop his personality, to improve his abilities, thus paving the way for him to become, in the future, an active member of his society, and to contribute to the civilization of his nation."

"A child is a gift from God." This saying, common throughout the Middle East for thousands of years, expresses a basic belief of Muslims, Christians and Jews of the area. Not only are children much desired and loved, their arrival has traditionally been regarded as a cultural statement of great importance: In many circles, an adult is not considered mature or a full-fledged member of society until he or she marries and has children. Children affirm a man's virility and a woman's fertility and become a living symbol that the family unit will continue, a link between the past and the present.

The vast differences between past and present throughout the Middle East make that linking role a difficult one, points out Dr. Mohammed Shoufani of Morocco's Ministry of Education office in Marrakech. "Children are the most important and the most complicated people in our society today, pulled as they are between two worlds. . . . At a time when old absolutes are crumbling and old values are disregarded, . . . young people . . . are endangered because they are, in terms of values at least, at sea."

Indeed, the future of the Middle East will be determined by the choices that young people like Lubna, Omar, Driss, Abdul Hamid, Hala and Nadia make, for they are the adults of the 21st century, being formed and shaped today in a world vastly different from that of their parents and grandparents.

Index

Index

Test Your Knowledge Form

We encourage you to photocopy and use this page as a tool to assess how the articles in *Annual Editions* expand on the information in your textbook. By reflecting on the articles you will gain enhanced text information. You can also access this useful form on a product's book support Web site at *http://www.mhcls.com/online/*.

NAME: DATE:

TITLE AND NUMBER OF ARTICLE:

BRIEFLY STATE THE MAIN IDEA OF THIS ARTICLE:

LIST THREE IMPORTANT FACTS THAT THE AUTHOR USES TO SUPPORT THE MAIN IDEA:

WHAT INFORMATION OR IDEAS DISCUSSED IN THIS ARTICLE ARE ALSO DISCUSSED IN YOUR TEXTBOOK OR OTHER READINGS THAT YOU HAVE DONE? LIST THE TEXTBOOK CHAPTERS AND PAGE NUMBERS:

LIST ANY EXAMPLES OF BIAS OR FAULTY REASONING THAT YOU FOUND IN THE ARTICLE:

LIST ANY NEW TERMS/CONCEPTS THAT WERE DISCUSSED IN THE ARTICLE, AND WRITE A SHORT DEFINITION:

We Want Your Advice

ANNUAL EDITIONS revisions depend on two major opinion sources: one is our Advisory Board, listed in the front of this volume, which works with us in scanning the thousands of articles published in the public press each year; the other is you—the person actually using the book. Please help us and the users of the next edition by completing the prepaid article rating form on this page and returning it to us. Thank you for your help!

ANNUAL EDITIONS: World History, Volume 2, 9/e

ARTICLE RATING FORM

Here is an opportunity for you to have direct input into the next revision of this volume.
We would like you to rate each of the articles listed below, using the following scale:

1. **Excellent: should definitely be retained**
2. **Above average: should probably be retained**
3. **Below average: should probably be deleted**
4. **Poor: should definitely be deleted**

Your ratings will play a vital part in the next revision.
Please mail this prepaid form to us as soon as possible.
Thanks for your help!

RATING	ARTICLE	RATING	ARTICLE
	1. Aztecs: A New Perspective		25. The 20th-Century Scientific-Technical Revolution
	2. The Peopling of Canada		26. On the Turn—Japan, 1900
	3. 400 Years of the East India Company		27. Home at Last
	4. The Ottomans in Europe		28. Gandhi and Nehru: Frustrated Visionaries?
	5. Death on the Nile		29. The Roots of Chinese Xenophobia
	6. Coffee, Tea, or Opium		30. The Dirty A-Word
	7. After Centuries of Japanese Isolation, a Fateful Meeting of East and West		31. Women in the Third Reich
	8. Chinese Burns: Britain in China, 1842–1900		32. Exposing the Rape of Nanking
	9. New Light on the 'Heart of Darkness'		33. His Finest Hour
	10. The First Feminist		34. Judgment at Nuremberg
	11. Benjamin Franklin: An American in London		35. The Plan and the Man
	12. George Mason: Forgotten Founder, He Conceived the Bill of Rights		36. Korea: Echoes of a War
			37. Coming to Terms with the Past
	13. This Is Not a Story and Other Stories		38. Iraq's Unruly Century
	14. From Mercantilism to 'The Wealth of Nations'		39. The USA in Vietnam
	15. The Return of Catherine the Great		40. The Common Currents of Imperialism
	16. As Good as Gold?		41. Like Herrings in a Barrel
	17. A Woman Writ Large in Our History and Hearts		42. The Weather Turns Wild
	18. Eyes Wide Open		43. Bombs, Gas and Microbes
	19. In God's Place		44. 10 Million Orphans
	20. The Workshop of a New Society		45. In God's Name: Genocide and Religion in the Twentieth Century
	21. The X Factor		
	22. Samurai, Shoguns & the Age of Steam		46. Terror in the Name of God
	23. The Transatlantic Telegraph Cable		47. A New Generation in the Middle East
	24. A Tale of Two Reputations		

BUSINESS REPLY MAIL
FIRST CLASS MAIL PERMIT NO. 551 DUBUQUE IA

POSTAGE WILL BE PAID BY ADDRESSEE

McGraw-Hill Contemporary Learning Series
2460 KERPER BLVD
DUBUQUE, IA 52001-9902

ABOUT YOU

Name   Date
_____

Are you a teacher? ❑ A student? ❑
Your school's name
_____

Department
_____

Address   City   State   Zip
_____

School telephone #
_____

YOUR COMMENTS ARE IMPORTANT TO US!

Please fill in the following information:
For which course did you use this book?
_____

Did you use a text with this ANNUAL EDIT   ❑ yes ❑ no
What was the title of the text?
_____

What are your general reactions to the Annual Editions concept?
_____

Have you read any pertinent   es re   ou think should be included in the next edition? Explain.
_____

Are there any articles that you feel shoul   e ced in the next edition? Why?
_____

Are there any World Wide Web sites that you feel should be included in the next edition? Please annotate.
_____

May we contact you for editorial input? ❑ yes ❑ no
May we quote your comments? ❑ yes ❑ no